L2 Learning as Social Practice: Conversation-Analytic Perspectives

Pragmatics & Interaction
Editor
Gabriele Kasper

PRAGMATICS & INTERACTION, a refereed series sponsored by the University of Hawai'i National Foreign Language Resource Center, publishes research on topics in pragmatics and discourse as social interaction from a wide variety of theoretical and methodological perspectives. P&I particularly welcomes studies on languages spoken in the Asian-Pacific region.

Talk-in-interaction: Multilingual perspectives
Hanh thi Nguyen & Gabriele Kasper (Eds.), (2009)
ISBN 978-0-09800459-1-8

ordering information at nflrc.hawaii.edu

L2 Learning as Social Practice
Conversation-Analytic Perspectives

edited by
Gabriele Pallotti
& Johannes Wagner

NATIONAL FOREIGN LANGUAGE RESOURCE CENTER
University of Hawai'i at Mānoa

2011 Gabriele Pallotti
Some rights reserved. See: http://creativecommons.org/licenses/by-nc-nd/2.5/
Manufactured in the United States of America.

The contents of this publication were developed in part under a grant from the U.S. Department of Education (CFDA 84.229, P229A100001). However, the contents do not necessarily represent the policy of the Department of Education, and one should not assume endorsement by the Federal Government.

ISBN (13) 978-0-9800459-7-0
Library of Congress Control Number: 2010938523

 All wood product components used in interior of this book are Sustainable Forestry Initiative® (SFI®) certified.

distributed by
National Foreign Language Resource Center
University of Hawai'i
1859 East-West Road #106
Honolulu HI 96822–2322
nflrc.hawaii.edu

About the
National Foreign Language Resource Center

The National Foreign Language Resource Center, located in the College of Languages, Linguistics, & Literature at the University of Hawai'i at Mānoa, has conducted research, developed materials, and trained language professionals since 1990 under a series of grants from the U.S. Department of Education (Language Resource Centers Program). A national advisory board sets the general direction of the resource center. With the goal of improving foreign language instruction in the United States, the center publishes research reports and teaching materials that focus primarily on the languages of Asia and the Pacific. The center also sponsors summer intensive teacher training institutes and other professional development opportunities. For additional information about center programs, contact us.

Richard Schmidt, Director
National Foreign Language Resource Center
University of Hawai'i at Mānoa
1859 East-West Road #106
Honolulu, HI 96822–2322
email: nflrc@hawaii.edu
website: nflrc.hawaii.edu

NFLRC Advisory Board 2010–2014

Robert Blake
University of California, Davis

Mary Hammond
East-West Center, Honolulu, Hawai'i

Madeline Spring
Arizona State University

Carol Chapelle
Iowa State University

Contents

About the Authors — ix

Acknowledgments — xiii

Transcription Conventions — xiv

Preface
Gabriele Kasper — xv

1 L2 Learning as Social Practice:
   Conversation-Analytic Perspectives
   Gabriele Pallotti & Johannes Wagner — 1

Language Learning as Development of Practices

2 A Longitudinal Microanalysis of a Second Language
   Learner's Participation
   Hanh thi Nguyen — 17

3 Engaging in Another Person's Telling as a Recipient in
   L2 Japanese: Development of Interactional Competence
   During One-Year Study Abroad
   Midori Ishida — 45

4 Expanded Responses of English-Speaking Korean
   Heritage Speakers During Oral Interviews
   Seung-Hee Lee, Jae-Eun Park, & Sung-Ock Sohn — 87

Doing Learning

5 Talk, Body, and Material Objects as Coordinated Interactional Resources in Repair Activities in One-on-One ESL Tutoring
  Mi-Suk Seo — 107

6 Doing Word Explanation in Interaction
  Kristian Mortensen — 135

7 Choral Practice Patterns in the Language Classrooms
  Keiko Ikeda & Sungbae Ko — 163

8 Language Learning Activities in Real-Life Situations: Insisting on TCU Completion in Second Language Talk
  Guðrún Theodórsdóttir — 185

Language Choice and Participation in Second Language Talk

9 Language Choice and Participation: Two Practices for Switching Languages in Institutional Interaction
  Maurice Nevile & Johannes Wagner — 211

10 Employing Multilingualism for Doing Identity Work and Generating Laughter in Business Meetings: A Case Study
  Monika Vöge — 237

Bridging the Interactional/Linguistic Divide

11 Italian Learner Varieties and Syntax-in-Interaction
  Michela Biazzi — 267

12 The L2 Inventory in Action: Conversation Analysis and Usage-Based Linguistics in SLA
  Søren Wind Eskildsen — 327

Index — 365

About the Authors

Michela Biazzi has a PhD in Linguistics from the University of Pavia, Italy. She wrote her dissertation within the framework of interactional linguistics, working on reformulations and co-constructions in naturally occurring interactions among first- and second-language speakers of Italian. Her research interests include second language acquisition (Italian and English) and sociolinguistics. She has worked as a teacher of Italian as a second language to university students and has been actively involved in teacher training programs. She teaches English as a foreign language in Italy and is a teaching assistant for the foundation course in sociolinguistics at the University of Pavia.

Søren W. Eskildsen primarily investigates developmental issues in second language (L2) learning from the perspective of usage-based linguistics, with special reference to the role played by multi-word expressions. His research interests include the interplay between social interaction and L2 development, as well as the ontological nature of constructions and other kinds of linguistically defined units in L2 use and learning. He received his PhD from the University of Southern Denmark. His recent publications include "Constructing Another Language—Usage-Based Linguistics in Second Language Acquisition" (*Applied Linguistics*, 2009).

Keiko Ikeda is an associate professor at Kansai University, Japan. Her research interests include microanalysis of L2 classroom discourse, political discourse in Japan, and mass media and politics. Her most recent publications are "Advanced learners' honorific styles in emails and telephone calls" (*Pragmatic Competence*, Mouton de Gruyter, 2009), "Audience Participation Through Interjection: Japanese Municipal Council Sessions" (*Journal of Language and Politics*, 2009), and "Use of Third Party Involvement in Japanese Political Television Interviews (*Talk-in-Interaction: Multilingual Perspectives,* National Foreign Language Resource Center, 2009).

Midori Ishida earned her PhD in Second Language Acquisition at the University of Hawai'i at Mānoa. Her research interests include second language pragmatic development, the application of conversation analysis to interlanguage pragmatics research, and the roles of interaction in second language acquisition. She has published articles in *Language Learning* and edited books, including *Pragmatics and Interaction, Volume 1*. She is currently conducting a study on the development of interactional competence in Japanese as a second language during study abroad from a conversation-analytic perspective.

Sungbae Ko is a research fellow at the Korea-Australasia Research Centre, the University of New South Wales, Australia. He has carried out various research projects in the field of language classroom interaction, second language acquisition, and language education. His most recent publications are "Implicit and Explicit Disagreeing Multiparty Talk in Classrooms" (*Making a Difference: Challenges for Applied Linguistics*, Cambridge Scholars Publishing, 2008), "Multiple-Response Sequences in Classroom Talk" (*Australian Review of Applied Linguistics*, 2009), and "Sequential Patterns of Multi-Party Talk in TESOL Classrooms" (*Korean Journal of Applied Linguistics*, 2008).

Seung-Hee Lee (PhD, University of California, Los Angeles) is an assistant professor in the Department of English Language and Literature, Yonsei University, Seoul, Korea. She studies the various language practices that underlie social interaction using conversation analysis. Her current research interests focus on sequential and interactional practices of talk that are particular to institutional contexts. She is currently working on designs of responses in ordinary conversation as well as on calls for service.

Kristian Mortensen (PhD, University of Southern Denmark) is a post doctoral researcher at the Unit for Sociocultural Research on Learning and Development (LCMI) at the University of Luxembourg. His research interests include social aspects of talk-in-interaction in classroom settings. He is interested in how participants verbally and visually display and co-ordinate their emerging understanding of ongoing activities.

Maurice Nevile (PhD, Australian National University) teaches in the Centre for Educational Development and Academic Methods (CEDAM) at the Australian National University. Previously he has researched and published extensively on features of language and interaction for pilots' collaborative work in the airline cockpit, and also on communication as a factor in human error for aviation accidents. His current projects examine linguistic and interaction practices in the multilingual international university and interaction in cars and other sources of distraction in driving.

Hanh thi Nguyen (PhD, University of Wisconsin-Madison) is an associate professor at Hawai'i Pacific University. Her research interests include the development of interactional competence in second language acquisition and in professional settings, second language socialization, and Vietnamese applied linguistics. Her recent works appear in *Text & Talk*, *Communication & Medicine*, *The Canadian Modern Language Review*, *Studies in Second Language Acquisition*, and *Language and Education*, among others. She is also the co-editor (with Gabriele Kasper) of *Talk-in-Interaction: Multilingual Perspectives* (National Foreign Language Resource Center, 2009).

Gabriele Pallotti is an associate professor of language teaching methodology at the University of Modena and Reggio Emilia, Italy. He is member of the executive committees of the European Second Language Association (EUROSLA) and the Second Language Acquisition and Testing in Europe (SLATE) network. His research focuses on second language interaction and socialization, methodology and epistemology in applied linguistics, and cross-cultural and intercultural conversation analysis. He has coordinated projects on the four-year development of interactional competences in learners of Italian as a second language and on telephone calls in five European languages.

Jae-Eun Park received her PhD from University of California, Los Angeles. Her research interests include conversation analysis and second language learning.

Mi-Suk Seo is an assistant professor in the English Department at California State University, Sacramento, where she teaches courses in second language acquisition, sociolinguistics, and research methods. She received her PhD from the University of Illinois, Urbana-Champaign. Her research interests include conversation analysis, second language acquisition, gesture, and English as a Second Language pedagogy.

Sung-Ock Sohn (PhD, University of Hawai'i) is a professor of Korean Language and Linguistics at UCLA. Her research areas include functional linguistics, discourse and grammar, and second language acquisition. She is the author/co-author of six books including *Integrated Korean* and *Tense and Aspect in Korean* (University of Hawai'i Press).

Guðrún Theodórsdóttir teaches Icelandic as a second language at the University of Iceland. She recently completed her PhD at the University of Southern Denmark (*Conversations in Second Language Icelandic: Language Learning in Real-Life Environment*). Her research interests are second language use and learning in everyday interaction within the research framework of conversation analysis-second language acquisition. Portions of her longitudinal data on naturally occurring second language interaction in everyday settings are available for researchers on TALKBANK.org.

Monika Vöge is currently teaching at the Institute for Germanic Studies at the University of Potsdam. She earned her PhD at the University of Southern Denmark, investigating the interactional implications of laughter in multilingual business meetings. Her research interests in conversation analysis focus on business communication, laughter in interaction, and local identity construction.

Johannes Wagner (PhD, Odense University) is a professor at the Institute of Business Communication and Information Science at the University of Southern Denmark. He is currently involved in three larger projects: He directs a project on electronic conversation analysis (CA) databases which makes first and second language conversations as well as high quality CA transcriptions available for the research community, he is part of participatory innovation group at the Sønderborg Participatory Innovation Research Centre (SPIRE, www.sdu.dk/spire), and he is also involved with the Research Center for Cultural and Linguistic Practices in the International University (CALPIU, calpiu.dk).

Acknowledgments

We are grateful to the following external reviewers for their insightful comments on the chapters in this volume:

Birte Asmuß, *Aarhus University*
Catherine E. Brouwer, *University of Southern Denmark*
Tim Caudry, *Aarhus University*
Asta Cekaite, *Linköping University*
Dennis Day, *University of Southern Denmark*
Paul Drew, *York University*
Roberta Grassi, *Bergamo University*
Hartmut Haberland, *Roskilde University*
Joan Kelly Hall, *Penn State University*
John Hellermann, *Portland State University*
Numa Markee, *University of Illinois at Urbana-Champaign*
Lorenza Mondada, *Université Lyon 2*
Junko Mori, *University of Wisconsin, Madison*
Janus Mortensen, *Roskilde University*
Simona Pekarek-Doehler, *Université de Neuchâtel*
Arja Piirainen-Marsh, *University of Jyväskylä*
Fritjof Sahlström, *University of Helsinki*
Paul Seehouse, *Newcastle University*
Richard Young, *University of Wisconsin, Madison*

Transcription Conventions

Simultaneous utterances
    [Point of overlap onset
    ]   Point of overlap ending

Continuous utterances
    =   No break or gap in speech (latched speech), or continuation of the same turn by the same speaker even though the turn is broken up in the transcript

Breaks and gaps between and within utterances
    (.)   Brief pause of about 0.1 s
    (0.3)   Silence measured by 0.3 s

Characteristics of speech delivery
.	Falling intonation
,	Slightly rising intonation
?	Rising intonation
↑	Shift into especially high pitch in the next sound
↓	Shift into especially low pitch in the next sound
:	Prolongation of the immediately prior sound; the longer the colon row, the longer the prolongation
word	Emphasized speech
WORD	Especially loud sounds compared to the surrounding talk
°word°	Especially quiet sounds compared to the surrounding talk
word	A focal linguistic item [in **boldface**]
(word)	Transcriber's best guess of the words or speaker
word-	Cut-off sound
<word>	Slowed down sounds compared to the surrounding talk
>word<	Speeded up sounds compared to the surrounding talk
.hhh	Audible inbreath
hhh	Audible outbreath
(h)	Plosiveness, associated with laughter, crying, breathlessness, etc.

Transcription issues
xxxx or ( )	Unintelligible speech or unidentifiable speaker to transcriber
((description))	Transcriber's description
→	Focal line in analysis

Source
Jefferson, G. (2004). Glossary of transcript symbols with an introduction. In G. H. Lerner (Ed.), *Conversation analysis: Studies from the first generation* (pp. 13–31). Philadelphia: John Benjamins.

Preface

The second volume in the *Pragmatics & Interaction* series contributes to the fast growing research domain of developmental conversation analysis (CA) within two core traditions of applied linguistics: the study of multilingualism and second language acquisition. The chapters assembled by editors Gabriele Pallotti and Johannes Wagner examine how multilingual participants engage and develop their interactional competencies in ordinary conversations and a range of institutional activities: service encounters, business meetings, medical consultations, a group examination in an academic program, oral language tests, second language tutorials, and second and foreign language classrooms. As the editors note in their introductory chapter, most of the research reports build on two active lines of developmental CA in multilingual contexts: second language (L2) learning as a social activity and the development of interactional competencies over time.

The first research direction has predominantly focused on settings dedicated to language learning and language practice, such as second and foreign language classrooms and tutorials. In this volume as well, several chapters address the overarching ethnomethodological question of how the participants accomplish the "local educational order" of teaching and learning in these specialized settings. So far, less analytic attention has been paid to settings that are not arranged for language instruction or practice, and in which the participant(s) orient to the activity in progress as an opportunity for L2 learning (Wagner, 2010). Some of the studies in this volume contribute to an incipient research program on "L2 learning in the wild." They seek answers to such questions as, How do temporary shifts to L2 learning come to pass? Are they tied to the participants' institutional or "transportable" identities, such as those of novice L2 speaker and more expert speaker? How do the participants manage the competing orientations to the main activity and L2 learning? Is the learning done as an insert sequence of sorts, putting the main activity on hold? Or do the participants pursue language learning and the main business of their talk simultaneously? Through what interactional practices do participants accomplish "doing L2 learning," and what interactional consequences ensue from them?

The second research strand investigates how interactional competencies develop over time. The studies reported in the volume deploy either a longitudinal single case study design or a cross-sectional design comparing groups of L2 participants at different levels of L2 proficiency. They reveal how the L2 participants accomplish a specific practice—proffering topics and responding to topic proffers, engaging in a teller's story, and giving extended responses to questions—jointly with their co-participants, and how over several occasions of engaging in the same practice, or with higher L2 proficiency, the L2 participants increasingly take on a larger and more consequential share in moving the interaction forward. In other words, the L2 participants shift their discourse identities—reflexively constituted through their actions moment-by-moment—towards more substantial, equitable, and effective participation in the practice. As is evident from several chapters in this volume, CA's fine granularity enables analysts to document such changes in the details of sequence organization and turn formats with L2 resources.

CA's fundamental perspective on the relationship between interaction and grammar is that the two orders organize each other, a perspective shared by CA studies examining how L2 speakers' use of grammatical resources changes over time. Thus far, L2 researchers embracing the view of grammar as social practice have not crossed the line to linguistic and cognitive theories of grammatical development, although they may have drawn on linguistic theories of grammar for descriptive tools. This volume breaks new ground in CA research on L2 development by showing how different theories of language acquisition can enter a productive partnership with the analysis of interaction as situated social practice. Despite major differences in their views on language and development, the two selected theories, Usage Based Linguistics and the approach to L2 grammatical development as a series of learner varieties, furnish effective conceptual and descriptive tools to account for the use and development of linguistic resources in specific social practices. The initial outcomes reported in this book offer the first steps towards a research program on L2 speakers' evolving inventories of linguistic resources in the context of developmental CA, and invite SLA researchers of different theoretical persuasions to incorporate an interactional, praxeological perspective in the analysis of L2 development.

Gabriele Kasper

Reference

Wagner, J. (2010). Learning and doing learning in interaction: What do participants do in everyday out-of-school second language talk? In Y. Kite & K. Ikeda (Eds.), *Language learning and socialization through conversations* (pp. 51–59). Osaka: Kansai University, Center for Human Activity Theory.

1 L2 Learning as Social Practice: Conversation-Analytic Perspectives

Gabriele Pallotti
University of Modena and Reggio Emilia, Italy

Johannes Wagner
University of Southern Denmark

Introduction

Learning is a fundamental human condition. Understanding learning as a pervasive phenomenon, present in all kinds of human environments, is a fundamental object of research, which has been pursued in a number of scientific fields and disciplines interested in human behavior (e.g., Koschmann et al., 2005; Koschmann & Zemel, 2009; Lave & Wenger, 1991; Suchman, 1987). Human behavior builds on previous behavior, for which there is rich evidence, if one cares to look at human practice. Learning to drive a Segway by trial and error; observing how locals take the bus or handle knife, fork, or chopsticks; welcoming guests by kissing them at all, once, twice, or even three times; or accomplishing leave-taking—all these are experienced in situations. Future encounters can build on the sediments of earlier experiences. In this way, experiences and understandings can form new practices. This is what we call learning.

If you are used to driving on the right side of the road and arrive at a country that drives on the left side, the learning curve may not be too steep and a change of behavior will necessarily be fast, although it might be felt as a fundamental change. But what is the situation if you come to a country in which another language is spoken? Is second language learning fundamentally different from learning to drive or learning to take your leave? Is language infinitely more complicated than driving, but the way of learning is the same? The answer seems to depend on whom one asks.

One possible answer comes from sociolinguistics. For a long time, sociolinguists have studied multilingual societies in which several languages thrive in parallel. Members of these societies acquire in and through their everyday activities the competence to do certain things in one language—but not necessarily in another (e.g., Blom & Gumperz, 1972; Myers-Scotton, 1993).

Previously monolingual societies have become multilingual in the process of globalization, and the ecology of language acquisition and use has changed radically over the last decades. In today's world of intense international cooperation and competition, people move around. They pass through foreign societies as tourists, business travelers, or international students; or they stay for longer periods as a part of the workforce, as expats. Or they might stay on as migrants. Whatever their reason to move or their reason to stay, they meet people from other places, and all of these people speak different tongues. Meeting people means talking to people, and the first and basic challenge of interaction is to establish a common language for the participants in an encounter.

In the process of increased international mobility, English has permeated societies worldwide. In smaller countries, English may even have become a parallel language throughout the society. In Scandinavia, for example, it is common to switch into English whenever foreigners are around, and many people do this effortlessly. From having been the international language of some professional environments, English has gradually become the lingua franca of professions, business, and education, and is nowadays even a parallel language in everyday life. Although in the larger countries in Europe monolingual environments are still widespread, there is no doubt that English has been established as the default language for international matters. This is creating a new asset for English, but it is a challenge for local and regional languages that need to accommodate to a multilingual future where English will become a default second or third language in conversation.

Sociolinguists point at the many ways in which English has grown. Certainly, language politics has played a role (Phillipson, 1992). Over the past decades, English teaching in schools has started much earlier than in previous times. English dominates the global entertainment industry and the Internet. In general, English has become more available in societies worldwide, and members of modern societies have easy access to it. Sociolinguistics observes and describes how languages become available resources for the members of the society through increased contact and social practices.

Already in the early years of second language acquisition (SLA) research, Hatch (1978) underscored the important relationship between language learning and interaction. In her oft-cited words, "language learning evolves out of learning how to carry on conversations" (p. 404). Her call to conduct more empirical research on the relationships between language learning and conversational interaction inspired a number of approaches in SLA to collect evidence to show how language use and language learning are interwined. Taking the point of departure in the work of Long (1980, 1996), a number of scholars have developed the Interaction Hypothesis, according to which participation in conversational interaction facilitates second language acquisition (Gass, 1997; Mackey, 2007). The interaction hypothesis intends to "understand what types of interaction might bring about what types of changes in linguistic knowledge" (Gass, 1998), in other words the hypothesis is concerned with the interplay between psycholinguistic mechanisms and language use. Another productive approach has been neo-Vygotskyan research into L2 learning (Hall, 2004; Hall & Verplaetse, 2000; Lantolf, 2000; Lantolf & Thorne, 2006; Ohta, 2001), which has established such analytic concepts as *scaffolding*, *micro-genesis*, *internalization*, and *zone of proximal development*, and demonstrated their empirical relevance. Lately, dynamic systems theory (Larsen-Freeman 2006) and Usage Based Linguistics (Ellis & Cadierno, 2009; Ellis & Larsen-Freeman, 2009; Eskildsen, 2009) have bridged SLA's traditional distinction between language use and language acquisition.

Two other strands of research have problematised the distinction between language system and language use. Firstly, research on child language acquisition has brought forth rich evidence that language learning emerges from a complex social interplay between the child and its environment (Bates & MacWhinney, 1987; MacWhinney, 1999; Tomasello, 2003) and is not different from other forms of learning. Secondly, linguistic pragmatics, discourse analysis, speech act theory, and a range of approaches to interaction have argued that "language use" is part and parcel of socially configured action (Firth & Wagner, 1997, 2007). This claim has been developed predominately by conversation analysis (CA), which in turn has its roots in ethnomethodological theory. From an ethnomethodological or conversation analytic perspective, the research goal is to describe how participants create social order by understanding the ways and structures in which social practices are configured and what they can achieve. Social practices are very much bound in language. Language is one available resource that is deployed by the participants to achieve intersubjectivity as the basis of social action. But there are other resources, for example, bodily behavior, gaze, and the manipulation of material objects (cf. Goodwin, 1981, 2000, 2003; Kidwell, 2009; Nevile, 2004).

Although all chapters in this volume address second language use and learning from the perspective of conversation analysis, we do not want to give here a general presentation of CA, for which the reader may consult a number of relevant texts (for general introductions see Drew, 2005; Have, 2007; Hutchby & Wooffitt, 2007; Mazeland, 2006; for introductions with a special emphasis on second language talk see Kasper, 2009; Kasper & Wagner, 2011; Pekarek-Doehler, 2010; Wagner & Gardner, 2004).

If language use is a social practice, and if humans learn in and from their own and other humans' practices, then a conversation analytic take on L2 learning can go two ways: It can investigate changes in participants' practices over time, and it can look at the practices in which participants show an orientation towards gaining control of linguistic resources in interaction.

Regarding changes in participants' practices over time, language learning can be demonstrated and understood by documenting the activities of second language speakers over time, that is, by collecting longitudinal data and comparing how activities unfold, evolve, and develop. This approach has its roots in first language acquisition and has been demonstrated in several studies (Cekaite, 2007; Hellermann, 2008; Kanagy, 1999; Pallotti, 1996, 2001, 2005).

Regarding gaining control of linguistic resources, learning is a recognizable activity for participants and accountable in the typical ethnomethodological sense proposed by Garfinkel, that is, it is noticeable and remarkable for the participants. The participants demonstrate for themselves and for each other that they "do learning." A number of studies have described such practices inside and outside educational environments (cf. Gardner & Wagner, 2004; Nguyen & Kasper, 2009; Richards & Seedhouse, 2005).

The contributions to this volume have been grouped into four sections. The first section (*Language Learning as Development of Practices*) consists of three chapters (Nguyen; Ishida; Lee, Park, & Sohn), which look at the development of participation and language over time. The second section (*Doing Learning*) collects four chapters (Seo; Mortensen; Ikeda & Ko; Theodorsdóttír), which describe participants' accountable practices and procedures of language learning. The two chapters in the third section investigate *Language Choice and Participation in Second Language Talk* (Nevile & Wagner; Vöge). In the final section (*Bridging the Interactional/ Linguistic Divide*), the chapters by Biazzi and Eskildsen take linguistic structures as their point of departure and discuss language development with respect to social organization and practice.

Language learning as development of practices

Hanh thi Nguyen's contribution examines a second language speaker's interactional competence over time. Nguyen investigates the development of one well-defined interactional practice, topic proffers. Topic proffers are interactional moves where a speaker proposes a topic, which can be responded to by co-participants who act on the proffer in different ways. Obviously, launching a topic proffer or responding to one initiated by another speaker indicates a speaker's participation in talk.

Nguyen looks at the L2 speaker's response to and use of topic proffers over five consecutive meetings. In a line of research that had been initiated by Pallotti (1996, 2001), Pavlenko & Lantolf (2000), and Nguyen herself (2008), tracking changing participation over time has delivered evidence for the development of interactional competence. Nguyen shows that her target student went from minimal and delayed responses, to topic proffers, to immediate responses in later meetings. The focal student also launched more topic proffers herself in later meetings. Topic proffers and the increasing response to proffers shape interactional spaces in which second language speakers can use and acquire language. Nguyen's contribution shows how participation increases with respect to one interactional practice.

Midori Ishida works with data from five encounters between an American student and her Japanese host mother during a study abroad, collected over nine months. Ishida is especially interested in how over time, the L2 speaker of Japanese organizes responses to tellings. In some cases, listener responses and assessments can close down the topic. In other cases, second stories and comments show how the telling is understood. While the L2 speaker in the first encounter delivers minimal responses to tellings, she displays her understanding in the second encounter by a second story and by voluntary assessments. Over the nine months, the student's engagement and alignment to the L1 teller grows and she acts more engaged and in tight coordination with the teller, as well as handling a larger repertoire of listener responses during the end of her stay.

Ishida's work raises the question about the relation between interactional competence and social relations. During the stay in Japan, social relations between these protagonists evolve, and this is indicated in language and forms of interaction. In conversation analytic terms, the development of competence can be understood as reflexivity and indexicality. The growing repertoire allows complex and locally adapted listener behaviors, and this works back by creating possibilities of behaving as a more competent participant in interaction, which allows the growth of a more complex interactional repertoire. As Brouwer andWagner (2004) have argued, the development of interactional competence cannot be distinguished from the development of social relations.

Seung-Hee Lee, Jae-Eun Park, and Sung-Ock Sohn's data are oral proficiency interviews with intermediate- and advanced-level Korean heritage language speakers. It turns out that the advanced speakers produce more talk in the same interview time and produce (more) expanded responses to the interview questions, while expanded responses are less common in the interviews of intermediate speakers. In other words, the advanced speakers take the interview as an opportunity to talk while the intermediate speakers orient to the interactional force of the questions (e.g., giving a simple answer to yes/no or other straightforward questions).

Furthermore, the advanced speakers use grammatical resources, that is, clause final and sentence final suffixes that project further talk. Control of these linguistic resources affords the speakers with resources to construct expanded responses and, consequently, to present themselves as speakers on equal terms with first language speakers of Korean.

Doing learning

Mi-Suk Seo's contribution to the volume investigates the interplay between talk, gesture, bodily conduct, and material objects as resources for intersubjectivity. The chapter builds on a strand of research that investigates how participants draw on non-linguistic resources for understanding. Seo demonstrates that multimodal resources can be critical in the interaction of L2 and L1 speakers. She looks at the role of embodied resources in *multiples of repairs*. Such repeated repair initiations seem to be more common in L2 talk than in L1 interaction (cf. Egbert, Niebecker, & Rezzara, 2004). In Seo's data from ESL tutoring sessions with Korean and English speakers, bodily resources and material objects are made relevant as several consecutive verbal repair attempts do not succeed. In the case at hand, the tutor and student talk about a book. At one point, several repair attempts are made to explain a critical word. When the student eventually grasps the meaning and form of the word, she demonstrates her understanding by using the word on a different material object. The point of this research is to show how participants' bodies and the physical world are made relevant in attempts to understand new words. The physical world and visual information are resources always available and possibly made relevant in and through the talk and therefore relevant in the learning activity.

Kristian Mortensen's chapter is also concerned with vocabulary. Mortensen's angle, however, is on teaching lexical items. In his data, the teacher initiates the interactional uptake of a word through his or her talk. In the practice Mortensen describes, the teacher places a lexical item at the end of the turn and makes it hereby available for students' repeats or repair initiation. The lexical items highlighted by this practice are typically connected to new topics, that is, they are projecting further talk. So, compared to Seo's cases, the word explanations do not arise from interactional trouble and extended (multiple) repairs. Instead, possible new items are presented by the teacher in a "sequential format, which structurally gives her/him space to request a word explanation" (Mortensen, this volume) from the students.

Keiko Ikeda and Sungbae Ko describe choral practice in language classrooms (i.e., simultaneous or near simultaneous co-production of a response by several speakers). Their classroom data—in which they find the phenomenon frequently—are collected in Japanese and English language classrooms in Japan, Australia, and Korea. Choral production comes in different forms. Ikeda and Ko distinguish *complete unison production*; *shadowing,* where one speaker starts the TCU and the classmates follow on after a split second; and *echoing,* repeating the whole preceding turn or parts thereof. It turns out that turn allocation by the teacher is the central factor for initiating choral responses. If the teacher allocates the turn to one specific student, this student responds. But if the teacher produces a first action without allocating the turn, students frequently speak in choral coordination.

The last chapter in this section, Theodorsdóttir's description of the turn taking behavior of second language (L2) speakers, is based on a research line which analyzes how second language speakers create learning opportunities outside of the classroom. A major conclusion of these descriptions of second language talk in everyday life is that second language speakers orient towards intersubjectivity *and* towards details of language production (Kurhila, 2006; Mazeland & Zaman-Zadeh, 2004). Second language speakers initiate repairs not only because of trouble with intersubjectivity but also due to trouble with linguistic forms. Theodorsdóttir confirms Kurhila's results that repairs of language forms are often initiated by the second and not by the first language speakers. The first language speakers minimize the role of language form and stick to intersubjectivity (the business at hand) as the main objective of the talk. Theodorsdóttir's contribution to this volume shows that a novice second language speaker insists on bringing her ongoing TCUs to completion, although her co-participants have already indicated their understanding and have moved onwards to the next action. In several exchanges from her data, the second language speaker has not yet reached TCU completion, but the co-participant indicates understanding by providing a possible completion or by proceeding to the next projected action. In these cases, the L2 speaker finishes her projected turn constructional unit without acknowledging the L1 speaker's intervention in the talk. In other words, the second language speaker insists on keeping the floor to bring her turn to syntactic completion although intersubjectivity has been accomplished.

Language choice and participation in second language talk

The two chapters in this section describe issues of participation in multilingual talk and contribute to a better understanding of what "language use" entails. Both chapters draw on data from institutional environments with specific policies for language use. The chapters show that the use of a specific language is an achievement by the participants, as they act with sensitivity to the local contingencies of the situation. Policies are not neutral, nor can they be taken for granted, but they must be acted upon and built into practices of use in concert with co-participants.

Maurice Nevile and Johannes Wagner's data come from a multilingual group examination. Three students and two examiners negotiate the use of Danish (the local language and mother tongue of most participants), German (the language of the written examination report), and English (the preferred language of one of the students). The data show the tension between a language policy—to use English and German, but not Danish, as languages in the exam—and local contingencies of the talk. Of the three students in the group, two have officially chosen to speak German while one has chosen English. It turns out, however, that the policy of "one speaker-one language" is not easily upheld in practice. It conflicts with issues of alignment such that switching language when taking one's turn might appear as a disalignment from the previous speaker, while speaking the same language as the previous speaker may be seen as a display of alignment. Language choice thus becomes a resource for social practices of affiliation and disaffiliation.

What is the relevance of this observation? In multilingual settings, it is sometimes argued that participants should speak their "own" language that is understood but not spoken by the other participants, especially when such languages are typologically close (see, e.g., the European project Eurom4, Blanche-Benveniste, Bonvino, Mota, Simone, Valli, & Uzcanga Vivar, 1997). So, in bilingual encounters between, say, French and Italians, each national group should stick to its language in order for both languages to be used at the same time with minimal efforts on both sides. In conversational practice, however, it is difficult to make this work. Local issues of turn-taking, as shown here, can destabilize the clear-cut a priori decision and good intentions about the distribution of languages.

Monika Vöge's data are also drawn from multilingual institutional conversations. Her chapter analyzes three instances of laughter in which participants make their orientation to multilingualism apparent and use it as a resource in order to do identity work. Institutional identities such as *employee* and *boss,* are enriched by locally created identities (*foreign language learner*). In the setting analyzed by Vöge, too, a general language policy has been set up officially, that is, to speak German in order to give the Hebrew/English speaker a possibility for language practice. However, here as well, such a language distribution rule may conflict with local constraints and goals, so that the participants in the multilingual situation create their own order by strategically switching languages at relevant points.

Bridging the interactional/linguistic divide

The chapters by Biazzi and Eskildsen do not, as do the other chapters in this collection, take their point of departure in social practices but start instead from linguistic forms and formulations. In this way, they bridge the divide between more traditional SLA approaches and how an interactional approach typically proceeds.

Michela Biazzi builds on previous research on learner varieties to identify developmental stages in the acquisition of a second language. The framework is that of the "basic variety approach" (Klein & Perdue, 1997), a functionalist view of second language acquisition describing how learners gradually develop the linguistic means that are necessary to achieve their communicative goals. According to this research line, learners go through a series of linguistic varieties of increasing complexity, from the pre-basic variety to the basic variety to post-basic varieties, characterized by the systematic use of syntactic and morphological strategies to convey grammatical meanings, such as temporality, spatiality, or speaker's stance.

Biazzi's project is to investigate the relationship between the development of linguistic means and that of interactional structures. Biazzi's data come from visits at general practitioners by second language speakers of Italian. The analysis focuses on co-constructions and on the encounter's opening. Biazzi shows that the syntax of recycled parts of the other speaker's utterance in co-constructions correlates with the second language speaker's proficiency level: Speakers of the post basic variety produce more complex recyclings of linguistic material than the basic and pre-basic speakers. With respect to the openings of encounters, however, the morphosyntactic competence of a speaker does not correlate as clearly with interactional competence, which means that speakers of both *low* and *high* learner varieties can be more or less successful in accomplishing this task based on their lexical competence, rather than on their level on a morpho-syntactic developmental scale. Biazzi's conclusion is that "high morphosyntactic competence is not necessarily a predictor of a successful interactional performance" (this volume) in particular actions and situations.

Søren Wind Eskildsen traces a speaker's use of the linguistic pattern *what/ how do you say* over one year, and documents how different uses of this pattern appear over time. Eskildsen brings Usage Based Linguistics (UBL) as a fruitful approach into the discussion. UBL describes the emergence of language structure out of interaction/language use. As part of an emergentist approach to language acquisition, UBL strives to bridge some fundamental dichotomies of modern linguistics (e.g., the distinctions between syntax and lexis, and between performance and competence). According to UBL, language acquisition and language use are indistinguishable. Instead of a "minimal" structural language system, UBL conceptualizes a "maximalistic" model that supports the inclusion of patterns of varying complexity. In this way, patterns and expressions in language sediment into an experientially driven language resource where new structures and new forms of use expand but not cancel earlier meaning/form patterns. Eskildsen shows how the target linguistic pattern is used over time for different purposes in different environments. The change and development lie not in the linguistic form *per se* but in a slow extension of this pattern's potential for use.

Perspective

This collection builds on the anthologies and special issues that have appeared during the last decade and intends to advance the field further. We hope its main contribution is a clearer understanding of the research procedures that have developed in the field and which currently offer two main roads to study language acquisition in interaction. The first one, the study of the development of interactional competence over time, is much better understood. The studies in the first section of this book demonstrate several ways in which the development of interactional competence can be studied. The two studies in the last section add a linguistic angle to these sociologically oriented studies of interaction. There is still much work to do since longitudinal data are scarce and very complex to analyze. The second direction, the ethnomethodological study of doing learning in interaction, is not much better equipped when it comes to data that transcend the classroom environment. Here, more studies are needed that study multilinguality in action and show how language competence grows out of interactional behavior over time.

Acknowledgment
We are grateful to Maurice Nevile and Dennis Day for commenting on an earlier version of this chapter.

References

Bates, E., & MacWhinney, B. (1987). Competition, variation, and language learning. In B. MacWhinney (Ed.), *Mechanisms of language acquisition,* (pp. 157–194). Hillsdale, NJ: Erlbaum.

Blanche-Benveniste, C., Bonvino, E., Mota, M. A., Simone, R., Valli, A., & Uzcanga Vivar, I. (1997) *Eurom 4—Méthode d'enseignement de quatre langues romanes* [Eurom 4—Teaching method for four Romance languages]. Florence: Nuova Italia.

Blom, J-P., & Gumperz, J. J. (1972). Social meaning in linguistic structures: Code switching in Northern Norway. In J. J. Gumperz & D. Hymes (Eds.), *Directions in sociolinguistics* (pp. 407-434). New York, NY: Holt, Rinehart, and Winston.

Brouwer, C. E., & Wagner, J. (2004). Developmental issues in second language conversation. *Journal of Applied Linguistics, 1*(1), 29–47.

Cekaite, A. (2007). A child's development of interactional competence in a Swedish L2 classroom. *The Modern Language Journal, 91,* 45–62.

Drew, P. (2005). Conversation analysis. In K. L. Fitch & R. E. Sanders (Eds.), *Handbook of language and social interaction* (pp. 71–102). Mahwah, NJ: Lawrence Erlbaum.

Egbert, M., Niebecker, L., & Rezzara, S. (2004). Inside first and second language speakers' trouble in understanding. In R. Gardner & J. Wagner (Eds.), *Second language conversations* (pp. 178–200). London: Continuum.

Ellis, N., & Cadierno, T. (Eds.). (2009). Constructing a second language. *Annual Review of Cognitive Linguistics,* [Special section] *7,* 111–290.

Ellis, N., & Larsen-Freeman, D. (2009). Constructing a second language: Analyses and computational simulations of the emergence of linguistic constructions from usage. *Language Learning, 59* (Supplement 1), 93–128.

Eskildsen, S. W. (2009). Constructing another language—usage-based linguistics in second language acquisition. *Applied Linguistics, 30,* 335–357.

Firth, A., & Wagner, J. (1997). On discourse, communication and some fundamental concepts in SLA research. *The Modern Language Journal, 81,* 285–300.

Firth, A., & Wagner, J. (2007). Second/foreign language learning as a social accomplishment: Elaborations on a reconceptualized SLA. *The Modern Language Journal, 91,* 798–817.

Gardner, R., & Wagner, J. (Eds.). (2004). *Second language conversations.* London: Continuum.

Gass, S. M. (1997). *Input, interaction, and the second language learner.* Mahwah, NJ: Erlbaum.

Gass, S. (1998). Apples and oranges: Or why apples are not oranges and don't need to be. A response to Firth and Wagner. *The Modern Language Journal, 82,* 83–90.

Goodwin, C. (1981). *Conversational organization: Interaction between speakers and hearers.* New York, NY: Academic Press

Goodwin, C. (2000). Action and embodiment within situated human interaction. *Journal of Pragmatics, 32,* 1489–1522.

Goodwin, C. (2003). Pointing as situated practice. In S. Kita, (Ed.), *Pointing: Where language, culture, and cognition meet* (pp. 217–242). Mahwah, NJ: Lawrence Erlbaum.

Hall, J. K. (2004). Language learning as an interactional achievement. *The Modern Language Journal, 88,* 606–612.

Hall, J. K., & Verplaetse, L. S. (Eds.). (2000). *Second and foreign language learning through classroom interaction.* Mahwah, NJ: Lawrence Erlbaum Associates.

Hatch, E. M. (1978). Discourse analysis and second language acquisition. In E. M. Hatch (Ed.), *Second language acquisition: A book of readings* (pp. 402–435). Rowley, MA: Newbury House.

Have, P. t. (2007). *Doing conversation analysis: A practical guide* (2nd ed.). Thousand Oaks, CA: Sage Publications.

Hellermann, J. (2008). *Social actions for classroom language learning.* Clevedon: Multilingual Matters.

Hutchby, I., & Wooffitt, R. (2008). *Conversation analysis: Principles, practices and applications* (2nd ed.). Oxford: Polity Press.

Kanagy, R. (1999). Interactional routines as a mechanism for L2 acquisition and socialization in an immersion context. *Journal of Pragmatics, 31,* 1467–1492.

Kasper, G. (2009). Locating cognition in second language interaction and learning: Inside the skull or in public view? *International Review of Applied Linguistics, 47,* 11–36.

Kasper, G., & Wagner, J. (2011). Conversation analysis as an approach to SLA. In D. Atkinson (Ed.), *Alternative approaches to SLA* (pp. 117–142). New York, NY: Routledge.

Kidwell, M. (2009). Gaze shift as an interactional resource for very young children. *Discourse Processes, 46* (2&3), 145–160.

Klein, W., & Perdue, C. (1997). The basic variety. *Second language research, 13*(4), 301–347.

Koschmann, T., & Zemel, A. (2009). Optical pulsars and black arrows: Discoveries as occasioned productions. *Journal of the Learning Sciences, 18,* 200–246.

Koschmann, T., Zemel, A., Conlee-Stevens, M., Young, N., Robbs, J., & Barnhart, A. (2005). How *do* people learn? Member methods and communicative mediation. In R. Bromme, F. Hesse, & H. Spada (Eds.), *Barriers and biases in computer-mediated knowledge communication and how they may be overcome* (pp. 265–287). Amsterdam: Kluwer Academic Press.

Kurhila, S. (2006). *Second language interaction.* Amsterdam: John Benjamins.

Lantolf, J. P. (Ed.). (2000). *Sociocultural theory and second language learning.* Oxford: Oxford University Press.

Lantolf, J. P., & Thorne, S. L. (2006). *Sociocultural theory and the genesis of second language development.* Oxford: Oxford University Press.

Larsen-Freeman, D. (2006). The emergence of complexity, fluency, and accuracy in the oral and written production of five Chinese learners of English. *Applied Linguistics, 27,* 590–619.

Lave, J., & Wenger, E. (1991). *Situated learning: Legitimate peripheral participation.* Cambridge: Cambridge University Press.

Long, M. (1980). *Input, interaction, and second language acquisition.* Unpublished doctoral dissertation. University of California, Los Angeles.

Long, M. H. (1996). The role of the linguistic environment in second language acquisition. In Ritchie, W. C., & Bahtia, T. K. (Eds.), *Handbook of second language acquisition* (pp. 413–68). New York, NY: Academic Press.

Mackey, A. (2007). Interaction. In R. DeKeyser (Ed.), *Practice in second language learning: Perspectives from linguistics and psychology* (pp. 85–110). Cambridge: Cambridge University Press.

MacWhinney, B. (Ed.). (1999). *The emergence of language.* Mahwah, NJ: Lawrence Erlbaum Associates.

Mazeland, H. (2006). Conversation analysis. In *Encyclopedia of language and linguistics* (2nd ed., Vol. 3, pp. 153–162). Oxford: Elsevier Science.

Mazeland, H., & Zaman-Zadeh, M. (2004). The logic of clarification: Some observations about word clarification repairs in Finnish-as-a-lingua-franca interactions. In

R. Gardner & J. Wagner (Eds.), *Second language conversations* (pp. 132–156). London: Continuum.

Myers-Scotton, C. (1993). *Social motivations for codeswitching: Evidence from Africa.* Oxford: Clarendon.

Nevile, M. (2004). *Beyond the black box: Talk-in-interaction in the airline cockpit.* Aldershot: Ashgate.

Nguyen, H. t. (2008). Sequential organization as local and longitudinal achievement. *Text and Talk, 28*(4), 501–528.

Nguyen, H. t., & Kasper, G. (Eds.). (2009). *Talk-in-interaction: Multilingual perspectives.* Honolulu, HI: University of Hawai'i, National Foreign Language Resource Center.

Ohta, A. (2001). *Second language acquisition processes in the classroom.* Mahwah, NJ: Lawrence Erlbaum.

Pallotti, G. (1996). Towards an ecology of second language acquisition: SLA as a socialization process. In E. Kellerman, B. Weltens, & T. Bongaerts (Eds.), Proceedings of EuroSLA 6. *Toegepaste Taalwetenschap in Artikelen [Articles in Applied Linguistics], 55,* 121-134.

Pallotti, G. (2001). External appropriations as a participation strategy in intercultural multi-party interactions. In A. Di Luzio, S. Günthner, & F. Orletti (Eds.), *Culture in communication* (pp. 295–334). Amsterdam: John Benjamins.

Pallotti, G. (2005). Variations situationnelles dans la construction des énoncés en L2: Le cas des autorépétitions [Situational variations in L2 utterance structure: The case of self-repetitions]. *Acquisition et Interaction en Langue Etrangère, 22,* 101–130.

Pavlenko, A., & Lantolf, J. P. (2000). Second language learning as participation and the (re)construction of selves. In J. P. Lantolf (Ed.), *Sociocultural theory and second language learning* (pp. 155–177). Oxford: Oxford University Press.

Pekarek Doehler, S. (2010). Conceptual changes and methodological challenges: On language, learning and documenting learning from a conversation analytic perspective on SLA. In P. Seedhouse, S. Walsh, & C. Jenks (Eds.), *Conceptualising learning in applied linguistics* (pp. 105-126). Basingstoke: Palgrave Macmillan.

Phillipson, R. (1992). *Linguistic imperialism.* Oxford: Oxford University Press.

Richards, K., & Seedhouse, P. (Eds.). (2005). *Applying conversation analysis.* Basingstoke: Palgrave Macmillan.

Suchman, L. (1987). *Plans and situated actions: The problem of human machine communication.* New York, NY: Cambridge University Press.

Tomasello, M. (2003). *Constructing a language: A usage-based theory of language acquisition.* Cambridge, MA: Harvard University Press.

Wagner, J., & Gardner, R. (2004). Introduction. In R. Gardner & J. Wagner (Eds.), *Second language conversations* (pp. 1–17). London: Continuum.

Language Learning as

Development of Practices

2 A Longitudinal Microanalysis of a Second Language Learner's Participation

Hanh thi Nguyen
Hawai'i Pacific University

Introduction

A recent proposal in Second Language Acquisition (SLA) is that learning be conceptualized as participation (Pavlenko & Lantolf, 2000, following Sfard, 1998). This perspective stems from the dissatisfaction with the dominant view in SLA[1] that learning is a cognitive process to acquire linguistic rules and forms (see also Firth & Wagner, 1997; Zuengler & Miller, 2006). In arguing for a social approach to complement the cognitive approach (Pavlenko & Lantolf), the learning-as-participation perspective views language learning as the development of "ways of acting and different kinds of participation" rather than the mere mastering of linguistic codes and structures (Hanks, 1996, p. 222). Attempts to support this perspective have included examination of learners' personal narratives reflecting on their second language in order to demonstrate that language learning is a "struggle to reconstruct a self" (Pavlenko & Lantolf, p. 174) and, in another line of research, investigation of learners' participation and non-participation in communities of practice (through learner's self-reports in diaries or interviews) to show a causal relationship between participation and language learning success (Norton, 2001; Norton & Toohey, 2001). These studies sharply demonstrate that language learning involves important issues (such as access, investment, and agency) beyond the possession of forms and that participation is the condition for learning. To further understand second language learning as participation, rather than relying on learners' self-reports of their participation, this study examines the learner in actual interaction and addresses the question of how exactly a person learns to use interactional resources in order to participate in social interaction in a second language to begin with.

Participation in social activities itself involves the sophisticated maneuvering of an array of interactional resources such as when and how to take turns to talk and how to formulate turns that fit the ongoing flow of action in the conversation. More precisely, in order to participate in talk in a second language, the learner needs to develop *interactional competence*, that is, the ability to co-construct with the other participants interactional resources including the sequential organization of the activity at hand, turn-taking mechanisms, appropriate topics, linguistic forms, and participation frameworks, all of which are performed in ways that are sensitive to the context of specific practices (He & Young, 1998; Nguyen, 2003; Young, 1999). For instance, Pallotti (2001, 2002) demonstrated that as a child learned to participate in multi-party talk in a second language, she needed to develop several skills, that is, learn to use several interactional resources, including how to appropriate words from an exchange between other speakers in the ongoing interaction and to add one's own words, as well as how to initiate a turn that fits the sequential flow and the current topic of the interaction. With respect to adult second language learning, Young and Miller (2004) detailed how a learner increased his participation in the social practice of revision talk in writing conferences. Specifically, the learner was able to perform more acts in the sequential organization of this particular practice in later meetings, acts that were mostly performed by the teacher in early meetings. These longitudinal studies on how someone learns to participate in a second language confirm that there are specific interactional resources that a newcomer needs to learn to utilize in talk to develop his/her interactional competence (see also Brouwer & Wagner, 2004; Cekaite, 2007; Hellermann, 2006, 2007, 2008). Further, interactional competence needs to be developed over time through repeated participation in specific social practices. In other words, the ability to use interactional resources effectively is both the target and the means for language learning (see also language socialization theory, e.g., Duff, 2008, 2010; Duff & Hornberger, 2008; Peters & Boggs, 1986; Schieffelin & Ochs, 1986).

Contributing to this growing line of research, the present study traces the development of a second language learner's interactional competence over a period of time, with a focus on how this learner employed the interactional resources to participate in topic talk with a native speaker of English. Similar to Young and Miller (2004), this study involves a student's repeated participation in a series of office hours with a teacher. A difference between their paper and this chapter lies in the focus on evidence of increased participation: While Young and Miller took increased participation to be mainly an increase in the number of acts performed by the novice, I examine in depth both the initiation of interactional moves and the production of more elaborate (multi-unit) and effective (non-delayed) interactional moves.[2] Further, rather than focusing on the work-related phase (e.g., revision talk), I examine the learner's participation in casual chats at the beginning of these meetings.

The casual chats in the data are characterized by the participants' non-task related talk and body orientation (the participants generally faced each other rather than the desk during these openings). Further, there is a clear transition between these chats and the business of the meeting, usually signaled by the teacher's use of certain discourse markers, often said in a raised volume (e.g., "OKAY," "NOW") as well as a shift in body orientation (from facing each other to facing the desk). Such chatting has also been found elsewhere to be more relaxed than task-related talk in the main business of a meeting (cf. Erickson & Schultz, 1982; Schegloff, 1998) and bears features of both task-related talk and informal talk (Sarangi, 2000). While casual chats are still under an institutional framing, seen, for example, in the participants' choice of topics and turn-taking pattern, it is "informal" in the sense that it is usually not under the same constraints regarding activities, topics, and participation frameworks typical of institutional talk (Drew & Heritage, 1992). For example, such casual chats do not have an explicit agenda as in a meeting, and in such casual chats, people who are institutionally recognized as boss and employees may construct themselves as football fans or homeowners. Because of this more "open" nature of casual chats, participants need to negotiate more on what to talk about in the interaction. For this reason, it may be quite challenging for a newcomer to initiate and sustain topical talk in this type of interaction. The focus of this chapter is thus to examine how an adult learner of English contributed to topical talk in an under-studied type of social interaction in second language acquisition: casual chats at the beginning of a larger, task-oriented activity.

Participation in topical talk crucially involves initiating topics and contributing to an ongoing topic. On this, Schegloff's (2007) description of topic proffering sequences is particularly relevant, and it will be reviewed in the next section.

The generation of topical talk in social interaction

Topic proffer is a common way to enter topic talk in which "a speaker proposes a particular topic ... but does not actively launch or further develop the proposed topic" (Schegloff, 2007, pp. 169–170). This is different from, among other things, unilateral topic initiation, in which the speaker proposes a topic *and* develops it. Topic proffers usually involve topics that are "specifically, differentially, or even exclusively within the *recipient's* experience, or on which their view has special weight or authority" (p. 170, emphasis added). A second feature of topic proffers is that they tend to be questions or assertions *about the recipient*. As such, a topic proffer functions as a first pair part to project a next relevant slot for the recipient to take a turn to talk (to answer the question or to give confirmation/rejection of the assertion). In other words, after a topic is proffered, the burden to talk is on the recipient. In the second position after a topic has been proffered, the recipient can either (a) accept the topic via a positive response token or some other forms of alignment, or (b) decline the topic via a negative response token or some other forms of non-alignment.[3] Given the focus of this chapter, it is important to note that the response turn to a topic proffer can be (a) minimal, that is, having a single TCU, a brief TCU, or several brief (and repetitive) TCUs, or (b) expanded, that is, having "more than one TCU, including one whose grammatical composition is more elaborate or inflected and designed to add to what the prior TCU has done" (p. 171). Thus, the response to a topic proffer can be described along two dimensions: (a) whether it is a topic acceptance or rejection and (b) whether it is minimal or expanded.[4] While a topic-rejecting response can also be expanded, the preferred second position to a topic proffer is expanded topic acceptance. This last feature is of special relevance to this study, since expanded topic acceptance in a second position to topic proffers may indicate more active participation in conversations. Furthermore, there seems to be an asymmetry between initiating topic proffers and responding to them. That is, a person's participation can be said to be more active when s/he proffers a topic and less active when s/he only responds to a proffered topic. In this chapter, I aim to compare the learner's degree of participation in five consecutive office hour meetings and trace her changes over time with respect to topic management.

Methodology

The data consist of the openings of five weekly office hours between a native English-speaking teacher and an adult ESL student from Vietnam. The student, Lien,[5] was of intermediate level, and the teacher, Jeff, had had a few years of experience teaching English. Jeff and Lien agreed to meet once a week so that Jeff could help Lien with her writing and that videotapes of their meetings could be made. Prior to these encounters, they had interaction for three weeks but only in class. Before the training program, Lien had not participated in office hours in English or in Vietnamese. The office hours were videotaped in their entirety, but only the openings, in which the participants chatted more casually about Lien's academic life and general mundane topics, were analyzed for this chapter.

I rely on conversation analysis (CA) for its power to uncover details of interactional procedures emically from the participant's perspectives in order to characterize the observable interactional resources employed by the learner to contribute to topic talk. I then compare the learner's behaviors across time to determine whether and how her level of participation changed with respect to topic talk management.

This methodological strategy (also used in Brouwer & Wagner, 2004; Nguyen, 2003; Pallotti, 2001, 2002; and Young & Miller, 2004) has not gone without being questioned. Markee (2008) argued that to be true to CA's emic approach, researchers should not introduce their own focus on what is being learned but they need to show "how members orient to a language behavior that has occurred days or even months earlier as a resource for learning during a subsequent speech event" (p. 409). A key difference between what Markee proposed and other studies on the development of interactional competence is the emphasis on members' orientation to an interactional resource (a lexical item, pronunciation, or a type of sequence) *as a "learning object"* (Markee's term).

While I agree with Markee that longitudinal studies using CA to understand second language learning should not compromise CA's principles in any way, I find it methodologically problematic to draw a line between when a participant is orienting to an interactional resource *as a learning object* and when the participant is not. In Markee's study, this orientation is taken to be the participants' co-construction of a repair sequence involving a key word. However, there are cases where learning clearly has occurred, but orientation of this type (e.g., in a repair sequence) is not present. For example, in Brouwer and Wagner's (2004) study, a second language user was shown to have changed over time in three telephone openings involving the same interlocutor. Specifically, in the initial phone call, there was much disorderliness and non-fluency (seen in pauses, overlaps, re-starts, and language shifts) but in the last recorded phone call, the interaction flowed smoothly. The difference in the participant's observable behaviors attests that learning has occurred, but there was no specific "learning object" that was oriented to by the participants in the initial phone call. What could have been oriented to by the participants was the disorderliness and non-fluency in the first phone call, and it may have been this orientation that then triggered his modification of behaviors in subsequent interactions when similar interactional problems arose. The analyst, in performing this type of "vertical comparison" (Zimmerman, 1999), does not go beyond what members have access to in their history of interaction, and CA's emic approach is maintained. In this chapter, I do not look for instances when the participants orient to a "learning object" as in Markee's study; rather, I look for observable changes over time in the learner's interactional behaviors.

Analysis

In this analysis, I focus on (a) how the student responded to the teacher's topic proffers and (b) how she initiated topics. The student's responses to topic proffers and her initiation of topic proffers are taken as her contribution to topic talk in the conversation and, by extension, her participation in the openings of the meetings.

Responses to topic proffers

Following Schegloff (2007), Lien's responses to topic proffers will be described as either *minimal* with short, syntactically and lexically simple TCUs, or *expanded* with long, syntactically and lexically elaborate TCUs. A pattern that emerged in the data is that from earlier meetings to later ones, Lien changed her participation from initially providing minimal responses to providing expanded ones. In addition, Lien's early expanded responses to topic proffers were sequentially delayed while they tended to be sequentially immediate in later meetings. A sequentially delayed response is one that does not occur right after the first topic proffer but is produced either after some subsequent trials of the first topic proffer or after some closing or closing-implicating devices by either party. I will first describe the two patterns observed in early meetings, namely, minimal responses and sequentially delayed expanded responses, and then I will describe Lien's immediate expanded responses observed in later meetings.

Minimal responses in early meetings

In the first and second meetings, Lien's participation is mostly limited to minimal, single-TCU responses to the teacher's topic proffers,[6] as exemplified in Excerpt 1.

Excerpt 1, First meeting

```
01 →  J: ((clears throat)) how was your afternoon class,
02        J arranges pens and papers on desk,
03        looks up from desk to L
04    L: it's fine:. but it finished a little late,
05        L smiles
06        (0.3)
07    L: [yeah.
08        L sits down, looks at J
09 →  J: [what- which class are you taking.
10        J puts pen down, shifts in chair,
11        rests hand on chin with elbow on desk
12    L: I took (.) TOEFL
13    J: oh the TOEFL.
14    L: preparation [class.
15 →  J:             [with- ah (.) Shawn?=
```

```
16                              J smiles
17    L:  =Shawns
18        L nods, smiles
19    (0.2)
20    L:  [yes.
21        L smiles
22  → J:  [d'you like- you like the class.
23        J smiles
24    L:  I do.
25        L smiles, nods
26    J:  yeah. Shawn's a- (.) >he's a< nice guy.
27        J nods                J smiles
28    L:  uh huh.
29  → J:  U:HM. (0.5) have you taken the toefl before,
30        J ends smile, rubs hands together
31        L ends smile
```

In this very first meeting, Jeff's topic proffers resemble pre-topical sequences used in talk between unacquainted pairs: They include categorization or categorizing-activity questions (Maynard & Zimmerman, 1984) about Lien as a student. One difference is that while pre-topical sequences can develop into topical talk even between unacquainted participants, what we observe here is that the pre-topical sequences initiated by Jeff do not develop into topical talk. Specifically, at line 1 Jeff proffers a topic about Lien's class, which took place immediately before the meeting and about which Lien has exclusive experience. This turn thus makes it highly relevant for Lien to take a next turn to contribute to the topic. At line 3, Lien responds to Jeff's question, "it's fine," thus claiming access to the topic. She then expands her response with another TCU at line 4. The pause at line 6 together with Lien's "yeah" at line 7 signals that she treats the sequence as complete (Park, 2007).

Schegloff (2007) observed that after the initial topic proffer sequence (such as Jeff's line 1 in Excerpt 1), if the recipient of a topic proffer (in this case, Lien) does not develop it by adding further tellings, the topic profferer may produce a "second try," either to further pursue the ongoing topic or to "steer the talk toward a particular facet of the topic domain first broached" (p. 173). This seems to be what Jeff accomplishes at line 9, when he produces another question to pursue the topic further, making it relevant for Lien to talk next. Lien accepts the topic with a single TCU (lines 12, 14), which was intervened by Jeff's uptake (line 13). Another question from Jeff ("third try") follows to pursue the topic on the class, this time focusing on its teacher (line 15). Lien again accepts the topic but produces a single, minimal turn (line 17). The pause at line 19 and Lien's minimal "yes" at line 10 then serve to close this sub-sequence. At line 22, Jeff proffers another related topic ("fourth try") with a question about Lien's feeling about the class. Lien again claims access to the topic but produces only a single-TCU response (line 24). With the lack of further topic talk from Lien, Jeff makes a positive comment about the teacher (line 26) to align with Lien's response. Lien agrees with this comment but her turn again contains a minimal token (line 28), indicating that she has no further topic talk to contribute to the conversation at this point. The sequence thus closes up and Jeff takes a next turn to proffer another topic (line 29).[7] The transitioning to a new sequence can be seen in his turn-initial hesitation marker "uhm," produced with a louder voice and followed by a pause.

This excerpt shows that Lien participated minimally in topic talk although she continually claimed access to the topic. Except for the initial response, which contained two TCUs, her other responses were minimal. I submit that these minimal responses triggered Jeff to issue a series of "follow-up tries" after the first topic proffer. As a result, not only did Jeff become the steerer of what got talked about in the conversation,[8] he also produced more talk while Lien took a recipient role most of the time and produced less talk. It is important, however, to note that unlike previous observations with native speakers' data in which minimal responses often indicate nonalignment or topic rejection (e.g., Schegloff, 2007), Lien's minimal responses were accompanied by non-verbal affiliating actions including smiling and nodding. It seems that Lien used non-verbal resources to complement her verbal participation in the conversation with the teacher in this meeting.

Delayed response expansion in early meetings

In the first meeting, there are two moments when Lien produced multi-unit turns with (grammatically and lexically) elaborate TCUs. However, the expansions of Lien's responses to the teacher's topic proffers were sequentially delayed, as shown in Excerpts 2 and 3 below.

Excerpt 2, First meeting

Prior to this excerpt, Lien has told Jeff that she took the TOEFL once before but the score was "very poor" and now she needs to improve it. Before line 70, Lien was smiling as the sequence closed down.

```
71      J: when was the last time you took it.
72          J ends smile            J smiles
73            L ends smile
74      L: tsk. I think ah about (.) six months ago.=
75          L looks up, 'thinking face'
76      J: =okay.
77      L: yes.
78      J: ↑↓I'm sure. (0.2) it will- it will improve.
79          J smiles, nods rhythmically several times
80          es[pecially (.) being- [(.) studying here in
81      L:   [yeah.              [I hope so.
82            L nods, smiles
```

```
83      J:  an English program [(.) plus being surrounded
84      L:                     [mhm,
85          [(.) by <LOTS OF ENGLISH>.=
86              J smiles
87              J scratches cheek and then rests hand on chin
88      L:  [ye:s.
89              L nods
90      L:  =right. hh. [that's why I spend a lot of time
91      J:              [so.
92              J smiles, nods, hand remains on chin
93      L:  to (.) practice with ah  toefl (0.2) preparation
94          book, Hanh help me a lot to ah (.) to borrow
95              L smiles, points to Hanh
96          some books from ah the library (to use here).
97      (0.2)
98      J:  °mmm°. good.
99              J nods several times
100     (0.5)
101     J:  And then you have an expert like Shawn to ah
102         answer your questions too, right,
103             gazes down at desk
104     L:  Right.
105             L smiles
106     J:  ((coughs)) °That's nice.°
107             J smiles, gazes down at desk quickly
```

Before Excerpt 2 begins, Lien told Jeff about her "very poor" TOEFL score from the last time she took the test, and they then talked about her need to improve the score. Extract 2, then, is part of a troubles-talk sequence (Jefferson, 1988; Jefferson & Lee, 1992). After Lien's single-TCU response at line 73, Jeff produces a minimal receipt token (line 75). With Lien's subsequent minimal token at line 76, both participants seem to be signaling to each other that they are moving into the closure of this sequence. At line 77, Jeff initiates an optimistic projection which has been found to function as a closing move in a troubles-talk sequence (Jefferson & Lee, 1992). Lien seems to orient to this closure-implicative nature of Jeff's turn by responding with minimal tokens at lines 80–81 and 84–85 (see Maynard, 1980). Her turn at line 80 contains a short TCU, "I hope so," which does not forward the topic any further. However, at line 86, after a latched minimal token as a receipt of Jeff's turn and a subtle laugh,[9] Lien produces a multi-unit turn (lines 87–91) to continue the topic about her preparation for the TOEFL. This expansion of the response to contribute to the ongoing topic talk is thus sequentially delayed, as it occurs after the co-construction of the closing by both Jeff and Lien. The delayed nature of Lien's contribution at this point is evidenced by Jeff's continued orientation to the imminent closure of the troubles-talk sequence: As Lien produces the multi-unit turn, Jeff utters "so" with falling intonation (line 87), which has been found to function as a closing device (Schiffrin, 1987), and thus it seems that he is orienting to the closing of the sequence. Further, after Lien's expanded turn, Jeff did not pursue the topic introduced in Lien's turn. He does not take a turn during the pause (line 93) after Lien's turn, then utters only minimal tokens at line 94 (see Maynard, 1980), and continues with another optimistic projection (lines 97–98), followed by more small tokens (line 102) and non-verbal orientation to the work area (lines 99, 103). Lien's expanded topic talk during the closing phase of a sequence here resembles the introduction of new topics by lower-proficiency students at the closing of academic advising sessions (Bardovi-Harlig & Hartford, 1993).

Another sequential delay found in Lien's contribution to topic talk in the first meeting is the production of an account, and this can be seen in Excerpt 3 (immediately preceding Excerpt 2 above).

Excerpt 3, First meeting

```
38      J:  do you nee:d ah: (1.0) >are you gonna be
39          studying here, (.)   in the graduate program<
40                  J's index finger points down
41          in the fall?
42      L:  uh: (.) nn[nn
43          L looks up, 'thinking face'
44      J:            [no?
45      L:  no.
46          L shakes head
47      J:  undergraduate?
48      L:  yeah I'm planning. (.) but I'm not yet (.)
49          [uh-
50      J:  [you haven't been accepted (.) officially,
51      L:  yes.
52      J:  UH:M. (0.9) does the university- (.)
53          here want (0.6) you to have higher score:
54          J's index finger points down, then up
55      (1.0)
56      L:  ah    [no they doesn't-
57      J:         [°in order for:°
58      J:  okay.
59  →   L:  I- I- I just want to take ah the toefl for:
60          and then ah (.) tsk. maybe it- my idea (.)
61          look for the scholarship myself.=
62      J:  =okay.
63      L:  yeah.
64          L smiles
65      J:  so it might help your- your (.) chance
66                  L smiles
67           to get a scholarship.
68      L:  I hope so.
```

```
69      L smiles
70      (0.2)
```

At lines 38–41, Jeff asks a *yes/no* question about Lien's plan for graduate school in the fall semester. As Lien produces what seems to be a dispreferred response (Pomerantz, 1984) at lines 42–43 (with a hesitation marker, a pause, a thinking face, and a prolonged nasal consonant possibly beginning a "no"), Jeff offers a candidate answer (line 44), which is then accepted by Lien (line 45). However, Lien's negative response with the absence of an account (see Ford, Fox, & Hellermann, 2004) seems to trigger Jeff to reformulate his question at line 47 to be about her plans for an *undergraduate* degree. At lines 48–49, Lien produces a two-TCU response, but as she pauses and hesitates, Jeff again offers to complete her turn (line 50). Lien again accepts Jeff's understanding (line 51), thereby closing this sequence.

At line 52, after a louder discourse marker and a long pause signaling transition, Jeff proffers another, related topic based on the new information he just learned from Lien in the previous sequence: If Lien is not yet accepted by the school, and she is working on her TOEFL, perhaps it is because the school is requiring a score that is higher than her current score. Lien's response at line 56, then, contradicts her previous answer,[10] and thus it is highly relevant at this point for her to resolve the contradiction. Indeed, Lien's multi-unit turn at lines 59–61 provides the explanation: She is not going to graduate (nor undergraduate) school in the fall semester because she does not intend to apply; she is going to improve her TOEFL score first and then seek a scholarship. This expanded response is actually an account for Lien's negative response back at line 45. However, she has been withholding this account and producing minimal tokens or short TCUs to go along with Jeff's completions of her turns and with his questions[11] until there is interactional trouble that requires the account. In this sense, the account is sequentially delayed, and I submit that this delay reflects and constitutes Lien's limited participation in topic talk in this meeting.[12]

Sequentially delayed expansion of a response to topic proffers continued to be found in the second meeting. Excerpt 4 illustrates these delays.

Excerpt 4, Second meeting

```
01      J: so you- you were in class this afternoon.
02          J smiles
03      L: ((breathy)) Yea:h.
04      J: are you- I can't remember now.
05          you're taking the toefl class with
06          Shawn? yes?
07          L smiles, gazes at J
08      L: yes.
09      J: how was that.
```

```
10         J smiles
11      (0.4)
12      L: ↑↓mmm: (.)↑↓I think ah (.)
13                              L smiles
14         I think it's fi:ne. Yeah.
15      (0.5)
16  →  L: uh even I take that cla:ss,
17         and have more homewo:rk, (.)
18         [but it's necessary so I still have to take that.
19      J: [yeah:. right right
```

In Excerpt 4 (second meeting), Jeff proffers the familiar topic about Lien's afternoon class via an assertion about Lien's exclusive experience (line 1). At line 3, Lien accepts the topic with a positive response but does not produce further topical talk. Jeff then revises his previous topic proffer at lines 4–6 by naming the class as "the TOEFL class with Shawn." After Lien's confirmation (line 8), Jeff proffers the topic about the class once more (line 9), this time in the form of a question, making it highly relevant for Lien to take a next turn to talk. After a delay (line 11), a lengthened hesitation marker "Mmm," a micro pause, and another hesitation marker "ah" followed by a micro pause (line 12), Lien provides a single-TCU description, "it's fine" (line 14). Her use of a falling "yeah" after this TCU (line 14) indicates the closure of her turn (Park, 2007). The pause at line 15 confirms that the closing of this sequence is imminent. In this sequential context, then, Lien's expanded, multi-unit response at lines 16–18 is clearly delayed. Her turn is formulated to tie to Jeff's question with the use of "that class" to refer back to the class that Jeff asks about, and while it answers more than the question by mentioning the homework, something not asked for in the question (cf. Stivers & Heritage, 2001), it is a sequentially delayed expansion.[13]

In fact, a recurrent pattern that emerged in the second meeting and continued in the third meeting to some extent was *teacher's topic proffer—student's minimal response—(pre-closing/teacher's further pursuit of topic)—student's expanded response.* This sequential structure is illustrated in Excerpts 5–7.[14]

Excerpt 5, Second meeting

```
80      J: so just a- a little SUMMER VACATION [for you
81             J smiles
82      L:                                      [right. right
83                                               L smiles,
84                                               arms rest on desk,
85                                               chin on hand, looks at J
86      J: but not really. you're busy busy [busy
87             J smiles
88      L:                                   [Yes yes.
89      J: [but hopefully you have a little time=
```

```
90       L:  [uh huh
91       J:  = to- (.) [relax.
92       L:             [yes I hope so.
93                      L smiles
94       J:  okay.
95    →  L:  ah actually I have a three ah three weeks
96            L does self-grooming around neck and shoulders
97                     J closes door because of outside noise
98           vacation already.=
99       J:  =okay?
100      L:  because I came to Madison three weeks in advance.=
101           self-grooming
102      J:  =oh good
((lines omitted as the topic continues))
112      J:  oh that's good. you spent all your time here?
```

Excerpt 6, Second meeting

```
45       J:  and what are you doing in (.)
46                L rests arms on desk,
47                   chin on hand, looks at J
48           Vietnam in the fall.
49       (0.9)
50    →  L:  mmm (1.0) I have job there.
51       J:  Okay.
52    →  L:  uhm: I just quit my job there for three months.
53           I have to come back, I'm working for yew ess embassy.
54       J:  °o:h. okay°.
55            L smiles
56       J:  what do you do at the embassy.
```

Excerpt 7, Second meeting

```
108      J:  oh that's good. you spent all your time here?
109      (.)
110      L:  yeah.
111      J:  in Madison?
112   →  L:  yeah in Madison. because ah I traveled to ah
113          (.) Washington (.) already.
114      J:  okay.
115   →  L:  so now I will spend all the rest time (.)
116          here (.) in Madison.=
117      J:  =well it's a nice place to spend the time.
118                      J smiles, glances down at desk
                            then up at L
```

In Excerpt 5, Lien's delay in providing an expanded response (lines 95–100) to Jeff's topic proffer (line 86) can be seen in the fact that it occurs after several closing-implicating turns by both parties: Jeff's optimistic projection (Jefferson, 1988) at line 89, Lien's elliptic turn, which does not produce a new mentionable at line 92, and Jeff's minimal token in line 94. In Excerpt 6, Lien's expanded response (lines 52–53) to Jeff's topic proffer (lines 45–48) can be logged as sequentially delayed because it occurs after a complete answer that addresses the question (line 50) and this answer has been acknowledged by the teacher (line 51), signaling a potential closure of the sequence. In Excerpt 7, Lien's expanded response (lines 112–116) to Jeff's topic proffer (line 108) also seems delayed, because it occurs after she has provided a complete and minimal response at line 110, which triggers Jeff to pursue the topic further (line 111).

Lien's expanded responses in the above segments have sequential implications. In Excerpt 5, Jeff's next topic proffer (line 110) is built on Lien's newly provided information, and the same is true with Jeff's next topic proffer in Excerpt 6 (line 56).[15] Thus, the student's expanded responses constitute her participation not only at the point of these responses but also, given the co-constructed nature of talk-in-interaction (e.g., Jacoby & Ochs, 1995), in the shape of the conversation as a whole.

However, the above examples also show that Lien's production of expanded responses to the teacher's topic proffers often appeared after the closing of the current sequence was imminent or after the teacher had pursued the topic further. This suggests that she had access to the topics being proffered and could indeed contribute to topic talk—it was the timing of her contribution that did not fit the flow of the conversation well. In the next section, I will show a change in this timing.

Immediate expanded responses in later meetings

In contrast to the two patterns observed above in the early meetings (minimal responses and sequentially delayed expanded responses), in later meetings, Lien seemed to produce lengthier topic talk (with more multi-unit turns) and her expanded responses were sequentially immediate. This is illustrated in the following excerpt taken from the third meeting, in which the teacher proffers the same topic as in the first meeting; however, Lien's response was remarkably different.

Excerpt 8, Third meeting

```
18      J:  SO how- how things' been going.
19          J looks down         J looks up to L, eating
20          L opens folder to get paper out, looking down
21      (1.2)
22      L:  in the: toefl class?
23          gazes at J, then down to bag again
```

```
24          J gazes at L
25       J: toefl class. (.) ee ess ell classes. (.)
26          J looks down          J waves hand, looks up
27          (0.9) ((L puts paper on desk))
28       J: life in general.
29          J continues eating
30    →  L: I think it's fi:ne (.) especially to-
31          L smiles       L looks at J
32          yeah I think ah tomorrow I have to take the (.)
32          ezzay (.) ah exam.
33       J: u:h.
34          J chews cherries
35    →  L: I think it's reading.
36       J: for: ah:
37          J points thumb over shoulder
38          (1.0)
39       L: for ah (0.4) uh (.) Pete.
40       J: okay (0.9)
41          J nods, smiles, takes cherry pit out of mouth
42             and puts it on napkin,
43          [Pete's havin' an essay exam. °ok°,
44             J cleans fingers, folds napkin
45       L: [hhhhh
46          L gazes at J, moves closer to desk
```

At line 18, Jeff proffers a topic about Lien's general well-being. After a pause (line 21), probably due to the managing of papers, Lien responds with a question (line 22), showing her orientation to the type of topics that are relevant in this type of conversation (in the previous two meetings, Jeff and Lien had routinely talked about her TOEFL class). Jeff's answer at lines 25–28, in which he specifies three levels of topics from most specific to most general ("TOEFL class," "ESL classes," and "life in general"), serves to close this inserted adjacency pair and thus makes it relevant now for Lien to respond to Jeff's topic proffer. At line 30, Lien produces a TCU that answers Jeff's question ("I think it's fine"). After this TCU, there is only a micro-pause. Then, without the type of assessment, response token, or further questions from Jeff observed before, Lien continues her turn to add more specific details. What results is a multi-unit turn, which continues until line 35, while Jeff produces only a minimal token (line 33). In this long turn, Lien not only responds to Jeff's inquiry about her general well-being ("I think it's fine") but also extends the turn to talk about her ESL classes ("especially to- yeah I think ah tomorrow I have to take the essay ah exam. I think it's reading"). Lien's expanded answer then creates the opportunity for Jeff to develop the topic further by focusing on another aspect of the topic, the teacher of the course (line 36). Compared to Lien's minimal responses in the first meeting (Excerpt 1), which triggered Jeff to produce a series of follow-up tries in the form of questions, in this meeting, Lien is producing more talk and thus participating more actively in the conversation.

It should be noted that in this case, Lien's increased contribution can be seen not only in the increased number of TCUs but also in her selection of relevant topic talk. At lines 30–35, Lien is orienting to the list of topics that Jeff has just proffered and to the context of the meeting—since this is an academic encounter, she chooses to mention academic-related topics and does not talk about her "life in general." Also, at line 36, when Jeff extends Lien's turn with the preposition "for" but then pauses and gestures over his shoulder, the trajectory of the turn is ambiguous, as it is unclear what can fit into the slot after "for." At line 39, after a pause (showing that Lien does find the trajectory of Jeff's turn to be uncertain), Lien completes Jeff's turn by mentioning the name of the teacher of the ESL class, Pete. This turn invokes the history of interaction between the two participants: In a previous meeting, Jeff has asked Lien about or mentioned the teacher of Lien's other class (the TOEFL class).[16] Jeff seems to be satisfied with this turn from Lien and offers a receipt token (line 40) and a "post-completion musing" at line 43 (Schegloff, 2007). Thus, Lien's contribution to topic talk in this conversation is not only expanded but also immediate and appropriate.

This pattern continued in the later meetings and can be illustrated in Excerpt 9 from the fifth meeting.

Excerpt 9, Fifth meeting

```
01      J:  did you talk to your er-(.) [advisor?
02          J looks at L, torso turned towards L
03  →   L:                              [yeah, yeah, yeah
04                                      L smiles, not facing J
05          I [talked to her.
06      J:    [did she give you some help?
07  →   L:  yeah. she- she correct my ah (.)
08          L glances toward J, then turns to bag
09          statement of pur[pose
10          L turns and leans on arms on desk, torso facing J
11      J:                  [oh, goo:d,
12  →   L:  and then she wanted to ah (.) give it to her (.)
13          yesterday so [I gave it to her already,
14      J:               [okay, so good.
15      J:  so did she give you- did she give you a few
16          suggestions too?
17  →   L:  a:h ye[ah. she-
18          L rests chin on hand
19      J:        [things to [add,
20  →   L:                   [she assessed my ah
21          in- introduction.
```

```
22      J:  hmm.
23   →  L:  yeah. and add wan- add something
24      J:  [uh hmm,
25   →  L:  [that you want me to add in the intro-
26          introduction. and with- she keeps the second
27          parts and she's just change some grammar.
28      J:  mmm.
29   →  L:  and for the first time, she add some more
30          information about Vietnamese ah (.) um m- medical
31      J:  mmm.
32      L:  policy.
33      J:  mmm.
34      L:  and yeah.
35      (.)
36      J:  [good.
37   →  L:  [and she- she think that it doesn't matter with
38          the uh gra- uh with the- grammar,=
39      J:  =mm hmm.
40   →  L:  but she- she think that ahm the- the concept
41          in the=
42      J:  =mm[m.
43      L:     [statement's fi:ne.
44      J:  °okay good°.
45      (.)
46      J:  °good° I'm glad she could help you with,
47                          J smiles
48      L:  yeah.
49          L laughs
50      J:  she's the expert.
51          J smiles, shifts body in chair quickly,
52            crosses legs, touches hair
53      L:  uh.
54          L shifts in chair, self-grooming
55      J:  so she knows exactly what (.) the medical
56          school (.) you know (.) expects,
57              J smiles        J ends smile
58                            J's hand extends towards L
59          L ends smile, chin back on hand
60      L:  [ri:ght.
61      J:  [°you know in ah statements of purpose like that°.
62          L nods
```

At line 1, Jeff proffers a topic about Lien's "advisor." By formulating the referent "advisor" as such (i.e., without any identifying description), Jeff invokes their mutually shared prior experience in previous encounters. Lien's non-problematic response, with an enthusiastic "yeah" repeated three times (lines 3–5), aligns with Jeff in sharing this prior experience. (This display of prior experience is commonly found between acquainted participants in topic initiations [Maynard & Zimmerman, 1984].) Jeff then develops the topic further by asking whether the advisor helped Lien (line 6). To this, Lien produces a multi-unit turn (lines 7–13), during which Jeff assumes the role of the recipient by uttering receipt tokens (lines 11, 14). This active contribution by Lien to the current topic perhaps triggers Jeff to pursue the same topic further (rather than shifting to another related topic) at lines 15–16. Again, Lien's response is quite expanded (lines 20–42) with several TCUs that are syntactically and lexically rich. She continually builds on to the first TCU that responds to Jeff's question (lines 17, 20–21) by beginning a new TCU with "and" (lines 23, 26, 29, 37), a discourse marker used to connect similar events. Jeff's orientation to Lien's expanded response can be seen in his use of minimal receipt tokens throughout this segment (lines 22, 24, 28, 31, 33, 36, 39, 42). Of note, Jeff's assessment at line 46 (which continues at lines 50, 55–56, 61) serves to uptake Lien's telling rather than to introduce a new topic proffer.

To sum up thus far, the student changed to respond to the teacher's topic proffers with more expanded turns to contribute to topic talk in later meetings. While her responses in the first meeting were verbally minimal, her later responses contained more elaborate TCUs. It is important to note here that this change may not be a simple consequence of the participants becoming more familiar with each other; Lien's change in behaviors may reflect and constitute both her increased familiarity with Jeff and her increased ability to use interactional resources.

Responding to topic proffers, however, is still a passive way of participation: The student only had to provide a second pair part of an ongoing adjacency pair. Since the first pair part already projects certain next actions for the second pair part, the producer of the second pair part only needs to select from a limited number of choices. In addition, most of the topic proffers by the teacher were questions and questions typically contain or "model" the use of certain lexical items and syntactic structures for the answer (Pomerantz, 1988). From a language learning perspective, this should make responding to topic proffers a simpler interactional task than initiating topics. In Lien's meetings with Jeff, I did not observe any topic initiation in the early meetings. She only moved from responding to topic proffers to initiating one in a later meeting, and this will be the focus of the next section.

Topic proffer production
In the five meetings examined, Lien proffered a topic only once. It is meaningful that this one instance occurred in the fourth meeting. In fact, the data show that

a similar occasion occurred in the third meeting but Lien did not proffer a topic then (Excerpt 10).

Excerpt 10, Third meeting

```
01      L closes door
02      J: I was just eating cake.
03         J smiles, eating
04      (0.5)
05      L: yeah.
06         L looks up, laughs
07      J: so don't worry. there's a piece of cake
08         here if you like and really (.) good cherries.
09      (1.2)
10      L: huh.
11         L bends down sideways to take things out of bag,
12         not looking at J
13      (0.8)
14      J: thanks Hanh for (.) bringing in (.)
15              looks up to H, eating
16              L laughs, looks up to J
17         these snacks again.
18      H: you should go ahead and help yourself,
19         L takes papers out and puts on desk
20      J: °this is kind of nice,°
21      J: SO how- how things been going.
```

In this meeting, Lien came late to the office. Jeff's turns at lines 2 and 7 seem to orient to this fact as he tells Lien not to "worry." At the same time, Jeff invites Lien to some of the cake and cherries provided by Hanh, the researcher (lines 7–8). The pause after this invitation (line 9) may indicate the beginning of a dispreferred response (Pomerantz, 1984) by Lien or it may indicate her occupation with getting ready for the business of the meeting (lines 11–12). In any event, Lien's absence of an acceptance response to Jeff's invitation continues to be seen in the minimal token at lines 10 and another silence at line 13. Indeed, Jeff seems to read Lien's lack of uptake as a dispreferred response and shifts the invitation sequence to a thanking sequence addressed toward the researcher (line 14). This may indicate that he has abandoned the invitation. Lien's lack of orientation to the invitation continues when Hanh issues another invitation to the snack (line 18): Lien silently takes her papers out and put them on the desk.[17] At line 19, Jeff transitions to another topic altogether. In sum, what we see in this interaction is Lien's lack of uptake to invitations addressed toward her.

Interestingly, in the next meeting, a similar scenario occurred. This time, we see Lien proffering a topic (Excerpt 11).

Excerpt 11, Fourth meeting

```
06     J:  I have even brought a little treat today.
07         J smiles, showing a fortune cookie to T
08         L is chewing something (probably chewing gum)
09     (3.5)
10     J:  any one like fortune cookies?
11         J sits down, smiling
12     (1.0)
13     L:  oh you went to a Chinese restaurant again?
14         L sits down, smiling
15     (0.9) J nods
16     J:  no the food cart. > have you tried any of the
17         food carts?<
((conversation continues with Jeff and Lien talking
  about how Lien should try the food carts one day))
```

    As the meeting begins, Jeff shows a fortune cookie to Hanh, the researcher. As Hanh is the one who has been bringing snacks to the meeting, his turn seems to be designed for her. Jeff's turn at line 6 could also be an invitation to the cookie, as he refers to it as "a little treat." However, with no uptake from either Hanh or Lien, Jeff reissues his invitation, this time a little more explicitly (line 10). There is still a lack of uptake from the other participants, as evident in the pause at line 12.[18] At line 13, however, Lien takes a turn. This turn is not a second pair part to Jeff's invitation (i.e., it is neither an acceptance nor rejection). Rather, it is formulated as a topic proffer: It concerns an activity that Jeff has exclusive access to and it is produced with a rising intonation (see Schegloff, 2007). This topic proffer fits the sequential flow of the conversation as it ties to the fortune cookie and it shows Lien's cultural knowledge (that fortune cookies are usually served at Chinese restaurants).[19] Thus, Lien's topic proffer is relevant in this context. Evidence for its relevance can be seen in Jeff's non-problematic response (a nod, line 15). Jeff then modifies his answer and specifies that it was not a restaurant but a food cart (line 16). Subsequently, he proffers a related topic, "have you tried any of the food carts?" Thus, Lien's topic proffer back at line 13 can be said to have driven the conversation forward and shaped what gets talked about next. From only responding to the teacher's topic proffers, Lien now shows that she can proffer a topic that fits the flow of the conversation.

Discussion and conclusion

The above analysis indicates that the student changed from making minimal responses or sequentially delayed expanded responses to making immediate expanded responses, and eventually to initiating topic proffers herself. Table 1 roughly summarizes the occurrence over time of each type of response to topic proffers by the student. Although minimal responses were observed throughout the first four meetings, only in the first and second meetings were they the student's predominant way of response to topic proffers. Sequentially delayed expanded responses were observed alongside these minimal responses in the first and second meetings for about half or one-third of the times, but they are much less frequent in the third and fourth meetings, and none occurred in the last meeting. From the third meeting on, the student began to produce immediate expanded responses to the teacher's topic proffers, and in the last two meetings, this is her predominant way of responding. Finally, an instance of active topic proffer by the student was observed in the fourth meeting.

Table 1. The student's responses to topic proffers over time

time	minimal responses	sequentially delayed expanded responses	immediate expanded responses	topic proffer
first meeting	X (7)	X (4)		
second meeting	X (14)	X (4)		
third meeting	X (1)	X (1)	X (1)	
fourth meeting	X (3)	X (1)	X (6)	X (1)
fifth meeting			X (3)	

Note: X: observed; number in parentheses: number of occurrences

As time went on, the student also contributed more to topic talk, as indicated by the increased number of TCUs in her responses,[20] the higher grammatical and lexical elaboration of these TCUs, and the active role she played in shaping the content of the talk through topic proffer initiation. It is also evident in the data that over time, the student and teacher developed their familiarity with each other, such as in Excerpt 4, when Jeff used information from the first meeting to make an assertion about Lien's class before the meeting (line 1) and explicitly invoked his (lack of) memory concerning what they had talked about in a previous meeting (lines 4–6); in Excerpt 8, when Lien oriented to something that had been discussed in previous meetings—the TOEFL class (line 22); and in Excerpt 9, when Jeff's question in line 1 assumed that Lien had an advisor, information provided in their previous meetings. The fact that the learner utilized certain interactional resources in more active and effective ways in the context of the participants' increasing mutual familiarity suggests that language learning is intertwined with relationship management.

While specific opportunities for language learning were provided by topic proffers as interactional moves that allow for the production of expanded answers, the opportunities to construct a sequentially "delayed" answer were provided by the sequential development of the subsequent talk, more specifically, the teacher's minimal acknowledgment tokens after the student's minimal/limited answers. It was these (teacher's) turns (interactional moves) that allowed for the production of the student's delayed responses because they did not immediately introduce a new topic.

The student's increased participation in office hour openings with the teacher may be said to be part of her socialization (Schieffelin & Ochs, 1986) into the practice at hand as she learned specific ways of behaving—culturally and linguistically. This socialization process was largely facilitated by the organization of topic proffers, which, as a first pair part in an adjacency pair, created a second pair-part slot for the student to contribute to the conversations (first minimally then in an expanded fashion). Further, the teacher's ways of using topic proffers also facilitated the student's development. By producing minimal tokens after the student's initial responses to his topic proffers, for example, he was providing her with opportunities to expand her responses (in a delayed fashion). Topic proffers thus can be considered an *affordance* for second language socialization (Gibson, 1979; van Lier, 2000; see also Frazier, 2007 for examples of how interactional patterns may serve as affordances for particular actions by the participants). In an ecological perspective, an affordance "refers to the fit between an animal's capabilities and the environmental supports and opportunities (both good and bad) that make possible a given activity" (Gibson & Pick, 2003, p. 15). For second language learners, this ecological approach involves making active use of language and other semiotic systems to achieve social actions that fit their needs. The potential of the topic proffer as an affordance may be seen in the fact that it allows for minimal responses (as in the first and second meetings) as well as expanded responses (cases when the novice took multi-unit turns as in later meetings). Particularly, it also allows for sequentially delayed expanded responses (cases when the novice took multi-unit turns *after* producing a brief second pair part, as in Excerpts 5–7 above). Thus, it can be said that the student's increased participation can be observed in her changes in the way she responded to the same affordance in social interaction (namely, topic proffers) over time.[21]

Furthermore, in order to make these changes, the student employed specific abilities including the ability to come up with TCUs that are more grammatically and lexically elaborate as well as the ability to produce turns at the appropriate slot and the ability to speak about topics that are suitable at specific moments of talk. These specific abilities make up her interactional competence in the given practice. The findings in this study thus compel us to think that participation itself is the *target* of learning: A second language learner needs to develop the specific interactional resources to participate in conversations in the target language. This point thus complements the current understanding (from critical ethnographic studies, e.g., Norton, 2001; Norton & Toohey, 2001) that participation opens the door to language learning. In that regard, this study strengthens the *learning-as-participation* metaphor in SLA.[22]

In this chapter, I have used CA to investigate language learning as a social phenomenon. I have shown that CA can provide a detailed description of the learner's situated, local display of competence (Drew, 2004; Heritage & Atkinson, 1984) at different times. I have demonstrated that CA's analytical lens allows the researcher (a) to observe a learner's utilization of interactional resources in interaction and (b) to document evidence of increased participation. The observations from the analysis of talk-in-interaction form the basis for a comparison of different instances of the same discursive practice across time, which then enables the researcher to gain an understanding about how a learner's interactional competence (Hall, 1993, 1995; He & Young, 1998; Nguyen, 2003) develops over time. This last step, the comparison of different instances, is, in fact, *not* outside of CA's methodology. In the view of a prominent CA researcher, Zimmerman (1999), CA can be involved with both "horizontal comparison" (across-case comparison) and "vertical comparison" (across-time comparison; see also Kasper, 2009). Thus, although a comparison of instances across time ("vertical comparison") has not been topicalized in most CA works, it is consistent with CA's principles—and it is precisely here that CA is powerful for the study of language learning as *observable changes in competence* across time.

According to Zimmerman, CA at the turn of the millennium was informed about how talk-in-interaction works (i.e., how competences are displayed in talk; see Drew, 2004; Heritage & Atkinson, 1984), but it had not been as informed about how talk-in-interaction emerges (i.e., how these competences develop). A number of years later, researchers still find that CA longitudinal studies are needed to understand second language learning (Firth & Wagner, 2007; Markee & Kasper, 2004). This study has been an effort to respond to this call by focusing on *competence-in-interaction* not as stable and to be taken for granted, but as changing and developing continuously.

Notes

1 Apart from this dominant view in SLA is an important line of research that focuses on communicative competence (Canale & Swain, 1980) and interlanguage pragmatics (e.g., Kasper & Blum-Kulka, 1993).
2 Further elaborations on these concepts will be provided later in the chapter.
3 Similarly, Maynard and Zimmerman (1984) found that topic development may proceed from a pre-topical sequence to topical talk. A pre-topical sequence is a type of pre-sequence in the sense that it is "a device by which a speaker can produce a preliminary sequence that signals a forthcoming adjacency pair of a particular type" such as a pre-invitation (p. 306, following Sacks, 1995 [Lecture 1, 1972]). Unlike other pre-sequences, however, pre-topical sequences "do not prefigure topical adjacency pairs as such, but rather they introduce extended segments of topical talk whose organization is more complicated than the adjacency pair" (p. 306). According to Maynard and Zimmerman, unacquainted participants may

generate topical talk by using a pre-topical sequence, which involves two parts: (a) categorization or categorizing-activity question such as "What's your major?" or "Where you from?" and (b) answer.

4. Maynard and Zimmerman (1984) similarly observed that pre-topical questions (used between unacquainted participants) are invitations and they can be accepted or declined. Acceptances of topic invitations are achieved in "long-form replies to pre-topical questions" (p. 306). Rejections of topic invitations, in contrast, are accomplished by "short-form replies" plus an optional "return question" (p. 306).

5. Participants' names are pseudonyms.

6. To be exact, in the first meeting Jeff produced 11 topic proffers and subsequent trials, to which 7 of Lien's responses (64%) are minimal and 4 (36%) are expanded. In the second meeting, Jeff produced 18 topic proffers and subsequent trials of topic proffers, to which Lien produced 14 minimal responses (78%) and 4 expanded responses (22%). "Minimal responses" are defined in Schegloff's terms mentioned above.

7. This new topic is initiated via the procedure of topic shading, that is, the new topic is related to an aspect of the previous topic (in this case, the TOEFL).

8. See also Hauser (2003) for a discussion on the "conversation manager" role of the native speaker in NS-NNS conversations.

9. The fact that Lien rushes to produce the receipt token at line 86 may indicate her orientation to the imminent closing of the sequence: Since the sequence is closing up, in order to take a long turn at this point, she needs to grab the floor quickly.

10. Indeed, Lien's answer at line 56 is formatted as a dispreferred turn, with the preceding pause at line 55, and a hesitation marker at the beginning of the answer.

11. The reasons for Lien to do so may be her politeness or her misunderstanding of Jeff's questions—however, we do not have evidence to discuss these reasons.

12. This excerpt (as well as the others presented here) also shows how the teacher constructs himself as the manager of the interaction by asking questions and completing the student's utterances.

13. It should be noted that the relevance of the response to a topic proffer is different from the timing of the response. A relevant response can still be delayed, as in this case.

14. Excerpts 4–7 include all the instances of delayed expanded responses in the second meeting.

15. In Excerpt 7, after this sequence, Jeff repeats a part of his utterance at line 177 in a quieter voice, a pause occurs, and Jeff transitions the talk to the business of writing.

16. In a previous study, Maynard and Zimmerman (1984) found that acquainted pairs often display prior experience in their topic initiation.

17. Lien's lack of response to Jeff's invitation may be due to the fact that his invitation is indirect, while in Lien's culture (Vietnamese), invitations of this type tend to be more direct, with the word "invite" used explicitly and/or with the invitation being repeated multiple times. Sometimes, the inviter will even insist on serving the food despite the invitee's refusal (Nguyen, forthcoming). Lien's lack of uptake to Hanh's invitation

at line 17 may also be due to the shape of the invitation: Hanh mentions "you," which can be ambiguous to Lien—Lien may interpret it as addressing only Jeff and not including her.

18 At this point Hanh is perhaps trying to stay out of the interaction and selects to be behind the camera.
19 It is also possible that Lien's use of the word "again" displays her orientation to a previous encounter in which Jeff talked about going to a Chinese restaurant. However, this previous encounter was not in the recorded conversations.
20 To obtain a sense of the global change in Lien's contribution as manifested in her verbal production, I counted her turns and the number of words and non-words tokens (cut-offs and hesitation markers). In the opening of the first meeting, Lien's turns averaged at 4.7 words and non-word tokens, but in the opening of the fifth meeting, her turns averaged at 7.9 words and non-word tokens.
21 See also Peters and Boggs, 1986, on similar ideas about the learning of interactional routines among children.
22 Block (2007) also recognized that critical ethnographic research on second language learning would have much to gain if the researcher also examines the learner in actual (vs. reported) social interaction.

References

Bardovi-Harlig, K., & Hartford, B. (1993). Learning the rules of academic talk: A longitudinal study of pragmatic change. *Studies in Second Language Acquisition, 15,* 279–304.
Block, D. (2007). The rise of identity in SLA research, post Firth and Wagner (1997). *The Modern Language Journal, 91,* 863–876.
Brouwer, C. E., & Wagner, J. (2004). Developmental issues in second language conversation. *Journal of Applied Linguistics, 1*(1), 29–47.
Canale, M., & Swain, M. (1980). Theoretical bases of communicative approaches to second language teaching and testing. *Applied Linguistics, 1*(1), 1–47.
Cekaite, A. (2007). A child's development of interactional competence in a Swedish L2 classroom. *The Modern Language Journal, 91,* 45–62.
Drew, P. (2004). Conversation analysis. In K. L. Fitch & R. E. Sanders (Eds.), *Handbook of language and social interaction* (pp. 71–102). New York, NY: Routledge.
Drew, P., & Heritage, J. (1992). Analyzing talk at work: An introduction. In P. Drew & J. Heritage (Eds.), *Talk at work* (pp. 3–65). Cambridge: Cambridge University Press.
Duff, P. (2008). Language socialization, higher education, and work. In *Encyclopedia of language and education* (Vol. 8, pp. 257–270). New York, NY: Springer.
Duff, P. (2010). Language socialization. In S. L. McKay & N. Hornberger (Eds.), *Sociolinguistics and language education.* Clevedon: Multilingual Matters.

Duff, P., & Hornberger, N. (2008). *Encyclopedia of language and education* (Vol. 8). New York, NY: Springer.

Erickson, F., & Schultz, J. (1982). *The counselor as gatekeeper.* New York, NY: Academic Press.

Firth, A., & Wagner, J. (1997). On discourse, communication, and (some) fundamental concepts in SLA research. *The Modern Language Journal, 81,* 285–300.

Ford, C., Fox, B., & Hellermann, J. (2004). "Getting past no": Sequence, action and sound production in the projection of no-initiated turns. In E. Couper-Kuhlen & C. Ford (Eds.), *Sound patterns in interaction: Cross-linguistic studies from conversation (Typological Studies in Language 62*; pp. 233–269). Philadelphia, PA: John Benjamins.

Frazier, S. (2007). Tellings of remembrances "touched off" by student reports in group work in undergraduate writing classes. *Applied Linguistics, 28*(2), 189–210.

Gibson, J. J. (1979). *The ecological approach to visual perception.* Boston, MA: Houghton Mifflin.

Gibson, E. J., & Pick, A. D. (2003). *An ecological approach to perceptual learning and development.* Oxford: Oxford University Press.

Hall, J. K. (1993). The role of oral practices in the accomplishment of our everyday lives: The sociocultural dimension of interaction with implications for the learning of another language. *Applied Linguistics, 14*(2), 145–167.

Hall, J. K. (1995). (Re)creating our worlds with words: A sociohistorical perspective of face-to-face interaction. *Applied Linguistics, 16*(2), 206–232.

Hanks, W. F. (1996). *Language and communicative practices.* Boulder, CO: Westview.

Hauser, E. (2003). *"Corrective recasts" and other-correction of language form in interaction among native and non-native speakers of English: The application of conversation analysis to second language acquisition* (Unpublished doctoral dissertation). University of Hawai'i at Mānoa, Honolulu.

He, A. W., & Young, R. F. (1998). Language proficiency interviews: A discourse approach. In R. F. Young & A. W. He (Eds.), *Talking and testing: Discourse approaches to the assessment of oral proficiency* (Vol. 14, pp. 1–24). Philadelphia, PA: John Benjamins.

Hellermann, J. (2006). Classroom interactive practices for developing L2 literacy: A microethnographic study of two beginning adult learners of English. *Applied Linguistics, 27*(3), 377–404.

Hellermann, J. (2007). The development of practices for action in classroom dyadic interaction: Focus on task openings. *The Modern Language Journal, 91*(1), 83–96.

Hellermann, J. (2008). *Social actions for classroom language learning.* Clevedon: Multilingual Matters.

Heritage, J., & Atkinson, J. (1984). Introduction. In J. Atkinson & J. Heritage (Eds.), *Structures on social action: Studies in conversation analysis* (pp. 1–15). Cambridge: Cambridge University Press.

Jacoby, S., & Ochs, E. (1995). Co-construction: An introduction. *Research on Language and Social Interaction, 28*(3), 171–183.

Jefferson, G. (1988). On the sequential organization of troubles-talk in ordinary conversation. *Social Problems, 35*(4), 418–441.

Jefferson, G., & Lee, J. (1992). The rejection of advice: Managing the problematic convergence of a "troubles-telling" and a "service encounter". In P. Drew & J. Heritage (Eds.), *Talk at work* (pp. 521–548). Cambridge: Cambridge University Press.

Kasper, G. (2009). Categories, context, and comparison in conversation analysis. In H. t. Nguyen & G. Kasper (Eds.), *Talk-in-interaction: Multilingual perspectives* (pp. 1–28). Honolulu, HI: University of Hawai'i, National Foreign Language Resource Center.

Kasper, G., & Blum-Kulka, S. (Eds.). (1993). *Interlanguage pragmatics*. Oxford: Oxford University Press.

Markee, N. (2008). Toward a learning behavior tracking methodology for CA-for-SLA. *Applied Linguistics 29*(3), 404–427.

Markee, N., & Kasper, G. (2004). Classroom talks: An introduction. *The Modern Language Journal, 88*(4), 491–500.

Maynard, D. (1980). Placement of topic changes in conversation. *Semiotica, 30*(3/4), 263–290.

Maynard, D., & Zimmerman, D. H. (1984). Topical talk, rituals, and the social organization of relationships. *Social Psychology Quarterly, 47*(4), 301–316.

Nguyen, H. t. (2003). *The development of communication skills in the practice of patient consultation among pharmacy students* (Unpublished doctoral dissertation). University of Wisconsin-Madison.

Nguyen, H. t. (forthcoming). Inviting in Vietnamese and in English. In C. Röver & H. t. Nguyen (Eds.), *Vietnamese pragmatics*. Honolulu, HI: University of Hawai'i, National Foreign Language Resource Center.

Norton, B. (2001). Non-participation, imagined communities, and the language classroom. In X. Bonch-Bruevich, W. Crawford, J. Hellermann, C. Higgins, & H. t. Nguyen (Eds.), *Selected Proceedings of the Second Language Research Forum* (pp. 167–180). Somerville, MA: Cascadilla Press.

Norton, B., & Toohey, K. (2001). Changing perspectives on good language learners. *TESOL Quarterly, 35*(2), 307–322.

Pallotti, G. (2001). External appropriations as strategy for participating in intercultual multi-party conversations. In A. Di Luzio, S. Günthner, & F. Orietti (Eds.), *Culture in communication* (pp. 295–334). Amsterdam: John Benjamins.

Pallotti, G. (2002). Borrowing words: Appropriations in child second-language discourse. In J. Leather & J. van Dam (Eds.), *Ecology of language acquisition* (pp. 183–202). Dordrecht: Kluwer Academic Publishers.

Park, J. E. (2007). *Getting closure in talk-in-interaction: Conversation-analytic study of the token "yeah"*. Paper presented at the Pragmatics and Language Learning conference, Honolulu, Hawai'i.

Pavlenko, A., & Lantolf, J. P. (2000). Second language learning as participation and the (re)construction of selves. In J. P. Lantolf (Ed.), *Sociocultural theory and second language learning* (pp. 155–177). Oxford: Oxford University Press.

Peters, A., & Boggs, S. (1986). Interactional routines as cultural influences upon language acquisition. In B. Schieffelin & E. Ochs (Eds.), *Language socialization across cultures* (pp. 80–96). Cambridge: Cambridge University Press.

Pomerantz, A. (1984). Agreeing and disagreeing with assessments: Some features of preferred/dispreferred turn shapes. In M. Atkinson & J. Heritage (Eds.), *Structures of social action: Studies in conversation analysis* (pp. 57–101). Cambridge: Cambridge University Press.

Pomerantz, A. (1988). Offering a candidate answer: An information seeking strategy. *Communication Monographs, 55*(4), 360–373.

Sacks, H. (1995). *Lectures on conversation* (Vols. I & II). Oxford: Blackwell Publishers.

Sarangi, S. (2000). Activity types, discourse types and interactional hybridity: The case of genetic counselling. In S. Sarangi & M. Coulthard (Eds.), *Discourse and social life* (pp. 1–27). London: Pearson.

Schegloff, E. A. (1998). Body torque. *Social Research, 65*(3), 535–596.

Schegloff, E. A. (2007). *Sequence organization in interaction: A primer in conversation analysis (Vol. 1)*. Cambridge: Cambridge University Press.

Schieffelin, B., & Ochs, E. (1986). Language socialization. *Annual Review of Anthropology, 15*, 163–191.

Schiffrin, D. (1987). *Discourse markers*. Cambridge: Cambridge University Press.

Sfard, A. (1998). On two metaphors for learning and the dangers of choosing just one. *Educational Researcher, 27*, 4–13.

Stivers, T., & Heritage, J. (2001). Breaking the sequential mold: Answering "more than the question" during comprehensive history taking. *Text, 21*(1–2), 151–185.

van Lier, L. (2000). From input to affordance: Social-interactive learning from an ecological perspective. In J. Lantolf (Ed.), *Sociocultural theory and second language learning* (pp. 245–285). Oxford: Oxford University Press.

Young, R. F. (1999). Sociolinguistic approaches to SLA. *Annual Review of Applied Linguistics, 19*, 105–132.

Young, R. F., & Miller, E. (2004). Learning as changing participation: Discourse roles in ESL writing conferences. *The Modern Language Journal, 88*(4), 519–535.

Zimmerman, D. H. (1999). Horizontal and vertical comparative research in language and social interaction. *Research on Language & Social Interaction, 32*, 195–203.

Zuengler, J., & Miller, E. (2006). Cognitive and sociocultural perspectives: Two parallel SLA worlds? *TESOL Quarterly, 40*(1), 35–58.

3
Engaging in Another Person's Telling as a Recipient in L2 Japanese: Development of Interactional Competence During One-Year Study Abroad

Midori Ishida
University of Hawai'i at Mānoa

Introduction

This study investigates the development of interactional competence through the analysis of conversational data collected in a longitudinal design. It examines, using conversation analysis (CA), how a learner of Japanese as a second language (L2) engages in conversation as a story recipient, and identifies changes that suggest the learner's development. Despite recent rapid growth in the research on development of interactional competence over time (e.g., Brouwer & Wagner, 2004; Cekaite, 2007; Hellermann, 2006, 2007, 2008; Ishida, 2009; Mondada & Pekarek Doehler, 2004; Ngyuen, 2003; Pallotti, 2001; Wootton, 1997; Young & Miller, 2004), little research has been conducted on the competence of L2 learners as story recipients and their competence in using assessments (e.g., Goodwin & Goodwin, 1987) as a way to demonstrate understanding of co-participants' talk and a particular stance toward it (exceptions include Ishida, 2006; Ohta, 2001). In this chapter, I aim to demonstrate (a) that CA enables the analyses of these heretofore unexplored aspects of L2 learners' interactional competence, and (b) that comparison of different excerpts taken on different occasions in a span of seven months suggests the development of interactional competence as part of language socialization (Schieffelin & Ochs, 1986).

Assessment activities and story recipients' interactional competence

As Charles Goodwin (1986a) argues, responding to storytelling as a recipient is a complex task because one has to comprehend the current speaker's talk and give appropriate responses by anticipating the trajectory of the story. When the primary speaker's telling is still in progress, other participants present there (the audience) are free to self-select to respond to the talk-in-progress in a variety of ways. When a person in the audience self-selects to respond, the person is identifying himself or herself as an active recipient of the telling. Recipients can send *back-channels* (Yngve, 1970) such as *yeah, uh-huh,* and *mm hm,* to signal that they are following the telling or to acknowledge certain parts of the telling. In addition to using these minimal response tokens as *continuers* (Gardner, 1998; C. Goodwin, 1986b; Schegloff, 1982), recipients can show their involvement in an ongoing telling through various alternative actions: asking a question about a particular point of the telling; telling a comparable story to align with the teller; and providing *assessments* (Pomerantz, 1984a), which are evaluative comments that "display an analysis of the particulars of what is being talked about" (C. Goodwin, 1986b, p. 210). Participants who are in the audience thus demonstrate their competence in actively engaging in the talk-in-progress in a variety of ways, and such competence is to be regarded as an important part of one's *interactional competence* (Hall, 1995; He & Young, 1998; Young, 1999).

While a teller can make a *summary assessment* (C. Goodwin, 1986b, p. 305) as a "prototypical story-ending device" (Jefferson, 1978, p. 244), recipients can also display their understanding of the telling by providing assessments. A recipient can make assessment actions not only through assessment segments such as *that's great* and *taihen desu ne* [that sounds hard], but also through nonverbal actions (e.g., nods and headshakes, M. H. Goodwin, 1980) and non-segmental features of verbal actions (e.g., *hee* [wow], Mori, 2006). By using these resources, recipients can indicate their understanding that a telling comes to the end of a unit of telling (cf. Goodwin & Goodwin, 1987) and project withdrawal from recipientship before shifting topics (cf. C. Goodwin, 1986a; Jefferson, 1993), as well as display their interpretation of what is talked about.

The teller, in turn, may show an orientation to the recipient's assessment by agreeing or disagreeing with their displayed understanding of a possible telling closure. An *assessment activity*, which consists of at least one pair of an assessment and a response orienting to it, transforms a sequence of telling into an arena in which co-participants in a conversation negotiate their understandings of the telling. In such activities, recipients are not passive listeners but become active participants who co-construct the meaning of the telling.

Studies of recipient responses in Japanese

This aspect of competence that recipients demonstrate in co-constructing the meanings of others' tellings has not been investigated much in studies of recipient responses in Japanese. However, there is a small number of CA studies (e.g., Iwasaki, 1997; Mori, 2006; Saft, 2007) that have uncovered how speakers of Japanese use various resources to accomplish certain practices (cf. Mori, 1999) as recipients of tellings. Iwasaki (1997), for example, found that first language (L1) speakers of Japanese negotiate a closure of a telling sequence and the subsequent floor taking by exchanging a series of backchannels (e.g., *un* [yeah]), which constitute the *loop* sequence. Saft (2007) also found interactional functions of *aizuchi,* or backchannels. Through the study of multi-party televised discussions, he found that *aizuchi* are used by a moderator to self-select recipientship and, by doing so, to take a full turn as one member of a dyadic discussion and allocate turns for other members of the discussion. The use of a minimal response token as shift-implicature (cf. Jefferson, 1993) was also found in Mori's (2006) study of the non-lexical reactive token *hee*.

Although these CA studies have uncovered the procedural consequences of participants' actions, research on listeners' responses in Japanese has predominantly investigated competences in terms of frequencies of certain types of responses. For example, Clancy, Thompson, Suzuki, and Tao (1996) identified several types of non-turn-claiming *reactive tokens* (e.g., *un* [yeah], *aa* [oh]) used by non-primary speakers. By counting frequencies, they compared characteristics of the use of those tokens in three languages: Japanese, Chinese, and English. They found that L1 speakers of Japanese use non-turn-taking backchanneling tokens more frequently than L1 speakers of other languages. This seems to be a robust finding, supported by other studies such as LoCastro (1987), Maynard (1986), Tanaka (1999), and Yamada (1992). L1 Japanese speakers display this tendency when conversing also in L2 English (Maynard, 1990, 1997).

Using the same research approach, previous L2 studies of listener responses have compared L1 speakers' and L2 learners' data to find that more advanced learners and learners who stayed in the target community for an extended period of time approximate L1 speakers in terms of how frequently they use certain types of responses (e.g., Chinen, 2000; Fujii, 2001; Horiguchi, 1990, 1997; Watanabe, 1993). In these L2 studies, development is examined based on the average number of tokens within a group and compared cross-sectionally across groups. Because the precise timing with which response tokens are used and how they function in the development of on-going talk are not examined, such a simplistic counting of forms has the danger of misinterpreting the overuse of a particular type of response (e.g., *mm-hm* at a possible completion of a storytelling) as a sign of development (cf. Schegloff,

1993). In addition, by averaging out all the learners in one group for the sake of looking for a trend, researchers who use cross-sectional designs dismiss different actions that each individual learner takes on different occasions of talk.

Unlike these cross-sectional quantitative studies, Ohta (2001) documented the development of four learners of Japanese individually in a first-year foreign language classroom using a longitudinal design. She examined whatever responses the focal learners produced, including "no response," in the IRF (Initiation-Response-Follow up) sequence (e.g., a question, an answer, and an assessment). The development she found is not an approximation to native speakers in terms of frequency, but a change in the variety of responses the learners were able to produce. The learners, who did not produce any response at first, began to use short acknowledgment tokens such as *hai* [yes] and *un* [yeah], and then the acknowledgment expression *aa soo desu ka* [oh, I see]. In the next stage, learners were able to make not only acknowledgments but also aligning responses such as *soo desu ne* [that IS right indeed] and assessments such as *tanoshisoo desu ne* [that sounds fun]. Drawing on the theory of situated learning that emphasizes the significance of *legitimate peripheral participation* (Lave & Wenger, 1991), Ohta suggests that teachers socialized their students to become "good listeners" with their frequent use of acknowledging and aligning responses in the third turn of the IRF sequence. Although her study documented the incipient stage of providing listener responses, it did not provide analyses of such matters as how assessments and other kinds of responses are oriented to in a subsequent turn and how they affect the subsequent development or closure of a topical telling. This could suggest a limitation not of the study itself but of the first-year learners' interactional competence at this level, in which they develop their conversations simply by repeating the IRF sequence and not yet by expanding on the follow-up turn to develop further topical talks.

Theoretical frameworks for investigating L2 learning

Firth and Wagner's (1997) reconceptualization of SLA (second language acquisition), drawing on the CA view of language and interaction, aroused various reactions including heated refutation (e.g., Long, 1997) and problematization of some issues (e.g., Kasper, 1997). The fundamental problem that both Long and Kasper pointed out was the lack of theorization on how "acquisition," not "use," can be investigated within such a framework. Even some researchers who use CA in their L2 studies (e.g., He, 2004) argued against the possibility of using CA for acquisitional research. However, the fertility of using CA for developmental approaches such as language socialization (Schieffelin

& Ochs, 1986) and for work based on the sociocultural theory of learning (Lantolf, 1994), has been suggested, for example, by Kasper (1997) and Mori (2007) and empirically explored by a number of researchers (e.g., Mondada & Pekarek Doehler, 2004; Nguyen, 2003). Recently, Kasper (2009) has argued that CA's view of language and interaction can furnish a theory of learning without reliance on other learning theories, which is also the approach taken in the present chapter.

Study

The present study investigates the development of interactional competence that Sarah,[1] an L1 speaker of English and intermediate learner of Japanese, demonstrated as a recipient of topical tellings during nine months of her study-abroad period (the academic year between September, 2005 and May, 2006). The data for this study consist of five 20–minute conversations in which Sarah participated with her host mother, Honma-san,[2] once a month during her stay in Japan (T1, T2, T3, T5, T7). Although Sarah made a total of seven video-recordings (chronologically identified as T1 through T7) for my larger study, I exclude two of the conversations she had with her Japanese fiancé (T4, T6) from the present study.

The setting of the conversations that Sarah recorded with Honma-san was different from her usual practice, in which they talked while watching television (as Sarah reports in the post-study-abroad interview). Sarah wrote in a post-conversation report after T1, "I usually don't talk to my host mother for 20 minutes straight," while sitting on a couch in the living room of Honma-san's house only for the purpose of this recording. In this regard, the conversations recorded for this study provided Sarah relatively new situations in which she had to deal with sustaining a conversation by having something to talk about for "20 minutes straight." While I make use of these five recordings for *vertical comparison* (Zimmerman, 1999), that is, for the purpose of investigating development, the decision to collect comparable units of talk-in-interaction, in this case "conversations for the sake of recording," is consistent with CA's approach to collecting comparable sets of occasioned talk-in-interaction (e.g., telephone calls in Schegloff, 1979, 2002; pharmacy consultations in Nguyen, 2003).

The data analyzed here are a collection of instances in which Honma-san discontinued her ongoing topical telling and the main speaker changed from herself to Sarah. The collection also includes those instances in which Honma-san self-selects in the next turn after a *lapse* (Sacks, Schegloff, & Jefferson, 1974, p. 714).[3] The term "topical telling" is used to describe a topically coherent unit of telling rather than a mere presentation of information or description that extends over several turns (cf. *description* sequences, M. H. Goodwin, 1980; *informing* sequences, Mori, 1999). Although the term "telling" derives from a speaker's telling of a story (C. Goodwin, 1986b), a topical telling is not necessarily a story but can be a topically coherent unit of talk provided in response to a question.

Analyses of Sarah's actions at telling closure

Table 1 summarizes Sarah's (SM, in the table and in the transcripts) actions at the closure of Honma-san's (HM) topical tellings. The second column from the left describes Sarah's actions that followed the end of Honma-san's telling sequences. These actions are categorized into two main types: (a) telling-closing actions, which are minimally responded to by Honma-san and consequently lead to a topic closure, and (b) telling-continuing actions, which are still on Honma-san's topical telling but after which Honma-san ceases to be the sole provider of the telling. Samples of these action types will now be discussed according to the order of rows in the table from top to bottom.

Table 1. Number of Sarah's actions taken at the closure of Honma-san's topical telling

	SM's action at the closing of HM's topical telling	T1 10/31/05	T2 11/28/05	T3 1/16/06	T5 4/1/06	T7 5/xx/06
telling-closing actions	minimal response	2 (Ex 1)	6	3	4	2
	minimal agreement to HM's assessment/ commentary	1	2 (Ex 2)	4	3	2
	assessment/ commentary	0	5 (Ex 3)	3	0	0
telling-continuing actions	contrastive telling	1 (Ex 4)	0	0	1	0
	second story	0	4 (Ex 5)	0	0	5 (Ex 7)
	commentary	0	0	1 (Ex 6)	1	2

Note: SM=Sarah; HM=Honma-san; T=Time; Ex=Excerpt; xx= Sarah did not report date

Telling-closing actions

In this section, I will examine three types of Sarah's recipient actions using CA. **Minimal response token.** Through the use of minimal response tokens such as *un* [yeah] and *hee* [wow], Sarah displayed her understanding of the content of Honma-san's telling and her understanding that a unit of the telling is possibly completed. Excerpt 1 illustrates the procedural consequences of Sarah's use of minimal tokens (see the appendix for abbreviations used in the transcripts).

Excerpt 1, Activities of the day (T1 1'15", 10/31/05)

At the beginning of the recording, Honma-san (HM) asked Sarah (SM) to start talking, and Sarah asked her a question, "*Kyoo wa nani shita no?* [What did you do today?]." Honma-san began talking about a lecture on raising children which she attended in the morning.

```
1    HM   yarinasa:i tte iwanaidemo   (0.2)
          you do it  QT  even not saying
2         ii    n  ja   nai   no? tte yuu
          good  N  Cop  Neg   FP  QT  that
                                        N⁴
3         [ohanashi kana:, tto watashi wa omo]tta.
          talk     I guess QT  I       Top thought
                   N                       N
          "I thought that the talk sort of had a message
          saying that, even if you don't say 'Study!'
          all the time, it's still okay."


4    SM   [huu : : : : : : : : : : : n,] ((nodding))⁵
          ah
          "Ah."


5         (0.5) ((SM moves her hand toward her eye))


6    SM   un.=
          yeah
          N
          "Yeah."


7    HM   =[un.⁶
           N  N
```

```
8   SM   =[((begins scratching her eye))

9        (1.0) ((HM looks away from SM))

10  SM   hee[: ((still scratching her eye))

11  HM      [sore kara
             that from
             "After that,"
```

((Transcript of the following 21 seconds omitted, in which HM talks about a visitor and a violin lesson.))

```
12  HM   soshite sara  mo    kaetteki[ta.
         then    Sarah also  came back
                                      N
         "Then, you came home too."

13  SM                            [hai. (.)
                                   yes
                                   N

14       ehh hah hah [hh]
                      N
         "Yes."

15  HM              [un.]
                     N

16       (0.9) ((HM looks away from SM))
```

```
17  HM  sooyuu  ichinichi  deshita.
        such    one day    Cop-past
                     ((looks at SM)) N
        "That was my day."

18       (0.6)

19  SM  he[e]:,=
        ah
        N
        "Ah."

20  HM     [°un.°]
            N

21  HM  =sara   wa   kyoo   doo   datta?
        Sarah  Top  today  how  Cop-past
        "How was your day?"
```

This excerpt is comprised of two parts: the first part is on a lecture that Honma-san attended in the morning and the second part (from line 11) on other things that she did during the rest of the day. Sarah uses a response token *hee* [wow] at the end of both parts (lines 10, 19), not as an immediate response upon hearing news but as a resource for projecting withdrawal from recipientship (cf. Mori, 2006). At first, Sarah claims understanding of the content of the lecture (lines 1–3) by saying *huun* [ah] and nodding throughout (line 4). This is an initial response to the immediate informing. However, when Honma-san concludes the content of the lecture by saying *tto watashi wa omotta* [that's what I thought] in past tense (*-ta*),[7] Sarah begins withdrawing from recipientship by preparing to scratch her eye and saying *un* [yeah] in response. Honma-san aligns herself with Sarah with a corresponding *un* [yeah] and off-gaze. Such an exchange of minimal response tokens between co-participants at a possible closure of a telling sequence constitutes a *loop sequence* (Iwasaki, 1997) in which they negotiate who will take the next turn. Sarah says *hee:,* [wow] to display her understanding that a unit of telling is now completed while claiming her interest in the telling at the same time (cf. Mori, 2006).[8] This understanding is shared with Honma-san who at about the same moment begins a new unit of telling in line

11. While closure of a unit of the telling is indicated already by the loop in lines 6 and 7 before Sarah's utterance of *hee* in line 10, her utterance of *hee* in line 19 does not follow such a loop. Instead her second *hee* follows the concluding remark that Honma-san made. In this sequential position, Sarah uses *hee* as a "shift implicature" (Jefferson, 1993, p. 18), and Honma-san aligns with it by saying *un* in line 20 before asking a return question to Sarah (line 21).

As illustrated in Excerpt 1, Sarah used response tokens such as *un* and *hee* at possible completion points of Honma-san's telling. When Honma-san acknowledged these responses, the pair of utterances constituted a loop sequence, and indicated that the next turn is open to both participants. Although there were some instances in which Sarah took the next turn after the loop, it was typical that Honma-san took the floor to continue her telling on a related topic (e.g., line 11), to change topics, or to assign Sarah the next turn (e.g., line 21).

Minimal agreement to Honma-san's assessment. The second type of actions that Sarah took at the closing of Honma-san's topical telling (the second row in Table 1) is an agreement to Honma-san's assessment, as illustrated in Excerpt 2.

Excerpt 2, School trips at private high schools (T2 2'34," 11/28/05)

```
On the topic of school trips, Honma-san talked about
the destination of a school trip that she went on as a
student at a public high school. Then, she contrasted
it with that of private high schools, which had higher
budgets.


1    HM    motto ii    tokoro ni itte    ne:.⁹
           more good place to going      FP
           "Private schools took their students to better
           places, and"


2          (0.5)


3    HM    watashitachi no jidai no, kookooseetachi
           we              LK era  LK  high school students
           ((puts hands on chest))
```

```
4         wa:. (.) hawai °ni ittari shiteta    [yo,°
          Top      Hawaii to go-and would do    FP
                   ((turns to SM))  ((lips rounded))
          "I'm telling you, high school students in my
          day went to places like Hawaii."


5   SM                                         [((smiles))


6       (0.2) ((HM puts on a smile))


7   SM  °s: kka° ((smiling))=
        so   FP
        "I see."


8   HM  =<sugoi   desho[o:?> ((smiling, louder))
        amazing I suppose
                 N    N
        "Impressive, isn't it?"


9   SM                       [un.   sugo:i.((smiling))=
                              yeah amazing
                             "Yeah. That's something."


10  HM  =un. demo watashi wa, (.) shiritsu ja nakutte:.
        yeah but  I       Top     private  Cop Neg-and
                  N ((looks away from SM))
        "Yeah. But, I didn't go to a private school"
```

On the topic of destinations of school trips at private high schools, Honma-san provides an assessment (*sugoi* [amazing], line 8) latching on to Sarah's acknowledgment token *s: kka* [I see] (line 7). Her use of utterance-final *deshoo?* [isn't it?] makes an agreement a relevant response in the next turn, and Sarah shows agreement by saying *un* [yeah] and by repeating the assessment segment. After an agreement is established in this way, Honma-san shifts the topic back to the comparison between private and public schools.

This excerpt suggests how accomplishing intersubjectivity on the meaning of the on-going telling becomes an important step for closing a telling unit. While this excerpt presented an example of an assessment and an agreement to it, a topical telling can also be closed after a commentary and an agreement to it. A commentary is a presentation of an opinion about a matter dealt with in a telling. For example, after Honma-san talked about Tokyo Dome as a possible place to visit for sightseeing by presenting an attractive aspect of the place, she commented on the place as *demo ne: sore dake* [but that's all], *hoka ni nani ga aru wake demo nai shi* [there is nothing else to see, so] (T5, 5'36") and implied that this was the reason why she chose not to visit the place. After Sarah showed agreement by saying *un* in response to Honma-san's utterance of *ne:* [isn't that right?], the telling unit was closed and Honma-san shifted the topic to another possible sightseeing destination.

Assessments. While Sarah's assessment was provided as an agreement to Honma-san's assessment in Excerpt 2, there were instances where Sarah voluntarily provided assessments at a possible completion of Honma-san's telling, as illustrated in Excerpt 3.

Excerpt 3, Entrance exams for elementary schools (T2, 14'50")

Honma-san was telling Sarah about Japanese entrance exams. She started talking about her son's classmates from kindergarten who took entrance exams to enter elementary schools.

```
1   HM  gojuu-nin       no uchi (0.3) hutari     ka
        fifty people    LK within     two people or
        ((pointing to five fingers))
2       sannin        gurai wa (0.5) yoochien  o (0.3)
        three people  about  Top     kindergarten O
        ((looks at SM))               ((closes hand))
        "About two or three out of fifty people, for
        kindergarten,"

3   SM  hee:,
        ah
        "Wow."
```

```
4         (0.2)

5    HM   a   shoogakkoo            o:.  (.) nyuugaku      shi-
              oh  elementary school O         enter school do-
              ((moves hand))                  ((hands back together))
6         (0.2) juken-[shiteta.
                taking exam-Past
                       N
          "Oh, I mean for elementary school, they enter-
          took entrance exams."

7    SM                  [((nods))

8         (0.3)

9    SM   °n°
          mm
          N
          "Mm."
10        (0.5)

11   HM   °un°
          N    N

12        (1.0) ((HM looks away from SM))

13   SM   °u:n   [taihen°
          yeah    hard
          ((tilts head))
          "Ah, that's a hard task for them."
```

```
14  HM          [°u:n:.° (0.2)    taihen ne[::,  soo  ne:,
                                  yeah           hard FP     true FP
                                  N    ((looks at SM)) N            N
                                  "Yeah. It IS hard. That's right."

15  SM                                                       [((nods))

16       (0.6) ((HM sligtly nodding))

17  HM  ((looks down)) [un::::,  (((nodding))

18  SM                 [((nods))

19       (1.8)

20  HM  °moo    zen°zen jaa   nihon to   amerika to
        already at all  then  Japan and  America and
21      sore ga chigau      ne::,
        that S  different  FP
                           ((looks at SM, with a nod))
        "Even there, Japan and America are totally
        different, aren't they?"
```

When Sarah provides the response token *hee:* [ah], expressing some amazement with a rising intonation (line 3), Honma-san does not orient to it and instead continues her telling in line 5. Still within the turn-construction unit (TCU), the token *hee* consequently worked as a repair initiator (Mori, 2006). However, Sarah's nods and her utterance of *n* [mm] produced after the completion of the TCU (*juken-shiteta* [were taking exams], line 6) are acknowledged by Honma-san (line 11). It is after this loop sequence that Sarah provides the assessment *taihen* [hard] (line 13). Honma-san, who has begun withdrawing from speakership after the loop (line 12), looks at Sarah as soon as Sarah provides the assessment and expresses agreement in line 14. Then, after some turns of exchanging nods, Honma-san makes a comparative commentary in lines 20 and 21, which reflexively indicates that her telling about Japanese entrance exams at an early age and an activity of making assessments about it are over.

In this extract, Sarah demonstrated her competence in providing an assessment voluntarily (line 13) and getting it taken up as a legitimate assessment. However, she did not contribute to further development of the assessment activity after Honma-san displayed her orientation to mutual agreement (line 14). Thus, Sarah's assessment works as a "resource[s] for closing topics" (Goodwin & Goodwin, 1987, p. 38). Such a closure-implicating function of Sarah's assessment was also observed in some instances where Honma-san directed her turns to a closure of her telling after hearing Sarah's assessment (e.g., T2, 13'07"), instead of expressing agreement or disagreement.

As has been shown so far, Sarah indicated her understanding of both the content and the trajectory of Honma-san's tellings by using minimal response tokens, agreeing to Honma-san's assessments, and providing assessments. Although there were instances in which Honma-san counteracted Sarah's telling-closure implicative actions by not orienting to Sarah's response tokens or assessments (e.g., Excerpt 3, line 3), on other occasions Honma-san aligned with Sarah's actions and closed the unit of the telling that she was delivering.

Topic-continuing actions

While the previous section dealt with Sarah's recipient actions that consequently led to topic closure, this section shows analyses of her actions that are in direct response to Honma-san's telling but at the same time initiate a new sequence departing from Honma-san's telling sequence. Some of these actions follow some actions that we have seen above, namely, minimal response tokens and assessments.

Contrastive telling. Excerpt 4 presents a case that contrasts with Excerpt 1, in which Sarah displayed her orientation to the informative aspect of Honma-san's telling instead of treating Honma-san's reporting of her past thoughts as something to comment on.

Excerpt 4, Abominable *katakana* (T1 12'29," 10/31/05)

When asked by Honma-san what she thinks about the Japanese *katakana*,[10] Sarah did not start answering the question for more than 2 seconds. Then, Honma-san explained what *katakana* is and talked about her personal experience with regard to the use of *katakana* in her English classes at school. She said that she cannot identify English words in native speakers' speech because she has learned English by reading *katakana*-represented English words.

```
1    HM   dakara watashi wa ne, totemo katakana tte
          so      I     Top FP  very   katakana QT
          ((hands kept to show a note and a pen))
2         jama     da  na:, tte   °omotta no.°
          nuisance Cop FP    QT    thought FP
                         ((hands down))  N
          "So katakana is quite a nuisance, I thought."

3         (0.3)

4    SM   u:n. ((without a nod))

5    HM   °un:.°
           N

6         (0.3)

7    HM   sooyuu ji       ga atta    tame ni: (0.2)
          such   character S  existed cause for
          ((Looks away from SM))
          "Because of such a set of characters,"
```

((Transcript of the following 10 seconds omitted, in which HM says that she relied on *katakana*. After another loop, HM tells SM that her ability to listen to English got worse as a consequence. There is another loop.))

```
8    HM   dakara     nihongo tte
          therefore  Japanese QT
          "So, Japanese has. . . "
```

((Transcript of the following 10 seconds omitted, in which
HM mentions three sets of Japanese characters including
katakana, and uses a connective *kedo* [but] to continue
saying "*katakana:: (1.7)*"))

```
9    HM   jama       da na:,  (.)  to omo(h)otta.
          nuisance   Cop FP        QT thought
                                   ((looks at SM, then smiles))
          "it's a nuisance, I thought."


10        (0.7) ((SM leans head leftward))


11   SM   °aa so[o.°] ((head back a little))
          oh  so
          "Oh, I see."


12   HM          [u ][:  n [:.
                         N ((still smiling))


13   SM             [(0.5)[dakedo ne[:.
                          but    FP
                          ((head back in a normal position))
                          "But, you know"


14   HM                           [u:n:.
                                  N ((still smiling))


15        (0.6)


16   SM   nanka::  (0.7)  nihongo    wa
          like            Japanese   Top
          "Like, Japanese is"
```

((SM says that if Japanese is written only with the alphabet, Americans will read it with different pronunciation, and adds "*to omou* [I think that] *kara* [because of that]." Then, she also tells Honma-san that learning *katakana* helps her pronounce Japanese words properly.))

Receiving no answer to her question from Sarah for 2 seconds, Honma-san begins talking about her own experience as a "fishing device" (Pomerantz, 1980). When she begins her commentary with the causal connective *dakara* [therefore] (line 1), several features of the utterance make it clear that this is a concluding remark: It includes an assessment segment (*jama* [nuisance]), ends with a sentence-final form of the verb *omou* [I think] in the past tense [*omotta*] and the final particle *no*, delivered in a decreasing volume, and is accompanied with a discontinuation of hand gestures.

In reference to earlier analyses of the consequentiality of the loop sequence, the telling sequence might be closed after the exchange of *un* [yeah] between Sarah and Honma-san (lines 4, 5), and Sarah's presenting her opinion about *katakana* in response to Honma-san's question. However, the loop does not close the telling unit and Honma-san repeats the telling through paraphrases and elaborations. Jefferson's (1978) analysis of a storytelling is relevant to understand Honma-san's action. When recipients do not display interest or agreement to the teller's assessments, the teller continues telling in "search[ing] for recipient talk by reference to the story" (p. 232). Jefferson argues that, on such an occasion, recipients are not in alignment with the teller as *story recipients* although they are in alignment as recipients of informing. In line 4 of Excerpt 4, Sarah is not aligning herself as a story recipient. However, after Honma-san's pursuit of a more substantial response (cf. Pomerantz, 1984b), Sarah aligns herself as a story recipient. Sarah first acknowledges Honma-san's commentary (line 11) and then displays her perspective on *katakana*, which differs from Honma-san's. Such a response is similar to the structure of a disagreeing turn that consists of a provisionary agreement, a display of disagreement through a contrastive connective (e.g., *demo* [but]), and an account for the disagreement marked with a causal connective *kara* [because of that] (Mori, 1999). That is, Sarah treats Honma-san's telling as presenting a view contrastive of her own and thus uses Honma-san's telling as a point of reference for answering the question about *katakana* (line 13).

This excerpt illustrates how Sarah, who acknowledged Honma-san's telling merely with a minimal response token at first, later aligned herself to Honma-san by presenting her own view on *katakana* in a way that contrasts with Honma-san's view. The analysis of Excerpt 4 suggests the relevance of the context of the telling for the appropriateness of recipient actions. Honma-san's telling of her view on *katakana* began as a fishing device when Sarah did not present her view in response to her question. Having the telling contextualized in this way, an expected response was the presentation of Sarah's view in reference to Honma-san's, rather than an acknowledgment. This contrasts with Excerpt 1, in which Honma-san's telling of her activities of the day was provided in response to Sarah's request for information. In that sequential context, Sarah's acknowledgment indicating the informativeness of the telling was an appropriate response.

Second story. Sarah displayed her understanding of the content of Honma-san's telling and her orientation to it as a point of reference for her own turns by using comparative tellings as well as contrastive tellings, as in Excerpt 5.

Excerpt 5, Boring school trips (T2 1'14," 11/28/05)

At 1'01" Honma-san started talking about school trips to Kyoto at junior high schools in Japan. After she mentioned a recent trend of going to Universal Studios in Osaka, she said, "*Watashi no toki wa otera bakkari datta* [At that time, we did nothing but visit temples]." Sarah said, "*hee::,* [ah]" in response.

```
1    HM   atsui  toki  datta  kara  ne:
          hot    time  was    so    FP
2         (0.7) boikotto °shita no.°
                boycott   did   FP
          ((looks at SM seriously))
          "Because it was during the hot season,
          some boycotted."


3    SM   [hh ((starts smiling))]


4    HM   ["orinee:." ((acting out))
          get off-Neg
          "'We're not getting off the bus.'"


5         (0.3)((HM starts smiling))
```

```
6    SM   hh .hh [hh .hh ((looks down))


7    HM          [hehh .h h .hhh


8         (0.2) ((HM looks away from SM))


9    HM   [nanninka    moo    orinai         tte itte(h)=
           some people already get off-Neg QT saying
                                          ((looks at SM))
          "Some people said that they wouldn't get off, and"


10   SM   [((looks at HM))


11   SM   =[heh heh


12   HM   =[ehh heh heh (0.5) hh (.) hh (.) .hhh.
                ((looks down))   N         N


13        (0.6)


14   SM   ya[a ((still smiling))


15   HM     [konaida   mo
             last time also
            "Last time too,"
```

((Transcript of the following 6 seconds omitted, in which HM refers to students who were on a school trip in a cooler season, which HM and SM saw during their trip to Kyoto. She said, "*Ii toki ni itta ne* [We went in a good season, didn't we]," and Sarah replied *un* [yeah].))

```
16  HM  watashitachi atsui toki   ni itta mon (0.2)
        we           hot   season in went  FP
        ((looking downward))          ((tilts her head))
17      sugoku.
        very
        "We went during the hot season. It was really hot."

18  SM  [((lowers eyes))

19  HM  [motto kugatsu gurai ni °ittara° atsuk°atta.°
         more  September about in went-if  hot-Past
        ((looks at SM))
        "More... When we went around September, it was
        so hot."

20      (0.7) ((SM glances at HM one moment))

21  SM  [un:.]
         N   N

22  HM  [    ](0.8)
         N    N ((looks downward))

23  SM  °watashi:° (0.6) un. (.) firadelfia
         I                yeah   Philadelphia
                                 ((looks at HM))
24      itta koto   aru
        went matter exist
        "I... yeah...went to Philadelphia."

25      (0.3)

26  HM  [un.
```

27 SM   [chuugaku[see
            junior high school student
            "*during Junior high.*"

28 HM   [un un u[n   u]n.
                     N N N   N
                    ((raising her gaze up at SM))

29 SM   [°(n)°]

30   (0.3) ((SM starts smiling))

31 SM   **sugu chikai no ka(h)ra(h)**
            just close   Cop so
            "*It's really close, so*"

32 HM   un.
          N

33 SM   **omoshirokunai, h**
            interesting-Neg
            "*It's boring.*"

    Hearing Honma-san's telling of students boycotting temple visits on a school trip, Sarah shows her understanding of its content and aligns herself with Honma-san through a smile already from lines 3 through 11. However, before Sarah provides some kind of a verbal response in line 14, Honma-san begins elaborating on the season of her school trip (line 15). It is after Honma-san withdraws from this post-climax telling which elaborates on the season (lines 16–19) that Sarah starts talking about her boring school trip in line 23. Although this story at first appears to be only minimally related to Honma-san's telling on the point that they both went on a trip, it is constructed as a *second story* through an "*achieved similarity*" (Sacks, 1992, p. 253). Sarah first identifies the trip as a compulsory excursion from school that she participated in when she was a junior high school student (*chuugakusee*, line 27). In addition, her negative assessment of the trip (*omoshirokunai* [boring], line 33) is in alignment with

Honma-san's telling that implicitly presents her negative evaluation of her school trip: They did nothing but visit temples (*otera bakkari*) so that some students even boycotted joining the visits. Sarah's second story reflexively constructs Honma-san's post-climax elaboration of the weather as a mere appendix. While not orienting to the post-climax telling as a relevant reference for her second story, Sarah nevertheless acknowledges it in line 21 and starts her second story only after Honma-san completes the loop sequence in line 22.

As illustrated in Excerpt 5, Sarah sometimes told second stories as a way to demonstrate her understanding of the point of Honma-san's telling and show alignment to it.

Commentary. Another type of response that Sarah provided at the end of Honma-san's telling sequence is a commentary, which provides some "talking on the topic" (Jefferson, 1993, p. 18), as in Excerpt 6.

Excerpt 6, No point in getting angry (T3 14'02," 1/16/06)

Sarah talked about the difficulty of dating in a long-distance relationship with her boyfriend who has only three days off in a month. Honma-san provided an assessment, "*Kekkoo taihen da ne:.* [It seems quite tough]," and then began talking about her past experience. She talked about an episode of waiting for her husband-to-be for three hours at a station.

```
1   HM   tai°hen dat[ta      yo°,]
         hard    was         FP
                ((looks at SM)) N ((looks away))
         "It was tough."

2   SM                [nn : :    ][::, heh heh hh
                      ((smiling, leaning forward))

3   HM                        [°mo°o:   kaeroo
                                already  return-shall
                      ((vertical headshake facing left))
```

```
4         ka(h)na,  MOO      KAEROO ((laughing))
          I guess   already  return-shall
                    ((vertical headshake facing right))

5         kana,   tto omotte. ((laughing))
          I guess QT  thinking
          ((looks at SM, quickly shaking head))
          "I was thinking,'I'm leaving soon. I'm gonna
          leave NOW.'"

6         (0.7) ((SM still smiling, gaze on HM))

7   HM    u::n:. ((still smiling))
          N  N ((looks away from SM))

8         (1.2)((SM back to normal posture))

9   HM    sonna datta kara ne:°::°
          such  was   so   FP

10        (1.0) ((SM smiling))

11  SM    watashi tabun=
          I       probably
          "I would probably"

12  HM    =un.=
          N ((looks at SM))

13  SM    =okoroo            to  omou kedo
          get angry-shall    QT  think but
          "want to get angry, but"
```

```
14          (0.6) ((HM looks away from SM))

15   SM   aa [shoo ga nai        kara(h)[:. o- ]
          ah  way  S nothing because
                ((facing down leftward))
             "'Ah, it couldn't be helped, so'"

16   HM      [°u:n.°               [soo soo.] (0.2)
              yeah                  so   so
17           o[koritai              yo,
              get angry-want        FP
             ((crossing her arms))((looks at SM))
             "Yeah. Right. Sure, I want to get angry."

18   SM     [okora(h)na(h)i hoo ga i(h)i(h) hh hh (.) .h
             get angry-Neg  way S   good
             ((face further down leftward))  ((head up))
             "It's better not to get angry."

((Transcript of the following 12 seconds omitted, in which
HM says that getting angry would not help, and SM repeats
HM's words. After SM agrees with HM's reasoning that the
delay was not due to oversleeping, HM again says that
she cannot get angry because it would not help.))

19   SM   ok(h)ori(h)tai kedo(h)  ((shaking head))
           get angry-want but
          "You want to get angry but"
```

```
20  HM   [soo. okoritai        kedo]
          so   get angry-want  but
                   N    N       N
         ((looks away from SM))
         "Right. You want to get angry but"


21  SM   [okorena(h)i  hh   hh   .hh][hh hh
          get angry-can-Neg
         ((facing down))  ((face up))  ((looks at HM))
         "you can't."


22  HM                          [okorenai  no yo.
                                 get angry-can-Neg FP FP
23       soo soo. soo na no yo.
         so  so   so Cop FP FP
          N   N
         "you just can't. Right. That's right."


24       (0.5) ((SM starts moving body back and forth))


25  HM   °un°
          N


26       (2.4)


27  HM   °nhu:::::n.°


28       (0.5)


29  HM   de ano (0.3) tatoeba
         and well     for example
         "And, well, for example,"
```

```
((HM begins talking about another episode about dating
difficulty.))
```

Although Sarah shows orientation to Honma-san's summary assessment *taihen* (hard) in line 2, she does not give any verbal response to Honma-san's telling until Honma-san shows signs of withdrawal from her telling in line 6, where she looks away from Sarah, and in line 9, where she makes a concluding remark reflecting on the reported event as one instance. Sarah does not even acknowledge Honma-san's conclusion with a minimal response token or a nod before she starts talking about her probable emotional reaction to the situation having been told (line 11). The absence of an acknowledgment seems to suggest Sarah's avoidance of a loop sequence, which could lead to a collaborative closure of Honma-san's telling sequence, for the sake of providing her commentary while the telling is not closed. In contrast to Sarah's assessment found in Excerpt 3 (line 13), which led to a telling-closure soon after Honma-san's agreeing utterances, Sarah's commentary found in this excerpt (lines 11–18) initiates an extended sequence of mutual agreement. The sequence contains many extended overlaps, repetitions of words and phrases (Goodwin & Goodwin, 1987), and explicit markings of agreement with *soo* [right] by both parties, which all contribute to making this sequence part of an *assessment activity* (Goodwin & Goodwin). Throughout the sequence, Honma-san treats Sarah's commentary as being in alignment with her own emotional reaction to the described past instance, by the use of *soo* [right] (lines 16, 20, 23) and a final particle *yo* [I'm telling you] (lines 17, 22, 23) and another final particle *no* [it is true that] (lines 22, 23), which all assign herself epistemic authority (Heritage & Raymond, 2005). Although Sarah does not nod or say *un* [yeah] to align herself with Honma-san's concluding statement (lines 20–23) or her telling-closing *un* (line 25), thus not contributing to the construction of a loop sequence, Honma-san self-selects a turn after a lapse to initiate a new unit of telling that is thematically related to the content of the assessment activity.

In this excerpt, we observed a case in which "the prior speaker-on-topic now comes into alignment as a recipient" (Jefferson, 1993, p. 22) after Sarah's elaborated commentary. Although the assessment activity that was initiated with the commentary is still on the topic of Honma-san's telling, the co-participants depart from the sequence in which Honma-san is the main carrier of the topic as a teller, to a new sequence in which Sarah contributes to co-constructing the meaning of the telling.

So far, six types of recipient actions that Sarah took at the end of Honma-san's telling sequence have been described. Because these excerpts are all taken from Sarah's earlier conversations (T1–T3: October, 2005–January, 2006), one excerpt from her later conversation (T7: May, 2006) may help discuss a developmental issue. Excerpt 7 presents a case in which Sarah told a second story as a recipient of Honma-san's telling.

Excerpt 7, Foreigners speaking regional dialects (T7 3'44," 5/xx/06)

In response to Honma-san's question about her research paper for her linguistics class, Sarah was talking about her questionnaire study on Japanese people's view of dialect use. Sarah told Honma-san about the finding that Japanese people like foreigners' use of their own dialect while they have negative reactions to dialect use by Japanese people from other regions. Then, Honma-san started talking about her reaction to foreigners speaking regional dialects that are less popular.

```
1   HM   kawaisoo, tte omou.
         pitiable  QT  think
             ((looks at SM))
         "I feel like, 'Poor thing!'"


2        (.)


3   HM   moshi sochira no hoo de:.
         if    that way LK way in
4        gaikoku no hito ga kichatte:.
         foreign LK person S come-and
         "If a foreigner was sent to the area,"


5        (0.2)


6   SM   °hh [hh° ((facing down and smiling))
```

```
7   HM       [nihongo  o  benkyoo  shichatta  n  [da   na::,
             Japanese  O  study    did        N  Cop  FP
                                                  N
             "'Ah, he ended up studying that Japanese.'"

8   SM                                    [u::n uh hh hh hh
                                          ((looks up at HM))

9            (0.5)

10  HM   kawa[isoo ni:,  tte  [omotchatta.
             pitiable -ly QT  think-Past
             N                  N
             "'Poor thing!' I couldn't help thinking that
             way."

11  SM       [(uo)           [un:.
                   N     N

12           (0.2)

13  SM   sore  mo    atta:.  to:  gaikokujin ga:.
         that also existed well  foreigner  S
14       hoogen  shabettetara:.=
         dialect speak-if
         "I found that too. If a foreigner speaks a
         dialect,"

15  HM   =un:

16       (0.8) ((HM looks down))
```

```
17  SM  un   tabun      sono (0.4) un.  joozu-ni:
        yeah probably that         yeah well
18           shaberetara:.=
             speak-if
        "Yeah, it's probably that... Yeah. If he speaks
        it well,"

19  HM  =°un.°
         N

20       (0.6)

21  SM  n  sono tokoro ni: sunda koto (0.4) benkyoo
        um  that place in  lived experience  study
22         shita kara: to (0.3) omo[u.
           did because QT       think
        "people think that he's lived or studied
        there."

23  HM                          [soo soo.  soko de ne,
                                 so  so    there in FP
         "That's right. He studied there."
```

((HM says that she feels the person learned strange Japanese, using a modal expression indicating a negative view, *chau*, and ending the utterance with the contrastive connective *kedo* [but]. In response to HM's "*ne:.* [y'know]", SM says "*un:.* [yeah]." Then, HM says that she thinks he should re-learn Japanese, ending the utterance with *kedo*. Again, in response to HM's "*ne* [y'know]", SM says "*un.* [yeah].")))

In line 1, Honma-san negatively assesses foreigners' use of less popular regional dialects by using the adjective *kawaisoo* [pitiable], which expresses her pity for those foreigners. Receiving no immediate verbal or nonverbal response to this asssessment from Sarah, Honma-san elaborates on the telling and uses the assessment word also in line 10. Although she packages her assessment with a modal expression both in lines 1 and 10, the packaging (Pomerantz & Fehr, 1997) slightly differs. While she indicates her assessment as a stable view toward foreigners speaking regional dialects by using the present tense of *omou* [I think that] in line 1, in line 10 she utilizes the modal expression *chau*, which indicates one's feeling of regret or disappointment over an event or a state of matters, and selects the past-tense form of *tte omou* (i.e., -*ta*). The latter way of packaging weakens the assessment (*kawaisoo*) by appending a sense of regrettable feeling that occurred to her and by limiting it to a one time perception rather than an unchanging view. By mitigating her assessment after elaboration, Honma-san seems to be expecting from Sarah an agreement with, or an empathic understanding of, her assessment. However, Sarah does not orient to Honma-san's assessment actions, either in line 1 or line 10. Despite her apparent indication of agreement through nods and the utterance of *un* in line 11, Sarah's subsequent telling from line 13 reflexively makes it clear that in line 11 she is not showing affiliation to Honma-san's assessment *kawaisoo*. Rather than showing agreement or disagreement directly toward Honma-san's negative assessment, Sarah refers to some responses of Japanese people to her survey study by saying *sore mo atta* [I found that too]. This utterance reflexively indicates that her earlier nods and utterance of *un* were expressions of acknowledging Honma-san's idea of the dialect-speaking foreigner's language learning background as consistent with the survey result. In contrast to Honma-san's use of the modal expression *chau* (lines 4, 7), Sarah does not use it in her report of this survey response. Instead of affiliating herself with Honma-san's negative view on dialect-speaking foreigners, Sarah achieves similarity by presenting a second story.

This excerpt illustrates sophisticated ways in which Sarah and Honma-san negotiated agreement. Sarah's second story shows alignment rather than agreement, and Honma-san oriented to it as aligning to her own telling while still seeking Sarah's agreement of empathic understanding of her view.

Through the analysis of seven excerpts, we have observed various ways in which Sarah engaged in Honma-san's tellings as a recipient at the end of telling sequences. In these CA analyses, no interpretation was given of the development of interactional competence, which is the subject of the next pages.

Discussion of learning and development

In this section, issues of learning and development will be addressed by reexamining the excerpts from the point of view of language socialization

(Schieffelin & Ochs, 1986), Vygotsky's theory of psychological development (Vygotsky, 1978; Wertsch, 1979), and the view of language and interaction taken in CA.

First of all, Sarah's ways of engaging in Honma-san's telling as a recipient will be reviewed chronologically. As seen in Excerpt 1, after 2 months of her stay in Honma-san's house (at T1), Sarah showed alignment to Honma-san's telling as a recipient of informing, by acknowledging the telling with the minimal response tokens *un* [yeah] and *hee* [wow] at possible telling completion places, but not as a story recipient. Even when Sarah aligned herself as a story recipient (Excerpt 4), it was only after Honma-san's recurrent attempts to make her display her view on the matter at hand. However, in these excerpts, Sarah exhibited her interactional competence for appropriately providing minimal response tokens to show her understanding of the trajectory of Honma-san's telling. In Excerpt 1, she differentially used *hee* to project the end of Honma-san's telling as satisfactorily informative, and in Excerpt 4, she acknowledged Honma-san's view by saying *aa soo* [ah, I see] before presenting a contrastive view of her own.

What she did not exhibit in her T1 conversation is her competence in aligning herself as a story recipient by making assessments and commentaries and in telling second stories. In her T2 conversation, Sarah began telling second stories to display her understanding of the gist of Honma-san's telling (Excerpt 5) and also started providing assessments voluntarily (Excerpt 3) as well as agreeing to Honma-san's summary assessments (Excerpt 2). However, these assessments functioned as telling-closure implicative, without Sarah's further actions elaborating on the assessment or agreement. This is in contrast with Sarah's engagement in an assessment activity that was initiated with her recipient commentary (T3, Excerpt 6).

By orienting to Honma-san's agreement to the commentary, Sarah prevented the commentary from serving as telling-closure implicative and showed her involvement as a story recipient in co-constructing the meaning of Honma-san's telling. In her T5 and T7 conversations, Sarah continued using these six types of recipient actions.[11] What differed at T7 (Excerpt 7) was Sarah's ability to tightly relate her second story to Honma-san's telling, by marking the similarity (*sore mo atta* [I found that too], line 13) immediately, without inserting a loop sequence. Furthermore, in the ninth month of her stay at Honma-san's house (T7), we observed that Sarah used a second story as a useful resource for aligning herself with Honma-san without making a disagreeing response to Honma-san's assessment (Excerpt 7).

The question is whether these changes can be regarded as indications of development. Sarah's non-use of recipient assessments in her T1 conversation and her use of them in the subsequent conversation seemingly appear to indicate development, similar to the first-year learners of Japanese in Ohta's (1999, 2001) study who first used acknowledgments and then assessments in the third turn of the IRF sequence. However, the data available to us are limited to these five conversations, and it is possible that Sarah had already been using assessments, commentaries, and second stories along with acknowledgments even before T1. Moreover, the absence of observed assessments may not be a direct indication of incompetence in using assessments. For example, in Excerpt 1, Sarah's orientation through the use of *hee* [wow] to Honma-san's telling as containing new information matches her information-seeking question, and in Excerpt 4 her presentation of an opinion in comparison with Honma-san's is in alignment with Honma-san, who provided her telling as a fishing device. Therefore, the apparent emergence of assessments in Sarah's recipient actions should not be automatically interpreted as an indication of development.

Nevertheless, within this particular set of interactional practices that Sarah participated in with Honma-san, we were able to observe Sarah's growing engagement as a recipient in co-constructing the meaning of Honma-san's telling. My contention is that this is the manifestation of her development as part of language socialization, rather than instantiations of newly acquired skills. In the theory of language socialization, Schieffelin and Ochs (1986) propose that language learning is part of being socialized as a member of a social group, that is, a process of learning ways of interacting with one another, including ways of using language as resources which are particular to a community of practice (Lave & Wenger, 1991), while developing interpersonal relationships with other members of the community.

In social interactions, members of a social group are not only learning ways of interacting, but also "socializing each other into their particular world views as they negotiate situated meaning" (Schieffelin & Ochs, 1986, p. 165). In the context of this study, at first Sarah simply accepted Honma-san's worldviews without contesting them (Excerpt 1, T1; Excerpt 2, T2; except Excerpt 4, T1). In subsequent sessions, she began voluntarily presenting her own views, to which Honma-san agreed (Excerpt 3, T2), and Sarah responded to Honma-san with another agreement (Excerpt 6, T3). At T7, Sarah also dealt with different views on a matter at hand by orienting to commonalities through a second story (Excerpt 7). In Lave and Wenger's (1991) terms, Sarah was at first on the periphery of the activity of co-constructing the meaning of Honma-san's tellings, but she became more involved in such an activity by becoming a more central member of this dyadic community of practice.

Once we interpret the observed changes as Sarah's a centripetal movement from legitimate peripheral to full participation in specific practical activities and in mutually socializing particular world views, we are faced with the problem of what learning mechanisms are involved in the process. A relevant learning theory in this regard is Vygotsky's theory of psychological development, especially the concepts of *zone of proximal development* (ZPD) and *scaffolding* (e.g., Donato, 1994). The ZPD is "*the distance between the actual developmental level as determined by independent problem solving and the level of potential development as determined through problem solving under adult guidance or in collaboration with more capable peers*" (Vygotsky, 1978, p. 86, italics original). Applying the concept of ZPD to the present data, Sarah's "actual developmental level" at T1 was to accept Honma-san's world view by acknowledging her telling at possible completion points with the use of response tokens (*un* [yeah], *hai* [yeah]) and news receipts (*hee* [wow], Excerpt 1; *sokka* [I see], Excerpt 2; *aa soo* [oh, really], Excerpt 4). The "level of potential development" in this session is found in her presentation of her views (her view on *katakana*, Excerpt 4) as *scaffolded* with Honma-san's pursuit of her opinion presentation. At T2, the scaffolded assessment (*sugoi* [amazing], Excerpt 2) "blaze[d] the trail for development to follow" (Dunn & Lantolf, 1998, p. 419), with Sarah later providing assessments voluntarily (*taihen* [hard], Excerpt 3). In sum, using Vygotsky's concepts, Sarah's development, or her centripetal movement, can be considered to have resulted from Honma-san's provision of scaffolding within Sarah's ZPD.

Although such interpretation points to the role of a more competent partner's *scaffolding,* such scaffolding is just one of the factors contributing to the development of a learner's competence. From CA's point of view, scaffolding is a prevalent feature of discursive practices in which co-participants publicly display their understanding of what is going on at the moment of talk-in-interaction. As Cicourel (1974/1999, p. 95) notes, "The interpretive procedures and their reflexive features provide continuous instructions to participants such that members can be said to be programming each other's actions as the scene unfolds." Such "interpretive procedures" are the premise of "[t]he acquisition of language rules" (p. 90). In the present data, for example, Sarah's competence in providing acknowledgments (e.g., *hee* [wow], Excerpt 1) at a possible completion of a telling is co-constructed and scaffolded by Honma-san's indication of withdrawal from her telling with a particular formulation of her informing and nodding (lines 3, 17) along with the withdrawal of her eye gaze (lines 9, 16). In another instance, Honma-san's re-issuing of a possible completion point after elaboration (Excerpt 4) gave Sarah an additional opportunity to present her opinion. In addition to co-constructing Sarah's competence in making particular actions in these ways, Honma-san's actions served to inform Sarah of the sequential appropriateness of the action she took. For example, we can interpret Honma-san's agreement with Sarah's assessment found in Excerpt 3 (line 14) as confirming to Sarah that she provided the assessment at the right moment. Earlier in the conversation (T2, 13'44," 13'47"), Sarah had provided assessments (*chotto taihen* [a little hard]) using the same assessment word (*taihen*) twice while Honma-san was still in the middle of a TCU, and Honma-san continued her telling without orienting to them. These actions by Honma-san allowed Sarah to develop her interactional competence in providing assessment at the right moment. These observations suggest the possibility of extending the notion of *scaffolding* from active pursuits of responses to other features of talk-in-interaction which are not particular to interactions involving L2 learners but also applicable to interactions between native speakers.

Conclusion

In this chapter, CA has been used to investigate an intermediate Japanese learner's development of interactional competence, particularly focusing on ways of acting as a recipient. In Ohta's study (1999, 2001), which documented beginning learners' incipient use of assessments, assessments were confined to the third turn of the IRF sequence, and learners and their interlocutors did not engage in extended assessment activities in which their views on the assessed object could be negotiated. On the other hand, Sarah, who at T1 only oriented to the information status of Honma-san's tellings, gradually got more actively involved in co-constructing the meaning of Honma-san's tellings. While I refrain from characterizing the apparent emergence of recipient assessments as an indication of development, I still consider Sarah's centripetal movement in participating in the activity of negotiating world views as part of her language socialization. While the concept of scaffolding was applied to Honma-san's pursuit of particular actions, which enabled Sarah to take a more active role as a telling recipient, the concept can be extended to all the discursive practices that make participants' understanding of what is going on at the moment of interaction publicly visible.

The present study demonstrated "the developmental significance of social interaction" that is highlighted by "[i]ntegrating a CA perspective on interaction with a sociocultural perspective on learning" (Hall, 2004, p. 611). I would argue, in alignment with Kasper (2009), that CA provides us not only the tools for understanding the learner's language use, but also a perspective on social interaction that is relevant for language learning theories. As a response to Firth and Wagner's (1997) proposal of a different paradigm of SLA, Kasper (1997) wrote, "if the excellent microanalytic tools of CA were incorporated into a language socialization approach to SLA, we might be able to reconstruct links between L2 discourse and the acquisition of different aspects of communicative competence that have been largely obscure thus far" (p. 311). Since then, CA has matured as a fruitful approach to SLA, and the present study may illustrate how CA can be used to investigate second language learners' development of interactional competence and the process of learning through talk-in-interaction.

Notes

1. All names presented in this chapter are pseudonyms.
2. When Sarah talked to me, she referred to her host mother using the last name (Honma) and the address suffix (*san* [Ms.]).
3. Sacks et al. (1974) note that "[d]iscontinuities occur when, at some transition-relevance place, a current speaker has stopped, no speaker starts (or continues), and the ensuring space of non-talk constitutes itself as more than a gap—not a gap, but a lapse" (p. 714).
4. When the precise timing of nods is indicated in the third line of the transcript, "N" is used for one nod.
5. In general, nonverbal actions are noted in the first line along with the Japanese utterance in the transcripts. However, if the space is insufficient or the timing of the nonverbal action is relevant, it is noted in the third line of transcript after the gloss.
6. Henceforth, when the lexical item *un* [yeah] or its repetition occupies one turn, I will dispense with glosses and the English translation.
7. Japanese is a SOV (subject object verb) language in which the modifying elements are presented before the head of a phrase and in which the conjugated verb form comes in sentence final position.
8. According to Mori (2006), the utterance of "*hee* by itself appears to express its producer's stance or assessment towards the prior informing, including surprise, disbelief, appreciation and so on, whether such a stance is genuine or not. However, the exact kind of reaction signaled by the producer of this non-lexical token remains ambiguous when compared to other responses" (pp. 1188–1189).
9. Punctuation in the original Japanese transcripts are solely based on prosody and do not suggest any correlation with the meaning-based punctuation used in the corresponding English translation.
10. *Katakana* is a set of 46 Japanese characters that represent sounds (e.g., アメリカ for A-me-ri-ca).
11. Although Sarah used recipient assessments in T5 and T7, they were followed by Honma-san's continued telling and did not function as telling-closing implicative. Therefore I did not list them in Table 1.

References

Brouwer, C. E., & Wagner, J. (2004). Developmental issues in second language conversation. *Journal of Applied Linguistics, 1*(1), 29–47.

Cekaite, A. (2007). A child's development of interactional competence in a Swedish L2 classroom. *The Modern Language Journal, 91*(1), 45–62.

Chinen, K. (2000). *Comparative study of the listening response in Japanese casual conversation: Japanese and American learners* (Unpublished master's thesis). California State University, Long Beach.

Cicourel, A. V. (1999). Interpretive procedures. In A. Jaworski & N. Coupland (Eds.), *The discourse reader* (pp. 89–97). New York, NY: Routledge. (Reprinted from *Cognitive sociology: Language and meaning in social interaction*, pp. 51–58, by A. V. Cicourel, 1974, Harmondsworth: Free Press).

Clancy, P. M., Thompson, S. A., Suzuki, R., & Tao, H. (1996). The conversational use of reactive tokens in English, Japanese, and Mandarin. *Journal of Pragmatics, 26*, 355–387.

Donato, R. (1994). Collective scaffolding in second language learning. In J. P. Lantolf & G. Appel (Eds.), *Vygotskian approaches to second language research* (pp. 33–56). Norwood, NJ: Ablex Publishing.

Dunn, W. E., & Lantolf, J. P. (1998). Vygotsky's zone of proximal development and Krashen's *i* + 1: Incommensurable constructs; incommensurable theories. *Language Learning, 48*(3), 411–448.

Firth, A., & Wagner, J. (1997). On discourse, communication, and (some) fundamental concepts in SLA research. *The Modern Language Journal, 81*(3), 285–300.

Fujii, K. (2001). Changes in the listener responses of foreign learners of Japanese during their stay in Japan. *Journal of International Student Center, Yokohama National University, 8*, 79–91.

Gardner, R. (1998). Between speaking and listening: The vocalisation of understanding. *Applied Linguistics, 19*(2), 204–224.

Goodwin, C. (1986a). Audience diversity, participation and interpretation. *Text, 6*, 283–316.

Goodwin, C. (1986b). Between and within: Alternative sequential treatments of continuers and assessments. *Human Studies, 9*, 205–217.

Goodwin, C., & Goodwin, M. (1987). Concurrent operations on talk: Notes on the interactive organization of assessments. *IPrA Papers in Pragmatics, 1*(1), 1–54.

Goodwin, M. H. (1980). Processes of mutual monitoring implicated in the production of description sequences. *Sociological Inquiry, 50*, 303–317.

Hall, J. K. (1995). "Aw, man, where you goin'?" Classroom interaction and the development of L2 interactional competence. *Issues in Applied Linguistics, 6*(2), 37–62.

Hall, J. K. (2004). Language learning as an interactional achievement. *The Modern Language Journal, 88*(4), 607–612.

He, A. W. (2004). CA for SLA: Arguments from the Chinese language classroom. *The Modern Language Journal, 88*, 568–582.

He, A. W., & Young, R. (1998). Language proficiency interviews: Discourse approach. In R. Young & A. W. He (Eds.), *Talking and testing: Discourse approaches to the assessment of oral proficiency* (pp. 1–24). Philadelphia, PA: John Benjamins.

Hellermann, J. (2006). Classroom interactive practices for developing L2 literacy: A microethnographic study of two beginning adult learners of English. *Applied Linguistics, 27*(3), 377–404.

Hellermann, J. (2007). The development of practices for action in classroom dyadic interaction: Focus on task openings. *The Modern Language Journal, 91*(1), 83–96.

Hellermann, J. (2008). *Social actions for classroom language learning.* Clevedon: Multilingual Matters.

Heritage, J., & Raymond, G. (2005). The terms of agreement: Indexing epistemic authority and subordination in talk-in-interaction. *Social Psychology Quarterly, 68*(1), 15–38.

Horiguchi, S. (1990). Jookyuu nihongo gakushuusha no taiwa ni okeru kikite to shite no gengo koodoo [Listening behaviors of advanced level learners of Japanese]. *Nihongo Kyooiku, 71,* 16–32.

Horiguchi, S. (1997). *Nihongo kyoiku to kaiwa bunseki* [Japanese language teaching and conversation analysis]. Tokyo: Kuroshio.

Ishida, M. (2006). Interactional competence and the use of modal expressions in decision-making activities: CA for understanding microgenesis of competence. In K. Bardovi-Harlig, J. C. Félix-Brasdefer, & A. Omar (Eds.), *Pragmatics and language learning* (Vol. 11, pp. 55–79). Honolulu, HI: National Foreign Language Resource Center, University of Hawai'i.

Ishida, M. (2009). Development of interactional competence: Changes in the use of *ne* in L2 Japanese during study abroad. In H. t. Nguyen & G. Kasper (Eds.), *Talk-in-interaction: Multilingual perspectives* (pp. 351–385). Honolulu, HI: University of Hawai'i, National Foreign Language Resource Center.

Iwasaki, S. (1997). The Northridge earthquake conversations: The floor structure and the "loop" sequence in Japanese conversation. *Journal of Pragmatics, 28,* 661–693.

Jaworski, A., & Coupland, N. (Eds.). (1999). *The discourse reader.* New York, NY: Routledge.

Jefferson, G. (1978). Sequential aspects of storytelling in conversation. In J. Schenkein (Ed.), *Studies in the organization of conversational interaction* (pp. 219–248). New York, NY: Academic Press.

Jefferson, G. (1993). Caveat speaker: Preliminary notes on recipient topic-shift implicature. *Research on Language and Social Interaction, 26*(1), 1–30.

Kasper, G. (1997). "A" stands for acquisition: A response to Firth and Wagner. *The Modern Language Journal, 81,* 307–312.

Kasper, G. (2009). Locating cognition in second language interaction and learning: Inside the skull or in public view? *International Review of Applied Linguistics, 47*(1), 11–36.

Lantolf, J. P. (Ed.). (1994). Sociocultural theory and second language learning [Special issue]. *The Modern Language Journal, 78*(4).

Lave, J., & Wenger, E. (1991). *Situated learning: Legitimate peripheral participation.* Cambridge: Cambridge University Press.

LoCastro, V. (1987). Aizuchi: A Japanese conversational routine. In L. Smith (Ed.), *Discourse across cultures* (pp. 101–113). London: Prentice Hall.

Long, M. H. (1997). Construct validity in SLA research: A response to Firth and Wagner. *The Modern Language Journal, 81*(3), 318–323.

Maynard, S. K. (1986). On back-channel behavior in Japanese and English casual conversation. *Linguistics, 24,* 1079–1108.

Maynard, S. K. (1990). Conversation management in contrast: Listener response in Japanese and American English. *Journal of Pragmatics, 14*, 397–412.

Maynard, S. K. (1997). Analyzing interactional management in native/non-native English conversation: A case of listener response. *International Review of Applied Linguistics in Language Teaching, 35*(1), 37–60.

Mondada, L., & Pekarek Doehler, S. (2004). Second language acquisition as situated practice: Task accomplishment in the French second language classroom. *The Modern Language Journal, 88*(4), 501–518.

Mori, J. (1999). *Negotiating agreement and disagreement in Japanese: Connective expressions and turn construction.* Amsterdam: John Benjamins.

Mori, J. (2006). The workings of the Japanese token *hee* in informing sequences: An analysis of sequential context, turn shape, and prosody. *Journal of Pragmatics, 38*, 1175–1205.

Mori, J. (2007). Border crossings? Exploring the intersection of second language acquisition, conversation analysis, and foreign language pedagogy. *The Modern Language Journal, 91*, 849–862.

Nguyen, H. t. (2003). *The development of communication skills in the practice of patient consultation among pharmacy students* (Unpublished doctoral dissertation). University of Wisconsin, Madison.

Ohta, A. S. (1999). Interactional routines and the socialization of interactional style in adult learners of Japanese. *Journal of Pragmatics, 31*, 1493–1512.

Ohta, A. S. (2001). *Second language acquisition process in the classroom: Learning Japanese.* Mahwah, NJ: Lawrence Erlbaum.

Pallotti, G. (2001). External appropriations as a strategy for participating in intercultural multi-party conversations. In A. Di Luzio, S. Günthner, & F. Orletti (Eds.), *Culture in communication* (pp. 295–334). Amsterdam: John Benjamins.

Pomerantz, A. (1980). Telling my side: "Limited access" as a "fishing" device. *Sociological Inquiry, 50*(3–4), 186–198.

Pomerantz, A. (1984a). Agreeing and disagreeing with assessments: Some features of preferred/dispreferred turn shapes. In M. Atkinson & J. Heritage (Eds.), *Structures of social action: Studies in conversation analysis* (pp. 57–101). Cambridge: Cambridge University Press.

Pomerantz, A. (1984b). Pursuing a response. In M. Atkinson & J. Heritage (Eds.), *Structures of social action: Studies in conversation analysis* (pp. 152–163). Cambridge: Cambridge University Press.

Pomerantz, A., & Fehr, B. J. (1997). Conversation analysis: An approach to the study of social action as sense making practices. In T. A. van Dijk (Ed.), *Discourse as social interaction* (pp. 64–91). Thousand Oaks, CA: Sage.

Sacks, H., Schegloff, E., & Jefferson, G. (1974). A simplest systematics for the organization of turn-taking for conversation. *Language, 50*(4), 696–735.

Sacks, H. (1992). *Lectures on conversation* (Vol. II). Oxford: Blackwell.

Saft, S. (2007). Exploring *aizuchi* as resources in Japanese social interaction: The case of a political discussion program. *Journal of Pragmatics, 38*, 1290–1312.

Schegloff, E. A. (1979). Identification and recognition in telephone conversation openings. In G. Psathas (Ed.), *Everyday language studies in ethnomethodology* (pp. 23–78). New York, NY: Irvington.

Schegloff, E. A. (1982). Discourse as an interactional achievement: Some uses of "uh huh" and other things that come between sentences. In D. Tannen (Ed.), *Analyzing discourse: Text and talk (Georgetown University Roundtable on Languages and Linguistics*; pp. 71–93). Washington, DC: Georgetown University Press.

Schegloff, E. A. (1993). Reflections on quantification in the study of conversation. *Research on Language and Social Interaction, 26*(1), 99–128.

Schegloff, E. A. (2002). Beginnings in the telephone. In J. E. Katz & M. A. Aakhus (Eds.), *Perpetual contact: Mobile communication, private talk, public performance* (pp. 284–300). Cambridge: Cambridge University Press.

Schieffelin, B. B., & Ochs, E. (1986). Language socialization. *Annual Review of Anthropology, 15*, 163–191.

Tanaka, H. (1999). *Turn-taking in Japanese conversation: A study in grammar and interaction.* Amsterdam: John Benjamins.

Vygotsky, L. S. (1978). *Mind in society: The development of higher psychological processes.* Cambridge, MA: Harvard University Press.

Watanabe, E. (1993). Nihongo gakushuusha no aizuchi no bunseki: Denwa de no kaiwa ni oite shiyoosareta gengoteki aizuchi [An analysis of Japanese learners' *aizuchi*: On the verbal *aizuchi* used in telephone conversation]. *Nihongo Kyooiku, 82*, 110–122.

Wertsch, J. V. (Ed.). (1979). *The concept of activity in Soviet psychology.* Armonk, NY: M. E. Sharpe.

Wootton, A. J. (1997). *Interaction and the development of mind.* Cambridge: Cambridge University Press.

Yamada, H. (1992). *Americans and Japanese business discourse: A comparison of interactional styles.* Norwood, NJ: Ablex.

Yngve, V. H. (1970). On getting a word in edgewise. In M. A. Campbell (Ed.), *Papers from the Sixth Regional Meeting of Chicago Linguistic Society* (pp. 567–577). Chicago, IL: Chicago Linguistic Society.

Young, R. (1999). Sociolinguistic approaches to SLA. *Annual Review of Applied Linguistics, 19*, 105–132.

Young, R. F., & Miller, E. R. (2004). Learning as changing participation: Discourse roles in ESL writing conferences. *The Modern Language Journal, 88*(5), 519–535.

Zimmerman, D. H. (1999). Horizontal and vertical comparative research in language and social interaction. *Research on Language and Social Interaction, 32*(1), 195–203.

Appendix: Abbreviations in gloss translations

Cop	copula
FP	final particle
LK	linking particle
N	nominalizer
Neg	negative morpheme
O	object marker
QT	quotation marker
S	subject marker
Top	topic marker

4 Expanded Responses of English-Speaking Korean Heritage Speakers During Oral Interviews

Seung-Hee Lee
Yonsei University, South Korea

Jae-Eun Park

Sung-Ock Sohn[1]
University of California, Los Angeles

Introduction

A growing number of studies on language proficiency interviews (LPIs) suggest the significance of investigating the nature and practices of interaction in the assessment of oral language performance (e.g., Kasper, 2006; Kasper & Ross, 2003, 2007; Kim & Park, 1999; Lazaraton, 1992; McNamara, 1997; McNamara, Hill & May, 2002; Young, 1995a, 1995b). Because LPIs are an interactional event co-constructed by the participants (McNamara, 1997; Okada, 2010; Young & He, 1998), the assessment of speaking skills may relate to the particular ways in which participants including the interviewer(s) manage their linguistic and interactional conduct during the interview. For instance, Lazaraton (1996) identified different types of linguistic and interactional support offered by interviewers and discussed the effects of such support on proficiency ratings. Similarly, Brown (2003, 2005) and Brown and Hill (1998) documented the impact of interviewer styles, defined by different language behaviors of the interviewers, on proficiency ratings (see also Ross, 2007). Ross

(1998), Kim and Suh (1998), and He (1998) examined how interviewees' social and cultural characteristics can create difficulties for the management of various oral performance norms and expectations in the interview setting. Finally, Kim and Park (1999) demonstrated the significance of "interactional competence," as examined by Young and He (1998), in interviewees' responses to interviewers' confirmation requests.

This chapter examines interactional practices used by English-speaking Korean heritage speakers with different levels of proficiency during oral interviews, focusing on the heritage speakers' constructions of expanded responses to the interviewer's questions. We define expanded responses as responses that provide information beyond what was projected by the form of the question. For instance, in answering a yes-no question such as *cikum hakkyo keysok tanisinayo* [are you still at school?], the interviewee may respond with *anio cikum hakkyonun ichennyendoey coluphaysskwuyo kuliko ku twiputhenun sosyel sikhurethi ophiseyse ilhako isseyo* [no, I graduated in 2000, and after that I'm working at a social security office]. This response provides more information (i.e., that the interviewee is working at a social security office) than was projected by the form of the question (i.e., a "yes" or "no" answer), and thus is considered an expansion.[2]

Our examination of expanded responses is based on the premise that grammar is a linguistic choice designed for practices of talk-in-interaction (Ochs, Schegloff, & Thompson, 1996), as shown in increasing research on Korean grammar and interaction (Kim, 1999; Park, 1999; Young & Lee, 2004). Using data from Korean oral interviews with English-speaking Korean heritage speakers, we will show that advanced heritage speakers often deploy Korean-specific grammatical resources to expand their responses, similar to native speakers of Korean. In contrast, intermediate level heritage speakers seldom use these resources in their expansions. The analysis will suggest that interviewees' access to particular grammatical morphemes can affect how they construct responses to the interviewer's question, which in turn affects how their proficiency level and interactional skills are evaluated.

Data and method

This chapter stems from a pilot study that assessed the oral proficiency of students enrolled in UCLA's Korean Flagship program. This program was implemented in 2004 with the aim to produce students with professional proficiency (Interagency Language Roundtable level 3) in the language. As part of the admission process, the Flagship program administers a series of diagnostic tests, which include the American Council on the Teaching of Foreign Languages (ACTFL) Oral Proficiency Interview (OPI), a measurement of reading and writing skills designed by the UCLA Korean Flagship team, and telephone interviews. To be admitted to the program, students must demonstrate at least level 2/2+ (ACTFL advanced level; see ACTFL, n.d.) proficiency in the target language.[3]

The data for this study are drawn from audio-recordings of eight Korean telephone interviews with three advanced and two intermediate level speakers, and face-to-face interviews with one advanced and two intermediate level speakers. There were two interviewers, both of whom were native speakers of Korean. One interviewer conducted the telephone interviews and the other conducted the face-to-face interviews. The eight interviewees were all English-speaking Korean heritage speakers. Two interviewees were born in the US. The other six were born in Korea but grew up and were educated in the US; the average age of their arrival in the US was about 7 years.

Like other heritage speakers who grew up in a home where a non-English language was spoken (Brinton, Kagan, & Bauckus, 2007), Korean heritage speakers are often highly proficient conversing about everyday topics but lack knowledge of vocabulary and a more formal register required in many situations outside the home domain, such as discussions of academic topics (see Sohn & Shin, 2007, for the linguistic profiles of Korean heritage and non-heritage speakers.). Given that heritage and non-heritage speakers display quite distinct patterns in their development and use of Korean, including oral and discourse-related skills (S. Sohn, 1997; Sohn & Shin, 2007), only heritage speakers were selected for this pilot study. Korean heritage speakers whose language proficiency was beyond the target proficiency of the program, that is, level 3 (ACTFL superior level) did not participate in the program.

The proficiency level of the interviewees in our study—advanced and intermediate—is based on the ACTFL rating scale. The rating was conducted by a certified Korean OPI rater. While both the advanced and intermediate levels can be divided into three sub-categories of high, mid, and low according to the ACTFL scale, we focused on the common features of the major level for the purpose of this chapter. The university's human subject protection committee approved the use of the data for research purposes. The data were transcribed and analyzed using the conventions of conversation analysis. The data were also coded for expanded responses as well as for the use of clause-final suffixes. We performed a quantitative analysis of the coding and calculated the total number of words by using Uniconcordance and *Kkamccaksay* programs.

In the data excerpts, Korean is romanized according to the Yale system. The list of abbreviations of the morphological categories used in the excerpts is provided in the appendix.

Results

Interviews with both advanced and intermediate speakers lasted approximately 60 minutes (Table 1). Despite the similar duration of the interviews, the compiled corpus size for each group showed an asymmetrical pattern. The total number of words produced by the advanced level speakers was significantly higher than that produced by the intermediate level speakers. More specifically, the advanced speakers produced about 1.6 times more talk than the intermediate speakers.

Table 1. Number of words produced by the interviewees

interviewee	OPI rating	time length (min:sec)	corpus size (number of words)
1	intermediate	16:59	978
2	intermediate	12:55	568
3	intermediate	14:14	734
4	intermediate	15:47	861
	total: intermediate	59:15	3141
5	advanced	13:22	886
6	advanced	19:11	1517
7	advanced	15:30	1675
8	advanced	11:32	962
	total: advanced	59:35	5042

This quantitative difference suggests the need for a closer look at what advanced level speakers are doing that is qualitatively different in their production of talk to produce this variation. In the remainder of this chapter, we examine this issue by focusing on the interviewees' responses to questions.

Expanded responses

In responding to the interviewer's questions, interviewees may simply produce a single item requested by the question, for instance a *yes* or *no* answer to a yes-no question, or alternatively, they may provide more information than what the form of the question is requesting and thus "expand" the response. The term "expansion" is used to describe a response that provides information beyond what was projected by the form of the question, as defined above. This may be a type of response that manifests participants' orientations to the goal of the OPI activity in which interviewees' oral performance is assessed through their speech samples obtained during the interview.

The advanced level speakers in our dataset often expanded their responses (Table 2). They constructed expanded responses to almost 42% of the interviewer's questions.[4] Example 1 illustrates a typical way in which advanced level speakers expanded their responses.

Expanded Responses of English-Speaking Korean Heritage Speakers

Example 1, Advanced level interviewee

```
1   IR:       um: 'hh kulemyen  mwe      hankul hakkyo  tani-si-myense
              um       then     what     Korean school  attend-SH-while
2             paywu-ko   kule-si-ci-nun       anh-usi-ss-kwu-yo?
              learn-and  do.so-SH-COMM-TOP    not-SH-PAST-and-POL:Q
              'Um: 'hh then you didn't go to Korean language school or
              anything to study it?'

3   IE:  ->   e   han    yuk kaywel cwunghakkyo    ttay yuk kaywel
              uh  about  six month  middle.school  time six month
4             tanye-ss(h)-na?
              attend-PAST-FML:Q
              'Uh about six months when I was in middle school I
              we(h)nt) for about six months?'

5   IR:       [um::
               mm
              'Mm::'

6   IE:  ->   [kuntey nemwuna:
               but    much
              'But it was so:'

7   IR:       ney=
              yes:POL
              'Yes='

8   IE:  ->   =cey-ka hankuk-eyse cala-     thayena-ss-unikka
               I-NOM  Korea-LOC   grow.up   be.born-PAST-because
9             com       swiw-e.kaciko[:
              a.little  easy-and
              ' =Because I grew- I was born in Korea it was a little
              easy and:'

10  IR:                              [a::
                                      oh
                                     'Oh::'

11  IE:  ->   sikan nangpi-i-n:  [(kes-kath-ase)]   an
              time  waste-be-REL  thing-be.like-so  not
12            tanye-ss-eyo.
              attend-PAST-POL:DEC
              'I didn't go because it felt like a waste: of time.'

13  IR:                              [a  :  :  ]
                                      oh
                                     'Oh:::'

14  IR:       ney:     kulemyen  cengsikulo  tasi    hankuke-lul
              yes:POL  then      formally    again   Korean-ACC
15            kongpwuha-si-n  ke-nun  ((school name))  o-si-e.kaciko
              study-SH-REL    thing-TOP                come-SH-and.then
              'that you began to study Korean formally?'
```

In lines 1–2, the interviewer (IR) produces a yes-no question. While the form of the question makes relevant a (dis)confirmation about whether he had Korean learning experience in an instructional setting, the interviewee (IE) does not simply produce a (dis)confirmation. Instead, this advanced speaker provides an expanded response, which is expected in this particular context as described above. He first describes his earlier exposure to instructed Korean, saying that his learning experience was insignificant in terms of its time frame as well as duration (lines 3–4). Then he continues with an account for the lack of education in an instructional setting (lines 6–12), which provides information that was not projected by the interviewer's question.

By contrast, the intermediate level speakers infrequently expanded their responses, usually providing only the information that was directly elicited by the question. They constructed expanded responses to 17% of the questions, a notable difference from the percentage of expanded responses produced by the advanced learners (Table 2).

Table 2. Use of expanded responses

interviewee	OPI rating	no. of questions	no. of expanded responses	% of expanded responses
1	intermediate	92	15	16.30
2	intermediate	40	8	20.00
3	intermediate	68	18	26.47
4	intermediate	41	5	12.19
	total: intermediate	241	41	17.01
5	advanced	47	9	19.15
6	advanced	50	28	56.0
7	advanced	37	17	45.95
8	advanced	47	22	46.81
	total: advanced	181	76	41.99

Example (2) illustrates the recurrent pattern found in the intermediate level speakers' responses.

Example 2, Intermediate level interviewee

```
1  IR:      um: 'hh kulemyen e: tayhak   wa-kaciko,
            uh       then      uh college come-and
            'Um: 'hh then uh: when you entered college'

2  IE:      ney=
            yes:POL
            'Yes='
```

```
3  IR:      hankwuke-lul ilehkey    mwe   cengsikulo: ttalo
            Korean-ACC   like.this  what  formally    further
4           kongpwuha-si-n cek-un    eps-usey-yo?
            study-SH-REL   event-TOP not.exist-SH-POL:Q
            'You never studied Korean formally:?'

5  IE:  ->  kunyang  (0.8) tullu-kimayn ha-ko:   (0.2) kekise ss- em:
            just           stop.by-only do-and         there  um
6           study-nun an  hay-ss-eyo
            study-TOP not do-PAST-DEC:POL
            'I just dropped by a Korean class and: (0.2) there
            ss- um: I didn't study.'

7  IR:      a   ttalo   mwe   Korean swuep-ul   tut-ko   kuleci-nun
            oh  further what  Korean class-ACC  take-and do.so-TOP
8           anh-usi-ss-ney-yo
            not-SH-PAST-I.see-POL
            'Oh so you didn't take Korean classes or anything?'

9  IE:  ->  anyo
            no:POL
            'No'

10 IR:      e   kulem ((name of school)) kyeysi-l ttay-to  an
            oh  then                     be-REL   time-also not
11          tul-usi-ss-eyo?   hankwke swuep-un?
            take-SH-PAST-POL:Q Korean  class-TOP
            'Oh then you didn't take any when you were in ((school
            name))? Korean classes?'

12 IE:  ->  ani-yo hh!
            not-POL
            'No hh!'
```

The interviewer produces a negative yes-no question (lines 1–4), similar to the one in lines 1–2 in Example 1. The interviewee describes her lack of formal Korean language education, establishing a "no" answer, without further account or information (lines 5–6). When the interviewer asks for confirmation in the next turn (line 7–8), thus possibly inviting expansion, the interviewee again produces a minimal "no" response (line 9). In lines 10–11, the interviewer produces another question on the same topic. This again can provide an opportunity for the interviewee to expand the response, elaborating on the topic. But the interviewee again produces a simple "no" response rather than an expansion (line 12). Thus the interviewee provides a "no" answer throughout these response turns (lines 5–6, 9, 12), addressing only what was projected by the form of the interviewer's yes-no question.

Expanding a response with grammatical resources
As a verb-final agglutinative language, Korean has various verbal suffixes which may be attached to predicate stems (H. Sohn, 1999, pp. 15–16). For instance,

in *hankwuk-eyse thayena-si-ess-e-yo?* [Were you born in Korea?], after the locative expression *hankwuk-eyse* [in Korea], the verb stem *thayena-* [be born] is followed by a chain of verbal suffixes in the following order—the subject honorific suffix *-si*, the past tense suffix *-ess*, the informal suffix *-e*, and the polite suffix *-yo*. Due to the agglutinative morphology, clausal connectives in Korean (e.g., "if," "because," "while," "and," etc.) are attached to predicate (verb or adjective) stems, as in *tani-ko* [attend-and], *tani-myen* [attend-if], and *tani-taka* [attend-while]. As a result, it is not possible for a recipient to predict whether an unfolding clause will be turned into a compound or complex sentence until a clausal connective is attached to the end of the verb. Due to this delayed grammatical projectability, speakers can expand an otherwise possibly complete turn by utilizing various clausal connectives at the end of a clause. That is, instead of finishing an utterance with a sentence-final suffix (e.g., a declarative suffix *-ta*), speakers can attach a clausal connective to the utterance-in-progress, thereby making relevant subsequent talk. In this way, clausal connectives can serve as a grammatical resource for constructing an expanded response in that they allow speakers to reserve a space for further talk at a point where the turn-so-far can otherwise be possibly complete (cf. Park, 1999).

Sentence-final suffixes,[5] such as *-canha(yo)* [you know; you see?] and *-cyo/-ciyo* [right?] (tag questions) in Korean are similarly utilized as a grammatical resource for building expanded responses. These sentence-final suffixes are used to convey the speaker's attitude toward the proposition of the current utterance. When delivered with continuing intonation, these suffixes simultaneously solicit the recipient's participation, frequently in the form of a minimal token (S. Sohn, 2008). More specifically, *-canha(yo)* can be used to index the speaker's conviction that the recipient will agree with the information being provided. Similarly, *-cyo/-ciyo*, whose function is somewhat similar to that of a tag question in English, can be used to solicit an alignment from the recipient.

The advanced level speakers in our dataset frequently used these grammatical resources in building expanded responses (Table 3; Figure 1). Example 3 illustrates the use of *-ketun* [you see] (→) by an advanced speaker in constructing an expanded response.

Table 3. Use of clause-final and sentence-final suffixes

interviewee	OPI rating	clause-final and sentence-final suffixes				
		-canha	-ciyo	ketun	-nuntey	-eyo/-ayo
1	intermediate	0	5	0	3	45
2	intermediate	0	0	1	5	28
3	intermediate	0	5	0	13	37
4	intermediate	0	4	2	6	61
	total: intermediate	0	14	3	27	171

5	advanced	1	6	14	8	34
6	advanced	5	3	1	24	24
7	advanced	7	25	7	10	38
8	advanced	3	1	6	13	25
	total: advanced	16	35	28	55	121

Example 3, Advanced level interviewee: *-ketun*

```
1  IR:       kulem cheum-pwuthe  pa:lo wan-o-thwu-bi-lo tul-ss-eyo?
             then  beginning-from directly 102B-LOC     take-SH-PAST-Q
             'Then uh did you take 102B from the very beginning?'

2            (0.3)

3  IE: ->    yey     [kulay-ss-eyo.=yekise sihem-ul pwa-ss-ketun-yo,
             yes:POL  be.so-PAST-DEC here   exam-ACC take-PAST-you see-POL
             'Yes, I did.=I took an exam here, you see?'

4  IR:               [a:::
                      oh
                     'Oh:::'

5  IE:       (.) kka      pass-lul   hay-kac-kwu,
                 I.mean   pass-ACC   do-and.then
             'I passed and then'

6  IR:       nye:,
             yes:POL
             'Yeah,'

7  IE:       ye:. wan-o: wan-o-thwu:ei-ey tule ka-ss-eyo
             yes:POL 1-0  1-0-2   A-LOC        enroll-PAST-DEC:POL
             'Yeah. I enrolled in 1-0 1-0-2A.'
```

After the interviewer's question (line 1), the interviewee provides a "yes" answer and expands his response by providing an additional account for his enrollment in the 102B course (line 3). In building the account, the interviewee deploys *-ketun* to set up the context (I took a placement exam) for the upcoming talk (i.e., I passed the exam, line 5). He thus projects a further unit of talk while simultaneously inviting the recipient's acknowledgment through the use of continuing intonation.[6] Example 4 illustrates this same advanced speaker's use of *-nuntey* as well as *-cyo/-ciyo* in constructing an expanded response.

Example 4, Advanced level interviewee: *-nuntey* and *-ciyo/-cyo*

```
1  IR:       kuntey    hasi-nun cwungey sihem: cwungey
             ha ha     by the way take-REL midst  exam   midst
2            com   elyewe-ss:-te-n           cem-un     eps-usey-yo?
             a bit difficult-PAST-RETRO-REL  thing-TOP  not exist-SH-Q
             'By the way, was there uh something difficult while uh
             taking the exam?'
```

```
3  IE: ->  elyewess-te-n          kes-un       eps-nuntey-yo,
           difficult-RETRO-REL thing-TOP not exist-but-POL
           'There was nothing difficult really'

4  IR:     [ney:.
           yes:POL
           'No'

5  IE: ->  [(ney:)    ku listening comprehension iss-cyo?
              yes:POL that listening comprehension be-COMM:POL
           '(Yeah) you know the listening comprehension part, right?'

6  IR:     yey yey
           yes:POL yes:POL
           'Yes yes'

7  IE:     kukey cal an tullye-ss-eyo
           that  well not be audible-PAST-DEC
           'That was not very clear'
```

When the interviewee is asked if there were difficult parts of the test, he provides a negative response but also provides additional information. In line 3, he first deploys -*nuntey* at the end of the clause that establishes the "no" response, thus projecting a further unit of talk (Park, 1999). The interviewer does not proceed with a question but limits his turn to producing a minimal acknowledgment (line 4). In lines 5 and 7, the interviewee continues by describing another kind of difficulty he had during the exam. In so doing, he uses the suffix -*cyo* (line 5) to seek the recipient's recognition of the current talk, that is, "the listening comprehension" part. Upon the interviewer's confirming response (line 6), the interviewee specifies the problem (line 7) and completes the expanded response.

Example 5 illustrates the use of -*canha(yo)* [you know? you see?]. In response to a question that elicits the area the interviewee wants to improve (data not shown), the interviewee elaborates on the area in which she feels she is not proficient.

Example 5, Advanced level interviewee: -*canha(yo)*

```
1  IE:     kuntey ce kathun kyengwu-nun cwunghakkyo il  i haknyen
           but    I  like   case-TOP middle.school one two grade
2          ttay paywu-n hanca                sillyek-i ta-ko,
           time learn-REL Chinese.characters ability-NOM all-and
           'And in my case, the knowledge of Chinese characters I
           learned in my first and second year at middle school is
           all and,'

3  IR:     um
           mm
           'Mm hm'
```

```
4    IE:       tto    hankwukmal-i  tto    swunswuhan  hankwukmal-man  iss-nun
               also   Korean-NOM    also   native      Korean-only     exist-REL
5                     key       ani-la::
                      thing.NOM not-but
               'And also when it comes to Korean, there is not only
               native Korean but also::'

6    IR:       ney
               yes:POL
               'Yes'

7              (0.4)

8    IE:       palum-un            kath-untey way  ilehkey
               pronunciation-TOP   same-but   why  like.this
9              hanmwun-ulo              pwa-ss-ul     ttay  thullin    kulen
               Chinese.characters-at    see-PAST-REL  time  different  such
        ->     key       manh-canh-ayo?
               thing:NOM a.lot-you.know-POL:Q
               'Although the pronunciation is the same if you look at
               Chinese letters there are lots of them that are different
               you know?'

10   IR:       kuleh-cyo
               be.so-COMM:POL
               'Of course'

11   IE:       kulen ke-lul    ce-nun cey-ka kakkum      molu-l
               such  thing-ACC I-TOP  I-NOM  sometimes   not.know-REL
12             ttay-ka  kakkum      iss-eyo.
               time-NOM sometimes   exist-POL:DEC
               'Those things I- there are times that I don't know them'
```

In lines 4–9, the interviewee first describes a particular aspect of Korean vocabulary. In line 9, the interviewee deploys *-canha*, soliciting the interviewer's agreement. The interviewer produces an agreement (line 10), inviting the interviewee to continue with the ongoing talk. The interviewee proceeds by describing her lack of proficiency (lines 11–12). Through the use of *-canha*, she foregrounds her upcoming utterance in the expanded response.

In contrast to the advanced speakers, the intermediate level speakers infrequently employed grammatical resources that can indicate an upcoming unit of talk (Table 3; Figure 1). The clause-final suffixes described above, such as *-ketun* [you see; because], *-nuntey/-(u)ntey* [and] or [but], *-canha(yo)* [you know? or you see?], and *-ciyo/-cyo* [right?], were used by the intermediate level speakers less frequently than by the advanced level speakers (Kim, 2009). Notably, the use of the informal ending suffix, *-eyo/-ayo*, was more frequent in the speech of the intermediate level speakers than of the advanced speakers. This is interesting considering that the suffix *-eyo/-ayo* can mark the completion of an utterance without projecting any further talk. The different use of these suffixes suggests an asymmetry among the advanced and intermediate level speakers in their access to Korean-specific grammatical features that can facilitate the construction of expanded talk.

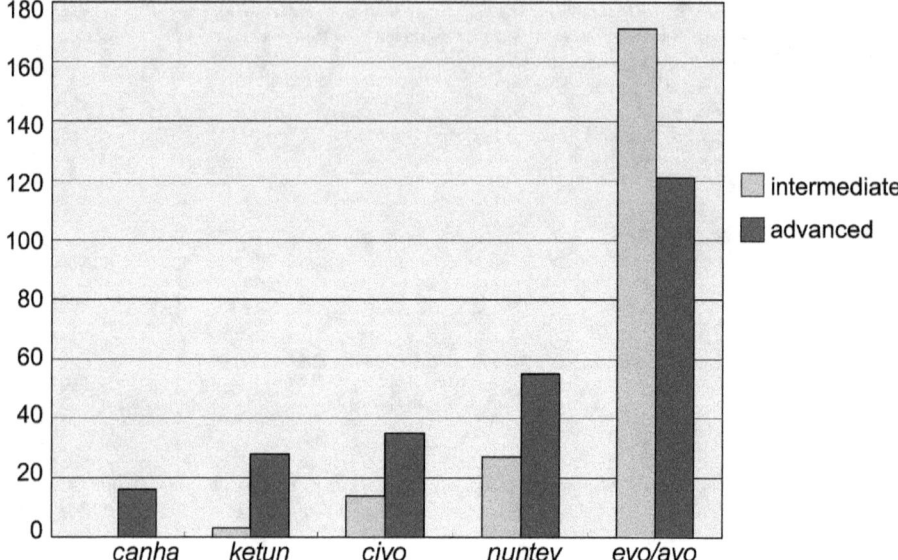

Figure 1.

In Example 6 (introduced as Example 2), the intermediate level interviewee, while expanding on the previous response, does not deploy a clause-final suffix that can project a further unit of talk.

Example 6, Intermediate level interviewee: *-eyo/-ayo*

```
1  IR:      a  ttalo     mwe  Korean swuep-ul   tut-ko    kuleci-nun
            oh formally  what Korean class-ACC  take-and  do.so-TOP
2           anh-usi-ss-ney-yo
            not-SH-PAST-I.see-POL:DEC
            'Oh so you didn't take Korean classes or anything?'

3  IE:      anyo
            no:POL
            'No'

4  IR:      e  kulem ((name of school)) kyeysi-l ttay-to    an
            oh then                     be-REL   time-also  not
5           tul-usi-ss-eyo?      hankwke  swuep-un?
            take-SH-PAST-POL:Q   Korean   class-TOP
            'Oh then you didn't take any when you were in ((school
            name))? Korean classes?'

6  IE: ->   ani-yo
            not-POL
            'No'
```

```
 7  IR:         a:- um::      ['hh kulem-
                oh um                then
                'Oh:- um::  'hh then-'

 8  IE:  ->                  [kuntey [cikum yeki apply (0.2)=
                              But     now   here  apply
                'But (I) apply here (0.2)='

 9  IR:                                      [ney
                                              yes:POL
                'Yes'

10  IE:         =ce-nun paywu-ko  siph-eyo. kunikkan    cikum-yo
                 I-TOP  learn-and want-POL  so:because  now-POL
                '=I'd like to learn. I mean now'

11  IR:         a: kulemyenun (1.8) cikum (0.7) pwumoni-malko phyengsoey
                oh then              now         parents-except usually
12              hankwuke kulemyenun nwukwu-lang manhi ssu-sey.yo?
                Korean   then       who-with    a.lot use-SH.POL:Q
                'Oh: then (1.8) now (0.7) besides your parents who do you
                usually speak Korean with?'
```

In response to the interviewer's question (lines 4–5), the interviewee completes the turn by producing "no" with the informal polite ending suffix (line 6). As the interviewee does not project any further talk but completes the turn with the informal ending suffix (line 6), the interviewer moves on to produce a next turn, probably a next question (line 7). However, the interviewee, in overlap, starts her turn with the use of a connector, *kuntey* [but] (line 8), which can function as a marker of topic development. Rather than designing the negative turn (line 6) with a clause-final suffix such as *-nuntey/-(u)ntey* [but] that can project a further unit of talk, the interviewee completes the response with "no" as one unit (line 6), and then initiates another unit of talk (line 8) after the interviewer has started his turn (line 7).

In sum, the advanced level speakers frequently use clause-final suffixes to project upcoming talk, thus reserving space for building an expanded response. The interviewer collaborates in the interviewee's construction of expanded responses by limiting their turn and producing only minimal acknowledgment/ agreement tokens. The intermediate level speakers, on the other hand, infrequently deploy such grammatical resources to expand their responses. This can lead to the interviewer's movement to a next question.

Discussion

We compared the construction of responses by advanced and intermediate level speakers. The advanced speakers often expanded their responses, whereas the intermediate speakers infrequently did so. Additionally, when expanding their responses, the advanced level speakers frequently used clause-final and sentence-final suffixes that can project further talk, which was not observed in the elaborated turns of the intermediate level speakers.

The use of grammatical suffixes and the production of expanded responses are related to one another, especially given that Korean is a verb final language. The advanced level speakers are more skillful at using clause-final and sentence-final suffixes, which can facilitate their construction of expanded responses. This is especially so given that the interviewer may start their turn once the interviewee completes his/her turn without the use of one of these suffixes. On the other hand, the intermediate level speakers' infrequent use of clause-final suffixes can deprive them of an opportunity to build an expansion. Additionally, if speakers do expand, this avoidance can limit their expansions because the interviewer is likely to produce subsequent talk.

This analysis suggests that speakers' interactional skills may be affected by their access to grammatical resources.[7] Oral interviews aim to obtain a speech sample that includes an adequate sample of talk from interviewees. Interviewers thus strive to elicit more talk from the interviewee, mostly through the use of questions. When interviewees are not forthcoming on a certain topic, interviewers often develop lines of questioning and provide several opportunities for interviewees to construct a more expanded response (cf. Example 2). At the same time, interviewees often strive to produce more talk, given that it is their oral performance that is being assessed. However, interviewees' responses can be restricted because interviewers are in a sense "ready" to take a turn and ask another question upon completion of the interviewee's response. Thus, one effective strategy on the part of interviewees is to produce expansions before bringing the response to completion.

As mentioned above, the advanced level speakers deploy this interactional strategy, which is facilitated by their use of Korean-specific grammatical resources that can reserve space for further talk. The intermediate level speakers, in contrast, display limited skills in building expanded talk in an effective way, in part because their access to relevant grammatical resources seems to be restricted. Our pilot data thus suggests that speakers' grammatical and interactional competences are related and that oral performance assessments measure both areas of language use.

Notes

1   The authors' names are alphabetically ordered. The authors would like to express their gratitude to Gabriele Pallotti and two anonymous reviewers for their insightful comments.
2   Note that answering a yes/no question with a "yes"or "no" only can be disaffiliative in certain OPI contexts (Kasper & Ross, 2003; Ross 1998). The concept of expansion

in this chapter is used to refer to the construction of response that provides information beyond what was projected by the form of the question.

3   The following descriptions characterize the speaking skill for the Interagency Language Roundtable (ILR) Level 2 and Level 3, respectively (ILR, n.d.).
    Level 2 (Limited Functional Proficiency)
    Able to handle routine daily interactions that are limited in scope. Able to handle confidently, but not fluently, most social conversations on such topics as current events, work, family, etc. Examples: can typically ask and answer predictable questions in the workplace and receive and provide straightforward direction.
    Level 3 (General Functional Proficiency)
    Able to speak the language with sufficient fluency and accuracy to participate effectively in most formal and informal conversations on practical, social and professional topics. However, there are noticeable linguistic and cultural imperfections that limit the individual's ability to participate in more sophisticated interactions such as high-level negotiation. Can typically discuss particular interests and special fields of competence with ease. Example: can use the language as part of normal professional duties such as answering objections, clarifying points, justifying decisions, conducting meetings, delivering briefings, etc. Can reliably elicit information and informed opinion from native speakers.

4   As Table 2 shows, one advanced level speaker (Interviewee 5) shows an exception. He expanded his responses to only 19% of the questions posed to him. This relatively low proportion may be accounted for by the fact that when the interviewee produced expanded responses to questions, he did so as multi-unit turns. For instance, most of his expanded answers to yes-no questions were rather long and elaborated. In other words, he produced few expansions but when he did, they were quite elaborate and lengthy. In addition, the interviewee frequently used clause-final suffixes in building his responses, which shows the complexity of his talk (cf. Section 3.2).

5   Clause-final suffixes are typically non-finite conjunctive suffixes while sentence-final suffixes (e.g., *-canha(yo)* and *-cyo/-ciyo*) are sentence enders which denote a sentence type (e.g., declarative, interrogative) and a speech level (e.g., polite, plain).

6   The utterance-final *-ketun-yo* in line 3 is marked with a high boundary tone, which launches an expanded response and at the same time allows the recipient to provide an alignment token. See Park and Sohn (2002) for the role of high boundary tone marked with *-ketun-yo* in Korean conversations.

7   Differences in proficiency described in the data—the differences in the use of expanded responses—can also be attributed to the interviewees' interpretation of the interview as a discursive practice in which they are evaluated on the length and complexity of their talk. While advanced level speakers may understand that the complexity and length of their response is significant in the assessment of their oral proficiency, and thus strive to produce expanded responses, intermediate level

speakers may not. This difference in understanding the purpose of the task may partially explain the dissimilar use of expanded responses.

References

American Council on Teaching Foreign Languages (ACTFL). (n.d.). Language Testing International (Proficiency guidelines). Retrieved November 1, 2008, from http://www.languagetesting.com

Brinton, D., Kagan, O., & Bauckus, S. (2007). (Eds.). *Heritage language acquisition: A new field emerging.* New York, NY: Routledge.

Brown, A. (2003). Interviewer variation and the co-construction of speaking proficiency. *Language Testing, 20,* 1–15.

Brown, A. (2005). *Interviewer variability in oral proficiency interviews.* Frankfurt: Peter Lang.

Brown, A., & Hill, K. (1998). Interviewer style and candidate performance in the IELTS oral interview. *IELTS Research Reports, 1,* 1–19.

He, A. W. (1998). Answering questions in LPIs: A case study. In R. Young & A. W. He (Eds.), *Talking and testing: Discourse approaches to the assessment of oral proficiency* (pp. 101–116). Amsterdam: John Benjamins.

Interagency Language Roundtable (ILR). (n.d.). Introduction to ILR. Retrieved November 1, 2008, from http://www.govtilr.org/Skills/ILRscale1.htm

Kasper, G. (2006). When once is not enough: Politeness of multiple requests in oral proficiency interviews. *Multilingua, 25,* 323–350.

Kasper, G., & Ross, S. (2003). Repetition as a source of miscommunication in oral proficiency interviews. In J. House, G. Kasper, & S. Ross (Eds.), *Misunderstanding in social life* (pp. 82–106). Harlow: Longman/Pearson Education.

Kasper, G., & Ross, S. (2007). Multiple questions in language proficiency interviews. *Journal of Pragmatics, 39,* 2045–2070.

Kim, K. (1999). Phrasal unit boundaries and organization of turns and sequences in Korean conversation. *Human Studies, 22,* 425–446.

Kim, K., & Park, Y. (1999). A study of communicative competence assessment in Korean as a foreign language with reference to language proficiency interviews. *The Sociolinguistic Journal of Korean, 7*(1), 5–49.

Kim, K., & Suh, K. (1998). Confirmation sequences as interactional resources in Korean language proficiency interviews. In R. Young & A. W. He (Eds.), *Talking and testing: Discourse approaches to the assessment of oral proficiency* (pp. 297–332). Amsterdam: John Benjamins.

Kim, Y. (2009). Korean discourse markers -*nuntey* and -*kuntey* in native-nonnative conversation: An acquisitional perspective. In H. t. Nguyen & G. Kasper (Eds.), *Talk-in-interaction: Multilingual perspectives* (pp. 317–350). Honolulu, HI: University of Hawai'i, National Foreign Language Resource Center.

Lazaraton, A. (1992). The structural organization of a language interview: A conversation analytic perspective. *System, 20*, 373–386.

Lazaraton, A. (1996). Interlocutor support in oral proficiency interviews: The case of CASE. *Language Testing, 13*, 151–172.

McNamara, T. (1996, March). *Interaction in second language performance assessment.* Paper presented at the American Association for Applied Linguistics Annual Conference, Chicago, IL.

McNamara, T. (1997). "Interaction" in second language performance assessment: Whose performance? *Applied Linguistics, 18*, 444–466.

McNamara, T., Hill, K., & May, L. (2002). Discourse and assessment. *Annual Review of Applied Linguistics, 22*, 221–242

Ochs, E., Schegloff, E. A., & Thompson, S. A. (1996). *Interaction and grammar.* Cambridge: Cambridge University Press.

Okada, Y. (2010). Role-play in oral proficiency interviews: Interactive footing and interactional competencies. *Journal of Pragmatics, 42*, 1647–1668.

Park, M.-J., & Sohn, S.-O. (2002). Discourse, grammaticalization, and intonation: The analysis of -*ketun* in Korean. *Japanese/Korean Linguistics, 10*, 306–319.

Park, Y.-Y. (1999). The Korean connective *nuntey* in conversational discourse. *Journal of Pragmatics, 31*, 191–218.

Ross, S. (1998). Divergent frame interpretations in language proficiency interview interaction. In R. Young & A. W. He (Eds.), *Talking and testing: Discourse approaches to the assessment of oral proficiency* (pp. 333–353). Amsterdam: John Benjamins.

Ross, S. (2007). A comparative task-in-interaction analysis of OPI backsliding. *Journal of Pragmatics, 39*, 2017–2044.

Sohn, H. (1999). *The Korean language.* Cambridge: Cambridge University Press.

Sohn, S. (1997). Issues and concerns in teaching multi-level language classes. In Y.-H. Kim (Ed.), *Proceedings of the Second National Conference on Korean Language Education* (pp. 139–158). Honolulu, HI: American Association of Teachers of Korean.

Sohn, S. (2008). *Grammar, grammaticalization, and discourse: The development of sentence-final suffixes in Korean.* Paper presented at the 18th Japanese/Korean Linguistics Conference, Graduate School of City University of New York, NY.

Sohn, S., & Shin, S. (2007). True beginners, false beginners, and fake beginners: Placement challenges for Korean heritage speakers. *Foreign Language Annals, 40*(5), 353–367.

Young, R. (1995a). Conversational styles in language proficiency interviews. *Language Learning, 45*(1), 3–42.

Young, R. (1995b). Discontinuous interlanguage development and its implications for oral proficiency rating scales. *Applied Language Learning, 6*, 13–26.

Young, R., & He, A. W. (Eds.). (1998). *Talking and testing: Discourse approaches to the assessment of oral proficiency.* Amsterdam: John Benjamins.

Young, R., & Lee, J. (2004) Identifying units in interaction: Reactive tokens in Korean and English conversations. *Journal of Sociolinguistics, 8*(3), 380–407.

Appendix: List of abbreviations

ACC	accusative particle
CIRCUM	circumstantial connective suffix
COMM	committal suffix
DEC	declarative suffix
FML	familiar speech style
HON	honorific suffix
LOC	locative particle
NOM	nominative particles (-i or -ka)
PAST	past tense suffix
POL	polite
PROG	progressive marker
Q	question suffix
REL	relativizer suffix
RETROS	retrospective suffix
SH	subject honorific suffix
TOP	topic particle

Doing

Learning

5   Talk, Body, and Material Objects as Coordinated Interactional Resources in Repair Activities in One-on-One ESL Tutoring

Mi-Suk Seo
California State University, Sacramento

Introduction

The importance of gestures and other embodied practices in social interaction as well as in cognitive development has been noted recurrently from various perspectives (e.g., Goodwin, 1986; Goodwin & Goodwin, 1986; Heath, 1986; Kendon, 1990, 2004; Lantolf, 2000; McNeill, 1992; Schegloff, 1984; Streeck, 1993, 1994, 2003). With the increasing availability of multimedia technology, there has been an upsurge of interest in the coordination of multiple semiotic resources—talk, gaze, gesture, body orientation, and material objects—in face-to-face interaction (e.g., Goodwin, 2000; Hayashi, 2003, 2005; Murphy, 2005; Sidnell 2005). However, to date, second language acquisition (SLA) studies have not devoted adequate attention to whether, when, and how non-vocal resources may be utilized to facilitate learning. As Lazaraton (2004) pointed out, SLA researchers have been overwhelmingly preoccupied with verbal aspects of second language discourse, viewing language as a disembodied set of linguistic rules and thereby mostly relying on audio-recorded and written data.

Given the paucity of studies in the SLA field that examine the role of gesture and other bodily conduct, recently a number of studies have started to explore the role of nonverbal behaviors in second language (L2) interaction[1] from different perspectives (see Gullberg, 2010, for an extensive review): experimental studies from cognitive perspectives (e.g., Gullberg, 2006; Hardison, 2003; Sueyoshi & Hardison, 2005), descriptive studies from sociocultural perspectives (e.g., McCafferty, 2002, 2004; McCafferty & Ahmed, 2000), and microanalytic studies from conversation analytic perspectives (e.g., Belhiah, 2005; Carroll, 2004; Lazaraton, 2004; Markee, 2004a, 2004b, 2005; Mori & Hayashi, 2006; Olsher, 2004, 2007). The findings from these studies, regardless of the differences in their approaches, have suggested that nonverbal aspects deserve more analytic attention in L2 studies in order to better understand interactional practices and processes of L2 use and learning. Especially, it has been argued that more research needs to be done to discover how gesture actually works in concert with talk in various interactions in which L2 learners participate in their everyday lives (Belhiah, 2005).

Aligning with the view of language learning as "an emergent, socially constructed phenomenon" (Markee, 2004a, p. 593) and using conversation analysis (CA), this study aims to enhance our understanding of how nonverbal resources may be used to facilitate language learning in naturally occurring L2 interaction. It provides a detailed description of sequential development and a close analysis of the interplay between verbal and nonverbal resources in a specific interactional context. In particular, it investigates how diverse semiotic modalities are coordinated to resolve an interactional contingency that emanates from the lack of shared linguistic resources between the participants in an ESL tutoring session. More specifically, it focuses on the important role of nonverbal resources in repair sequences.

In what follows, after briefly reviewing relevant literature on nonverbal behaviors in L2 interaction and on repair, I provide an in-depth analysis of long repair sequences in an ESL tutoring session, which demonstrates a crucial role of non-vocal components of interaction in resolving problematized mutual understanding and in facilitating language learning. Specifically, I investigate in detail how the tutor, faced with the tutee's repair initiation, deploys diverse extra-linguistic resources, and how the tutee displays moment-by-moment changes in her knowledge status as the tutor enhances her multimodal efforts by expanding and diversifying the use of gestures and material objects in the surround. Finally, based on the findings, I discuss what kinds of insights CA can provide into ESL teaching and SLA research.

Study

Nonverbal behavior in L2 interaction

There has been a widespread assumption that, since L2 learners do not yet have a good command of the target language, both the learners and their interlocutors frequently mobilize gestures to assist their communication. However, few SLA studies have discussed the relevance of gestures to language learning and their specific role in L2 interaction, since the majority of data collection procedures in SLA studies fail to capture nonverbal behaviors. Gestures have been treated simply as part of strategic competence and as a way to compensate for the L2 learners' insufficient ability to resolve communication breakdowns (e.g., Bachman, 1990; Canale & Swain, 1980). An adequate account for how they actually work in L2 interaction has yet to be provided. Considering the findings in other fields, such as communication, sociology, anthropology, and psychology, which show the importance of nonverbal behaviors in social interaction, it stands to reason that researchers have started to problematize this noticeable gap in second language research and made empirical contributions to address the gap (e.g., Belhiah, 2005; Carroll, 2004; Lazaraton, 2004; Markee, 2004a, 2004b, 2005; McCafferty, 2002, 2004; McCafferty & Ahmed, 2000; Mori & Hayashi, 2006; Olsher, 2004). For example, Lazaraton (2004) contended that neither SLA researchers nor language teacher educators can afford to overlook any longer the fundamental role that nonverbal behaviors play in second language interaction. Also, Belhiah (2005) argued that SLA research will not be characterized as having fully come of age until it becomes engaged in an earnest analysis of how spoken and non-vocal actions work in concert in L2 interaction.

Given this challenge to SLA scholarship, CA is considered to be well suited to address the marginalized aspects in L2 use and learning. As one of the CA tenets states that no detail of interaction, however small or seemingly trivial, may be discounted a priori as not pertinent or meaningful to the participants (Heritage, 1984b), it has been suggested that CA enables researchers to examine meticulously the dynamic coordination of interactional details, including participants' bodily movements as well as their utterances. As such, there have been a few CA or CA-informed studies to date that merit special attention in order to understand the role of gestures and other nonverbal behaviors in L2 interaction.

Advocating potential benefits that can be obtained by applying CA to applied linguistics and SLA studies, Markee (2004b) demonstrated how close attention to the participants' nonverbal behaviors can help us to better understand the organizational structure of learning activities and the socially distributed nature of human cognition. Specifically, he juxtaposed two transcripts of the same data segment, one with and one without detailed description of the participants' nonverbal behaviors. By capturing the critical moment in which the emergence of learning is visibly facilitated through the participants' use of nonverbal resources, he argued that CA-inspired views on the role of nonverbal behaviors in L2 interaction can provide an essential platform for reexamining verbally-oriented key concepts in SLA, such as comprehensible input and output.

In a similar vein, Lazaraton (2004) pointed out that L2 learners receive considerable input in nonverbal form, which may modify and make verbal input more comprehensible. She thereby implied that one of the main SLA concepts, "comprehensible input," needs to be respecified in more participant-relevant terms by including the nonverbal details that participants themselves orient to as relevant. She described how one ESL teacher used gesture, eye gaze, and facial expressions in coordination with her talk in incidental vocabulary explanation sequences. She found that the teacher's nonverbal behaviors added important information to the verbal explanation being given, possibly facilitating L2 learners' construction of lexical knowledge. Her findings suggested that gestures and other nonverbal behaviors are important forms of input to classroom L2 learners and should not be neglected in L2 classroom-based research.

Olsher (2004) explored the potential importance of nonverbal behaviors by focusing on a practice called "embodied completion," which was used by the students in small group activities in an EFL classroom at a Japanese University. In his examples, L2 learners were often observed to launch a turn at talk and, at a point where some trajectory of the turn is projectable, cease to talk and complete the turn through gesture or embodied display. Adding to our understanding of the kinds of communicative practices occurring in L2 classrooms, his analysis proposed an interactionally well-grounded view on L2 learners' nonverbal behaviors. That is, although these behaviors of L2 learners can be viewed as a kind of failure or limitation from the point of view of much SLA research, they seem to demonstrate L2 learners' interactional competence in deploying, parsing, and projecting the interactional trajectory of turns-in-progress, and in successfully engendering the recipient's relevant next action.

Expanding Olsher's (2004) findings, Mori and Hayashi's (2006) study provided a close analysis of two focal cases that highlight the potential role of the participants' embodied practices in L2 learning. Excerpted from casual conversations between L1 (first language) and L2 Japanese speakers, their examples show a dynamic coordination of verbal and nonverbal resources deployed in a moment-by-moment fashion by the participants. In particular, they described (a) how L1 speakers—not L2 speakers as in Olsher's examples—consider their L2 interlocutors' lack of linguistic resources and use "the embodied completion" in a recipient-designed way; (b) how L2 speakers demonstrate their understanding of L1 speakers' gestures through their production of corresponding gestures as well as their verbalization of gestures; and (c) how L1 speakers provide refined linguistic expressions, recasting the L2 speakers' prior verbalization of their gestures. Mori and Hayashi's convincing explication enables us to understand how nonverbal behaviors can be instrumental in occasioning a critical opportunity that may facilitate language learning in situ.

Belhiah (2005) also reported notable cases that exemplify the important role of nonverbal behaviors in L2 interaction. Through a fine-tuned analysis of the coordination of gaze, gestures, and speech in ESL tutorial dialogues, he argued for the importance of viewing the use of body language as a positive and influential component of communication, not only as a sign of linguistic incompetence. Specifically, he described how the students and the tutors coordinate their speech and manual gestures strategically to amplify the meaning of verbal utterances, to disambiguate the meaning of lexical items, and to display alignment through corresponding gestures. Based on his findings, he contended that a careful examination of the participants' nonverbal behaviors can inspire us to reconceptualize the traditional concept of "language" and the dichotomy of "native/nonnative" in a more interactionally relevant way.

Olsher's more recent study (2007) bears specific relevance to the current study as it focuses on the use of gesture in the sequential context of repair. In his study, L2 learners, in responding to their fellow learners' repair initiations in small group activities, were observed to add gestures to enhance the comprehensibility of their talk while repeating their prior utterances (i.e., the trouble source). Since Olsher's study showed how L2 learners, given their own (and their interlocutors') statuses as language learners, may use gestures to resolve contingent problems in interaction, it inspired research on whether L1 speakers, in response to L2 speakers' repair initiations, use similar practices in similar sequential contexts. As such, the current study expands Olsher's investigations to different interactional contexts.

In addition to these studies, there have been other studies that have actively incorporated the participants' nonverbal behaviors in their analyses. For example, Mori (2004) included in her analysis of L2 Japanese classroom interaction a close examination of "how non-vocal conduct serves as a critical resource at different stages of negotiation including indicating and noticing a trouble, as well as pursuing different levels of understanding" (p. 161). Also, while showing that even beginner level L2 learners are able to use a very wide range of interactional resources, Carroll (2004) stated that L2 learners are found to deploy gaze as a useful resource to establish mutual understanding of the sequential development and to negotiate recipiency of the ongoing utterance. Similarly, Mortensen (2009) described how L2 learners competently deploy various nonverbal resources to claim speakership and establish recipiency with a coparticipant in specific sequential contexts (e.g., when the next speaker is not selected by the current speaker in order). Markee's (2005) study further argued for the necessity of carefully attending to the embodied aspects of L2 classroom interaction. His analysis illustrated how the students' nonverbal behaviors can be important clues in understanding the sequential organization of L2 classroom interaction, and it delineated how the students attempt to manage off-task talk while still orienting to the ongoing class activity by artfully deploying linguistic and extra-linguistic resources.

Pursuit of understanding through repair practices

Repair deals with troubles in speaking, hearing, or understanding while temporarily halting the ongoing main activity (Schegloff, Jefferson, & Sacks, 1977). As such, problems due to L2 learners' incomplete mastery of the target language can be resolved through repair practices, although L2 learners' lack of understanding or linguistic problems do not necessarily result in repair. According to Schegloff et al. (1977), repair can be initiated on any part or aspect of talk-in-interaction, and it can be divided into four different types depending on who initiates repair (i.e., self-initiated vs. other-initiated) and who completes repair (i.e., self-completed vs. other-completed). Among these different types, the current study focuses on other-initiated repair that concerns a participant's problem understanding another participant's prior talk.

Referring to studies on repair in L1 interaction (e.g., Drew, 1997; Schegloff et al., 1977), repair sequences initiated by the recipient of the talk (i.e., other-initiated repair) tend to be very brief: (a) the recipient of the talk signals the trouble (i.e., repair initiation); (b) the original speaker of the trouble source attempts to resolve the trouble by repeating or reformulating the prior talk, or by confirming the proposed understanding or hearing (i.e., repair completion); and (c) the repair initiator may produce a success marker, such as "oh" (Heritage, 1984a), when the repair operation is successful. However, it may also be the case that the repair operation is not sufficient. In this case, the recipient may launch a second repair initiation, expanding the repair sequence. This phenomenon is referred to as "multiples" (Schegloff et al., p. 369). They have been found to be relatively uncommon in L1 conversation and tend not to stretch over more than two rounds (Shen, 1998).

In contrast, several studies (e.g., Egbert, Niebecker, & Rezzara, 2004; Shen, 1998) on L2 interaction have suggested that multiples may occur more often in L2 interaction than in L1 interaction. These studies described complex cases in which multiple rounds of repair operation are engendered due to L2 speakers' lack of linguistic resources. For example, Egbert and her colleagues (2004) investigated long repair sequences that involved an L2 speaker's problematic linguistic performance in a conversation among L1 and L2 German speakers. On the one hand, they illustrated how repair sequences may turn out to be complex when trouble sources concern participants' differential linguistic resources and divergent cultural understanding. On the other hand, they also demonstrated how participants can eventually resolve the problem through persistent deployment of available resources, refuting the common belief that communication breakdowns occur frequently in L2 interaction. Shen (1998), based on her analysis of conversations between L1 English speakers and L2 English speakers from Taiwan, claimed that a complex sequential trajectory of multiple other-initiated repair can be one defining feature of L2 interaction. She reported that in her data, when L2 speakers initiated repair on L1 speakers' utterances due to their incomplete knowledge of cultural concepts and target linguistic elements, it more often resulted in multiples than when L1 speakers initiated repair on L2 speakers' utterances.

Joining these efforts to understand the distinctive sequential characteristics of repair in naturally occurring L2 interaction, this study attempts to expand the scope of previous research on repair by incorporating nonverbal aspects of interaction in the analysis, and thus to pursue a more encompassing view on repair in L2 interaction. In the following, I will briefly introduce the data set before presenting the main analysis.

Data

The excerpt examined in this study is extracted from a larger data set, which consists of 23.5 hours of one-on-one ESL tutoring sessions by eight English native-speaker tutors and eight nonnative-speaker tutees whose native language is Korean. The tutors are experienced ESL teachers, and the tutees' proficiency levels vary from high-beginner to advanced. Each session was video- and audio-recorded, and relevant portions were transcribed according to the conventions of CA (e.g., Atkinson & Heritage, 1984).[2] As an informal type of second language instruction, the tutoring sessions analyzed in this study occurred when ESL learners hired native speakers with TESOL training to improve their English. Although it is empirically unsustainable to claim that there is a clear distinction between institutional talk and ordinary conversation in all instances of interactional events or at all points of a single interactional event (Drew & Heritage, 1992), ESL conversation tutoring seems to have characteristics that are distinctively associated with both institutional talk and ordinary conversation. It can be described as an informal type of institutional talk between a language teacher and a student that is arranged to achieve specific institutional goals (i.e., L2 teaching and learning) through some predictable practices such as error correction, linguistically-oriented questions and answers, and the like. Also, it is similar to ordinary conversation between two peers since it is very flexible in turn taking and topic choices, and there is not as much power asymmetry between the participants as there is between students and teacher in formal classroom talk. As such, the participants seem to move flexibly in and out of different speech exchange systems in a moment-by-moment fashion, negotiating their roles both as peers and as teacher and student.

The following data segment is excerpted from a session in which the tutee wanted to practice reading a children's book on the lives of sea creatures. The reason why she wanted to study this book was that she found it hard to read and understand while trying to read it aloud to her 3-year-old daughter. She had been concerned about how to teach her daughter English and how to answer her daughter's English-related questions since she herself is a beginner-level ESL learner. Thus, she asked the tutor to check her pronunciation while she was reading each paragraph in the book and to confirm her understanding while she was explaining the meaning of the paragraph in her own words after reading it. Occasionally, the tutee asked vocabulary questions when she encountered new words, and the tutor provided explanations to assist the tutee's understanding and corrected the tutee's pronunciation. Also, their talk often became digressive and closer to ordinary conversation between peers when they felt like talking about their own personal experiences related to the content of the paragraph.

Analysis

Emergence of trouble and preliminary resolution

Let us first consider how the trouble source (which engenders an almost three-minute repair activity and stretches over more than 100 lines of transcript) emerges in the conversation. The tutee, SH, had just finished reading one paragraph about the physical description of catfish and had encountered a new word, *gill*, about which she explicitly said, "It's very difficult word," after pronouncing it. So, right after the tutee finished reading the sentence, the tutor corrected her pronunciation of *gill* and the tutee practiced pronouncing the word several times. Then the tutee said that she did not understand the word, but the tutor, instead of giving a direct definition, asked a series of display questions, such as: "How do fish breathe?" and "How do they get their air?"

In the transcript below, I use both verbal delineation and frame grabs to describe the participants' nonverbal behaviors, depending on their characteristics. For example, it seems to be more effective to describe headshakes verbally than to capture them on a frame grab because the repetitive movement may not be easily represented in a still picture. It should also be noted that, given the prolific use of nonverbal conduct by both participants, it is practically impossible to describe all their nonverbal behaviors. Thus, only some distinctive forms of nonverbal conduct that are believed to be critical in understanding the ongoing developments of actions and sequences are included.

Excerpt 1 [Slit/TL&SH1009]

```
01    SH:     [brea-
02    TL:     [how do they get their air.
03            [where.
04            [((TL moves her pen around the picture of
05               the fish in the book))
06            (0.5)
07            you know hehhh .hhh heh
```

```
08                 [you have a science background.
09      SH:        [gi:ll.
10      SH:        [gill.
11      TL:        [gill.
12                 [((TL moves her left index finger across
13                    the picture of the gill))
14      SH:        [ah::::::::::::::::::::=
15      TL:        [these (.) are gills.*
16                 [((TL repeats her prior gesture))
17      SH:        =yea::::h.
18      TL:        so they're:=
19      SH:        =ah::  [ah
20      TL:               [slits.
21      SH:        sli:ts
22      TL:        slit is a small cut.
```

```
23      SH:        small cut?
24      TL:        mm hm,
25                 (0.5)
26      SH:        [eh I don' °(     )°
27                 [((SH shakes her head several times, gazing
28                     at TL))
29      TL:        [tch! so::::
30                 [((TL opens the cap of her pen and looks to
31                     her left with frowning face))
32                 (0.5)/((TL closes the cap of her pen))
33      ??:        (    )
34                 (5.0)/((TL reopens cap and cut paper with
35                         pen while SH gazing at it closely))
36      TL:        a sma:ll [cut.
37                          [((TL moves gaze to SH while
38                             holding the paper))
```

```
39      SH:        ah huh::::::
```

```
40                  (0.5)
41     SH:     [yeah,
42     TL:     [you can see through. heh
```

```
43     SH:     ah::::  .hhh
44             (0.5)
```

Faced with the tutee's request for the definition of the word *gill*, the tutor, in line 2, asks a display question while leading the tutee's attention to the picture of the fish in the book by circling around it with her pen, so that the tutee herself can find on the picture what the word refers to. With the expected response delayed as shown in the half-second pause in line 6, the tutor says *you know* followed by laughter tokens, thus further soliciting a response from the tutee. In line 9, the tutee provides the answer to the tutor's question, but she finds it overlapped with the tutor's talk. In the subsequent turn, while the tutee repeats the word again (*gill*), the tutor moves her left index finger across the gill on the picture of the fish in the book along with her utterance *gill*, thereby nonverbally providing the answer to the tutee's original question of what the word *gill* means. As such, the tutee produces an elongated "change of state token" (Heritage, 1984a), which claims that understanding of the word *gill* has come about. In line 17, the tutee adds an acknowledgment token, *yeah*, possibly confirming her understanding of the tutor's talk (in line 15) accompanied by a pointing gesture toward the picture of the gill in the book.

Even though the tutee claimed her understanding of the target word, the tutor adds a verbal description of the physical shape of a gill by using the word *slits*, in line 20, and locates the word in the paragraph the tutee has just read with a pointing gesture. In line 21, the tutee acknowledges the word by repeating it with an elongated vowel, seemingly marking it as new vocabulary to her, and thus the tutor, in line 22, provides a brief definition of the word (*slit is a small cut.*) along with a manual gesture in the area of their mutual orientation. In the next turn, the tutee again repeats the defining phrase, *small cut*, but this time with rising intonation. The tutor's minimal confirmation in line 24 shows her orientation to the tutee's partial repeat of her previous talk as proffering a candidate hearing or understanding. Faced with the tutor's potential misalignment as shown in a half-second pause and the absence of following elaboration, the tutee directly claims that she does not understand the phrase *small cut* or, ultimately, its role in explaining the word *slit*. Knowing that the trouble emerged from the tutee's lack of linguistic resources, the tutor resorts to more sophisticated bodily enactments in lines 30 through 35. First, she opens the cap of her pen and looks around to find some material in the surround, signaling her quandary with a frown on her face. Then she seems to give up the idea of using the pen by returning the cap, but she quickly reopens the pen and uses it as a tool to cut the paper in front of her while the tutee is intently gazing at it. With the cut completed, the tutor attempts to make it more visible by lifting up the paper and, showing the cut to the tutee with the pen through it, in line 36 she repeats her prior verbal description, *a small cut*. This is somewhat similar to what Olsher (2007) refers to as "gesturally enhanced repeats" as the tutor, while repeating the same utterance, uses gestures that are more complex than her prior gesture by utilizing the material objects in addition to her body.

The tutor's nonverbal illustration in lines 30 through 38 seems to be successful to some extent in bringing about the tutee's preliminary understanding of the trouble source as indicated by the tutee's receipt token *ah huh:::::* in line 39. This token is very similar to the "change of state token," "oh," as it is used as a repair receipt token (Heritage, 1984a), showing the speaker's changed state from not-understanding to understanding as a successful outcome of the repair. Even after the tutee's signal of understanding, the tutor adds more information by dynamically coordinating talk, body, and the material object in line 42. Her utterance *you can see through* is physically enacted through her synchronized deployment of her body and the material object in order to ensure the tutee's understanding. Subsequently, the tutee again displays her changed understanding of the added information, and/or the target word, by producing another change of state token in line 43.

So far, it has been shown how the trouble source (*slits/small cut*) emerged in the ongoing interaction and how the tutee's problem of understanding became resolved at least at a preliminary level as shown in her claim of understanding. During these preliminary resolution processes, nonverbal behaviors were used as critical resources as the tutee's claimed understanding appeared to occur as a consequence of changes in the tutor's gestures.

Pursuing further understanding and unsuccessful outcome

If participants were exclusively oriented to communication and mutual understanding, the repair sequence might end at this point, given the tutee's claim of understanding, and the participants might move on to the next activity. However, the following excerpt shows how the participants' orientation to this speech event as institutional talk arranged for the purpose of language learning becomes more observable as the tutee pursues more linguistic knowledge on the trouble source beyond mere understanding and invokes the interlocutor's expertise in the given domain as relevant.

Excerpt 2 [Slit/TL&SH1009]

```
45    SH:    ah:::- [kurumyen (0.2) ah::
46                  [((Korean, meaning "if so"))
47                  (3.8)
```

48   SH: .h whe:re? where use to::: this word.
49   TL: um:::[::
50   SH: [the other- I want to
51   [the other:: sentence.]=
52   TL: [another (.) situation?]=
53   SH: =[yeah.
54   TL: =[um::: (°okay.°)
55   (0.5)
56   TL: maybe i:f we're:: (2.8)
57   making something with paper::?

58   SH: mm [hm,
59   TL: [or fabric too.

60   SH: mm,
61   TL: if you're making so:me
62   SH: mm,
63   TL: costu:me?
64   SH: mm,

```
65  TL:   or outfit,
66  SH:   mm,
67  TL:   you can put (.) uh::: (1.0) can cut two::
```

```
68  SH:   mm,
69  TL:   in this (0.5) fabric?
70  SH:   mm,
71  TL:   you can cut (0.5) two:: [slits,
72  SH:                           [mm,
```

```
73  SH:   mm
74  TL:   e:n you can make (.) a: (0.2)
75        [ma:sk.
76        [((TL repeats her prior gesture))
```

```
77        (2.0)
78  TL:   so:
79  SH:   yeah. I'm sorry I (h) don' [underst(h)and.
80  TL:                              [heh heh heh heh hh
```

In line 45, after cutting off the token *ah*, the tutee abruptly produces a Korean connective, *kurumyen* [if so]. As this connective is produced to pursue the construction of further knowledge in response to the interlocutor's prior talk and appears to be self-addressed (i.e., it is produced in a think-aloud fashion in her L1), it provides a window onto the ongoing processes of her cognition that occur as a consequence of social interaction. Although the tutor is not expected to understand the connective, the tutee's "thinking face" (Goodwin & Goodwin, 1986) with her fingers on her lips and her eye gaze away from the tutor—as shown in the accompanying frame grab—helps the tutor to understand what the tutee is engaged in at the moment. Hence, the long silence in line 47, which the tutor does not interrupt to take the floor. This is similar to phenomena that often occur in word search activities in which, as Goodwin and Goodwin have shown, the coparticipant comes in to help only after the speaker signals that the search is unsuccessful and/or solicits candidate solutions directly or indirectly.

After giving thought to the problem as shown in the long pause in line 47, the tutee explicitly appeals for assistance by asking the tutor where she can use the word *slit* and by requesting more example sentences (lines 48, 50–51). In response to the tutee's request, the tutor starts a long sequence of illustrations by strategically orchestrating diverse resources available at the moment. First, during her utterance in lines 56 and 57, the tutor shifts her gaze to her hands as she starts moving them over the paper, possibly indicating to the tutee that the emerging manual demonstration merits special attention. According to Streeck (1993), speakers initiating a gesture commonly bring their gaze to their hands at the onset of gesticulation and thereby convey the message to the recipients that the forthcoming hand movements will be relevant to the understanding of the emerging talk, and therefore that the recipients should attend to them. After directing the tutee's gaze to her gesture, the tutor shifts her gaze back to the tutee possibly to make sure that the tutee's attention is secured. Then, in line 59, the tutor slightly turns her body to her left and touches the sofa cover with her right hand in coordination with her utterance, *fabric*, while the tutee also moves her gaze toward the sofa.

In lines 61 through 76, the tutor embodies the semantic content of her talk by mobilizing her body and the material objects in concert with her talk. Each phase of her nonverbal enactment enables her to achieve important actions, such as specifying the meaning of lexical items, materializing the meaning of verbal utterances, and disambiguating the meaning of her prior talk especially with her verbal self-repair. Specifically, in line 65, when she says *outfit*, (a generic word), she lifts both of her hands over her face and thereby specifies which kind of outfit she means (i.e., an outfit that covers someone's face). Also, with her talk *can cut two::* in line 67, she enacts the verb *cut* by lifting both of her hands right in front of her torso and using two fingers of her right hand as if they were scissors while using her left hand as if it were material like paper or fabric. However, she leaves her utterance in line 67 grammatically, prosodically, and pragmatically incomplete as she produces a prepositional phrase in her next turn, *in this (0.5) fabric?* Then she restarts her utterance abandoned in line 67, but this time she makes it a complete utterance by adding a required noun component, *slits*. It is notable how she changes the nonverbal behavior she used in her prior talk, which turns out to be repairable, when she delivers the repair proper in line 71. She grabs her pen and draws an oval on the paper, draws two short horizontal lines in the oval that seem to represent eyes on a mask, and sweeps the lines with each of her index fingers from the center toward the outline of the oval. This nonverbal enactment accompanying her repair not only enables the tutor to show the physical shape of the trouble source, *slits*, in a visually better-contextualized way, but also to disambiguate the meaning of her prior utterance, *can cut*, which may have been ambiguous to the tutee regarding exactly which part of the outfit can be cut and in which way it can be cut. In lines 74–76, disengaging herself from the physical action on the paper, the tutor delivers a final sentence that seems to complete her long illustration sequence. While delivering her talk, she sweeps down her face with both of her hands as a nonverbal iconic rendition of the word *ma:sk*.

However, this long illustration does not seem to be successful in bringing about the tutee's understanding as indicated in the 2-second pause in line 77. Considering that the tutor sequentially completed her second pair part to the tutee's request for another sentence or situation that includes the word *slit*, the silence can be attributed to the tutee and thus it may foreshadow an emerging problem on the tutee's part. Dealing with the tutee's lack of response, the tutor produces a stand-alone *so* in line 78, possibly reconfirming that her multi-turn illustration has been completed and it is the tutee's turn to respond to the illustration as a whole. According to Raymond (2004), when a recipient's conduct displays some incipient problem regarding how a prior bit of talk figures in a larger course of action, the stand-alone *so* can be used to prompt the recipient to acknowledge the action import of that prior talk for that larger course of action and thereby to initiate the next relevant action. As such, the tutee produces her delayed response to the larger course of action—that is, the tutor's illustration—starting with *yeah* in line 79. However, as foreshadowed in line 77, what follows this receipt token is the tutee's explicit statement that she does not understand the tutor's illustration and/or the full semantic content of the word *slit*, thereby initiating repair on the tutor's whole action as a second pair part to her original request. Given all the trouble that the tutor had to go through by mobilizing multiple resources, including talk, body, and material objects, the tutee displays embarrassment through her bodily conduct: She averts her eye gaze from the tutor and puts her left hand on her chin with her face slightly down. Also, she delivers her talk with a slight laugh (*I (h) don' underst(h)and.*), trying to mitigate the unease she might be experiencing. In line 80, with the tutee's emerging negative response projected by an apology and the beginning of a negative sentence, the tutor also displays some embarrassment on the undesirable outcome of her extended multimodal efforts. She produces mild laughter with her eye gaze away from the tutee, right after the negative auxiliary verb *don't* in the tutee's talk.

The way in which the participants deal with the unsuccessful outcome of the interactional efforts deserves more discussion from a socio-pragmatic perspective on language learning. The tutee's pursuit to further the linguistic knowledge of the new lexical item (i.e., the trouble source) demands considerable work on her interlocutor's part and potentially creates a change in interactional dynamics between the participants. That is, through the tutee's request for more information, the tutor is put in a position to demonstrate her linguistic expertise in a way that suits the tutee's need. Thus, although the interactional trouble emerged due to the tutee's lack of linguistic competence, now the tutor's competence to perform the requested action is on trial. As such, when the tutee could not accomplish further understanding of the trouble source after the tutor's responsive action, the tutor is also responsible for the failure. Hence, we see both participants displaying discomfort and embarrassment. In sum, these sequences show how an active pursuit of language learning may entail the risk of socio-pragmatic infelicities depending on the context, illustrating the complex nature of the interactional processes of language learning.

This section has shown how the participants encounter another trouble as the tutee solicits more linguistic information on the trouble source even after her claimed understanding, displaying her orientation for language learning. While providing an illustration of the trouble source, the tutor made visible attempts to enhance the comprehensibility of her verbal illustration by mobilizing diverse resources (e.g., gaze, posture, manual gestures, material objects) and also by changing her bodily enactments in order to represent the similar verbal utterances. However, all these efforts by the tutor turned out to be unsuccessful in bringing about the tutee's further understanding. The following section shows how the participants deal with this undesirable outcome and make further efforts to resolve the trouble.

Enhancing multimodal efforts and final resolution
Now that the tutee explicitly announced her problem understanding the tutor's prior turns, the tutor's repair proper is sequentially due. Technically, there seem to be two potential directions in performing the repair, especially because the tutee's utterance in line 79 does not have an object for the verb *understand*. Although the understanding of the word *slit* and that of the tutor's illustration are not two separate things, the following sequential development can be slightly different depending on what the participants orient to as a main problem. Given the format of the tutee's turn, it is unclear whether she does not understand

the original trouble source, *slit,* (even after the tutor's explanation) or the tutor's illustration. Her *yeah* may target the tutor's illustration so far, meaning, *I understand your illustration, but I'm still not sure about the word "slit."* Thus, the tutor can provide a different example, in which case the focus of the repair will be on the original trouble source, *slit.* Or, she can redo her first illustration with the same content, identifying the trouble with the form of her explanation. The following segment shows that the tutor displays her orientation to the problem as located in her construction of the example. She redelivers her original illustration basically with the same semantic content, but with a slightly different organization and nonverbal conduct.

Excerpt 3 [Slit/TL&SH1009]

```
81      TL:     oh::  I need some fabric.
82              but we- if we take the fabric,
83      SH:     mm,
84      TL:     maybe we want to make
85              [the:::
86              [((TL moves both hands over her head and
87                slowly moves them down her face.))
88      SH:     mas[kuh?
89      TL:        [like a: [ma:sk.=
90                          [((TL repeats gesture))
91      SH:     =eyeah?
```

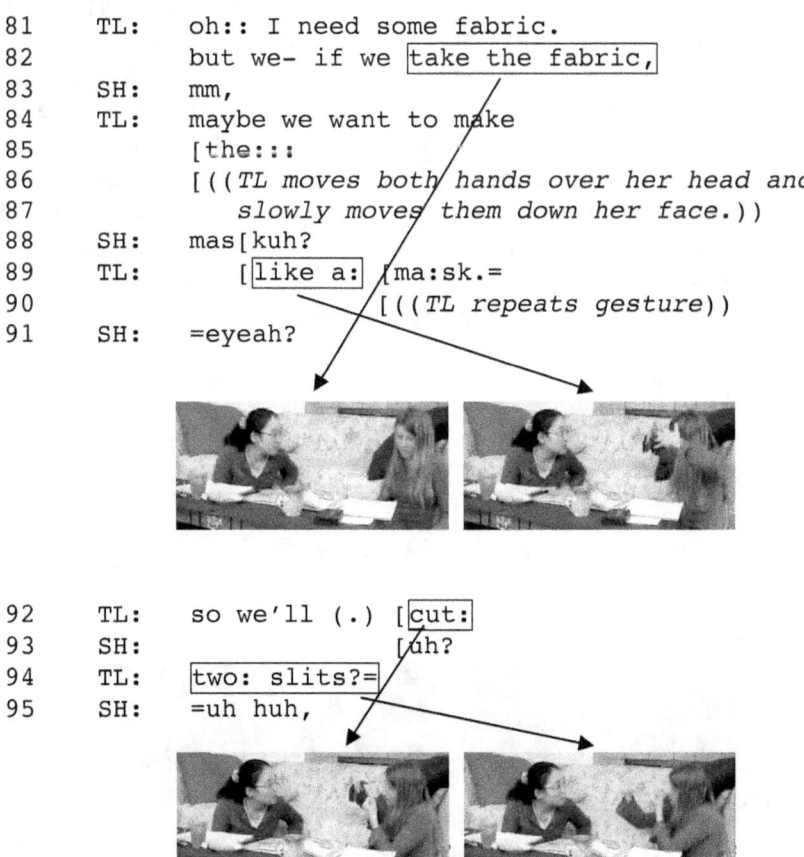

```
92      TL:     so we'll (.) [cut:
93      SH:                  [uh?
94      TL:     two: slits?=
95      SH:     =uh huh,
```

```
96      TL:     en then [I can see.
97      SH:             [AH::::::::: I: understand.
```

In line 81, starting with a response cry *oh::* (Goffman, 1979), which indicates her affective stance toward the difficult situation, the tutor projects the direction of her illustration by mentioning the need for fabric. In line 82, as she begins to redo the illustration, specifically with the word *fabric*, she holds and slightly lifts the tablecloth instead of the sofa cover as she did in her first try. After the tutee's continuer (Schegloff, 1982; *mm* in line 83), the tutor, in line 84, constructs the main clause for her conditional clause in line 82, but she gets into trouble producing the last noun component as indicated by the prosodically marked article, *the::*. Subsequently, the tutee rather quickly jumps in with a candidate item in line 88 and ends up getting overlapped with the tutor's own completion. The tutor uses the same iconic gesture for the word *mask* as she used for *outfit* in the previous illustration sequence (line 89). However, notable changes occur in her subsequent gestures. That is, she utilizes different gestures for the same verbal utterances—that is, *cut two slits*. If we compare the frame grabs for line 71 in Excerpt 2 and lines 92 and 94 in Excerpt 3, the differences can be easily detected.

Excerpt 2, "Cut two slits."

Excerpt 3, "Cut two slits."

First, there is a difference in the spatial organization of the gestures and the kinds of resources. The tutor uses a different area of the interactional space for delivering her gestures, upgrading the dimensionality of the represented target (e.g., two-dimensional on the paper à three-dimensional in the air).[3] Her manual gestures for cutting slits with scissors are produced right in front of her eyes, clarifying the exact cutting spot on the mask, whereas her gestures in Excerpt 2 involved using a pen and paper along with her body and was performed in the lower interactional space. Second, she produces the cutting gestures in a more elaborate way in Excerpt 3; she adds another cutting gesture by moving the direction of her fingertips toward her eyes, which can be the actual direction when we cut slits to make eye parts while keeping the surrounding part of the fabric uncut. Also, instead of using the material objects to support her gestures as in Excerpt 2, she extends her gestures as a continuing activity within the same focal space, toward which the tutee's gaze is already established. At the onset of her turn in line 96, the tutor quickly starts to move her fingers to make circles in front of her eyes. Thus, even before she completes her verbal utterance, *I can see*, in line 96, the tutee produces a big change of state token in a prosodically distinctive way with her mouth wide open, claiming that her long delayed understanding has just occurred. The accompanying frame grab for lines 96 and 97 clearly shows the co-occurrence of the tutee's display of her understanding and the tutor's circling gesture with her fingers.

This section has focused on how the tutor upgraded her gestures, while providing similar verbal descriptions used in her prior unsuccessful illustration, and succeeded in engendering the tutee's delayed understanding of the trouble source. It has shown that nonverbal behaviors that accompany repair can make observably positive consequences for the repair initiator's achievement of understanding.

Demonstrating full understanding and closing the sequences
Now that the tutee's pursuit of further understanding has been successful, the participants might proceed to the next activity. However, there follows another sequential expansion that can be attributed to the tutee's orientation for language learning. As a novice, to make sure that she understood the original trouble source correctly, the tutee initiates another repair on the tutor's illustration, proffering a candidate understanding with another example and thereby asking the tutor to confirm her understanding of the lexical item "slit."

Excerpt 4 [Slit/TL&SH1009]

```
98    TL:    (    )
99    SH:    ah:: okay. .hh uh::::: you mean um::::: tch!
100          we::: sometimes we:: ma:ke uh: sometimes
101          we::: uh:: when we: make uh::: clothe?
102   TL:    mm hm,
103   SH:    e:n we need to::: uh::: (0.2) take- uh OH-
104          uh you: we: nee:d we: need to::: button.
105   TL:    mm hm,
```

```
106    SH:    yeah? so butto:n, uh put on? (0.8) put (.)
107           >into<? put into: this.
108    TL:    yeah.=this is kind of a slit.
```

```
109           [but we [have a specific word.
110    SH:    [yeah.  [yeah.
111    TL:    this is a button ho:le.
112    SH:    ah::: ye[s. (another word.)
113    TL:            [we don' say slit.
114           [but it i:s (.)  [a slit
115    SH:    [yeah.   kin' of. [yea:h. kin' of=
```

```
116    SH:    =[yea:h. sli:t.
117    TL:    =[eh heh
118    SH:    ah:: okay. yea:h okay. ah o:kay. °yeah.°
119           I understa(hh)nd.=
120    TL:    =heh hhh
121    SH:    yeah. thank you.
```

In line 99, the token *okay* (Beach, 1993; Gardner, 2001) marks the transition from the tutee's claim of understanding to a demonstration of her understanding, or from her discourse identity as a recipient of an illustration to that of a producer of an illustration. Immediately after the token, the tutee launches a corresponding illustration sequence as a way of proffering a candidate understanding starting with a reformulation marker, *you mean*. The tutor shows her understanding of the tutee's ongoing illustration by producing continuers (in lines 102 and 105) at each prosodic and grammatical juncture of the tutee's talk. To briefly rephrase the tutee's talk in lines 99–101 and 103–104, she seems to try to say that when we make clothes, we need to put buttons on. In line 106, after using the discourse marker *so*, and thus presenting her emerging talk as a consequence of her prior information (Schiffrin, 1987), the tutee reestablishes the referent *button* with rising intonation, which turns out to function as an object for her emerging sentence. After a hesitation marker, *uh*, the tutee produces the verb phrase *put on* with rising intonation, indicating her uncertainty about its linguistic accuracy. Willey's (2001) study provided a thorough analysis of how ESL learners use this way of prosodic performance as an interactional device to elicit help from native speakers. With no assistance coming from the tutor as shown in the 0.8 second pause in line 106, the tutee restarts the verb phrase, but as the micro pause after *put* indicates, she is still having trouble producing the preposition. Finally, she produces a new preposition, *into*, in a rushed manner with rising intonation, but quickly repairs it in the next line by adding a demonstrative pronoun, *this*. It is notable that she shifts her eye gaze to her cardigan and slightly pulls up one of the buttonholes with both of her hands in order to specify what *this* refers to.

Orienting to the tutee's pronoun and accompanying gestures as an example for the word *slit*, the tutor provides positive feedback (in line 109) starting with *yeah*, and points to the buttonhole pulled up by the tutee with her index finger. However, she reserves a full confirmation for the proposed understanding as shown in the inserted qualifier, *kind of*, and the subsequent account in line 108. In line 110, the tutee vehemently acknowledges the tutor's positive feedback, while overlapping with the tutor's account. In the next turn, the tutor provides the alternative, more accurate word *buttonhole* for the tutee, and subsequently the tutee acknowledges and accepts the tutor's corrective action. Interestingly, in lines 113 and 114, the tutor reconfirms that the tutee's understanding is technically correct by stressing and elongating the verb (*i:s*). Overlapping with the tutor's reconfirmation, the tutee repeats the qualifier *kind of*, originally used by the tutor in line 108 with the agreement token *yeah* (line 115), and completes the noun phrase by adding the word *slit* in line 116. The tutee's full understanding of the trouble source, *slit*, which has already been demonstrated in her illustration,[4] once again gets verbally proclaimed in line 119. Finally, the tutee's appreciating remark in line 121, accompanied by her physical action of turning to the next page in the book, officially closes the extended sequence.

Summary and discussion

By analyzing a considerably long repair sequence excerpted from an ESL tutoring session, this study shows how diverse semiotic modalities—talk, gaze, gestures, body orientation, and material objects—are deployed in a repair activity as coordinated interactional resources to facilitate L2 learning as well as intersubjective understanding. More specifically, it demonstrates (a) how nonverbal behaviors emerge as critical modalities in repair sequences that started from the lack of shared linguistic resources between the participants; (b) the kinds of important actions that are performed by nonverbal behaviors (e.g., specifying, disambiguating the meaning of verbal utterances); (c) how an L2 learner's moment-by-moment changes in the status of lexical knowledge observably occur in concert with the tutor's enhanced multimodal practices; and (d) how gestures are also consistently negotiated as reciprocal means in a way that is similar to the negotiation of verbal utterances.

From an SLA perspective, given the small body of studies in the SLA field that focus on the role of gestures, this study addresses the question of whether, when, and how gestures are mobilized to facilitate L2 learning. Although this study does not intend to provide any generalizable answers, some preliminary claims can be made based on the findings. First, it is evident that the participants' nonverbal behaviors contribute to the L2 learner's construction of new lexical knowledge, as seen in the tutee's demonstrated understanding, at least within the episode analyzed here. Second, the conducive role of gestures in L2 learning may become more observable in particular sequential contexts, such as repair that is performed in the form of "gesturally enhanced" (Olsher, 2007) repeats, especially when it is clear that the troubles originate from the learners' limited linguistic resources in the target language. In other words, in these repair sequences, the participants themselves orient to gestures as locally relevant resources in their attempts to resolve the troubles by adding or changing gestures while repeating the trouble sources or producing similar utterances. Last, gestures make the conveyed meaning of utterances and the intended communicative actions more accessible to participants in L2 interaction and sometimes facilitate intersubjective understanding in a publicly observable manner. Thus, their incorporation into our analysis of interaction can allow us a more encompassing view of how L2 interaction is linked to L2 learning and enable us to go beyond the predominant SLA theories and concepts that are grounded mainly in the analysis of verbal aspects of interaction.

The findings from this study can be instrumental in advocating potential benefits that CA can offer to SLA studies and ESL teaching. As "a dynamic, empirical, emic, bottom-up approach rooted in the details of the interaction" (Seedhouse, 2004), CA requires researchers to closely attend to what the participants themselves orient to as relevant in real time L2 interaction, regardless of preexisting social contexts and theories. As such, it offers "an epistemological stance and analytical method" (Kasper, 2004) to investigate various "affordances" (van Lier, 2000) that become contingently relevant to L2 learning as the interaction unfolds. In this regard, this study provides a sequentially-grounded analysis of how participants' nonverbal behaviors, which have been so far overlooked by most SLA researchers, become critical resources in engendering the L2 learner's understanding of new vocabulary.

Following Markee's (2000) convincing example of an L2 learner's new vocabulary learning through extended interaction with her interlocutors, this study offers another example of how CA can provide a powerful approach to point out in detail the link between interaction and L2 learning. Although the data presented here cannot speak to the tutee's vocabulary development in the long term, the example in this study shows that the tutee was able to access the semantic content of new vocabulary through an active engagement in repair activities, as she demonstrated through her own illustration. Also, as shown in the above analysis, CA not only allows researchers to present the processes of (coming to) understanding, but also enables them to describe potential socio-pragmatic risks that L2 learning may involve (e.g., lines 79 and 80, also see Markee, 2004a), suggesting that language learning does not occur as information transfer in a social vacuum. Thus, CA supports the view of language learning as "socially distributed practices" (Markee, 2004a) that are situated in specific social, interactional contexts, by complementing the widely-spread view that regards L2 learning as a solely cognitive phenomenon that occurs in the mind/brain of individuals (Long, 1996).

Among other insights from CA that may influence future SLA studies is CA's multimodal approach to language. As a number of researchers noted (e.g., Belhiah, 2005; Fox, 1999; Lazaraton, 2004), CA argues for the significance of treating language as an embodied activity in which gaze, gesture, and body orientation practices are coordinated with talk in meaningful ways. This view of language can extend notions of "comprehensible input" and "comprehensible output," which so far have been mainly constructed based on verbal utterances. In fact, the above examples (i.e., different gestures for *a small cut* in line 22 vs. line 36 and for *cut two slits* in line 71 vs. lines 92 and 94) illustrate how the same verbal input can become comprehensible to the learner supported by the interlocutor's changes in her bodily conduct. It is reasonable that a new perspective on language can also change how we view language learners. As noted in Firth and Wagner's (1997) proposal to reevaluate a long held perception of L2 learners as "deficient communicators" by getting over the obsession with *linguistic* competence, CA-inspired studies focus on L2 learners' *interactional* competence, describing how L2 learners achieve their communicative goals by deploying various resources with their limited linguistic competence. This study portrays the image of an L2 learner as a persistent learning agent. While pursuing further knowledge of new vocabulary and ensuring the accuracy of her final understanding, the tutee was observed not only to react sensitively to the tutor's nonverbal behaviors, but also to use her body and material objects competently, in a way that facilitated her learning as well as mutual understanding.

Finally, how can we apply the findings on the importance of nonverbal behaviors in L2 interaction to ESL teaching? The findings challenge us to consider what constitutes good language teaching. It is certain that language teachers' sensitivity to the potential influence of gestures on language learning can be conducive to maximizing the benefits that L2 students get from L2 classrooms. Also, if we include nonverbal aspects in the concept of "language," L2 teachers are required to demonstrate the use of gestures and are responsible for improving students' competence to use and understand gestures that commonly accompany the new language. As such, the results of my analysis confirm other researchers' suggestion (e.g., Allen, 2000; Sime, 2006) that teacher trainers should actively consider incorporating discussions of the role of nonverbal behaviors in their curricula. For the discussions in teacher training programs, it might be helpful to use examples from real time interaction like the ones presented in this chapter. The questions of to what extent and in what manner L2 teachers should use gestures require further empirical exploration in consideration of other factors, such as pedagogical goals, learner characteristics, and so on. All in all, exploring in depth the role of nonverbal behaviors in L2 teaching and learning is an area worthy of future studies.

Notes

1. The term "L2 interaction" refers to any interaction in which one or more participants are L2 speakers.
2. For this chapter, 12.5 hours of data were roughly transcribed and went through a preliminary investigation for the selection of the target phenomenon. The example presented below was chosen because it illustrates the complexity of the organization of nonverbal behaviors in relation to the unfolding talk and demonstrates the important role that nonverbal behaviors play in resolving interactional troubles due to an L2 learner's unfamiliarity with the target language.
3. Note that the tutor already tried a three dimensional representation in line 67, Excerpt 2 although she ended up repairing the accompanying talk by aborting it before completion. Thus, it is also analytically worthwhile to compare the gestures in Excerpt 3 to the gestures used in line 67, Excerpt 2.
4. Sacks (1992) distinguishes between claiming an understanding and exhibiting an understanding. As Sacks regards it as exhibiting an understanding when a recipient of a story responds with a relevant second story, I argue that the tutee exhibits or demonstrates her understanding of the trouble source by providing a relevant illustration that includes the trouble source.

References

Allen, L. (2000). Nonverbal accommodations in foreign language teacher talk. *Language Learning, 11*, 155–176.

Atkinson, J. M., & Heritage, J. (1984). Transcription notation. In J. M. Atkinson & J. Heritage (Eds.), *Structures of social action: Studies in conversation analysis* (pp. ix-xvi). Cambridge: Cambridge University Press.

Bachman, L. F. (1990). *Fundamental considerations in language testing.* Oxford: Oxford University Press.

Beach, W. A. (1993). Transitional regularities for casual "Okay" usage. *Journal of Pragmatics, 19*, 325–352.

Belhiah, H. (2005). *The partnership between vocal and nonvocal aspects of language use in ESL tutorials: A conversation analytical approach* (Unpublished doctoral dissertation). University of Wisconsin, Madison.

Canale, M., & Swain, M. (1980). Theoretical bases of communicative approaches to second language teaching and testing. *Applied Linguistics, 1*, 1–47.

Carroll, D. (2004). Restarts in novice turn beginnings: Disfluencies or interactional achievements? In R. Gardner & J. Wagner (Eds.), *Second language conversations* (pp. 201–220). London: Continuum.

Drew, P. (1997). "Open" class repair initiators in response to sequential sources of troubles in conversation. *Journal of Pragmatics, 28*, 69–101.

Drew, P., & Heritage, J. (1992). Analyzing talk at work: An introduction. In P. Drew & J. Heritage (Eds.), *Talk at work: Interactions in institutional settings* (pp. 3–65). Cambridge: Cambridge University Press.

Egbert, M., Niebecker, L., & Rezzara, S. (2004). Inside first and second language speakers' trouble in understanding. In R. Gardner & J. Wagner (Eds.), *Second language conversations* (pp. 178–200). London: Continuum.

Firth, A., & Wagner, J. (1997). On discourse, communication and (some) fundamental concepts in SLA research. *The Modern Language Journal, 81*, 285–300.

Fox, B. (1999). Directions in research: Language and the body. *Research on Language and Social Interaction, 32*, 51–59.

Gardner, R. (2001). *When listeners talk*. Amsterdam: John Benjamins.

Goffman, E. (1979). Response cries. In M. von Cranach, K. Foppa, W. Lepenies, & D. Ploog (Eds.), *Human ethology* (pp. 203–240). Cambridge: Cambridge University Press.

Goodwin, C. (1986). Gesture as a resource for the organization of mutual orientation. *Semiotica, 62*, 29–49.

Goodwin, C. (2000). Action and embodiment within situated human interaction. *Journal of Pragmatics, 32*, 1489–1522.

Goodwin, M. H., & Goodwin, C. (1986). Gesture and coparticipation in the activity of searching for a word. *Semiotica, 62*, 51–75.

Gullberg, M. (2006). Handling discourse: Gestures, reference tracking, and communication strategies in early L2. *Language Learning, 56*, 155–196.

Gullberg, M. (2010). Methodological reflections on gesture analysis in second language acquisition and bilingualism research. *Second Language Research, 26*, 75–102.

Hardison, D. M. (2003). Acquisition of second language speech: Effects of visual cues, context, and talker variability. *Applied Psycholinguistics, 24*, 495–522.

Hayashi, M. (2003). Language and the body as resources for collaborative action: A study of word searches in Japanese conversation. *Research on Language and Social Interaction, 36*, 109–141.

Hayashi, M. (2005). Joint turn construction through language the body: Notes on embodiment in coordinated participation in situated activities. *Semiotica, 156*, 21–54.

Heath, C. (1986). *Body movement and speech in medical interaction*. Cambridge: Cambridge University Press.

Heritage, J. (1984a). A change-of-state token and aspects of its sequential placement. In J. M. Atkinson & J. Heritage (Eds.), *Structures of social action: Studies in conversation analysis* (pp. 299–345). Cambridge: Cambridge University Press.

Heritage, J. (1984b). *Garfinkel and ethnomethodology*. Cambridge, MA: Polity Press.

Kasper, G. (2004). Participant orientations in conversation-for-learning. *The Modern Language Journal, 88*, 551–567.

Kendon, A. (1990). *Conducting interaction: Patterns of behavior in focused interaction*. Cambridge: Cambridge University Press.

Kendon, A. (2004). *Gesture: Visible action as utterance*. Cambridge: Cambridge University Press.

Lantolf, J. P. (2000). Second language learning as a mediated process. *Language Teaching, 33*, 79–96.

Lazaraton, A. (2004). Gesture and speech in the vocabulary explanations of one ESL teacher: A microanalytic inquiry. *Language Learning, 54*, 79–117.

Long, M. (1996). The role of the linguistic environment in second language acquisition. In W. C. Ritchie & T. K. Bhatia (Eds.), *Handbook of second language acquisition* (pp. 414–468). New York, NY: Academic Press.

Markee, N. (2000). *Conversation analysis*. Mahwah, NJ: Lawrence Erlbaum.

Markee, N. (2004a). Zones of interactional transition in ESL classes. *The Modern Language Journal, 88*, 583–596.

Markee, N. (2004b). Conversation analysis for second language acquisition. In E. Hinkel (Ed.), *Handbook of research in second language teaching and learning* (pp. 355–374). Mahwah, NJ: Lawrence Erlbaum.

Markee, N. (2005). The organization of off-task talk in second language classrooms. In K. Richards & P. Seedhouse (Eds.), *Applying conversation analysis* (pp. 197–213). New York, NY: Palgrave Macmillan.

McCafferty, S. G. (2002). Gestures and creating zones of proximal development for second language learning. *The Modern Language Journal, 86*, 192–203.

McCafferty, S. G. (2004). Space for cognition: Gesture and second language learning. *Interactional Journal of Applied Linguistics, 14*, 148–165.

McCafferty, S. G., & Ahmed, M. (2000). The appropriation of gestures of the abstract by L2 learners. In J. P. Lantolf (Ed.), *Sociocultural theory and second language learning* (pp. 198–218). Oxford: Oxford University Press.

McNeill, D. (1992). *Hand and mind: What the hands reveal about thought*. Chicago, IL: University of Chicago Press.

Mori, J. (2004). Pursuit of understanding: Rethinking "negotiation of meaning" in view of projected action. In R. Gardner & J. Wagner (Eds.), *Second language conversations* (pp. 157–177). London: Continuum.

Mori, J., & Hayashi, M. (2006). The achievement of intersubjectivity through embodied completions: A study of interactions between first and second language speakers. *Applied Linguistics, 27,* 195–219.

Mortensen, K. (2009). Establishing recipiency in pre-beginning position in the second languageclassroom. *Discourse Processes, 46,* 491–515.

Murphy, K. M. (2005). Collaborative imagining: The interactive use of gestures, talk, and graphic representation in architectural practice. *Semiotica, 156,* 113–146.

Olsher, D. (2004). Talk and gesture: The embodied completion of sequential actions in spoken Interaction. In R. Gardner & J. Wagner (Eds.), *Second language conversations* (pp. 221–245). London: Continuum.

Olsher, D. (2007). Gesturally-enhanced repeats in the repair turn: Communication strategy or cognitive language-learning tool? In S. G. McCafferty & G. Stam (Eds.), *Gesture: Second language acquisition and classroom research* (pp. 109–130). New York, NY: Routledge.

Raymond, G. (2004). Prompting action: The stand-alone "so" in ordinary conversation, *Research on Language and Social Interaction, 37,* 185–218.

Sacks, H. (1992). *Lectures on conversation. Volumes 1 & 2* (Gail Jefferson Ed.). Oxford: Blackwell.

Schegloff, E. A. (1982). Discourse as an interactional achievement: Some uses of "uh huh" and other things that come between sentences. In D. Tannen (Ed.), *Georgetown University Roundtable on language and linguistics* (pp. 266–296). Washington, DC: Georgetown University Press.

Schegloff, E. A. (1984). On some gestures' relation to talk. In J. M. Atkinson & J. Heritage (Eds.), *Structures of social action: Studies in conversation analysis* (pp. 266–296). Cambridge: Cambridge University Press.

Schegloff, E. A., Jefferson, G., & Sacks, H. (1977). The preference for self-correction in the organization of repair in conversation. *Language, 53,* 361–382.

Schiffrin, D. (1987). *Discourse markers.* New York, NY: Cambridge University Press.

Seedhouse, P. (2004). The Interactional architecture of the language classroom: A conversation analysis perspective. *Language Learning, 54,* Supplement 1.

Shen, C. (1998). *Other-initiated repair in native-nonnative English conversation and its interactional consequences* (Unpublished doctoral dissertation). University of Texas, Austin.

Sidnell, J. (2005). Gesture in the pursuit and display of recognition: A Caribbean case study. *Semiotica, 156,* 55–88.

Sime, D. (2006). What do learners make of teachers' gestures in the language classroom? *International Review of Applied Linguistics, 44,* 211–230.

Streeck, J. (1993). Gesture as communication I: Its coordination with gaze and speech. *Communication Monographs, 60,* 275–299.

Streeck, J. (1994). Gesture as communication II: The audience as co-author. *Research on Language and Social Interaction, 27,* 239–267.

Streeck, J. (2003). Body taken for granted: Lingering dualism in research on social interaction. In P. Glenn, C. LeBaron, & J. Mandelbaum (Eds.), *Studies in language and social Interaction* (pp. 427–440). Mawwah, NJ: Lawrence Erlbaum.

Sueyoshi, A., & Hardison, D. M. (2005). The roles of gestures and facial cues in second language listening comprehension. *Language Learning, 55*, 661–699.

van Lier, L. (2000). From input to affordance: Socio-interactive learning from an ecological perspective. In J. P. Lantolf (Ed.), *Sociocultural theory and second language learning* (pp. 245–259). Oxford: Oxford University Press.

Willey, B. (2001). *Examining a "communication strategy" from a conversation analytic perspective: Eliciting help from native speakers inside and outside of word search sequences* (Unpublished master's thesis). University of Illinois, Urbana-Champaign.

6 Doing Word Explanation in Interaction[1]

Kristian Mortensen
Université du Luxembourg

Introduction

One of the things teachers in the second/foreign language classroom are faced with is how to teach new lexical elements. Since the days of grammar-translation, where formal structures and lexical items were taught explicitly and out of context (see, e.g., Kumaravadivelu, 2006; Larsen-Freeman, 2000; Richards & Rodgers, 2001), different teaching methodologies, and communicative language teaching in particular, have sought to incorporate vocabulary teaching in more meaning-oriented discourse. Research on vocabulary teaching has used dichotomies such as implicit or explicit (DeCarrico, 2001) and planned or unplanned (Hatch & Brown, 1995) to refer to whether vocabulary is taught as separate activities or dealt with as part of the ongoing activity. Special tasks, such as filling-the-blank, semantic associations, and language games, may be designed specifically to practice new vocabulary. However, vocabulary, as well as other formal linguistic aspects, is always a possible and relevant aspect to be extracted "on the fly" from the ongoing course of action in the language classroom and made a subject for explicit teaching. Focus on form (e.g., Doughty & Williams, 1998) argues for meaningful classroom interaction with occasional shift[s] of attention to linguistic code features—by the teacher and/or one or more students—triggered by perceived problems with cowmprehension or production (Long & Robinson, 1998, p. 23).

In this way, teaching linguistic material is embedded within the ongoing (meaningful) interaction and is therefore highly context dependent.

Extracting linguistic material "on the fly" can be described in terms of repair[2] (Schegloff, 1997b, 2000; Schegloff, Jefferson, & Sacks, 1977): Either the teacher locates a part of his/her turn as a *possible* problematic word and provides an explanation of the word (i.e., self-repair) or she or he explicitly asks the students whether or not they understand the word. Alternatively, the lexical item is located and pointed out by the students as problematic, and the teaching sequence thus takes the form of an other-initiated repair. In both ways, a word or words are identified in the ongoing interaction and made relevant for more or less formal instruction. These practices may evoke the institutional character of the language classroom and define the ongoing activity as "doing (vocabulary) teaching."

Vocabulary learning is an important aspect of second language acquisition (e.g., Carter & McCarthy, 1988; Schmitt, 2000). A substantial part of vocabulary-learning research focuses on how new vocabulary is processed and memorized and is primarily conducted within a psycholinguistic framework. On the other hand, teaching methodologies (see, e.g., Larsen-Freeman, 2000; Richards & Rodgers, 2001), either explicitly or implicitly, provide suggestions for how to teach vocabulary to second/foreign language students in the classroom. These suggestions are often based on a theoretical set of assumptions about the nature of language and learning rather than on an emic perspective based on interactional analyses of classroom interaction (e.g., Evaldsson, Lindblad, Sahlström, & Bergqvist, 2001; Seedhouse, 1996, 1997, 2004). As a contrast, this study shows, by means of transcripts of recorded classroom interaction, *how* vocabulary is extracted from the ongoing course of action "on the fly." In which sequential environments does this occur? How is the vocabulary selected from the range of possible "teachable" words from the flow of classroom interaction? Drawing on conversation analysis (CA), I will describe a social practice that I call "doing word explanation."[3]

This chapter focuses on cases where the word explanation is jointly extracted and explained by teacher and students. In other words, I will not examine cases where the teacher teaches vocabulary without including the students. As we will see later, the social phenomenon that is described here is based on a sequential environment in which the students provide a candidate understanding of the word. I will show how the teacher sets up a frame in which a relevant action for the students is to display orientation to particular lexical item(s), and how this display provides for a word explanation to be requested. The analysis therefore highlights the joint accomplishment of vocabulary teaching as being constructed in and through interaction. Henceforth, I will refer to this interactional practice as "doing word explanation".

The data material consists of 25 hours of video recordings of Danish second language (L2) classrooms with adult learners. The recordings are part of the cross-institutional research project "Learning and Integration—Adults and Danish as a Second Language" conducted by three Danish universities. The recordings were made in 2005–2006 with two individual cameras that were placed on tripods since the researcher was not present in the classroom during the recording. Transcription conventions follow Jefferson (see, e.g., Hutchby & Wooffitt, 1998, for overview), and include additional information about visual features (in particular gaze and gesture).

Looking at the examples in this article gives the impression that the vocabulary that is taught is part of the teacher's lesson plan. Most of the lexical items emerge from the ongoing interaction and are left again after a short formal explanation. The word explanations occupy a short sequence within whole class interaction and are embedded within the ongoing task accomplishment. However, although the lesson plan has been prepared prior to the lesson, it nonetheless has to be carried out during the lesson in front of, and in collaboration with, the students (cf. Suchman, 2007). Consequently, rather than treating the lesson plan as a "task-as-workplan" (Breen, 1989), I will examine how it is made relevant and included in the interaction.

Presenting "doing word explanation"

In this section, I will present the sequential format through which word explanation emerges. Example 1 is a typical example of the sequential structure that is central to the interactive construction of doing word explanation. Prior to the example, the class had a group discussion about fines, and Angela told a story about "a plain clothes police officer." The teacher circled among the students and, among other things, wrote "a plain clothes officer" on the board.

Example 1 [O620U2—34:40]

```
1       Te:    Mia hun havde:: nej ikk Mia undskyld (.)
               Mia she had no not Mia sorry (.)

2       Te:    Angela havde fået e:n bøde af (.)
               Angela had got a fine by (.)

        geTe:  /gazes and points towards "en betjent i
               civil"(a plain clothes police officer)
               on the blackboard

3 ->    Te:    /en (1.4) en <betjent i civi:l>
               a (1.4) a plain clothes police officer
               "Mia she had no not Mia sorry (.) Angela
               had got a fine by (.) a (1.4) plain
               clothes police officer"
```

```
4     Ps:    (0.4)

5     Te:    hørte je
             heard I
             "I heard"

      gaTe:  /gazes towards students
6     Ps:    /(.)

7     Ca:    °(En) betjent (i civil)°
             A plain clothes police officer
             "A plain clothes police officer"

8     Ps:    (2.0)

9     Ca:    En betjent i civi[:l
             A plain clothes police officer
             "A plain clothes police officer"

10    Te:                     [Ja hva betyder det hva-
                               [Yeah what means that what

11    Te:    en betjent i civi:l hva er det
             a plain clothes police officer what is that
             "Yeah what does that mean what a plain
             clothes police officer what is that"

12    Ps:    (0.5)

13    Al:    De:::t en betjent uden uniform
             It an officer without uniform
             "It is an officer without a uniform"

14    Te:    Det en betjent uden uniform ja
             It an officer without a uniform yeah
             "It is an office without a uniform yeah"
```

A few comments should be noted about the sequence that leads up to the word explanation (line 13). (a) The first time the "noun phrase-to-be-explained" is produced is in line 3 after a hesitant turn by the teacher; the turn includes a micro pause as well as a substantial 1.4 second pause and a restart (the repetition of the article). The specific noun phrase is placed in a possible turn constructional unit (TCU)-final position and is produced at a slower pace than the surrounding talk. (b) The turn is followed by a 0.4 second pause and an increment (Ford, Fox, & Thompson, 2002) that provides a new transition relevant position. (c) A student repeats the noun phrase twice (lines 7 and 9), and the teacher asks for a word explanation (lines 10–11). In this way, the noun phrase is oriented to as *relevant* to the ongoing activity by both participants. (d) The word explanation by a student, Ali, follows the consistent three-part IRF (Initiation-Response-Follow-up) pattern in classroom interaction as described, among others, by Sinclair and Coulthard (1975) and Mehan (1979): In lines 10–11 the teacher requests a word explanation (Initiation), a student explains the word in line 13 (Response), and the teacher, in line 14, accepts the student's explanation (Follow-up).

In the following sections, I will elaborate on this pattern characterized by the following moves: (a) The teacher emphasizes a specific part of the turn, which (b) a student repeats, and (c) the teacher then asks for a word explanation, which (d) the student provides in the following turn. I will show how the participants collaboratively prepare the ground for the word explanation and discuss the context(s) in which this social practice is found. The sequence is interactively constructed, and I will show how the students orient to the teacher's emphasis of a part of the teacher's turn-at-talk, and how they contribute to the lexical explanation sequence.

Highlighting the target word

In the prior paragraph, we saw that the teacher highlights a part of his/her turn, and that the highlighted words therefore hold a prominent position within the turn. This seems to be an important aspect of "doing word explanation." Examples 2 to 4 show examples of how the teacher emphasizes a particular part of the turn.

```
1      Ps:    (2.4)

2      Te:    He:r i spørgsmål fem hvo::r han spør hvorfor
              Here in question five where he asks why

3      Te:    hun ikke køber en ny cykel, (0.3) så det
              she not buy a new bike (0.3) then it

4      Te:    fordi hun ikke har råd til det li´e nu (.)
              because she cannot afford it right now (.)

5  ->  Te:    også fordi hun skal betale <e:n bø:de>
              also because she has to pay a fine
              "Here in question five where he asks why
              she doesn't buy a new bike (0.3) so it's
              because she can't afford it right now
              (.) also because she has to pay a fine"

6      Ps:    (0.7)
```

Example 2 [O620U1—55:25]

```
1    Ps:   (2.4)

2    Te:   He:r i spørgsmål fem hvo::r han spør hvorfor
           Here in question five where he asks why

3    Te:   hun ikke køber en ny cykel, (0.3) så det
           she not buy a new bike (0.3) then it

4    Te:   fordi hun ikke har råd til det li´e nu (.)
           because she cannot afford it right now (.)

5 -> Te:   også fordi hun skal betale <e:n bø:de>
           also because she has to pay a fine
           "Here in question five where he asks why
           she doesn't buy a new bike (0.3) so it's
           because she can't afford it right now
           (.) also because she has to pay a fine"

6    Ps:   (0.7)

7    Ca:         Ehrm::[:: °en bøde°]
                 Ehrm:::: a fine
                 "Ehrm a fine"

8    Te:         [E- e:n bøde] hva er det en bøde er
                 [A- a fine what is it a fine is
                 "A a fine what's that a fine is"

9    Ps:   (0.6)

10   Al:   Multa ((Spanish for fine))
           Fine
           "Fine"

11   Ps:   (1.1)

12   Al:   Ehrm: når du: DU LAVer no:get du skal betale
           Ehrm: when you you do something you must pay
           "Ehrm when you you do something you have to pay"
```

Example 3 [O620U2—27:15]

```
1    Te:   Hva hedder det=ehrm::::::::::::::::::, Monika
           What do you say ehrm:::: Monika
```

Doing Word Explanation in Interaction 141

```
 2 -> Te:   hun kørte (0.5) forkert (.) i en=eller kørte
            she drove (0.5) wrong (.) in a or went

 3 -> Te:   ind i en ensrettet gade
            into a one way street
            "What do you say ehrm Monika she drove (0.5)
            wrong (.) in a or went into a one way street"

 4    Ps:   (0.3)

 5    Al:   E:ns↓redde[::d¿
            One way
            "One way"

 6    Te:              [Ensrettet hva er det¿
                       [One way what is that
                       "One way what is that"

 7    Ps:   (0.5)

 8    Al:   De::t e[r
            That is
            "That is"

 9    Ke:              [ONE way.
                       [One way
                       "One way"

10    Te:   (Ja) one wa:y
            (Yeah) one way
            "(Yeah) one way"

11    Ke:   °One way.° [hm
            One way hm
            "One way hm"

12    Te:              [One way jaer
                       [One way yeah
                       "One way yeah"

13    Ps:   (1.0)

14    Te:   Å fik en bøde,
            And got a fine
            "And got a fine"
```

Example 4 [O620U2—25:20]

```
1    Te:   Eh::: å så hørte je at Monika hu:n kørte
           Eh::: and then heard I that Monika she passed

2    Te:   forbi: en eh:: (.) hun kørte f::- h̲urtigt
           by a eh:: (.) she drove t::- fast

3    Te:   (.) >alt alt< for hurtigt i bi:l
           (.) way way too fast by car
           "Eh and then I heard that Monika she passed
           by a eh (.) she drove t::- fast (.) way way
           too fast by car"

4    Ps:   (0.6)

5    Te:   eh:::: <midt om na̲tten>
           eh:::: middle of the night
           "eh in the middle of the night"

6    Ps:   (0.3)

     moTe: /walks towards blackboard
7    Te:   /(Det den her hedder) midt om natten her
           (that's this one it's called) in the
            middle of the night here
           "(That's this one it's called) in the
            middle of the night here"

     geTe: /points at blackboard
8    Ps:   /(0.3)

9    Te:   forbi en sko:le (0.8) å blev=eh::: he- eh
           by a school (0.8) and was eh::: xx- eh

10   Te:   sto̲ppet a:f (0.3) Du fik e:n (0.7)
           stopped by (0.3) You got a (0.7)

     geTe: /picks up chalk   /starts writing on
                             the blackboard
11-> Te:   /Hun fik en <fa̲:rt/bøde>
           she got a speeding ticket
           "by a school (0.8) and was eh eh stopped
           by (0.3) You got a (0.7) She got a
           speeding ticket"

     geTe: /writes "hun fik en fartbøde" (she got a
           speeding ticket) on the blackboard
```

```
12   Ps:   /(3.2)

13   Al:   °En fartbøde°
           A speeding ticket
           "A speeding ticket"

14   Ps:   (5.8)

15   Al:   Fartbøde (0.2) hva er [det
           Speeding ticket (0.2) what is that
           "Speeding ticket (0.2) what is that"

16   Te:                           [Fartbøde
                                   [Speeding ticket
                                   "Speeding ticket"

17   Ps:   (0.6)

18   Te:   Fartbøde betyder du har kørt for hurtigt
           Speeding ticket means you have going too fast
           "Speeding ticket means you were going too fast"

19   Ps:   (.)

20   Te:   [Fart betyder s:peed (.) spe[ed (.) ikk
           [Speed means 'speed' (.) 'speed' (.) right
           "Speed means 'speed' (.) 'speed' (.) right"

21   ?:    [Nå:[:
           [Oh::
           "Oh"

22   Al:          [Ah: okay
                  [Oh okay
                  "Oh okay"
```

In these examples, we see that the teacher's turn is designed so as to emphasize a part of the ongoing turn. Several resources make the target word stand out from the ongoing TCU by framing it as productionally isolated (cf. Brouwer, 2000, ch. 6, 2004). In the following paragraphs, I will outline the resources that the teacher relies on in order to emphasize a part of the turn. Then I will show how the students orient to the emphasis. The resources will be described according to self-repair, prosodic resources, and visual resources in relation to the blackboard. As will be seen, the highlighting is frequently done through a combination of these resources. For instance, a pause does not highlight the following turn elements in and by itself but may serve other interactional business, for example, requesting and securing the gaze of the co-participant (Carroll, 2004; Goodwin, 1980, 1981; Heath, 1984; Mortensen, 2009). However, when the element(s) that follow the pause in other ways are made relevant, the pause is one of the resources used to emphasize the words and produce them as productionally isolated.

It is to be noted that Examples 1, 3, and 4 all come from the same lesson related to a specific topic, namely, traffic (violations) and fines. The activity is centered on the students' prior stories during group work; the task is framed as, and organized in relation to, "fines" as the central word; and during the following whole class interaction, the teacher uses the opportunity to deal with relevant vocabulary with which the students may not be familiar. In these examples, the teacher has prepared vocabulary teaching prior to the lesson, and she includes the blackboard as a visual resource in selecting and explicating the relevant vocabulary.

TCU-final position

According to Sacks, Schegloff, and Jefferson (1974), TCUs are the basic building blocks of turns and central to the ways in which turn-organization is managed. Participants rely on recognizable (possible) completions of TCUs, since these positions constitute places where transfer from one speaker to another may be relevant (see, e.g., Jefferson, 1984). To project a possible completion of a TCU, current non-speakers rely on the action that the TCU accomplishes, on grammar/syntax (Lindström, 2006; Schegloff, 1996; Steensig, 2001), on intonation (Ford & Thompson, 1996; Selting, 2000), and on gesture (Klippi, 2006; Mondada, 2006; Olsher, 2004).

The emphasized words occur in a (possible) TCU-final position. In Examples 2, 3, and 4 the teacher's turn is completed by the target word, and the highlighted word is followed by a substantial pause, which displays that turn-transition is relevant and that the students should or could do something at this point. In Example 1, the teacher continues her talk after the emphasis of a possible TCU-completing element by expanding the turn with an increment in line 5 *hørte jeg* [I heard]). Schegloff (1996) describes increments as RE-completing a possible completion, and the TCU has therefore come to a possible completion by the end of the emphasized noun phrase.

Self-repair

One way in which the teacher can highlight a part of the current turn-at-talk is through changes in the ongoing or projected turn. This can be described in terms of self-initiated repair, which according to Schegloff, Jefferson, and Sacks (1977, p. 367) has the following properties:

Self-initiations within the same turn (which contains the trouble source) use a variety of non-lexical speech perturbations (e.g., cut-offs, sound stretches, "uh's etc.) to signal the possibility of repair-initiation immediately following.

Through modifications such as hesitations and pauses, the speaker may initiate self-repair of the turn and the target element can be productionally isolated, although it may be syntactically integrated in the ongoing TCU. In Example 3, the teacher self-repairs and restarts the turn where the target words could be produced syntactically (after *forkert (.) i en* [wrong in a]). She thus changes the projected course of the turn by producing a self-repair, lines 2–3, which substitutes *kørte forkert i* [drove wrong in] with *kørte ind i* [drove into]. In this way, the target words are highlighted through a lexical modification of the turn-design. In lines 9–10 in Example 4, the teacher restarts the ongoing TCU after *stoppet af* [stopped by] and changes the direction of the TCU with *du fik en* [you got a] which changes the projection of the next-possible element from, for example, *a policeman* to *fartbøde* [speeding ticket]. Through this method she modifies the turn-design to syntactically prepare for the word *fartbøde* [speeding ticket]. Additionally, she produces another restart, which changes the pronoun from *you* to *she*, thus changing the recipient roles of the turn from *you*, that is, Monika, to the whole class, and thereby highlights the relevance of the turn to the whole class. This changes the activity from initiating a story through reporting a prior conversation to teaching relevant vocabulary in a contextualized and syntactically appropriate sentence.

Hesitations such as pauses, prolongations, and (variations of) *ehrm*s are frequently used during word searches (Goodwin & Goodwin, 1986; Helasvuo, Laakso, & Sorjonen, 2004; Lerner, 1996; Schegloff, 1979), in which the progressivity towards TCU completion has been halted, but the search is organized to show that an ongoing attempt is being made to continue the TCU (Lerner, 1996, p. 261).

Additionally, many turn units that end up containing word searches are designed in such a way that the search is placed near the end of the unit, thereby providing a place for candidates which will concomitantly be terminal item completions (Lerner, 1996, p. 262). So the hesitations seen in doing vocabulary explanation have several similarities with those in word searches. However, the collection does not include cases where the student(s) provides a candidate word, so the students do not seem to orient to the hesitations as word searches. And neither does the teacher, during the hesitations, visibly display that (s)he is engaged in a word search, for example, by withdrawing the gaze from the students or producing a "thinking face" as described by Goodwin and Goodwin (1986). Despite the similarities in the turn-design, this makes the activity seem different from a word search.

Prosodic resources
In Examples 2 and 5, the target word is marked *prosodically* by producing the noun phrase significantly more slowly than the surrounding talk and stretching the words by prolongations of vowels (Example 2) and stressing the word

(Example 5). These are interactionally common ways of attributing a "special status" to a part of the turn.

Example 5 [O620U2—38:20]

```
1      Te:    Eh:::: (.) å man bruger det osse::
              Eh:::: (.) and you use it also

       geTe:  /writes "ordre, plan, fremtid"
              (order, plan, future) on the blackboard
2      Ps:    /(7.4)

3      Te:    når man har en plan om noget
              when you have a plan about something
              "Eh (.) and you also use it (7.4) when
              you plan to do something"

4      Ps:    (0.6)

5      Te:    Når jeg kommer hjem så s:kal jeg
              When I get home then will I

6      Te:    ha (0.5) e:n kop kaffe
              have (0.5) a cup coffee
              "When I get home then I will have
              (0.5) a cup of coffee"

7      Ps:    (0.9)

8  -> Te:     å en lu:r
              and a nap
              "and a nap"

9      Ps:    (1.0)

10     Al:    Lur
              Nap
              "Nap"

11     Te:    En lur
              A nap
              "A nap"

       geTe:  /writes "en lur" (a nap) on the blackboard
12     Ps:    /(3.2)
```

```
13   Te:   That's a nap
            "That's a nap"

14   Ps:   (0.4)

15   Al:   Lur
            Nap
            "Nap"

16   Te:   Man lige sover lidt
            You just sleep little
            "You sleep for a short time"
```

The blackboard

The teacher often relies on *visual* resources to highlight the target word. In this regard, the blackboard plays an important role. Although the blackboard is an important socio-cultural artefact of the classroom, few studies have analyzed how it is used by participants to organize their ongoing courses of action (e.g., Pitsch, 2007). The approach adopted by Pitsch follows studies within linguistic anthropological research, which show how written documents are included in the interaction, and how participation is shaped by the participants' mutual orientation to texts, books or figures (Goodwin, 2000, 2003, 2007; Mondada, 2007; Nevile, 2004).

The blackboard may be used in two fundamentally different ways. On the one hand, the teacher may write on the blackboard during a turn-at-talk that includes the written version of the verbal talk. In Example 4, we see how the teacher uses the blackboard by *writing* the target words *hun fik en fartbøde* [she got a speeding ticket]. Writing, talk, and movement are delicately coordinated: After the first restart in line 10, the teacher walks towards the blackboard, picks up a piece of chalk from the chalk tray, and clearly projects that she is about to write on the board. However, at this point she makes another restart by changing the pronoun from *you* to *she* (see above). She thereby projects an activity in which the written words are relevant to the ongoing activity rather than related to just one of the students—that is, *you*. The TCU that is initiated through the restart prosodically emphasizes the word *fartbøde* [speeding ticket]. The writing is initiated in overlap with the verbal production of the word, and projects that *fartbøde* [speeding ticket] will be written on the board. However, the teacher writes the entire verbal phrase on the board, and thus embeds *fartbøde* [speeding ticket] within a syntactically complete sentence. Although the teacher prosodically emphasizes the word *fartbøde* [speeding ticket], it is up to the students to locate whether the particular lexical item or the entire written sentence is the relevant unit for the ongoing activity (see below).

On the other hand, the teacher may use what is already on the blackboard by including it into the ongoing course of action, for example, by *pointing*. Since what is written on the board is potentially relevant during the lesson, the blackboard is used as a resource to structure the activities in the lesson. For instance, in Example 3 the teacher uses gesture to point to the blackboard where she has written *ensrettet gade* [one-way street] at the beginning of the lesson. In this way, the teacher makes a specific part of the blackboard relevant through pointing and projects the turn-completion visually before producing the lexical affiliate, that is, the lexical item whose meaning the gesture is conveying (cf. Klippi, 2006; Schegloff, 1984). The text written on the board is thereby included in the ongoing interaction. Similarly, in Example 1 the teacher wrote *en betjent i civil* [a plain clothes police officer] during the prior group work. With this action, she projects that this is a relevant noun phrase to be included in a later part of the lesson. By pointing towards the text while reading it aloud, she invokes the conversation of the prior group work as well as the relevant participants—the members of the particular group. However, she does not specify which aspect of the written noun phrase is to be dealt with at this point.

As shown in the example, the teacher relies on *linguistic* as well as *visual/embodied* resources, including physical artefacts, to emphasize the target word(s) during the turn, and thus makes it relevant to the ongoing interaction. Prosody seems to play a particular role in the highlighting and is a resource used in all the cases in the collection. Whereas pointing, writing, and self-repair may be present, they do all occur in relation to *prosodic emphasis*. This may be done through stressing the word or a part of the word, or by producing it at significantly slower speed than the preceding talk.

Turn-transition
The emphasized part of the teacher's turn is followed by a pause, which constitutes a possible completion point of the ongoing TCU. By not continuing the turn, the teacher provides space for the students to take a turn through self-selection (Sacks et al., 1974). In Example 1, the teacher turns the gaze towards the students after the noun phrase *en betjent i civil* [a plain clothes police officer] has been produced. She orients to the students as relevant recipients of the turn and thus as relevant next-speakers (Mortensen, 2010). A general feature of talk-in-interaction is what Sacks calls *contiguity* (Sacks, 1987 [1973]). He describes how speakers orient to next-position (Sacks, 1992, vol. 2, part viii, lecture 4) as a relevant position for dealing with the prior turn. On a sequence organization level (Schegloff, 2007), this means that a second pair-part (e.g., "an answer") is relevantly placed in the next-turn in relation to its initiating first pair-part (e.g., "a question"). This does not mean that a second pair-part will actually follow, but if it does not, the turn that comes "instead" of the second pair-part orients to the first pair-part by producing a relevant action. The second pair-part can

therefore be said to be conditionally relevant (Schegloff & Sacks, 1973) in the turn following the first pair-part. At the same time, Sacks (1987 [1973]) argues, if a speaker orients to another turn but the prior one, (s)he needs to do extra work (e.g., *what you said before...*) to display that the incipient turn is not orienting to the immediate prior one. However, contiguity is also relevant at another level of organization. If a turn is designed to include a multi-question turn (Sacks, 1987 [1973]; e.g., *What's your name and where are you from?*) recipients tend to deal with the last question of the prior turn *first*. There is thus a preference for proximity, or what Jefferson (1972) calls "item-adjacency," in interaction.

If we return to "doing word explanation," we saw that the teacher designs his/her TCU to highlight a specific part of the turn in a (possible) TCU-final position. For instance, we saw how the teacher changes the course of the projected TCU to prepare the ongoing syntax for a particular lexical element (see Example 4 above). We now move on to the next-turn in the sequential structure and see how the students orient to the teacher's turn and the emphasized lexical item(s).

Repeating (a part of) the highlighted word(s)

Following the teacher's turn with the target word and the pause, one of the students repeats the target word. By repeating parts of the prior turn, the students treat the highlighted word(s) as response-worthy (Schegloff, 1997a) and display an understanding of the target word(s) as *relevant* to the ongoing course of action. They orient to this position as a relevant position for self-selection (Sacks, et al., 1974). Two things should be noted in relation to the design of the student's turn. Firstly, only the "target," that is, emphasized, words from the prior turn, are repeated.

Example 6 [O620U2—38:20]

```
1      Te:   Ud over fremtid så bruger vi det nå-
              In addition to future then use we it wh-

2      Te:   når det noget med en ordre
              when it about an order
              "In addition to future then we use it
              when it is about an order"

3      Ps:   (1.2)

4  ->  Ay:   °Ordre°
              Order
              "Order"
```

5	Te:	En ordre (.) it's an order (0.2) du s:kal
		An order (.) it's an order (0.2) you have to
		"An order (.) it's an order (0.2) you have to"
6	Ay:	Okay
		Okay
		"Okay"
7	Ps:	(0.2)
8	Te:	vaske op
		wash up
		"do the dishes"

The students display an understanding of the repeated word(s) as being emphasized by the teacher. The teacher's syntactic construction is repeated, and (syntactic) modifications occur only within the repeated noun phrase. For instance, in Examples 5 and 6 the students do not repeat the entire noun phrase, but leave out the definite article and repeat only the head of the noun phrase. What is relevant for whether or not all the highlighted words are repeated is the *sequential distance* between the teacher's highlighted word and the student's repeat. When the repeat follows immediately after the highlighted words, the repeat does not necessarily include the entire noun phrase that was highlighted, but only a part of it as in Examples 3 and 5. When the repeat does not follow immediately after the highlighted words, the students often repeat the syntactic structure that was highlighted by the teacher (see, e.g., Example 1).

Secondly, the repeat does not display the students' understanding of what should be done with the target word, and in this sense the repeat seems to be an acknowledgment of the teacher's prior turn and the highlighted words. By repeating the target word, the students play the ball back to the teacher. At this point, they display a mutual understanding of the target word as being central to the ongoing action, but they have not specified what they are going to do with it.

Requesting a word explanation

Following the students' repeat, the teacher requests a word explanation. The teacher's "request for a word explanation" turn is constructed by a repetition of the target word and the request itself. By repeating the target word, the teacher acknowledges that the students have located the emphasized word in the teacher's prior turn. In Example 1, this is done explicitly through the teacher's overlapping *yeah*, line 10. By overlapping the student's repeat, the teacher does not provide space for the student to explain what the repeat is doing (e.g., displaying that it is a problem of understanding or pronunciation). In this way, the teacher orients to the repeat as locating the relevant words in her own prior turn, which is necessary for the continuation of the word explanation sequence.

The request builds on the student's repeat, and this is an important step in the word explanation sequence. If the students do not repeat the target words, they do not participate in locating the word, and this is crucial for the word explanation to be built up interactionally. In Example 7, the teacher emphasizes the noun phrase *p-skive* [parking disc] by hesitating immediately before it is produced, stressing the word, and writing the word on the board.

Example 7 [O620U2—31:40]

```
1      Te:    .tsk Å så får man en bøde hvis man ikk har
              .tsk And then get you a fine if you not have

2      Te:    sat sin=ehh pe skive
              put your=eh parking disc
              ".tsk And then you get a fine if you
              don't use your parking disc"

       geTe:  /writes "p-skive" (parking disc) on the board
3      Ps:    /(1.5)

       geTe:         /gestures "clock"
4 ->   Te:    Det /den der pe ski[ve
              It is this one parking disc
              "It is this one parking disc"

5      Ay:                         [°Pe skive°
                                   [Parking disc
                                   "Parking disc"

6      Ps:    (0.2)

7      Te:    Det hedde:r de:n lille: (.) tidstæller
              That's called the little (.) time
              indicator
              "That's what it's called the little (.)
              time indicator"

8      Ps:    (0.4)
```

```
9       Te:     på [bi:len
                on the car
                "on the car"

10      St:            [↑Ah::: (den der)
                       [Ah that one
                        "Ah that one"

11      Te:     Jaer
                Yeah
                "Yeah"
```

However, the students do not repeat the word and after a 1.5 second pause, the teacher provides a repetition of the word (line 4) as well as an iconic gesture (e.g., McNeill, 1992, 2000) resembling a watch. In overlap with *p-skive* [parking disc] in line 4, a student repeats the word, and the teacher then provides an explanation of the word (line 7). In this way, the teacher orients to the repeat in line 5 as a display of non-understanding of the word.

Previously, I described the teacher's turn as preparing the ground for his/her request for a word explanation. Giving the students the opportunity to provide the word explanation seems to be pedagogically motivated: Rather than explaining the word, the teacher uses a sequential format which structurally gives space to request a word explanation by relying on the local context. The students thus have the opportunity to display whether they understand the word or not. By repeating the target word, the students extract the target word from the teacher's prior turn, and following the students' repeat, the teacher uses the local context to request a word explanation. However, the students may project non-understanding of the target word. In Example 4, a student initiates repair after the highlighted word has been produced in the teacher's prior turn. In the turn following the repair initiation, it is therefore conditionally relevant for the teacher to provide a word explanation.

Example 4, fragment [O620U2—25:20]
```
5       Te:     eh::::: <midt om natten>
                eh::::: middle of the night
                "eh in the middle of the night"

6       Ps:     (0.3)

        moTe:   /walks towards blackboard
7       Te:     /(Det den her hedder) midt om natten her
                (that's this one it's called) in the
                    middle of the night here
                "(That's this one it's called) in the
                    middle of the night here"
```

```
      geTe:   /points at blackboard
8     Ps:     /(0.3)

9     Te:     forbi en sko:le (0.8) å blev=eh::: he- eh
              by a school (0.8) and was eh::: xx- eh

10    Te:     stoppet a:f (0.3) Du fik e:n (0.7)
              stopped by (0.3) You got a (0.7)

      geTe:   /picks up chalk    /starts writing on
                                 the blackboard
11->  Te:     /Hun fik en <fa:rt/bøde>
              she got a speeding ticket
              "by a school (0.8) and was eh eh stopped
              by (0.3) You got a (0.7) She got a
              speeding ticket"

      geTe:   /writes "hun fik en fartbøde" (she got a
              speeding ticket) on the blackboard
12    Ps:     /(3.2)

13    Al:     °En fartbøde°
              A speeding ticket
              "A speeding ticket"

14    Ps:     (5.8)

15    Al:     Fartbøde (0.2) hva er [det
              Speeding ticket (0.2) what is that
              "Speeding ticket (0.2) what is that"

16    Te:                         [Fartbøde
                                  [Speeding ticket
                                  "Speeding ticket"
```

In line 13, a student repeats the target word. However, this is produced in a low volume while the teacher is writing the target word on the blackboard. Since the teacher does not react to the repeat of the target word, the student repeats it again in line 15 and pursues a response from the teacher. During the 0.2 second pause in line 15, the teacher turns towards the student, but before she has completed the bodily re-orientation, the student initiates a repair by requesting an explanation and specifies the trouble source as a problem of understanding the target word in the teacher's prior turn. In line 18, the teacher responds to the request by providing an explanation.

A repair initiation from the students creates a sequential environment in which it is relevant for the teacher to explain the word. The teacher orients to (possible) repair initiation in the turn following the highlighted word. In Example 2, a student projects repair in the turn following the teacher's introduction of the target word.

Example 2, fragment [O620U1—55:25]

```
5    Te:   også fordi hun skal betale <e:n bø:de>
           also because she has to pay a fine
           "Here in question five where he asks why
           she doesn't buy a new bike (0.3) so it's
           because she can't afford it right now
           (.) also because she has to pay a fine"

6    Ps:   (0.7)

7 -> Ca:   Ehrm::[:: °en bøde°]
           Ehrm:::: a fine
           "Ehrm a fine"

8    Te:         [E- e:n bøde] hva er det en bøde er
                 [A- a fine what is it a fine is
           "A a fine what's that a fine is"
```

In line 7, the student projects a repair initiation by hesitating and repeating the highlighted word in a low volume. She thereby displays trouble in relation to the prior turn. However, the trouble source has not been located when the teacher initiates a new turn (line 8). In overlap with the hesitation, the teacher repeats the target word and requests a word explanation that builds on the projected repair by the students.

What we have seen here is that participants orient to the normative character of the sequential structure. They orient to a repeat of the target word by the student in next-turn position. In Example 4, we saw that the student who produces the repeat orients to the repeat as providing the teacher the opportunity to request a word explanation. However, the teacher may not necessarily request a word explanation but provide it him/herself. This is the case in Examples 5 and 6. In both cases, she relies on an English translation to explain the target words. By explicating the word, the teacher minimizes the break away from the ongoing focal activity. In this way, she does not turn it into an interactional word explanation sequence, which provides the students the opportunity to display their understanding of the lexical item. By explicating the word(s) through a self-repair, the teacher does not initiate such a sequence and therefore does not turn the explanation into an interactional pedagogical task of teaching and/or testing the student's knowledge of the particular vocabulary.

The students' repeat as a repair-initiation?

On the basis of the analyses presented here, it makes sense to ask whether the students' repeat of the target word(s) is a repair-initiation (Schegloff, 1997a; Schegloff et al., 1977), that is, whether it orients to interactional *trouble* in terms of hearing or understanding that is impairing intersubjectivity, or whether the teacher sets up a frame in which it is relevant (cf. Schegloff & Sacks, 1973) for the students to produce a next-turn repeat of the emphasized elements. Mazeland (1986, reported in Brouwer, 2000, p. 78; Mazeland, 1987) describes the actions that a next-turn repair initiation performs: (a) It signals that there is interactional trouble; (b) it locates the trouble source; (c) it identifies the kind of trouble that is causing problems; (d) it displays how the repair is to be accomplished, that is, by self or other (Schegloff et al., 1977); and (e) it suggests a repair method. A crucial point to the present analysis is the location of the trouble source, and maybe even more importantly, *who* locates the trouble source—teacher or student. The students do this in and through the repeat. We have seen that the students' repeat reuses the same elements that the teacher emphasized in a possible TCU-final position in the prior turn. However, in Example 4, the teacher does not respond to the repeat and the student produces it again, but this time without the determiner. In this way, the student locates the exact word, *fartbøde* [speeding ticket], which is central to the ongoing business. However, we sometimes find cases where the teacher points out the target word. In Example 3, the teacher emphasizes the noun phrase *ensrettet gade* [one way] by pointing to a written version of the phrase on the blackboard. However, as a student repeats the noun phrase (line 5), the teacher overlaps the student's repeat. The overlap is initiated towards the end of the word *ensrettet* [one way], which is not the final element of the noun phrase. Here, the teacher does not orient to the entire noun phrase as the relevant words to be explained, but only to the word *ensrettet* [one way]. Both teacher and student can therefore be said to collaborate in selecting which of the possible emphasized words are relevant to be explained.

In the above, we saw that if the students do not repeat the emphasized words, the teacher may orient to the lack of a turn by the students and set up a frame in which it is possible and relevant for the students to "do something" with the emphasized words. By providing a repeat, the students take part in locating the key word(s) and participate in the sequential unfolding of the word explanation sequence. Without the students' repeat of the emphasized word(s), the teacher may or may not request and pursue a word explanation or provide the explanation him/herself, but in that instance the word explanation is not interactively produced, depending solely on the teacher.

Word explanation and sequence closing

The teacher does not select a next-speaker to provide the word explanation but allows the students to self-select. It is therefore up to the students to find out who will, or is able to, provide an explanation. If the teacher accepts the student's explanation, (s)he evaluates the response as in Example 1, where the teacher repeats the student's explanation and evaluates it with a *yeah* in line 14. Following the sequence-closing, the teacher resumes the sequence, which was expanded by the word explanation sequence. After the assessment (line 12) and a 1.0 second pause in Example 3, the teacher resumes the turn she initiated in lines 1–3 and frames it as a continuation of the introduction with *and* (line 14). She thereby treats the word explanation sequence as a side sequence (Jefferson, 1972) which emerges from the ongoing activity and is left as a secondary activity.

Discussion and implications for language teaching

So far we have conducted a sequential analysis of a particular social practice: how teacher and students collaboratively extract lexical elements from a turn-at-talk and treat it as an opportunity for vocabulary teaching. The word explanation sequence has been described as a side sequence that puts the ongoing interaction on hold while dealing with a parenthetical, linguistic issue. This analysis suggests some implications for language teaching, in particular the teaching of vocabulary.

(Un)planned word explanation and pedagogical intentions

The analysis shows how participants interactionally negotiate (a) *that* they initiate a word explanation sequence, (b) *how* they do it, and (c) *which* lexical items are relevant for explanation. The word explanation sequence emerges from the ongoing activity, for example, a post-task activity during a storytelling (Examples 1, 2, 3, and 4), which is (briefly) put on hold while the relevant vocabulary is explained (cf. Doughty & Williams, 1998). In this way, although the lexical item(s) is already present in the lesson (e.g., has been written on the blackboard prior to this point) it is made relevant "on the fly" at this moment.

In the beginning of this chapter, I referred to the common distinction in the vocabulary teaching literature of planned versus unplanned teaching of lexical items (e.g., Hatch & Brown, 1995). This distinction is primarily based on *pedagogical intentionality* and preparation (or not) of the lesson. However, the present analysis reveals how the participants deal with the accomplishment of the task *in situ* (cf. Coughlan & Duff, 1994; Hellermann, 2007, 2008; Mondada & Pekarek Doehler, 2004; Mori, 2002, 2004; Szymanski, 2003). In the above, I noted that several of the examples come from the same lesson. For instance, Examples 1, 3, and 4 all occur within a period of approximately seven minutes.

It therefore seems that the lesson and the ongoing activity are organized so as to *facilitate* vocabulary teaching, and that the vocabulary teaching is related to a specific topic, namely traffic (violations) and fines. By selecting key-words in advance and organizing the activity around a well-defined topic, the teacher makes vocabulary learning a central aspect of the lesson.

Topic initiation
In several of the analyzed examples, the highlighted word(s) is intimately tied to the initiation of a new activity. In Examples 1, 3, and 4, the highlighted words invoke the students' stories during the prior group work and become part of initiating a new activity. The highlighted word in Example 5 emerges from an explanation about how future tense is grammatically constructed in Danish. The highlighted word, *lur* [nap], provides an example of how this can be done. The teacher uses the grammatical teaching context to include a lexical item which might be unfamiliar to the students and embeds a vocabulary sequence within the grammatical explanation.

Teaching linguistic material which emerges from the immediate context is always potentially relevant in the (second/foreign) language classroom. By using the ongoing activity as a point of departure for a (brief) "formal teaching sequence" like "doing word explanation," the teacher takes what is already contextually present to teach formal aspects of the second language. Therefore, it does not (necessarily) break with the pedagogical intentions of the ongoing activity but rather builds on it and expands the activity in sequentially relevant ways.

In this chapter, I have shown how vocabulary explanation may occur in one such sequential environment and how the ground which leads to the word explanation is interactionally constructed between the teacher and the students. The pedagogical implications that can be drawn from this analysis are twofold. On the one hand, it shows how vocabulary is taught not necessarily due to interactional problems but rather due to teachers' pedagogical aims. On the other hand, the way in which the word explanation sequence is constructed includes the students as relevant participants—the students' lack of participation has implications for the teacher, since their repeat of the emphasized lexical items is a relevant sequential step in creating an interactionally shaped word explanation sequence. Through different forms of participation, the students display strong interactional awareness. Not only do they orient to the teacher's turn-design and provide a coherent and relevant next move, they also do this in cases where they may know the meaning of the particular emphasized words (see Example 3, in which the student who repeats the lexical items is the same student who produces the word explanation). The present analysis of the "doing word explanation" practice thus adds to the range of studies that show how students participate in creating the frames for their own learning opportunities (e.g., Hellermann, 2007; Koole, 2007; Koshik, 2002; Markee, 2005; Mori, 2004; Ohta, 2001; Sahlström, 1999).

Notes

1. Thanks to Catherine E. Brouwer, Gabriele Pallotti, Johannes Wagner, and one anonymous reviewer for constructive criticisms on earlier versions of this article.
2. For repair in classroom interaction, see for example, Kasper (1985), Macbeth (2004), McHoul (1990), and Seedhouse (2004).
3. As described in this chapter, "doing word explanation" has some (sequential) similarities with what Brouwer (2000, 2004) calls "doing pronunciation."

References

Breen, M. (1989). The evaluation cycle for language learning tasks. In R. K. Johnson (Ed.), *The second language curriculum* (pp. 187–206). Cambridge: Cambridge University Press.

Brouwer, C. E. (2000). *L2 listening in interaction* (Unpublished doctoral dissertation). University of Southern Denmark, Odense.

Brouwer, C. E. (2004). Doing pronunciation: A specific type of repair sequence. In R. Gardner & J. Wagner (Eds.), *Second language conversations* (pp. 93–113). London: Continuum.

Carroll, D. (2004). Restarts in novice turn beginnings: Disfluencies or interactional achievements? In R. Gardner & J. Wagner (Eds.), *Second language conversations* (pp. 201–220). London: Continuum.

Carter, R., & McCarthy, M. (Eds.). (1988). *Vocabulary and language teaching*. New York, NY: Longman.

Coughlan, P., & Duff, P. (1994). Same task, different activities: Analysis of a second language acquisition task from an activity theory approach. In J. P. Lantolf & G. Appel (Eds.), *Vygotskian approaches to second language research* (pp. 173–194). Norwood, NJ: Ablex Press.

DeCarrico, J. S. (2001). Vocabulary learning and teaching. In M. Celce-Murcia (Ed.), *Teaching English as a second or foreign language* (pp. 285–299). Boston, MA: Heinle & Heinle.

Doughty, C., & Williams, J. (Eds.). (1998). *Focus on form in classroom second language acquisition*. Cambridge: Cambridge University Press.

Evaldsson, A.-C., Lindblad, S., Sahlström, F., & Bergqvist, K. (2001). Introduktion och forskningsöversikt [Introduction and research overview]. In S. Lindblad & F. Sahlström (Eds.), *Interaktion i pedagogiska sammanhang* [Interaction in pedagogical context] (pp. 9–35). Stockholm: Liber.

Ford, C. E., Fox, B. A., & Thompson, S. A. (2002). Constituency and the grammar of turn increments. In C. E. Ford, B. A. Fox, & S. A. Thompson (Eds.), *The language of turn and sequence* (pp. 14–38). Oxford: Oxford University Press.

Ford, C. E., & Thompson, S. A. (1996). Interactional units in conversation: Syntactic, intonational, and pragmatic resources for the management of turns. In E. Ochs, E.

A. Schegloff, & S. A. Thompson (Eds.), *Interaction and grammar* (pp. 134–184). Cambridge: Cambridge University Press.

Goodwin, C. (1980). Restarts, pauses, and the achievement of a state of mutual gaze at turn-beginning. *Sociological Inquiry, 50*(3–4), 272–302.

Goodwin, C. (1981). *Conversational organization: Interaction between speakers and hearers.* New York, NY: Academic Press.

Goodwin, C. (2000). Practices of color classification. *Mind, culture and activity, 7*(1–2), 19–36.

Goodwin, C. (2003). The body in action. In J. Coupland & R. Gwyn (Eds.), *Discourse, the body, and identity* (pp. 19–42). London: Palgrave Macmillan.

Goodwin, C. (2007). Participation, stance and effect in the organization of activities. *discourse & society, 18*(1), 53–73.

Goodwin, M. H., & Goodwin, C. (1986). Gesture and coparticipation in the activity of searching for a word. *Semiotica, 62*(1–2), 51–75.

Hatch, E., & Brown, C. (1995). *Vocabulary, semantics, and language education.* Cambridge: Cambridge University Press.

Heath, C. (1984). Talk and recipiency: Sequential organization in speech and body movement. In J. M. Atkinson & J. Heritage (Eds.), *Structures of social action. Studies in conversation analysis* (pp. 247–265). Cambridge: Cambridge University Press.

Helasvuo, M.-L., Laakso, M., & Sorjonen, M.-L. (2004). Construction of word search in conversations of Finnish speakers with aphasia. *Research on Language and Social Interaction, 37*(1), 1–37.

Hellermann, J. (2007). The development of practices for action in classroom dyadic interaction: Focus in task openings. *The Modern Language Journal, 91*(1), 83–96.

Hellermann, J. (2008). *Social actions for classroom language learning.* Clevedon: Multilingual Matters.

Hutchby, I., & Wooffitt, R. (1998). *Conversation analysis. Principles, practices and applications.* Cambridge: Polity Press.

Jefferson, G. (1972). Side sequences. In D. Sudnow (Ed.), *Studies in social interaction* (pp. 294–338). New York, NY: The Free Press.

Jefferson, G. (1984). Notes on some orderlinesses of overlap onset. In V. D'Urso & P. Leonardi (Eds.), *Discourse analysis and natural rhetoric* (pp. 11–38). Padua: Cleup Editore.

Kasper, G. (1985). Repair in foreign language teaching. *Studies in second language acquisition, 7,* 200–215.

Klippi, A. (2006). Nonverbal behavior as turn constructional units. *Texas Linguistic Forum, 49,* 158–169.

Koole, T. (2007). Parallel activities in the classroom. *Language and Education, 21*(6), 487–501.

Koshik, I. (2002). Designedly incomplete utterances: A pedagogical practice for eliciting knowledge displays in error correction sequences. *Research on Language and Social Interaction, 35*(3), 277–309.

Kumaravadivelu, B. (2006). *Understanding language teaching: From method to postmethod*. Mahwah, NJ: Lawrence Erlbaum Associates.

Larsen-Freeman, D. (2000). *Techniques and principles in language teaching*. Oxford: Oxford University Press.

Lerner, G. H. (1996). On the "semi-permeable" character of grammatical units in conversation: Conditional entry into the turn space of another speaker. In E. Ochs, E. A. Schegloff, & S. A. Thompson (Eds.), *Interaction and grammar* (pp. 238–276). Cambridge: Cambridge University Press.

Lindström, J. (2006). Grammar in the service of interaction: Exploring turn organization in Swedish. *Research on Language and Social Interaction, 39*(1), 81–117.

Long, M. H., & Robinson, P. (1998). Focus on form. Theory, research, and practice. In C. Doughty & J. Williams (Eds.), *Focus on form in classroom second language acquisition* (pp. 15–41). Cambridge: Cambridge University Press.

Macbeth, D. (2004). The relevance of repair for classroom correction. *Language in Society, 33*(5), 703–736.

Markee, N. (2005). The organization of off-task talk in second language classrooms. In K. Richards & P. Seedhouse (Eds.), *Applying conversation analysis*. London: Palgrave.

Mazeland, H. (1986). Repair srganisatie in onderwijs interakties [Repair organisation in classroom interaction]. In A. Scholtens & D. Springorum (Eds.), *Gespreksanalyse* [Conversation analysis] (pp. 233–246). Nijmegen: Instituut Nederlands.

Mazeland, H. (1987, August). *A short remark on the analysis of institutional interaction: The organization of repair in lessons*. Paper presented at the International Pragmatics Association (IPrA) Conference, Antwerp, Belgium.

McHoul, A. (1990). The organization of repair in classroom talk. *Language in Society, 19*, 349–377.

McNeill, D. (1992). *Hand and mind: What gestures reveal about thought*. Chicago, IL: The University of Chicago Press.

McNeill, D. (Ed.). (2000). *Language and gesture*. Cambridge: Cambridge University Press.

Mehan, H. (1979). *Learning lessons: Social organization in the classroom*. Cambridge: Harvard University Press.

Mondada, L. (2006). Participants' online analysis and multimodal practices: Projecting the end of the turn and the closing of the sequence. *Discourse Studies, 8*(1), 117–129.

Mondada, L. (2007). Multimodal resources for turn-taking: Pointing and the emergence of possible next speakers. *Discourse Studies, 9*(2), 194–225.

Mondada, L., & Pekarek Doehler, S. (2004). Second language acquisition as situated practice: Task accomplishment in the French second language classroom. *The Modern Language Journal, 88*(4), 501–518.

Mori, J. (2002). Task design, plan, and development of talk-in-interaction: An analysis of a small group activity in a Japanese language classroom. *Applied Linguistics, 23*(3), 323–347.

Mori, J. (2004). Negotiating sequential boundaries and learning opportunities: A case from a Japanese language classroom. *The Modern Language Journal, 88*(4), 536–550.

Mortensen, K. (2009). Establishing recipiency in pre-beginning position in the second language classroom. *Discourse Processes, 46*(5), 491–515.

Mortensen, K. (2010). Selecting next-speaker in the second language classroom: How to find a willing next-speaker in planned activities. *Journal of Applied Linguistics, 5*(1), 55–79.

Nevile, M. (2004). *Beyond the black box: Talk-in-interaction in the airline cockpit.* Aldershot: Ashgate.

Ohta, A. S. (2001). *Second language acquisition processes in the classroom: Learning Japanese.* Mahwah, NJ: Lawrence Erlbaum

Olsher, D. (2004). Talk and gesture: The embodied completion of sequential actions in spoken interaction. In R. Gardner & J. Wagner (Eds.), *Second language conversations* (pp. 221–245). London: Continuum.

Pitsch, K. (2007). Unterrichtskommunikation *revisited*. Tafelskizzen als interaktionale Ressource [Classroom communication revisited. Blackboard drawings as intractional resource]. *Bulletin Suisse de Linguistique Appliquée, 85*, 59–80.

Richards, J. C., & Rodgers, T. S. (2001). *Approaches and methods in language teaching.* Cambridge: Cambridge University Press.

Sacks, H. (1987 [1973]). On the preference for agreement and contiguity in sequences in conversation. In G. Button & J. R. E. Lee (Eds.), *Talk and social organization.* Clevedon: Multilingual Matters.

Sacks, H. (1992). *Lectures on conversation. Volumes 1 & 2* (Gail Jefferson Ed.). Oxford: Blackwell.

Sacks, H., Schegloff, E. A., & Jefferson, G. (1974). A simplest systematics for the organization of turn-taking for conversation. *Language, 50*(4), 696–735.

Sahlström, F. (1999). *Up the hill backwards.* Uppsala: Uppsala Studies in Education.

Schegloff, E. A. (1979). The relevance of repair to syntax-for-conversation. In T. Givón (Ed.), *Syntax and semantics volume 12: Discourse and syntax* (pp. 75–119). New York, NY: Academic Press.

Schegloff, E. A. (1984). On some gestures' relation to talk. In J. M. Atkinson & J. Heritage (Eds.), *Structures of social action. Studies in conversation analysis.* (pp. 266–296). Cambridge: Cambridge University Press.

Schegloff, E. A. (1996). Turn organization: One intersection of grammar and interaction. In E. Ochs, E. A. Schegloff, & S. A. Thompson (Eds.), *Interaction and grammar* (pp. 52–133). Cambridge: Cambridge University Press.

Schegloff, E. A. (1997a). Practices and actions: Boundary cases of other-initiated repair. *Discourse Processes, 23*, 499–545.

Schegloff, E. A. (1997b). Third turn repair. In G. R. Guy, C. Feagin, D. Schiffrin, & J. Baugh (Eds.), *Towards a social science of language 2* (pp. 31–40). Amsterdam: John Benjamins.

Schegloff, E. A. (2000). When "others" initiate repair. *Applied Linguistics, 21*(2), 205–243.

Schegloff, E. A. (2007). *Sequence organization in interaction: A primer in conversation analysis* (Vol. 1). Cambridge: Cambridge University Press.

Schegloff, E. A., Jefferson, G., & Sacks, H. (1977). The preference for self-correction in the organization of repair in conversation. *Language, 53*, 361–382.

Schegloff, E. A., & Sacks, H. (1973). Opening up closings. *Semiotica, 8*, 289–327.

Schmitt, N. (2000). *Vocabulary in language teaching.* Cambridge: Cambridge University Press.

Seedhouse, P. (1996). Classroom interaction: Possibilities and impossibilities. *English Language Teaching Journal, 50*(1), 16–24.

Seedhouse, P. (1997). The case of the missing "No": The relationship between pedagogy and interaction. *Language Learning, 47*(3), 547–583.

Seedhouse, P. (2004). *The interactional architecture of the language classroom: A conversation analysis perspective.* Oxford: Blackwell Publishing.

Selting, M. (2000). The construction of units in conversational talk. *Language in Society, 29*(4), 477–517.

Sinclair, J., & Coulthard, M. (1975). *Towards an analysis of discourse.* Oxford: Oxford University Press.

Steensig, J. (2001). *Sprog i virkeligheden: Bidrag til en interaktionel lingvistik* [Language in reality: Contributions to an interactional linguistics]. Århus: Aarhus Universitetsforlag.

Suchman, L. A. (2007). *Human-machine reconfigurations: Plans and situated actions* (2nd ed.). Cambridge: Cambridge University Press.

Szymanski, M. H. (2003). Producing text through talk: Question-answering activity in classroom peer groups. *Linguistics and Education, 13*(4), 533–563.

7 Choral Practice Patterns in the Language Classrooms

Keiko Ikeda
Kansai University, Japan

Sungbae Ko
The University of New South Wales, Australia

Introduction

Within conversation analysis (CA) (e.g., Markee, 2000, Markee & Kasper, 2004), it has been pointed out that classroom interaction is composed of many subsets of talk that are not adequately described by the generic label "classroom talk." Other recent CA-based studies of classroom talk (e.g., He, 2004; Ko, 2005, 2009; Lazaraton, 2003; Mori, 2002, 2004; Seedhouse, 2004) have pointed out that just as many pedagogical focuses may exist as there are various shapes of talk beyond the well-recognized three-part pedagogical sequence (Initiation-Response-Follow-up [or Evaluation]; Mehan, 1979, Sinclair & Coulthard, 1975). Through classroom talk, the participants—both students and teachers—construct a complex, fluid interactional space (Seedhouse, 2004).

The primary purpose of this study is to build up a comprehensive notion of choral practices by exploring how they are activated in two different types of language classroom settings, that is, JFL (Japanese as a Foreign Language) and TESOL (Teaching English to Speakers of Other Languages) classrooms, by employing recent CA approaches and perspectives.

Choral practices

Previous studies

Schegloff (1995) refers to "choral talk" as sets of talk and activities which are treated by interactional co-participants as not to be done serially (one after another) but to be done *simultaneously*. Overlapping talk is, in general, seen as problematic; in other words, it is typically treated as a phenomenon to be resolved immediately upon occurrence in order to observe the "one party at a time" rule of conversation (Sacks, Schegloff, & Jefferson, 1978). However, particular situations call for simultaneous utterances. The literature recognizes that there are various activities in our everyday lives which are produced chorally, for instance, collective greetings and leave-takings or congratulations in response to an announcement of personal good news (e.g., Jefferson, 1979, Lerner, 1993; Schegloff, 1995, 2000).

Simultaneous talk (or choral talk) also is a recurrent feature of classroom talk-in-interaction. Lerner (1993, 1995, 2002) remarks that students' response patterns can be affected by the teacher's techniques of turn-allocation in his/her question-in-turn. After a teacher's question to more than two students, several students may self-select chorally, producing the same utterance(s) with other speakers, as shown in the following extract:

Lerner, 1993

```
1       Teacher:    How many chapters in the book?
2       Student B:  [((raises hand))
3       Student C:  [Ele[ven
4  ->   Class:         [Eleven ((mostly in unison))
```

A choral response is found in line 4. Students producing the choral talk are not building linguistically on prior students' turns (e.g., Student C in line 3) but are providing the linguistic form and pragmatic meaning at the same time.

For ESL (English as a Second Language) and EFL (English as a Foreign Language) classrooms, Ko (2005) examined what he called "multiple responses." One of the various patterns of multiple responses is produced in a choral mode (p. 129). In his study, he points out that choral responses requested by the teacher are a specific pedagogical technique and potential aid to language learning. That is, choral responses are presumably designed by teachers to reinforce the learning point by inducing all class members in the production of an utterance with a word or structure to be learnt or being learnt.

In this study, we will not only examine the students' simultaneous participation upon a cue produced by the teacher but also explore various types of choral productions, for example, a collaborative sentence construction together with the teacher. Such choral activities will be referred to as a "choral practice" (hereafter, CP) in this study.

CPs in second/foreign language classrooms have not been systematically investigated from a CA perspective, although the present study demonstrates that they are a pervasive practice in a number of different contexts and countries such as Australia, Japan, and Korea. As such, they deserve to be carefully analyzed to uncover some of the inherent features in language classroom settings.

Defining the choral practice
In this study, we define the CP observed in the language classroom as a collective activity in which more than one person talks at one time and where these speakers treat their production as properly simultaneous. Lerner (2002) remarks that, at times, participants are not aiming to produce a separate turn at talk but are aiming to simultaneously co-produce part or all of a turn constructional unit (TCU), more or less in unison with another participant (p. 226). Drawing upon his remark, we suggest that in the course of CPs co-participants simultaneously co-produce a TCU or TCU element(s) which can be projected from the TCU in progress. In the following sections, we delineate in detail how CPs are constructed and used.

Study

The data used in this study were collected from classrooms of Japanese and English as second/foreign languages. The Japanese data was drawn from approximately 40 hours of language classroom recording, either audio or video, from two different language classrooms for beginning students of Japanese, both taught in Toronto, Canada. One is a class for beginners held in a private language school; the other is an introductory university-level language course. Both courses ran for an entire school year. The teachers were both female and trained language teachers. The TESOL data (audio and video recordings) was drawn from a corpus of approximately 40 hours of different proficiency level Korean TESOL classes (from elementary to intermediate) collected in Australia and in Korea. In the corpus, 145 adult Korean students, seven Korean teachers (four male and three female), and seven native English-speaking teachers (one American, one Canadian, and three Australian men; one American and one Canadian women) participated.

In the following subsections, we first portray the general characteristics of CPs and then discuss three main types of CP patterns: *complete unison*, *shadowing*, and *echoing*. In the subsequent section, the focus will then shift to how participants collaboratively realize, engage in, and manage CPs in classroom talk-in-interaction.

Three types of choral practice patterns
Complete unison

The prototypical example of CPs is what we call *complete unison,* in which the class as a whole produces a new utterance simultaneously. There is no obvious delay from anyone among the students in the beginning of the production of the utterance. The flow of complete unison is performed by the whole class or a number of self-selecting students speaking for the class as a team (Lerner, 1993). It typically occurs after a teacher's question or other kind of elicitation. Let us consider the following two examples (Extract 1 [TESOL classroom] and Extract 2 [JFL classroom]).

Extract 1, TESOL: Taekwondo

```
1       KT:    can you give me one examp:le of martial arts?
2              (0.2)
3  ->   S1:    [Taekwondo
4  ->   S2:    [Taekwondo¿
5              (0.2)
6       KT:    yeah (.) that's Korean martial art
```

In this extract, the teacher's question (line 1) is initiated and targeted at all six students in the class. The absence of the insertion of a name in the question leads to the possibility for self-selection by any student. The two self-selecting students (S1 and S2) produce the same response simultaneously in lines 3 and 4. After this, the ratifying token *yeah* and a short further commenting turn *that's Korean martial art* are provided by the teacher in line 6.

A complete unison can also be a newly created utterance by the class. In Extract 2, the class composes the sentence *maiasa shinbun o yomimasu* [every morning I read a newspaper] without answering a teacher's question, even though the teacher does promote the production of a CP in various ways.

Extract 2, JFL: University

```
1       JT:    okay. Ja:a:! (.) maiasa:, .hh every morning,
                 so             every morning
               "Okay. So! Every morning,"

2              (0.5)

3  ->   SS:    [maiasa: (0.5)]
               Every morning

4       JT:    [maiasa: (0.5)]
               Every morning
```

```
5 ->   SS:    sh[inbun    o:   ]
              newspaper   O
              "Newspaper"

6      JT:    [>shinbun<  o]
              newspaper   O
              "Newspaper"

7      S1:    yomimasu=
              read
              "I read a newspaper every morning."

8 ->   SS:    =[°yomi° masu.
              read
              "I read a newspaper every morning."

9      JT:    =[yomimasu:
              read
              "I read a newspaper every morning."
```

The production of the target sentence is divided into three chunks, each made by a CP. We find the first CP in line 3 *maiasa* [every morning], the second in line 5 *shinbun o* [newspaper Object-marker], and finally the third in line 8 *yomimasu* [read]. The three choral productions together compose a full sentence, "I read a newspaper every morning." Each utterance is produced in a slow tempo, coordinating the rhythm together. This coordination is achieved by the way each word is enunciated. In lines 3 and 5, for example, we find a lengthening of the last vowel of the utterance, which indicates that the completion of a full production is still forthcoming. The participants can also monitor each other for their pace of speaking. In between the CPs, we observe that the instructor (JT) inserts her turns, either immediately after or simultaneously with each choral production. At each turn, JT repeats verbatim what the students said, acknowledging that the students' chorally produced turns are "on the right track."

Shadowing

When participants construct a CP, its production is not always in complete unison. A CP can also be produced through what we call shadowing. By shadowing, we refer to the case where a co-participant begins to repeat a prior speaker's utterance immediately after the prior speaker has produced one or two syllables of the utterance. In the end, such multiparty talk eventually generates a more or less unified CP.

The following extract provides an example of this. In Extract 3, the class is reviewing the expressions for dates, months, and years using an enlarged monthly calendar posted on the blackboard.

Extract 3, JFL: University

```
1    JT:   kongetsu      wa↓ nangatsu     desu ka?
           this month    TP  what month   CP   Q
           "What month is this month?"

2    S1:   juu:[ga:tsu: desu ]
           October        CP
           "It's October."

3 -> SS:        [juugatsu desu]
                 October   CP
                 "It's October."
```

In line 1, the teacher prompts the class by asking a display question, "What month is this month?" In line 2, we see that S1 starts to answer, pronouncing the first syllable of the word *juu* in *juugatsu* [October]. Immediately after the other students hear the beginning, they participate in the choral production of the whole sentence *juugatsu desu* [it's October] in line 3. Upon the other students' merger to the production, the speaker (S1) changes his articulation of *gatsu* [month] by inserting a vowel lengthening in *ga:* and *tsu:* to adjust the pace with the others. With this adjustment, S1's turn eventually merges into complete unison with the other students.

In Extract 4, the class is practicing to compose the sentence *mearii wa yojihan ni (kimasu)* [Mary comes at four thirty]. *Yojihan ni* [at four thirty] is a newly learned expression for the students at the time of the recording.

Extract 4, JFL: Language school

```
1    JT:   un=Mearii wa¿
           yes=Mary    TP
           "Yes Mary,"

2    S1:   uh:
           HES
           "Uhm"

3          (1.5)

4    S2:   yo=
           Four

5    S3:   =yo[ji::    ]
              Four o'clock
```

```
6       JT:     [yoji:,   ]
                Four o'clock

7       SS:     [(yoji:,)]
                Four o'clock

8 ->    JT:     yoji [han ni: ]
                four hour half at
                "At four thirty"

9 ->    SS:          [yoji han] ni:
                     four hour half at
                     "At four thirty"
```

In lines 8–9, we find shadowing between the teacher and students. To compose the phrase *yojihan ni* [at four thirty], S2 produces *yo* [four] in line 4, then S3 *yoji* [four o'clock] in line 5. JT and the class follow the S3's lead and produce *yoji* [four o'clock] together, constructing a CP. The intonation of the word *yoji* in the CP has a non-final rising intonation, which tells us that the speakers are still in the process of producing an utterance. In line 8, JT speaks first to produce the full form of the target expression *yojihan* [four thirty]. As soon as the previously chorally generated part *yoji* [four o'clock] is heard, the shadowing by the whole class takes place, chorally producing the full expression.

The following extract displays another case. The TESOL teacher's pedagogical purpose now is to get the students to produce a string of question forms beginning with "How many + X" and "How much + X."

Extract 5, TESOL: Hospital

```
1       ET:     y'genna a:sk her one more question?
2               (0.3)
3       S1:     [how m-
4       S2:     [(°come on°)
5               (0.4)
6       S1:     ho:w muchee::¿=
7       S2:     =°hih ↑hihhehh°  ·HHH
8               (0.2)
9       S1:     how much (0.2) how much:: (1.2)
10              ↑hos:↓p'tal is: the:re.
11              (0.7)
12      S2:     ↑how [↓ma:ny¿
13      ET:          [how-
14              (0.2)
15      ET:     [how- (    )-
16      S1:     [how man:y
17              (0.2)
18      ET:     ho:s:pitals; (.) [a:re the:re.
```

```
19      S1:                     [yeah
20              (0.4)
21      S2:         °are the[:re° ¿
22      S1:                [are th[ere
23  -> ET:                       [how many hos[pita:ls      [are there.
24  -> S2:                                      [h[ospitals [are there.
25  -> S1:                                         [hospitals [are there.
```

Here, before a CP is forthcoming (lines 24–25), there is an explicit correction by a fellow student and the teacher collaboratively. More specifically, when the nominated student, S1, produces two repairables in her response turn in lines 6–10, S2 initiates and carries out a next-turn other-repair which treats the first grammatical error, the incorrect form "how much" instead of "how many" (line 12). In line 18, the teacher also performs other-repair work *ho:s:pitals; (.) a:re the:re.* on another grammatical error in the original utterance (line 10: ↑hos:↓p'tal is: the:re.). In lines 16 and 21, S1 shows her acceptance of the next-turn other-repairs. Thereafter, the teacher produces the complete TCU (line 23), and the two students (lines 24–25) produce a CP by partially repeating the teacher talk (line 23).

In Extract 6, the shadowing appears in two places (lines 6–7 and 14–15). In this scene, everyone is now looking at the same exercise in the textbook. The task is to describe what the main character, Mary, does every day. In this particular example, they are describing at what time she wakes up in the morning.

Extract 6, JFL: Private school

```
1       JT:     Mearii san wa   nan   ji   ni okimasu ka?
                Mary    Ms. TP  what  hour at wake up  Q
                "What time does Mary wake up?"

2       S1:     °shichi° [ji    han
                seven    hour   half
                "Seven thirty"

3       JT/SS:           [°°shichi ji°° han=
                         seven    hour  half
                         "Seven thirty"

4       JT:     =so!=
                Right!

5       S2:     =°°shichi ji    han°°
                seven    hour   half
                "Seven thirty"

6   ->  JT:     go[zen:(.)
                Morning
```

```
7  -> SS:      [gozen    shichi ji   han:
                morning  seven  hour half
               "Seven thirty in the morning"

8     JT:      gozen    shichi ji   han:
               morning  seven  hour half
               "Seven thirty in the morning"

9     S1:      ni=
               At

10    JT:      =[ni!
                At

11    S3:      =[ni!
                At

12             (0.2)

13    S1:      o- kimasu.
               w- wake up
               "She wakes up."

14 -> JT:      °oki[masu.°
               wake up
               "she wakes up."

15 -> SS:          [°okimasu.°
                    wake up
                   "She wakes up."
```

The first case of shadowing appears immediately after the students produced the expression of time *shichiji han* [seven thirty]. This answer still lacks an indication of either morning or evening. JT, in line 6, initiates the repair *gozen* [morning]. As soon as the first syllable of this word *go* is pronounced, the students also engage in a repaired production *gozen shichijihan* [seven thirty in the morning]. In lines 9–15, S1 (in lines 2 and 9) and S3 (in line 11) speak in solo turns to produce the remainder of the target sentence. However, these individual responses do not terminate the construction of the target sentence. In line 14, JT produces the first two syllables of the verb *oki* in *okimasu* [wake up], then the remainder of the class performs shadowing in line 15.[1]

In the practice of shadowing, there is always a first speaker, and co-participants' collaborative production lags behind only a syllable or two from him or her. This may appear to violate the simultaneous nature of choral production; however, as the analysis above has shown, the collectivity in action is hearably and very carefully focused on by the participants. We can observe that the co-participants following the first speaker produce mostly in unison exactly what has not been yet said. In this sense, we regard the occurrence of shadowing as a kind of CP based on the high projectability of talk in pedagogical interactions.

Echoing

In the course of CPs, a speaker or multiple speakers may immediately repeat a prior turn partially or entirely. We call this pattern echoing. It resembles shadowing, and it also tends to result in choral talk. Determining an exact demarcation between shadowing and echoing is sometimes difficult, because overlaps of turns by the first and the following speakers commonly occur in both patterns.

In shadowing, the followers do not wait to hear a prior speaker's completion of the target expression. In contrast, during the occurrence of CPs in the form of echoing, the followers wait until the completion of a prior speaker's turn before they speak together. They then self-select to produce the same utterance(s) chorally as spoken by the prior speaker. To illustrate this, Extract 7 (TESOL classroom) and Extract 8 (JFL classroom) are provided below.

Extract 7, TESOL: The guy

```
1        KT:   do you remember the guy's name?
.
.              ((a few lines omitted))
.
17       KT:   a::nd (0.7) what abo:ut (.) his wife.
18             (0.9)
19       S1:   Helen?
20             (.)
21  ->   S2:   [Helen
22  ->   S3:   [Helen
23       KT:   [Helen (.) goo:d a:nd (0.7) there're
24             two daughters (0.5) oka:y
```

After the teacher has provided a question in line 1, it is incremented by the teacher's further question in line 17 *a::nd (0.7) what abo:ut (.) his wife..* In lines 19–22, three students provide the same response to the question. After S1 provides a response in line 19 *Helen?*, S2 (line 21) and S3 (line 22) echo the prior response produced by S1 with upward intonation in line 19 *Helen?*. The teacher then repeats the response *Helen* and offers the assessment *goo:d* and further information *a:nd there're two daughters* in lines 23–24.

In Extract 8, students are composing the sentence *erueru de teepu o kikimasu* [she listens to the tapes in the language laboratory room].

Extract 8, JFL: Language school

```
1      JT:   un  er[ueru de:, (.)]
             yes  L    L   LOC
             "Yes, at the Language Laboratory"

2      SS:          [erueru de:   ]
                     L    L   LOC
                    "At the Language Laboratory"

3      S1:   uh:
             HES
             "Uhm"

4      JT:   what- what she does?

5      S2:   bi- (.) bi

6      JT:   te[epu:       ]o:?
             tape           O
             "Tape"

7      SS:      [°teepu: o°]
                 tape   O
                 "Tape"

8 ->   S3:   kikimasu.
             listen
             "She listens"

9            (0.5)

10 ->  SS:   [kikimasu.
              listen
              "She listens"

11     JT:   [kikimasu. (.) teepu o kikimasu. (.) okay. (.) tsugi¿
              listen         tape  O listen                    next
              "Listen. She listens to the tape. Okay. Next."
```

In this extract, we find examples of echoing by the class in line 10, repeating *kikimasu* [listen] after S3's complete production in line 8. There is half a second pause between S3's turn and the CP. During the course of CP, JT also joins the students in the production of the verb *kikimasu* [listen] in line 11, and then she continues to recapitulate the full constituent *teepu o kikimasu* [she listens to the tape]. After a micro pause, JT ends this particular exercise by saying "okay" in English, and urges the students to move on to the next exercise.

In echoing, the first speaker provides the expected elements to complete the turn construction in a full form; however, we observe that their contribution can be treated as a sufficient move only after the teacher performs a closing move with an assessment or at least an acknowledgment token. Here, we learn that, as a type of CP, echoing can be considered as a didactic activity in the language classroom.

When the students echo a peer speaker in the class, echoing by the class is still in need of the teacher's feedback, whether it is the expected answer or not. We may find the teacher offering an assessment and/or further elicitation moves after the chorus. It is common that the first speaker's production is not treated as a legitimate completion of the exercise which has taken place. As seen in the extracts above, only after the occurrence of a CP does the particular activity meet its completion.

Interplay among different choral practices

Previously, we have observed three types of CP patterns: complete unison, shadowing, and echoing. As was mentioned earlier, however, the patterns of CP are not always distinguishable from each other. The following extract is an example of a CP occurring in shadowing and/or echoing mode in TESOL classroom talk-in-interaction.

Extract 9, TESOL: How often

```
1        KT:   I'm complaining about my electric bill
2              (0.7)
3        KT:   next question?
4              (0.4)
5   ->   S1:   how often[: do you complain[:
6   ->   S2:          [how often         [complain=
7        S1:   =about
8              (0.2)
9        S2:   abo:ut=
10       S1:   =it (.) about it
11             (0.3)
12       KT:   okay once aga:in?
13             (0.3)
14       SS:   how often do you complain about it
```

In lines 1–3, the teacher first introduces an answer form and then asks the students to produce a sentence as a follow-up question to that answer (i.e., "how often do you complain about it?," a *reordering the sentence* task given in their textbook). In this extract, the occurrence of shadowing and/or echoing provided by S2 in line 6 is interesting. In line 5, S1 attempts to construct a sentence, which is overlapped by S2 in line 6. In some respects, the verbatim repetition produced by S2 can be seen as instantiating two types of CP. Firstly, in terms of shadowing, S2 partially repeats S1's continuing utterance in line 6. S2 here attempts to re-produce key elements of S1's TCU without waiting to hear S1's completion of the target expression. In echoing, on the other hand, S2 waits until

S1 has produced the key elements of the target expression. In this respect, S2's utterance in line 6 displays both shadowing and echoing.

An illustration of how shadowing and echoing may occur concurrently is also found in the Japanese data. In Extract 8, in which we earlier discussed lines 8–10 as a case of echoing, we also observe two cases of shadowing in line 2 and line 7. The complete target sentence aimed at in this extract is *eru eru de teepu o kikimasu* [she listens to the tapes in the language laboratory room]. Up to *teepu o* [tape Object-marker] in line 7, the students are able to detect what to produce when they hear one syllable of the targeted word; however, to produce the verb *kikimasu* [listen], they lag behind for 0.5 seconds after S3 has first provided the expected form, resulting in a case of echoing. What we observe in this extract is that, regardless of the type of CP, the students orient to their production not as individuals but as a collective, that is, as a class.

Mechanism of choral practice

Thus far, we have portrayed the three patterns of CPs. To further investigate the organization of CPs, this section treats distributional phenomena commonly occurring in the course of the CP (i.e., how these collective actions are elicited.).

Question design and addressee allocation

One of the most relevant features which elicit a CP from the class is the turn design and addressee allocation of the teacher's questions. When a CP is on demand, the teacher projects his or her question without explicitly selecting a next speaker. When the teacher's turn does not specify an addressee, students treat themselves as an associated addressee (Lerner, 1993), that is, they respond to the question as a team. Let us illustrate this point with examples. In Extract 10, we can compare a case of shadowing (lines 3–4) with a case in which an individual student speaks (lines 5–6). The class is practicing with a classroom activity resource named "Mr. Hayashi's schedule" that has some memos written in it, and these memos indicate "what Mr. Hayashi is going to do in that week."

Extract 10, JFL: University class

```
1     JT:   >soo< desu ka:    (.) hai.  (0.2) ↑Hayashi
            so   CP   Q           ok          Hayashi

2           san wa (.) nijyuuyokka wa  hataraki<masu> ka:?
            Mr  Top    24th        TP  work           Q
            "Really? Okay, Mr Hayashi, does he work on the 24th?"

3     S1:   ii [e
            no
            "No"
```

```
4      Ss:     [>ii e< hatarakimasen.]
               no      work-neg
               "No he does not work."

5      JT:     [>ii e< hatarakimasen.] jaa   nan  desu ka:
               no      work-neg        then  what  CP   Q
               "No he does not work, then what is it?"

6  ->          ↓Hoorii san.
               Holly  Ms.
               "Ms. Holly."

7      S2(H):  e:: (.) deeto (.)  °ki:   ki: (.) kimasu°
               HES     date       come-  come-   come
               "Uh:: there's a date."
```

Let us first discuss the prompt for the shadowing. In lines 1–2, the teacher projects a question with a rising intonation, *hayashi san wa nijyuu yokka hatarakimasu ka?* [does Mr. Hayashi work on the 24th?]. Upon this question, S1 initiates to answer *iie* [no] and before completion of S1's turn, the rest of the class composes a CP (shadowing) *iie hatarakimasen* [no he does not work]. In line 5, we see that the teacher joins the students' shadowing, *iie hatarakimasen* [no, he does not work], then continues her turn *jaa nan desu ka* [then what is it]? This question, in comparison with the question which prompts a CP (lines 3–4), is produced differently. The volume is louder, and it has a falling intonation and a vowel lengthening at the end. In line 6, without any pause, she summons a specific student's name *Hoorii san* [Ms. Holly]. This prompts Holly to speak solo, and the rest of the class listens to her turn. The intonation-contour of the question in line 5 as well as the specific summoning of a single student is utilized to break out of the CP.

Extract 11 is another example. In this episode, we can observe more spontaneously emerging CPs. The teacher intercedes in an emerging CP and re-selects one student to speak. When the teacher wishes to avoid a CP, the teacher may allocate the next turn to a specific student to minimize the response turn (i.e., by eliciting a single response) as in the turn shown below.

Extract 11, TESOL: Not everybody

```
1       ET:    how was- what's intonation here
2              (1.0)
3       Ss:    I hoped you would come to me last night
4  ->   ET:    oh not everybody at once
5              (0.5)
6  ->   ET:    okay Ann (     )
7              (0.2)
8       S1:    yeah?=
9       ET:    =what's thee intonation here?
```

When a number of self-selecting students provide the same response at the same time in line 3, the teacher allocates a turn to S1 in line 4 in order to avoid a CP. Through this, the question and answer sequence is resumed between the teacher and a single student (S1).

These two extracts may indicate that a CP is heavily dependent upon the teacher's next speaker-selection techniques, but in fact, they usually exercise little control over the emergence of CP in our data set: Every student tends to have a potential opportunity to take the floor and produce multiple occasions of CP. In brief, the occurrence of CPs is made possible because the teacher normally allows students to self-select.

Explicit elicitation

In the practice of incidental complete unison, the teacher's question is not intended to sustain a conversation or to elicit new information, but rather to permit the teacher to pre-test the students' knowledge of what they have learned in the previous lesson. Furthermore, each question from the teacher does not permit a large number of possible answers but is likely to be designed to have only one or few acceptable answers. Such a *closed* question is an important factor in providing an incidental choral response. Extracts 1 and 3 are repeated below as Extracts 12 and 13, respectively, for illustration of this point.

Extract 12, TESOL: Taekwondo

```
1 ->   KT:   can you give me one examp:le of martial arts?
2            (0.2)
3      S1:   [Taekwondo
4      S2:   [Taekwondoと
```

Extract 13, JFL: University

```
1      JT:   kongetsu     wa    ↓nangatsu    desu ka?
             this month   TP    what month   CP   Q
             "What month is this month?"

2 ->   S1:   juu:[ga:tsu: desu ]
             October      CP
             "It's October."

3      SS:        [juugatsu desu]
                  October  CP
                  "It's October."
```

Asking the students for an example of Korean martial arts in Extract 12 and asking a display question "What month is this month?" in Extract 13 facilitate incidental choral responses by the students, as answers to both questions are relatively straighforward and predictable. The following extract shows that a CP may also be produced following a request by the teacher to review earlier utterances that the class already practiced.

Extract 14, TESOL: Dictionary

```
1        ET:    more vocabulary down here...
.
.               ((a few lines omitted))
.
7        ET:    dictionary
8               (0.2)
9        SS:    dictionary=
10       ET:    =English dictionary=
11       SS:    =English dictionary
12              (0.4)
13       ET:    ma'am do you have an English dictionary?
14              (0.6)
15       ET:    do you?
16              (0.2)
17       S1:    I- I have a dictionary in my house=
18       ET:    ='kay mmhm (0.2) in my house goo:d
19              or at home (0.4) at home (0.3)
20 ->           everybody. I have a dictionary at home
21              (.)
22 ->    SS:    I have a dictionary at home
```

In lines 1–11, the teacher draws the students' attention to the new word "dictionary" provided in their textbook before reading the vocabulary item and a possible combined form (i.e., English dictionary). Students provide CPs for each item (line 9: *dictionary*; line 11: *English dictionary*) even where the teacher does not directly request them to do so. Thereafter, the teacher provides a question using the word "English dictionary" with S2 in line 13 (*ma'am do you have an English dictionary?*). After an expansion of the question (line 15: *do you?*), S1 produces a response turn in line 17 *I- I have a dictionary in my house*, which is immediately followed by the teacher providing agreement, repetition, and assessment *kay mmhm (0.2) in my house goo:d,* and an alternative version *or at home (0.4) at home* in lines 18–20. The teacher then calls on all students to provide a CP (line 20: *everybody. I have a dictionary at home*) and all students speak together in line 22.

Code-switching

In the JFL classroom data, code-switching (from Japanese to students' common language, English) by the teacher in her orchestration for a CP was observed. Extract 15 (a repeat of Extract 2) is an illustration. The target sentence is *maiasa shinbun o yomimasu* [I read a newspaper every morning]. It is important to know that the adverb *maiasa* [every morning] must come at the beginning of the sentence.

Extract 15, JFL: University

```
1      JT:    okay. Ja:a:! (.) maiasa:, .hh every morning,
                              so         every morning
              "Okay. So! Every morning,"

2             (0.5)

3  ->  SS:    [maiasa: (0.5)]
               Every morning

4      JT:    [maiasa: (0.5)]
               Every morning

5  ->  SS:    sh[inbun    o:   ]
               newspaper  O
              "Newspaper"

6      JT:    [>shinbun<  o]
               newspaper  O
              "Newspaper"

7      S1:    yomimasu=
               read
              "I read a newspaper every morning."

8  ->  SS:    =[°yomi° masu.
                read
              "I read a newspaper every morning."

9      JT:    =[yomimasu:
                read
              "I read a newspaper every morning."

10            (0.5)

11 ->  JT:    if you don't read, (0.3)

12     SS:    yo[mimasen     ]
               read-NG
              "I don't read."

13     JT:    [>yomi<masen.]
               read-NG
              "I don't read."
```

In the turn by JT immediately prior to the complete unison which starts from line 3, we observe a case of code-switching from Japanese to English. JT provides the first word of the target sentence, *maiasa*, followed by its English equivalent "every morning," said with continuing intonation. Following this, we observe a CP in lines 3–5. Another instance of code-switching is found in line 11. Upon students' completion (and JT also joins the chorus) of the verb *yomimasu* [read], JT addresses the whole class in English "if you don't read," asking the students to produce the negative form of *yomimasu* [read] this time. After a short pause, the students provide the desired response *yomimasen* [do not read] in complete unison (line 12). What we observe in this example is how the teacher orchestrates the whole class by addressing them as a team, using code-switching as a resource to prompt a CP.

Nonverbal cues

Prompting for a CP can also be done by non-verbal cues. In Extract 16, lines 5 and 8 are the key turns. Up to line 3, the students and the teacher work on the expression *kongetsu* [this month], and now they have to move on to express the rest of the target phrase, that is, *kongetsu no nijyuu yokka* [24th of this month]. For a CP of this phrase, the teacher prompts the students non-verbally, by pointing to cue the production of the target words.

Extract 16, JFL: University class

```
1       S1:     kon[getsu
                this month
                "This month"

2       Ss:         [kongetsu
                this month
                "This month"

3       JT:         [kongetsu:: >°desu°<
                this month      CP
                "It's this month"

4       JT:     hai(.) kongetsu:
                okay   this month
                "Okay, this month"

5  ->           *(0.5) *((JT: 'bracket' gesture))

6       SS:     n[o:
                of
                "of"

7       JT:      [no
                of
                "of"

8  ->           *(0.5) *((JT: pointing to the date '24th'))
```

```
9    SS:    [nijuu  yokka
             twenty  fourth
             "Twenty  fourth"

10   JT:    [°nijuu  yokka°
             twenty  fourth
             "Twenty  fourth"
```

Prior to this example, the teacher had just finished reviewing the small components of a phrase *kongetsu* [this month] and *nijuu-yokka* [24th] and now the task is to compile them to produce "the 24th of this month" in Japanese. In order to combine two noun phrases, the genitive marker *no* [of] is required. We see in line 4 that JT says *hai* [okay], which is a disjunctive marker to project an upcoming transition to a new action. During the pause in line 5, the teacher makes a gesture with her right hand. The video captures the teacher's posture, with her left hand towards the calendar on the blackboard and right arm bent in front of her torso, making an upward open bracket-like figure with her thumb and index fingers. Upon seeing this gesture, the class detects what is to be produced next in the sentence, generating a chorus construction of *no* [of] in line 6. Immediately after the students begin producing the sound *n* in the genitive marker *no* [of], the teacher joins the chorus in line 7. Another means of gestural cueing is found in line 8: The teacher points again to the 24th of the month on the calendar on the blackboard, prompting non-verbally again for the next word. Expectedly, in line 9, the students produce in complete unison *nijyuu yokka* [24th]. The teacher also joins the chorus in a slightly lowered voice in line 10.

As this example shows, at times the teacher orchestrates CPs through non-verbal cues. The successful CPs (complete unison) of the target expressions (lines 6 and 9) tell us that the students are highly attentive and responsive to the teacher's non-verbal prompts, monitoring for an appropriate time for a CP.

Conclusion

In this study, we defined the CP observed in the language classroom as a collective activity in which more than one person talks at one time. To delineate how CPs are constructed and used, we portrayed the general characteristics of CPs and discussed three main types of CP patterns: complete unison, shadowing, and echoing. The focus then shifted to the mechanism of CP to analyze and consider how participants collaboratively realize, engage in, and manage CPs in classroom talk-in-interaction. We claimed that one of the most relevant features which elicit a CP from the class is the turn design and addressee allocation of the teacher's questions: The occurrence of CPs can be made possible because the teacher normally allows students to self-select. Prompting for a CP can also be done by explicit elicitation from the teacher: A CP can occur when a question from the teacher is likely to be designed to have only one or few acceptable answers. We also observed how the teacher orchestrates the whole class by addressing them as a team, using code-switching as a resource to prompt a CP. Finally, we showed that students are highly attentive and responsive to the teacher's non-verbal prompts, monitoring for an appropriate time for a CP.

CPs occur in the contingent development of social interactional architecture: Participants mutually orient to, and collaborate, in order to complete orderly and meaningful sequences. CPs reflect the intended pedagogical foci of the language classroom in which the teacher and students display attentiveness towards the "same" learning objects.

Although we have attempted to provide a close look at various features of CP throughout this study, there is still plenty of room for research in this area. Studying CPs is a new phenomenon for CA research on language classroom talk-in-interaction. Along with contributing to a deepening and broadening of empirical understanding of the CP, we would like to present some suggestions of areas for future research.

The first is a concern to further probe the question of where in the course of a language classroom activity CPs emerge and how they relate to other learning practices. Since this study examined adult beginners and early intermediate level TESOL and JFL classroom talk-in-interaction, we cannot claim that the CP is a plausible learning practice in all language classrooms.

Similar to the first concern, the sequential features of CPs may differ across languages, cultures and classrooms. Attitudes towards CPs may also vary or be similar depending on the cultural backgrounds of the participants and different teaching approaches, which would effect CPs' frequency and structure.

Acknowledgments

We sincerely thank our editors, Dr. Gabriele Pallotti, Dr. Johannes Wagner, and Dr. Gabriele Kasper for their astute critiques and constructive suggestions during the refinement process of this chapter.

Note

1   Lines 14 and 15 are spoken more softly than the first shadowing. This is perhaps related to the fact that S1 in line 13 already has spoken the target line once.

References

He, A. W. (2004). CA for SLA: Arguments from the Chinese language classroom. *The Modern Language Journal, 88*, 519–535.

Jefferson, G. (1979). A technique for inviting laughter and its subsequent acceptance/declination. In G. Psathas (Ed.), *Everyday language: Studies in ethnomethodology* (pp. 79–96). New York, NY: Irvington Publishers.

Ko, S. (2005). *Multiple-response sequences in adult Korean TESOL Classrooms* (Unpublished doctoral dissertation). University of New South Wales, Sydney, Australia.

Ko, S. (2009). Implicit and explicit disagreeing multiparty talk in classrooms. In H. Chen & K. Cruickshank (Eds.), *Making a difference: Challenges for applied linguistics*. (pp. 109–124). Newcastle: Cambridge Scholars Press.

Lazaraton, A. (2003). Incidental displays of cultural knowledge in the no-native-English-speaking teacher's classroom. *TESOL Quarterly, 37*, 213–245.

Lerner, G. (1993). Collectivities in action: Establishing the relevance of conjoined participation in conversation. *Text, 13*, 213–245.

Lerner, G. (1995). Turn design and the organization of participation in instructional activities. *Discourse Processes, 19*, 111–131.

Lerner, G. H. (2002). Turn-sharing: The choral co-production of talk-in-interaction. In C. E. Ford, B. A. Fox, & S. A. Thomson (Eds.), *The language of turn and sequence* (pp. 225–256). Oxford: Oxford University Press.

Markee, N. (2000). *Conversation analysis*. Mahwah, NJ: Lawrence Erlbaum.

Markee, N., & Kasper, G. (2004). Classroom talks: An introduction. *The Modern Language Journal, 88*, 491–500.

Mehan, H. (1979). *Learning lessons: The social organizations of classroom behavior.* Cambridge, MA: Harvard University Press.

Mori, J. (2002). Task design, plan, and development of talk-in-interaction: An analysis of a small group activity in a Japanese language classroom. *Applied Linguistics, 23*, 323–347.

Mori, J. (2004). Negotiating sequential Boundaries and learning opportunities: A case from a Japanese language classroom. *The Modern Language Journal, 88*, 536–550.

Sacks, H., Schegloff, E. A., & Jefferson, G. (1978). A simplest systematics for the organization of turn taking for conversation. In J. N. Schenkein (Ed.), *Studies in the organization of conversational interaction* (pp. 7–55). New York, NY: Academic Press.

Schegloff, E. A. (1995). Parties and talking together: Two ways in which numbers are significant for talk-in-interaction. In P. ten Have & G. Psathas (Eds.), *Situated order: Studies in the social organization of talk and embodied activities* (pp. 31–42). Washington, DC: University Press of America.

Schegloff, E. A. (2000). Overlapping talk and the organization of turn-taking for conversation. *Language in Society, 29*, 1–63.

Seedhouse, P. (2004). The interactional architecture of the language classroom: A conversation analysis perspective. *Language Learning, 54* (Supplement 1).

Sinclair, J., & Coulthard, M. (1975). *Towards an analysis of discourse: The English used by teachers and pupils.* London: Oxford University Press.

Appendix

Specific abbreviations used in the word-by-word translation

- CP   copula
- HES   hesitation marker
- IP   interactional particle
- LOC   locative
- NG   negative
- Nom   nominalizer ("that + clause")
- O   object marker
- Q   question marker
- QT   quotative particle
- S   subject marker
- TP   topic marker

Keys to identify who is speaking

All names in the present study have been fictionalized to ensure teachers' and students' anonymity.

- ET   native English speaking teacher
- JT   native Japanese speaking teacher
- KT   native Korean speaking teacher
- S1   identified student: "S1," "S2," etc. indicate an individual's turn order within an extract.
- S?   unidentified student
- Ss   subgroup of class
- SS   whole class

A symbol used for picture cues

*   An asterisk indicates simultaneous verbal and non-verbal actions.

8 Language Learning Activities in Real-Life Situations: Insisting on TCU Completion in Second Language Talk[1]

Guðrún Theodórsdóttir
University of Iceland

Introduction

The study reported here is part of a project which investigates second language learners' conversations outside of the classroom. The second language (SL) speakers' participation in different activities in the second language community may be relevant for their success as language learners. It is, however, unclear in what ways and to what degree second language speakers deploy activities in mundane talk that orient towards linguistic norms, forms, and correctness. Do they use specific practices or does this orientation simply emerge from their interactions with other speakers so that, as Firth and Wagner (2007) argue, language learning comes out of participation in second language interaction? More knowledge about learners' activities outside of the classroom is relevant for language teaching as well as for a better understanding of language learning practices, and is beneficial to the development of language learning/teaching material.

This chapter looks specifically at a practice where the second language speaker struggles for the floor and insists on completing a turn construction unit (TCU; Sacks, Schegloff, & Jefferson, 1974) while intervening talk by another speaker has made it clear that he or she has already been understood. This is shown in the following excerpt:

Excerpt 1, Fishing boat, fragment

```
01    An:   þ↑ú vinnur (0.4)
            y↑ou work   (0.4)
            you work
02    Ma:   ég er (.[hh)]
            I am  (.[hh)]
            I am
03    An:         [Á]fiskibát. bátur
                  [ON] a-fishing-boat. boat
                  on a fishing boat boat
```

In line 2, the co-participant enters the second language (SL) speaker's ongoing turn. As shown later in this chapter (cf. pp. 196–200), line 2 is a correction of Anna's candidate formulation in line 1—but Anna ignores the correction. She competes for the floor by overlap and increased volume and finishes, in line 3, the TCU she had begun in line 1.

I will refer to this practice as *insisting on TCU completion*, analyze it in its interactional details, and discuss it with regard to a general orientation towards language learning.

The chapter is organized as follows: A description of the data used in the study is followed by a presentation of an example of *insisting on TCU completion* in SL talk. This example will be analyzed in detail in order to describe what precisely is involved in this practice in terms of turn organization (Sacks, Schegloff, & Jefferson, 1974). It will be shown that this practice is embedded in environments where the SL speaker orients to features of the language being learned. Next is a discussion on more examples displaying some variations of the first one. These will be analyzed and matched against the first instance. This part of the chapter is followed by a discussion of the interactional significance of this practice with respect to a preference for progressivity (Stivers & Robinson, 2006). The final section of the chapter contains some concluding remarks.

Data

In order to study learners' activities outside of the classroom, a few foreign students at the University of Iceland were asked to make audio recordings of their daily life interactions on a regular basis. This method was first described by Brouwer and Nissen (2003). The data used in this study were taped by Anna, a Canadian student. She is a beginner of Icelandic who came to Iceland in the fall of 2005. Anna started recording herself after having been in Iceland for a month. When listening to her recordings, it turned out that she recorded both service encounters (e.g., in stores, offices, banks) and also private talk (e.g., dinner table conversation, talk while driving in a car).

Anna taped approximately half an hour of interaction a week for three years[2] in her daily life. The corpus of her audio recordings comprises 55 hours of talk. This study uses transcribed data from the first five months (approximately seven hours).

Insisting on completing one's TCU: A prototypical case

The sequential organization
In the next excerpt, we see an example where a SL speaker insists on finishing her TCU (lines 2–9). This is part and parcel of a rather intensive orientation to features of language in the talk.

When this conversation takes place, Anna has been in Iceland for two months. She is at a public office to pick up her monthly check (her grant). Prior to the excerpt, Anna had asked for the person (by name) in charge of the grant and was informed that this person was available. Anna might now have asked whether she can see her, but instead she raises the issue of the check and claims that this person sometimes leaves a check in a certain place at the front desk (cf. lines 2–9). This shift from asking for a person to referring to the check might indicate that Anna's business is not the person herself, but the grant. In that light, Anna's asking for the person in charge of the grant seems to be an attempt to indicate her business, rather than wanting to see the person. In other words, the clerk at the front desk has been given a clue to what Anna is doing there[3] and may be expected to pick up on it. The pause in line 1 may be indicative of Anna waiting for the clerk to act. When no such action is forthcoming, indicating that the clerk has not understood her, Anna makes another attempt to make herself understood:

Excerpt 2a, Grant

```
01              (0.9)
02     An:      uh:uh:m:: (.ts) (0.4) °uh° uh::: (0.2) uh
03              s (0.2) t uh:: stund↑um: .hh (0.3) h↑ún:
                s(0.2) t uh:: sometim↑es: .hh (0.3) sh↑e:
                sometimes she
04              (0.9) uh::: (0.9) leggja::: (.) affí- (0.2)
                (0.9) uh::: (0.9) put::: (.) che- (0.2)
                put che
05              ávís::::[:sun]
                che::::[:ck]
                check
```

```
06   C1:              [Ávís]un (.) já
                      [Che]ck (.) yes
                 check yes
07   An:    [uh::::::]
08   C1:    [þe-  j ]á ÞÁ ertu að sæ[kja]
            [the- y]es THEN are-you to pi[ck-up]
            The- yes then you are picking up
09   An:                              [HÉR]na. hérna.
                                      [HER]e. here.
            here here
10   C1:    þá ertu að sækja styrkinn þinn.
            then are-you to pick-up grant-the your.
            Then you are picking up your grant
```

Anna starts her turn with a long stretch of hesitation markers interspersed with pauses (line 2), before uttering *s* and then *t* after a short pause, but she abandons this attempt and produces another hesitation marker. Then she utters *stundum* [sometimes] (line 3), which she possibly started to produce in the first segments of this line. Following an in-breath and a short pause, Anna refers with *hún* [she] with rising pitch to the person who normally handles the grant. After stalling for nearly 2 seconds, she produces *leggja* [put] stretching the final vowel (line 4). This might indicate trouble in finding the proper next element in her TCU (word search). After a micro pause, Anna utters *affí-*, and then, following a short pause, she repairs the pronunciation to *avís:::::sun* [check] (Hutchby & Wooffitt, 1998, p. 64). The stretched *s* in *avís:::::sun* can be heard as an indication that Anna still has trouble with the word: She has abandoned and then repaired an earlier version of it. The initial trouble may have been in the pronunciation, since that is what she repaired. The stretching of the *s*, however, may have something to do with the form of the word, more specifically the part of the word still to come. During the stretching of the *s* and the possible search for the form of the word, the clerk overlaps Anna, treating what she is doing as a possible search for the relevant form of the word, and offers the correct form of the word *ávísun* [check], which Anna actually produces herself in the overlap.

At the start of the turn, Anna was at pains to keep her turn with hesitation markers and pauses without actually starting it. When she has managed to produce *Stundum hún leggja avís:::* [sometimes she put che:::] (lines 2–5), the clerk takes the turn. Anna's TCU is not finished; she has not yet arrived at a transition relevance place (TRP; Sacks, Schegloff, & Jefferson, 1974), but it is quite clear what she is going to say. She has arrived at a recognition point, that is, the point of a TCU where its trajectory is understood although it has not been completed. At precisely this point, the clerk responds to the possible word search (*ávísun*), which is a repaired version of the trouble word, confirms with *já*, and possibly closes the topic of the trouble word.[4]

Now both speakers move on. Anna produces a hesitation marker in overlap indicating that she is keeping her turn (line 7), and the clerk starts with Þe- (line 8), which he abandons. Then he produces a second *já* [yes] and restarts his turn. The raised volume of the word Þe [THEN] can be heard as the clerk claiming his turn. The clerk's: *ÞÁ ertu að sækja* [THEN you are picking up] (line 8) provides a candidate understanding of Anna's action. In terms of intersubjectivity, Anna's turn has been understood before the TCU has been finished completely. In Jefferson's (1984) words, "a recipient/next speaker seems to be orienting, not so much to completeness as to <u>adequacy</u>" (p. 2). The clerk's action is designed to move the interaction forward: His action of formulating Anna's business is the next relevant action following her talk and would, if accepted by Anna, discontinue her troubled turn, and speed up the interaction.

During the delivery of the word *sækja* [pick up], Anna overlaps the clerk's talk with the projected final element of the TCU she started in line 2: *hérna* [here]. The raised volume of *HÉRna* [HERe] suggests that Anna is insisting on completing her TCU and treating the clerk's contribution as an interruption. Once out of the overlap, Anna repeats the word *hérna* [here] in normal volume. The clerk abandons his talk and lets Anna finish. At this point in the conversation, Anna has finished her TCU, *stundum hún leggja ávísun hérna* [sometimes she puts the check here], but the final element in the clerk's TCU, *þá ertu að sækja* [then you are picking up], is still pending. In line 10, the clerk restarts for the third time and finally manages to finish his TCU, *þá ertu að sækja styrkinn þinn* [then you are picking up your grant].

In this segment, Anna, in line 9, is not responding to the preceding talk by the clerk, and the clerk, in line 10, is not responding to Anna's intervening talk. Both ignore the other speaker's talk and proceed with their own.

Interestingly, Anna never states her business, *I am here to pick up a check for my grant,* in the conversation. Instead, what she has uttered can be seen as clues to the nature of her business: She names the person in charge of the grant, and then she claims that this person sometimes leaves a check at the front desk. Furthermore, her hesitant and troubled turn may be indicative of her identity as a foreign student coming for her grant. The format of Anna's talk can be seen as inviting the clerk to formulate what her business is, and that is exactly what the clerk does. He is able to infer her business and to formulate it: *þá ertu að sækja styrkinn þinn* [then you are picking up your grant] (line 10). The clerk's turn-initial use of the word *þá* [then] supports this, as this word is often seen in *if-then* formulations (Jefferson, 1986), although in this case there is no *if*-part. The linguistic resources that Anna has delivered together with the context of the talk may, in other words, be seen as clues for the clerk to infer her business. This is indicated by the clerk's *then*, which treats Anna's talk as the *if*-part.

To conclude my observations thus far, in the excerpt, Anna managed to utter a complete phrase in Icelandic: *stundum hún leggja ávísun hérna* [sometimes she puts the check here]. She put great effort into producing every little detail of her TCU including the final part *hérna* [here], which seems somewhat unnecessary for the ongoing interaction, since the clerk had already displayed an understanding of her business. Anna, when pursuing her turn, indicates that she is not only picking up the check but orienting as well to features of the language.

Anna's TCU (seen in lines 2–9) is obviously a struggle for her: There are hesitation, several pauses, a search for a form of a word, and the pace is very slow. But it also seems to be a struggle with her co-participant for the right to talk. Anna's hesitation marker in line 7 is in overlap with the beginning of the clerk's further talk, and later Anna is overlapping the clerk's talk with the projected final element of her TCU.

In Excerpt 2a, we saw a pattern, insisting on TCU completion, that can be described as follows:
1. Anna produces a slow and hesitant turn.
2. When the other participant recognizes what Anna is doing, but not at a TRP, he starts to speak. He enters her turn by assisting her and then keeps the turn. His actions are designed to move the interaction forward.
3. Anna overlaps the incoming speaker, ignores his contribution, and insists on completing the TCU herself. A speaker has a right to utter one TCU (Sacks, Schegloff, & Jefferson, 1974), and Anna has now exercised that right.

In more general terms, we can see that Anna is very persistent in speaking Icelandic in a situation where the communication has real-life consequences; she is picking up the check to support herself for the next month. Even when lacking necessary vocabulary (i.e., the Icelandic word for "grant"), Anna sticks to speaking Icelandic, using the linguistic resources available to her to complete the TCU successfully. Anna is a native speaker of English and could have switched to English at any time during the interaction, which would have enabled her to complete her business quickly and safely. The Icelandic clerk would not have had any problem understanding English.[5] Furthermore, when faced with a candidate understanding of her business, she ignores it in order to complete her TCU. That is not necessary for the business since intersubjectivity had already been established. Obviously, she is doing more than picking up her check: She is also orienting to learning and using her new language.

Attending to some linguistic resources extracted from the preceding topical interaction

In the talk after Excerpt 2a, we see the participants attending to the language, more specifically to some linguistic resources used in lines 2–10 (Excerpt 2a).

I will discuss the talk following Excerpt 2a to demonstrate that Anna's insisting on TCU completion feeds into a longer interaction about features of language.

It turns out that Anna does not know the word *styrkinn* [grant]—a keyword in her business—which the clerk uses in line 10. This may explain the trouble in the beginning of her turn in lines 2–4; lacking the word for "grant," she was unable to state her business in the simplest way, "I'm here for my grant."

Excerpt 2b, Grant

```
10      C1:     þá ertu að sækja styrkinn þinn.
                then are-you to pick-up grant-the your.
                Then you are picking up your grant
11              (0.4)
12      AN:     uh:
13      C1:     (það) heitir styrkur.
                (it) is-named a-grant.
                It is called a grant.
14      AN:     styrkur [uh] hvað (0.5)
                grant        what
                Grant what
15      C1:             [já]
                        [yes]
                        yes
16      C1:     það er [það er s-]
                it is  [it is g-]
                It is it is a g-
17      AN:     >what does that mean<
18              (0.3)
19      AN:     (.hn)
20      C2:     >scholarship<
21              (0.3)
```

Anna is expected to act on the clerk's candidate formulation of her business (seen in line 10), but instead she hesitates, indicating trouble, which the clerk in line 13 apparently analyzes as a problem with the Icelandic word for grant. The clerk takes the word out of the context and introduces its base form (nominative singular): *það heitir styrkur* [it is called a grant]. The clerk confirms Anna's repeat (lines 14–15), but there is further trouble. In line 14, Anna starts a question with *hvað* [what]. The clerk makes two attempts at responding to Anna's unfinished question (line 16): *það er- það er s-*[it is- it is g-]. In line 17, we see what the problem is: Anna does not understand the meaning of the word, and she switches to English overlapping the clerk's response and asks for the meaning. The English translation comes from another clerk: *scholarship* (line 20).

Excerpt 2c, Grant

```
22     AN:    Aah JÁ JÁ styr- uh:uh s[:]
                  YES YES gran-        g[:]
                  Yes yes gran
23     C1:                             [s]tyrkur
                                       [g]rant
                                       Grant
24     AN:    styrkur
              grant
25     C1:    já
              yes
26     AN:    já já
              yes yes
27            (0.4)
28     C1:    do you have i dee.
29     AN:    jáh
              yesh
              yes
30     C1:    skírteini.
              id.
              ID
31            (0.5)
32     AN:    °skírteini já°
              °id yes°
              ID yes
33            (0.2)
```

Anna confirms and makes two rather hesitant attempts to say the word *styrkur* [grant] (line 22). The clerk overlaps her, assisting with the word, which Anna then repeats (lines 23–24). After confirmation from both participants, the clerk returns to the institutional business of delivering the check to Anna, and asks her in English whether she has her ID (line 28). This request for Anna's ID is formulated as a yes/no question; Anna is now expected to show her ID. Instead, she responds with *já* [yes], which can be a preface to her presenting her ID; she may have to look for it, and the *já* [yes] may serve as preannouncement of the presentation of the ID. Interestingly, Anna responds in Icelandic to the clerk's question, which is in English. This may be significant, not to the business at hand, but to the choice of language in which this business is conducted. Anna's response may be seen as an other-initiation of repair; they have been speaking Icelandic during most of the conversation, and Anna has made her identity as a language learner relevant. The clerk may thus be abandoning the "activity" of speaking Icelandic when he asks for her ID in English. This being the case, the next relevant action, following Anna's initiation of repair, is for the clerk to return to speaking Icelandic, which is precisely what he does in line 30 when offering the Icelandic word for ID, *skírteini*, as an other-initiated self-repair of line 28. Further support for this analysis comes from Anna's uptake of the word (line 32), which shows her continuing to orient to the language.

These findings are in agreement with Kurhila's (2004, p. 67) report that in institutional interaction between native speakers and non-native speakers in Finnish, the native speakers may focus on institutional aspects while the non-native speakers attend to the language.

Excerpt 2d, Grant

```
34     AN:    .h (0.8) uh is that the right word uh m .hh
35            orð (.h)(0.2) e:r (0.3) ávísun
              word            i:s       check
              word is check
36     C1:    ávísun já
              check yes
37            (0.4) (.h)
38     AN:    ávísun (.h) uh:[m:      ]
              check
39     C1:                   [that's a]check
40     AN:    já (.h)
              yes (.h)
              yes
41     C1:    °(já)°
              °(yes)°
              yes
```

In lines 34–35, Anna struggles to ask in Icelandic and English whether *ávísun* [check] is the right word to use. The clerk confirms (line 36) with a repeat of the target word. Anna's question regarding the usage of the word *ávísun* goes back to lines 4–6 (Excerpt 2a) where both participants attended to the pronunciation as well as to the form of the word. Apparently there were still problems regarding the word (when the clerk possibly closed the topic in Excerpt 2a, line 6, cf. endnote 4), as Anna's hesitation marker in line 7 (Excerpt 2a) indicates. Anna is thus reorienting to the topic of attending to the word *ávísun* in lines 34–38. In line 36, the clerk confirms the appropriate usage by repeating the word followed by a *yes* token, which can possibly function as a closing of the sequence regarding this word (cf. endnote 4). Anna, however, still has problems with this word, as can be seen in line 38. The clerk analyzes Anna's problem as having to do with the meaning of the word and explains it in English (line 39). Confirmations from both participants in lines 40–41 indicate that this problem now is solved.

Excerpt 2e, Grant

```
42    AN:   uh: (0.2)
43    C1:   scholarship that's a styrkur
                                grant
44          (1.1)
45    C1:   styrkur
            grant
46    AN:   Styrkur
            grant
47    C1:   °(já)°
            °(yes)°
            yes
48          (0.2)
49    AN:   ávísun (0.2) fyrir styrkur?
            a-check        for a-grant?
            A check for a grant
50    C1:   já
            yes
51    AN:   já (·h)
            yes
            yes
```

Excerpt 2e is the final stage in a series of operations on features of the target language; the participants have worked on aspects of pronunciation, morphology, appropriate usage, and finally the formulation of an utterance containing both words (line 49). This final stage relates to the beginning of the interaction as Anna has now managed, with help from the clerk, to get the necessary linguistic information to form the utterance she has been searching for to conduct her business in the simplest way (line 49),[6] after having taken care of that business without these resources (lines 2–9, Excerpt 2a). When scanning over this conversation, it is remarkable to see how focused and determined Anna is in reaching her goal, with regards to her business as well as the language.

The activities we have seen so far appear to have a certain sequential organization. An example of this sequence is in lines 22–26 (Excerpt 2c). In line 22, Anna tries to utter the word *styrkur* [grant] that both participants have been working on. She manages to utter *styr-* before cutting herself off. Then she utters hesitation markers before trying to say the word again. This is a clear indication of trouble to which the clerk responds with *styrkur* (line 23). The third action in the sequence is the response by Anna, who repeats the target word in line 24. Finally both participants confirm with *já* (lines 25 and 26).

In several instances, it is Anna who initiates these activities[7] by posing questions regarding the language (cf. lines 14, 17 [Excerpt 2b], line 34 [Excerpt 2d], line 49 [Excerpt 2e]), or indicating trouble as we saw in the example above (cf. line 12 [Excerpt 2b], line 38 [Excerpt 2d], line 42 [Excerpt 2e]). In this way, she appears as a language learner. The clerk participates as a reluctant language expert. He does not initiate linguistic assistance, and his participation is limited to responding to Anna's trouble indications. Furthermore, his responses are minimal: He offers the information asked for but nothing more. This we saw in lines 22–26 (Excerpt 2c).[8]

Summing this up in terms of second language (SL) and first language (FL) speakers, we can say that in cases like the one analyzed here, the SL speaker is responsible for the orientation towards features of language while the FL speaker responds. The first two contributions in these sequences are a prompt by the SL speaker and a minimal response from the FL speaker. The third part is an uptake/reaction from the SL speaker.

In lines 43–47 (Excerpt 2e), we can see that such an uptake/response from the SL speaker is expected: When the clerk (line 43) responds to Anna's indication of trouble (line 42) by offering the translation/meaning of the word *styrkur, scholarship that's a styrkur*, the next relevant action is for Anna to respond. The pause of one second in line 44 may be the clerk waiting for her response, but when no action is forthcoming, the clerk repeats the word *styrkur*, which is then repeated by Anna (lines 45–46). Finally, the clerk confirms: *já*.

The sequential organization of the language orienting activity seen in the excerpt can thus be described as follows:

Prompt by the SL speaker
Response (minimal) from the FL speaker
Uptake/response from the SL speaker
Confirmation from the FL speaker (and the SL speaker)

In the target practice and in the talk following it, we see the participants attending to the language rather intensely. They locally negotiate the identities of a language learner and a language expert and focus on some linguistic aspects of the talk in the preceding business interaction. These activities are initiated and driven by Anna (the language learner), while the participation of the clerk (the language expert) is limited to responding minimally to signs of trouble or questions about the language.

In the next section, we will look at some more examples in which Anna insists on finishing her TCU.

Further cases

The corpus for this chapter is a collection of 15 instances in which the SL speaker insists on completing her TCU in much the same way as shown in Excerpt 2. This section examines two more instances of this practice. Excerpts 3–4 are variations of Excerpt 2, especially with regard to the incoming speakers' actions, and may contribute to a more general description and a better understanding of the practice. We will also see how the practice of insisting on TCU completion is embedded in activities which orient to features of language.

Fishing boat

At the time of this conversation, Anna has been in Iceland for 2 months. She is talking to a new acquaintance, a man who offered to drive her to a distant post office to pick up a parcel. In the part of the conversation seen in lines 1–19 (Excerpt 3a), they are walking to his car, and in the part seen in lines 24–49 (Excerpts 3b and 3c), they are in the man's car.[9] The conversation revolves around the man's occupation.

The target practice can be observed in lines 40–42 (Excerpt 3c) when the next speaker delivers a correction to Anna's candidate formulation. Anna ignores him and insists on completing her own TCU. Before I proceed any further with an analysis of the target lines, I want to discuss the preceding talk to show how the target activity is embedded in some interesting language-oriented activities.

Language orientation embedded in the topical interaction

Prior to Excerpt 3a, the man and Anna discussed her occupation, and in line 1 she asks the man about his work.

Excerpt 3a, Fishing boat

```
01      AN:     UH::M: (0.3) en þú↑ hva- uh hvað gerir þú?
                                but you↑ wha-    what do you?
                What about you wha- what do you do
02      MA:     ég uh uhuh (0.7) ég er ↑útgerðarm↓aður
                I                I am a-f↑ishing-boat-↓owner
                I I am a fishing boat owner
03              (0.3)
04      MA:     ég á sv↑ona b↑áta
                I own k↑ind-of b↑oats
                I own kind of boats
                ((car sound))
05              (0.4)
06      ?:      (þessi hérna)
                (this-one here)
                 This one here
07              (0.9)
08      AN:     ↑AH t- t↓[ú:]
                         y- y↓[ou:]
                 y- you
09      MA:            [fi-] fiskibáta.
                       [fi-] fishing-boats.
                Fi fishing boats.
```

```
10              (0.4)
11      An:     F↑ISK↓IB↑ÁT↑A
                F↑ISH↓ING-B↑OAT↑S
                Fishing boats
12      Ma:     (h)já (h) ha ha [ha]
                (h)yes(h)  ha ha [ha]
                Yes
13      An:                     [J↑Á]
                                [Y↑ES]
                Yes
14              (0.5)
15      An:     UH:[:uh           ]
16      Ma:        [fishing-boa]ts
17              (0.9)
18      Ma:     fishing-boat (.) fiski>bát↓ur<=
                fishing-boat (.) fishing>boa↓t<=
                Fishing boat fishing boat.
19              =I am on this one.
```

In his response to Anna's hesitantly formulated question, the man starts his TCU with *ég* [I] and then stops talking. Hesitation markers and a rather long pause indicate possible trouble with the upcoming item. After the pause, the man resumes his TCU and finishes it: *ég er útgerðarmaður* [I am a fishing boat owner]. The man's turn beginning is surprisingly troubled given that the information asked for (what do you do for a living?[10]) is straightforward and should be readily available. The possible trouble might be that the man—having heard Anna's hesitant speech—does not expect her to know the word *útgerðarmaður*.

No response from Anna is forthcoming and, after a pause of half a second, the man goes on to explain what is involved in being *útgerðarmaður* [a fishing boat owner]: *ég á svona báta* [I own a kind of boat].

In line 8,[11] Anna utters *ah t- tú*, which is possibly a version of *þú* [you], but she is interrupted by the man's turn *fi- fiskibáta* [fi- fishing boats], which can be heard as a specification of a previously mentioned item (boats) in line 4. Anna's repeat of the word is try-marked with rising pitch and she receives a confirming response from her co-participant (line 12). However, the man does not seem to be convinced that Anna has understood him and offers the English translation, *fishing boats* (line 16), indicating that he analyzed Anna's trouble (line 15) as having to do with understanding the word *fiskibáta* [fishing boats]. When Anna is not responding, he repeats the translation after a pause of almost a second (line 18). Then he goes back to the Icelandic word *fiskibátur* [fishing boat] now as the base form of the word, the nominative singular, which is different from the accusative plural form he had started off with (cf. line 9).

Let us briefly summarize the operations that have been done on the word *fiskibáta* [fishing boats], which has now changed into *fiskibátur* [a fishing boat]. The FL speaker has (a) isolated the word from its grammatical environment, and

(b) presented it in its base form. Through the intervening talk the item has been isolated from the preceding talk (Brouwer, 2004), and (c) is offered as a lexical item to Anna.

These operations move the interaction from topical talk (what do you do for a living?) to talk about features of the language.

Excerpt 3b, Fishing boat

```
24              (7.3) ((car engine sound, traffic,
                slamming sound))
25      MA:     .h (slamming sound) I run this (2.5)
                ((sound of paper flipping)) can show you
                a picture of my boat. I thin(k)(3.5)
                ((sound of  paper wrappings)) no.
26              (3.9)
27      MA:     (I) own this boat. .hh he he he [he     ]
28      AN:                                     [°a:ah°]
29              (0.4)
30      MA:     yes
31              (1.3) ((sound of keys))
32      AN:     <fi[s]kib↑átur>=
                <fi[s]hing-b↑oat>
                Fishing boat
33      MA:        [( )]
34      MA:     =fiskibátur
                =fishing-boat
                Fishing boat
35      AN:     >fiskibátu[r]<
                >fishing-boa[t]<
                Fishing boat
36      MA:               [fi]shing-boat
37              (0.2)
38      AN:     °fiskibátur°=
                °fishing-boat°=
                Fishing boat
39      MA:     =fiskibátur
                =fishing-boat
                Fishing boat
```

After having switched to English, the man searches for a picture of his boat and shows it to Anna with the words *I own this boat* (line 27). Anna recognizes it with the word *fiskibátur* [fishing boat] (line 32). This looks very much like a traditional language learning activity: See the picture, say the word. Here she is orienting to two activities, naming the item in the photo as well as attending to the language; her slow delivery of the word may indicate that she is attending to its precise pronunciation. In lines 32–39, both participants engage in practicing the placement of the stress in the word. This activity takes place in a side sequence while other matters are put on hold as described by Brouwer (2004). As we will see in Excerpt 3c, line 40, Anna abandons this activity of attending to the pronunciation and moves on to do other things.

So far we have seen how the participants try to reach intersubjectivity regarding the man's work and his relationship to the fishing boat. But at the same time, they attend to linguistic matters, that is, the pronunciation of the word *fiskibátur*, its morphology, meaning, and syntax. These activities are integrated parts of the on-going interaction.

Insisting on TCU completion

Excerpt 3c, Fishing boat

```
40    An:    þ↑ú vinnur (0.4)
             y↑ou work
             you work
41    Ma:    ég er (.[hh)]
             I am
             I am
42    An:            [Á] fiskibát. b[átur]
                    [ON] a-fishing-boat. b[oat]
                     on a fishing boat boat
43    Ma:                            [NEI]
                                     [NO]
             No
44           ég er útgerðarmaður.
             I am a-fishing-boat-owner.
             I am a fishing boat owner.
45           útgerðarmaður,
             a-fishing-boat-owner,
             A fishing boat owner
46           (0.5) is the guy that's works (0.6)
47           in u:h on land.
```

In the context of the extensive "work" on the word *fiskibátur* [fishing boat] (cf. Excerpt 3b), Anna's utterance in line 40, *þú vinnur* [you work], can be heard as a beginning of a suggestion that the man works on a fishing boat. Previously, Anna apparently did not understand the man's explanation of his work (cf. Excerpt 3a, line 2) and may here be making a candidate formulation of what he does for a living and/or what his relationship to the fishing boat is.

The man moves into her ongoing TCU uttering *ég er* [I am] (line 41), thereby showing an understanding of Anna's unfinished turn (seen in line 40). He reformulates Anna's still incomplete TCU *þú vinnur* [you work] with *ég er* [I am], which can be seen as the beginning of the man's explanation of his relationship to the fishing boat.

In line 42, Anna ignores the man's intervening talk with the utterance *Á fiskibát bátur* [ON a fishing boat boat]. The raised volume of *Á* [ON] indicates that she is actually competing for the floor. Anna's insisting on finishing her TCU allows her to utter a complete phrase in Icelandic, *þú vinnur á fiskibát* [you work on a fishing boat]. If Anna had let the man finish, her ongoing TCU would have been discontinued: The part of her TCU in line 42, *á fiskibát* [on a fishing boat], would have been irrelevant. In Anna's self-repair (line 42), we see yet another instance of orientation to the language: Anna is attending to the morphology of the word with her repair, changing *bát* to *bátur* (from accusative to nominative). Interestingly, with her repair, she produces the form presented by the man earlier in the conversation (cf. Excerpt 3a, line 18): She is now using the (form of the) word they have been attending to, in a complete TCU[12] Anna has, in other words, again "insisted on TCU completion," allowing her to produce *þú vinnur á fiskibát* as opposed to the shorter *þú vinnur* after which the co-participant intervened in Anna's talk.

In line 43, the man utters *NEI* [NO] with raised volume as a response to Anna's statement *þú vinnur á fiskibát* [you work on a fishing boat] (lines 40 and 42). Then, in normal volume, he explains his relationship to the fishing boat: *ég er útgerðarmaður* [I am a fishing boat owner]. This can be seen as restart of the utterance *ég er* [I am] in line 41. Then he repeats *útgerðarmaður* [a fishing boat owner], and after a pause of half a second, he switches to English and explains what a fishing boat owner does: *útgerðarmaður* [a fishing boat owner] *is the guy that works on land*. It is worth noting that when the man explained this word previously (cf. Excerpt 3a, line 2), he did it in Icelandic, whereas now he does his explaining in English, indicating that his focus has shifted from the language to the topic of the talk, his work.

Throughout the conversation, we saw the participants work on reaching mutual understanding regarding the man's occupation. At the same time they engaged in another activity, intense orientation to the language, where the man and Anna adopted the roles of a language expert and a language learner respectively. Their dedication to this task and the effort they make is quite striking.

If we compare the two instances of *insisting on TCU completion* in Excerpts 2a and 3c, we see the incoming speakers in both cases responding to potential trouble in Anna's unfinished TCU. Their actions, however, are different. In Excerpt 2, the clerk attends to trouble (with the word *ávísun* [check]) in Anna's TCU. He delivers the correct form of the word *ávísun* and then attempts to take over the turn. In Excerpt 3, we can see in the incoming speaker's action that the trouble he sees in Anna's TCU has to do with her understanding of the previous talk, more precisely the relationship of the man and the fishing boat (cf. lines 2–4 [Excerpt 3a], line 27 [Excerpt 3b]). He offers a reformulation of her

TCU and appears to be attempting to take over her turn, but he only manages to deliver the first part of his TCU before Anna cuts him off. In both cases, the next speakers' attempts to take over Anna's turn are defeated by her insisting on finishing her TCU.

Post office
In the next excerpt, Anna is in a post office to pick up a parcel, but it turns out it has been sent to another post office in town by mistake. Prior to Excerpt 4, the clerk and Anna have been discussing how Anna can obtain her parcel. Anna asked the clerk if the postal service could deliver the parcel to her home. The clerk informed her that they could not. In the excerpt, they are working on a solution, and Anna suggests that she come back later to pick it up.

Excerpt 4, Post office

```
01      An:     uh:m:   (1.7)   uh:::   (4.7)   ég get:   (,)
                uh:m:   (1.7)   uh:::   (4.7)   I can:    (.)
                I can
02              (.ts::)  (1.0)  uh:uh:  (3.6)   kom:   (0.3)
                (.ts::)  (1.0)  uh:uh:  (3.6)   com:   (0.3)
                com
03      Cl:     komið af[tur hérna] já:
                come ba[ck here] ye:s
                Come back here yes
04      An:             [herna?]
                        [here?]
                        here
05              uh:::   (0.7)   á morgun,
                uh:::   (0.7)   tomorrow,
                tomorrow
```

In Excerpt 4, Anna utters hesitation markers and makes long pauses before starting her actual TCU as can be seen in line 1. There is even more trouble in this turn beginning than the one we saw in Excerpt 2a; the pauses are longer and there are extensive hesitations. Following these displays of trouble in the turn beginning, Anna utters *ég get* [I can], and after stalling for nearly 5 seconds, she utters **kom:* [com]. The stretching at the end the word **kom:* [com] may indicate that Anna is having trouble finishing the word (similar to what we saw in the word *ávísun* [check] in Excerpt 2a). Now she has uttered (simplified) *ég get *kom* [I can *come]. Anna is not at a transition relevance place (TRP), but in this context of picking up a parcel her turn so far suffices to makes it clear that she is going to say that she can come back to the post office to pick up the parcel.

In line 3, we see the clerk move into Anna's ongoing TCU repairing the form of the verb *kom* [*come] to *komið* [come] and offering a candidate completion to Anna's TCU with his utterance *komið aftur hérna* [come back here]. Interestingly, this is the same pattern as in Excerpt 2a: The co-participant enters the ongoing TCU to assist with a word and then takes over. The clerk's repair of the verb is embedded as a part of the candidate completion and thus designed not to be attended to (Brouwer, Rasmussen, & Wagner, 2004; Jefferson, 1987).

In line 4, we can see Anna overlapping the clerk, ignoring his repair of the word *kom* [*come] as well as the candidate completion. She insists on finishing the TCU herself (line 4) with the utterance of the word *hérna* [here].[13] Her TCU is now possibly finished, syntactically and pragmatically.

The next speaker's action, in line 3, has some characteristics of collaborative completion, namely that the incoming speaker finishes the first speaker's turn. One of the main features of many collaborative completions (Lerner, 2004) is that the "owner" of the turn responds to the co-participant's completion, either accepting or rejecting it. In the example presented here (Excerpt 4), however, Anna does not respond to the co-participant's completion of her TCU; instead, she simply ignores it, and insists on finishing the TCU herself.

Lerner (1989, 2004) reports a procedure in FL talk, *delayed completion*, which among other things is an alternative to the acceptance or rejection in collaborative completion, where the initiator of the turn can delay his turn completion in the case of an intervening speaker. This procedure has a similar sequential structure as *insisting on TCU completion*, that is, an incoming speaker starts to speak in the midst of a current speaker's turn and sometimes delivers a candidate completion. In SL talk, however, there is an obvious language imbalance between the participants: The SL speaker does not *delay* the turn completion; rather, the apparent delays come out of her slow and hesitant delivery of the language. Furthermore, we see the SL speaker actually struggle with her co-participant in order to finish her turn.

In line 5, Anna adds *á morgun* [tomorrow] after uttering hesitation markers and making a pause of 0.7 seconds. Instances of this type have been described by Schegloff (1996) as an add-on "which grammatically complements what had otherwise appeared to be possibly complete" (p. 91). Upon producing *á morgun*, Anna has succeeded in delivering the phrase *ég get kom hérna á morgun* [I can come here tomorrow].

In Excerpts 2–4, we saw Anna's hesitant turns. Even though her TCU is not complete with respect to syntax and prosody, it is possible for the co-participant to understand where she is heading at some point in the utterance before transition relevance has been achieved. The linguistic material she has produced combined with the context of the talk makes this early understanding possible. The next speaker moves into her ongoing turn, attending to trouble in her talk. He offers a candidate completion of her TCU (Excerpt 4) or corrects her as we saw him do in Excerpt 3e. The co-participant enters her turn assisting with a form of a word (Excerpts 2a and 4) or helping with trouble in understanding (Excerpt 3e) and then takes the turn. Anna ignores this talk and finishes her TCU, indicating that her orientation towards producing a complete utterance takes priority over the need to achieve mutual understanding smoothly and effortlessly.

The potential implication of some features of *insisting on TCU completion* for progressivity in second language interaction

This section sums up the main characteristics of the target practice of this study, makes some structural observations, and discusses the practice with respect to the more general question of forward movement in interaction.

A summary of the main features of *insisting on TCU completion*

In insisting on TCU completion, the FL speaker enters the SL speaker's hesitantly produced TCU at a point where FL understands where the SL speaker is heading. The FL speaker's actions, that is, a candidate formulation of the SL speaker's business (cf. Excerpt 2a), a correction in Excerpt 3e, and a candidate completion (cf. Excerpt 4), make it clear that intersubjectivity has been established even if the SL speaker has not yet completed her TCU and therefore not reached a TRP. The linguistic resources that the SL speaker has delivered together with the context of the talk make this early understanding possible. The FL speakers' actions are designed to end the SL speaker's TCU and move the interaction forward. The most interesting feature of this practice is the SL speaker's reaction: She actively ignores the incoming speaker and insists on finishing her TCU. With her action, she exercises her right to utter the TCU, which at the same time allows her to deliver a whole construction in the second language. Her actions are clearly not in favor of the topical interaction; rather, she attends to the delivery of the linguistics forms. This is especially remarkable in cases where there are real-life consequences, such as cashing a grant or receiving a parcel.

Insisting on finishing one's TCU and its implication for the progressivity of the interaction

In the preceding section we saw that the FL speakers' actions in the target SL practice are designed to move the interaction forward. Stivers and Robinson (2006) refer to this as "progressivity," that is, participants in interaction orient towards moving the interaction forward. They argue that there is a preference for progressivity in interaction and suggest that "a concern for progressivity is not restricted to certain contexts (such as institutional contexts) nor to certain participants" (p. 388). In the examples used in this study and presented in this chapter, however, we saw that the second language speaker did not show such orientation. In fact, her actions point in the opposite direction: She actively ignores the incoming speakers' attempts to advance the interaction and insists on finishing her TCU, thereby showing an orientation to language matters rather than the progressivity of the interaction. This suggests that the preference for progressivity in interaction may be temporarily suspended in some episodes of SL talk.

This leads to the conclusion that in SL conversation, the FL speaker and the SL speaker may have different interactional goals. The FL speaker's goals are mainly interactional (topical) while the SL speaker's goals are linguistic as well as topical. This implies that an orientation to language is omnipresent in second language talk and perhaps even more so in the beginning stages of the acquisition. With that in mind, we could say that a difference between FL talk and SL beginner's talk is that the former has a topical focus, while the latter has a dual nature where, along with the topic, there is a linguistic focus. Besides insisting on TCU completion, there are several other ways in which this language orientation is manifested, as we saw in Excerpt 2, Grant, and Excerpt 3, Fishing boat, where both participants in the interaction attend to matters of the language during long stretches of talk. This is not to say that SL talk is not normal talk (Wagner & Gardner, 2004) but simply to point out one thing that appears to work differently in SL talk than in FL talk.

Concluding remarks

This chapter set out to study second language interaction in a real-life environment, outside of the classroom, with regard to the learning of the second language: Can second language speakers be seen to orient to language learning in everyday talk? The short answer to that question is *yes*. In fact, the orientation to language matters in mundane SL talk is shown to be quite extensive at times, with participants adopting the roles of language learner and a language expert.

The main target of this study is the practice *insisting on TCU completion*, in which the SL speaker produces a troubled TCU, and the co-participant enters her unfinished TCU offering assistance and then attempts to take over. The SL speaker notices—but actively ignores—the intervening speaker and his unrequested help and insists on completing her turn. Her actions are clearly not in favor of the business at hand. Rather, they allow her to attend to language matters, more precisely to deliver a whole phrase in the second language.

The actions of the incoming speakers (FL speakers) are designed to move the interaction forward, while the SL speaker's actions at times may work against this progressivity and show her focusing on language issues.

The target practice is shown to be embedded in other language-oriented activities. The linguistic resources used in the target practice are the very items focused on in such activities, either after *insisting on TCU completion* or before it. In Excerpt 2, Grant, the linguistic resources used in the interaction fuel the following activities of attending to linguistic features. In Excerpt 3, Fishing boat, on the other hand, the preceding activities concerning language matters feed into the target practice: The SL speaker has gathered the linguistic resources in the preceding activities, sufficient to deliver a whole phrase in the SL on the topic. This is a clear indication that language orientation/learning activities are rooted and integrated in interaction, as other researchers have pointed out (Firth & Wagner, 2007; Hall, 2006).

A closer inspection of these language-oriented activities reveals their sequential order. It turns out that it is the SL speaker who initiates these activities. She indicates trouble or asks questions regarding the language. The FL speaker's participation as an expert is limited: Their responses are minimal and prompted by the SL speaker. The important point here is that it is the SL speaker who is the driving force in these activities.

One of the interesting points in this study concerns the striking level of persistence on the part of the second language speaker. Here—as in Egbert, Niebecker, and Rezzara (2004)—we see the SL speaker work hard on language comprehension and production; she perseveres in constructing utterances in the second language, which is obviously quite difficult for her. Despite her patent linguistic limitations, Anna sticks to speaking Icelandic even when switching to English seems (at least to the analyst) to be the obvious way for her to conduct her business (especially when the stakes are high, cf. Excerpts 2 and 4) quickly and safely.

Notes

1 Earlier versions of this chapter were presented at *The 17th International Conference on Pragmatics & Language Learning* at the University of Hawai'i at Mānoa, Honolulu, Hawai'i, in March 2007, and *The 8th Conference on Nordic Languages as Second Languages*, at the University of Helsinki, Finland, in May 2007.
2 During her travel abroad in the summer and sometimes at Christmas time, she did (obviously) not record. Apart from recording in her daily life, she recorded her weekly tutoring lessons with an instructor in Icelandic spanning the same period. These are not included in the 55 hrs. corpus and are not used in this study.
3 Anna sets up membership relations so that reference to the clerk can be heard as activating category-bound information. A closer analysis of this phenomenon however has to be done in a different paper.
4 I have, in my data, more instances of similar first language (FL) speakers' responses to trouble in second language (SL) talk, that is, delivery of a repaired version of the trouble word followed by *já* [yes]. The interesting part here is the significance of *já*, whether it functions as a topic closing device, or if, with *já*, the FL speaker is doing a part of the next action which is showing understanding of

the previous turn and moving on. In this case it may be a combination of both: After saying *já*, the clerk moves on to do the next action. He overlaps Anna's hesitation markers and thereby ignores a possible indication of trouble that the SL speaker may still be having. This suggests that he has closed the topic of the trouble talk. Kurhila (2006) reports similar activity in SL Finnish where the FL speaker straightens out anomalies in the SL speaker's talk by delivering a grammatical substitute followed by the affirmative particle *joo*, suggesting closure of the repair sequence (p. 223). The function of *já* in cases like the one described above needs further research. In this chapter we only mention the possibility of *já* being a topic-closing device.

5   Icelanders are well aware of the fact that very few foreigners speak or understand their language. Everyone learns at least two foreign languages in school: English and Danish. It is fair to say that knowledge of English is common among Icelanders.

6   Going back to the different focus of the SL speaker and FL speaker in interaction, linguistic vs. topical: In line 49, Anna proposes an utterance using both of the words (*check* and *grant*) that she and the clerk have been working on. The try-marking (raised intonation at the end) shows that the utterance requires a response from the clerk. As a language expert, the clerk is expected to guide Anna in the right direction, that is to give her correct information instead of misleading her (Grice, 1975). Instead, the clerk confirms (line 50) Anna's usage even if it is grammatically incorrect. This may indicate that at this point, the clerk is focusing on the business at hand and not participating in the language orientation: The utterance Anna produced is adequate for the business (since it has been understood) even if it is grammatically deviant.

7   Anna, as a language learner, initiates and drives these activities, which appears to be in contrast with classroom interaction where the teacher is the leading force (Mehan, 1979).

8   See also lines 36, 41 in Excerpt 2d; line 50 in Excerpt 2e.

9   Another activity is taking place simultaneously: finding and getting into the man's car. The lines relating to that have been deleted from the excerpt, except for *I'm on this one*, in line 15, referring to the car.

10 Some people's occupation may be a sensitive issue. The man, however, had asked Anna about her occupation. When asking her about her work he can expect to be asked a similar question about himself. The trouble the man is having in formulating his answer must therefore be for different reasons.

11 In line 6, it is either the man or someone else (passing by). It is difficult to determine what is being said, but clearly it is not on the "fishing boat" topic.

12 The accusative form is correct here.

13 Incidentally, it is the same word, *hérna* [*here*], that Anna is insisting on delivering in Excerpts 2 and 4. The significance of this is unclear.

References

Brouwer, C. (2004). Doing pronunciation: A specific type of repair sequence. In R. Gardner & J. Wagner (Ed.), *Second language conversations* (pp. 93–113). London: Continuum.

Brouwer, C., & Nissen, A. (2003). At lære dansk som andetsprog i praksis [To learn Danish as a second language in practice]. In B. Asmuß & J. Steensig (Eds.), *Samtalen på arbejde [Talk at work]* (pp. 52–72). Fredriksberg: Forlaget Samfundslitteratur.

Brouwer, C., Rasmussen, G., & Wagner, J. (2004). Embedded corrections in second language talk. In R. Gardner & J. Wagner (Eds.), *Second language conversations.* (pp. 75–92). London: Continuum.

Egbert, M., Niebecker, L., & Rezzara, S. (2004). Inside first and second language speakers' trouble in understanding. In R. Gardner & J. Wagner (Eds.), *Second language conversations* (pp. 178–200). London: Continuum.

Firth, A., & Wagner, J. (2007). Second/foreign language learning as a social accomplishment: Elaborations on a reconceptualized SLA. *The Modern Language Journal, 91*(Focus Issue), 800–819.

Grice, H. P. (1975). Logic and conversation. In P. Cole & J. L. Morgan (Eds.), *Syntax and semantics 3: Speech acts* (pp. 41–58). New York, NY: Academic Press.

Hutchby, I., & Wooffitt, R. (1998). *Conversation analysis: Principles, practices, and applications.* Cambridge, England. Malden, MA: Polity Press.

Jefferson, G. (1984). Notes on some orderlinesses of overlap onset. *Tilburg Papers in Language and Literature, 28.*

Jefferson, G. (1986). Notes on latency in overlap onset. *Human Studies, 9,* 153–183.

Jefferson, G. (1987). On exposed and embedded correction in conversation. In G. Button & J. Lee (Eds.), *Talk and social organisation* (pp. 86–100). Clevedon: Multilingual Matters.

Kurhila, S. (2004). Clients or language learners-being a second language speaker in institutional interaction. In R. Gardner & J. Wagner (Eds.), *Second language conversation* (pp. 58–74). London: Continuum.

Lerner, G. H. (1989). Notes on overlap management: The case of delayed completion. *Western Journal of Speech Communication, 53,* 167–177.

Lerner, G. H. (2004). Collaborative turn sequences. In G. H. Lerner (Ed.), *Conversation analysis: Studies from the first generation (pp. 225–256).* Amsterdam: John Benjamins.

Mehan, H. (1979). *Learning lessons: Social organization in the classroom.* Cambridge, MA: Harvard University Press.

Sacks, H., Schegloff, E., & Jefferson, G. (1974). A simplest systematics for the organization of turn-taking for conversation. *Language, 50*(4), 696–735.

Schegloff, E. (1996). Turn organization: One intersection of grammar and interaction. In E. Ochs, E. A. Schegloff, & S. A. Thompson (Eds.), *Interaction and grammar* (pp. 55–133). Cambridge: Cambridge University Press.

Stivers, T., & Robinson, J. D. (2006). A preference for progressivity in interaction. *Language in Society, 35*, 367–392.

Wagner, J., & Gardner, R. (2004). Introduction. In R. Gardner & J. Wagner (Eds.), *Second language conversations* (pp. 1–7). London: Continuum.

Language Choice and Participation

in Second Language Talk

9 Language Choice and Participation: Two Practices for Switching Languages in Institutional Interaction

Maurice Nevile
The Australian National University

Johannes Wagner
University of Southern Denmark

Introduction

In multilingual interactions, participants' language choices are informed by their second language (L2) competence and the L2 competencies of their co-participants. In institutional settings, such choices can be contingent also upon institutional goals and constraints. In this chapter, we are interested in the use of multiple languages in core activities for teaching, learning, and assessment. We study an oral university examination where German and English work as the official languages, while Danish is used occasionally by students in situations where certain words are not available. Conducting the examination in two languages requires a division of labor of some kind between these languages, which has to be organized on a local (here-and-now) basis. This creates particular challenges for participation and displays of competence by the students. As conversation analysts, we are interested in how participants manage language choice in situ, moment-to-moment, through processes of social interaction. We analyze both the audio recording on the basis of a detailed transcription, and the video data itself, to highlight those moments where language choice is made relevant or accounted for.

We consider the range of linguistic, interactional, and embodied (e.g., gestural) resources over the course of the examination, by which the participants manage issues of speakership, recipiency, and participation, while seeking to fairly present and determine the students' academic performance and competence, both as individuals and as a project team. Our analyses can inform understandings of both teacher-student and student-student relations in universities seeking increased linguistic and cultural diversity. We highlight how institutional, departmental, or program policies for creating the internationalized university as a complex multilingual and multicultural arena must attend to the demands faced by participants in authentic institutional settings, such as an examination. For example, an ideal or policy of free language choice, motivated to empower individuals, must be accomplished locally through processes of interaction. So, our consideration of the process and demands of internationalization involves recording and analyzing practices of staff and students in naturally occurring interactions.

Data

The data used in this chapter originate from a group oral examination in a Danish university in which a team of three students at the bachelor level is examined by two members of academic staff: the subject examiner (SE), who is a teacher on the students' subject; and a co-examiner (CoE), who is a staff member of the host university not teaching on the subject. The students are being examined on a written project, which they have completed jointly and for which they are assessed. The project is part of an international degree where the students do courses and examinations in a foreign language, which, however, is mainly English and to a much lesser degree German, French, and very rarely Spanish. This oral examination defends a paper on Berlin's recent history, which was written jointly by the students and is entitled *Die Mauer im Kopf* [*The Wall in the Head*]. The paper is written in German, and this indicates that all students must be able at least to read and write German. However, we note that the students' written competence in German is never referred to during the examination. In this sense, the staff members treat the students as having sufficient competence in written German.

The examination was captured by a video-recorder and an independent audio-recorder. These recordings last 75 minutes each and cover the whole oral examination.[1] Figure 1 shows the physical arrangement of the participants. The examination is held in a university classroom. The three students sit side-by-side along one side of a rectangular table, and the two academic staff members sit side-by-side along the table's other side. Students are indicated with "St" and reference to their location at the table as either on the left (i.e., StL), right (StR), or middle (StM). The examination was recorded with one fixed camera, aimed diagonally across the table. Always in view are all three students and the subject examiner, seated right, while the co-examiner, seated left, is mostly in partial view, but occasionally sits or leans forward to be in full view.

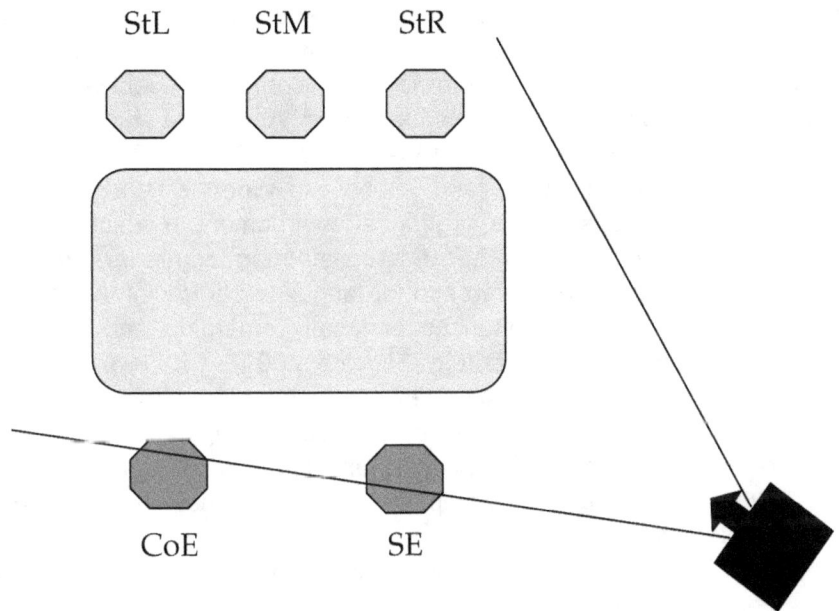

Figure 1. The physical arrangement of participants

During the first few minutes of the session, the two staff members make opening comments. First, SE speaks, then CoE. These comments include some words of welcome, followed by procedural details for how the examination will be conducted and the languages to be used. The three students then each make a presentation of around 10–15 minutes on some aspect of their joint project, including a few minutes of discussion. There are then approximately 25 minutes of general discussion, covering all three student presentations and general matters concerning the project overall. This discussion period involves mostly the staff asking questions and making comments, and the students offering responses.

Research questions

Generally, as conversation analysts, we are interested in uncovering the ordinary language, embodied conduct, practices, and processes of reasoning by which participants create and make sense of whatever it is that they are doing, of whatever is going on. We view naturally occurring interaction as the primordial site of sociality (see Have, 2007; Hutchby & Wooffitt, 2008; Schegloff, 2006). Auer's (1984) pioneering book employed a conversation-analytic angle on questions of language choice. Different from well established, linguistically oriented code-switching studies (e.g., Myers-Scotton, 1993; Muysken, 2000), Auer took a discourse perspective for which Gumperz (1982) had already laid the foundation. A range of studies followed in Auer's footsteps, most notably Li Wei (1998, 2002, 2005), Auer (1998), Gafaranga (2001, 2005, 2007), and Sebba and Wootton (1998). With this work, we share a focus on the sequential environment in which language switch is enacted. However, rather than considering language switches as reflecting forms of general preference for language choice (cf. Auer, 1984), we will view switches as instances of locally emerging and contingent alignments between participants (e.g., Higgins, 2009).

A number of specific research questions emerged as we developed and analyzed the transcription and video recording, concerning the participants' use of the two main languages for the examination, German and English.

- When and how do the participants switch languages during the course of interaction?
- What do the participants say explicitly about their language choice and use?
- What happens at moments of switching languages, and how do participants manage and accomplish such switches?
- How "smooth" is the process for switching between languages? Are there interactional "hiccups" at moments of switching?
- Do certain interactional positions with relation to language use change and settle over the course of the examination, or do participants' language choice behaviors remain unchanged over time?
- What do participants' language choices reveal about their sensitivities and orientation to managing participation and possible displays of content knowledge and academic competence?

Framing the language choice: A policy

The video recording begins before the start of the official examination. We see the three students lined up, shuffling papers, and the co-examiner (CoE) doing the same. After some silence, CoE addresses the students without establishing gaze contact. Due to some features of our data and our analytic interests, our transcription notation differs a little from other contributions to this volume.[2]

Excerpt 1, Summer holiday

```
01    CoE:    so heute habt /ihr sommer (.) urlAUb¿
              so today  have you summer      holiday
              so today you´re on summer holidays
      GES:                    /StM, StR GAZE -> CoE

02            (0.5)
      GES:    CoE GAZE -> STUDENTS

03    StM:    ja:
              yes

04    StR:    [mm ]

05    CoE:    [ehh ] hhe hhe.

06    StL:    not /yet, not [↑yet.
      GES:        /GAZE -> CoE

07    CoE:                  [NOT YET.

08    StR:    det ville vær' de:jligt¿
              that would be great
```

CoE's question in line 1 is answered by all three students in turn. StM replies positively (line 3), supported by StR (line 4). StL disagrees and refers in line 6 to the upcoming oral examination which stands between the holiday and the here and now. In line 8, StR, now aligning with the direction of StL's response, says, in Danish, that having summer holidays now would be great.

In these pre-exam, off-the-record exchanges, CoE asks his question in German. StM answers in German as well, while StL chooses English and StR in line 8 speaks Danish. All the three languages that will be used during the next 75 minutes are in place in this very first exchange on the recording. On the face of it, there seems to be a free language market where everybody speaks one of the languages available to all of the participants. We will return to this extract to consider it in detail.

Now, not all speakers involved in this examination are native or near-native speakers of Danish. StL is a native speaker of Dutch who speaks German and English and some Danish. CoE is a Dane. He has been chosen as an external examiner since he is willing to speak German. His language choice in the opening exchange deserves some comment:

Because the examination has not yet begun, Danish (the language of the socio-cultural environment) may be a choice. However, StL is a speaker of Dutch and CoE might not know whether she knows any Danish.

German is the language of the written text, which is the basis of the examination. CoE therefore treats the students as having at least some competence in written German.

Some seconds later, SE joins the group and opens the examination proper with a formal greeting *so. guten mor:gen¿* [well. good morning]. Again, from the examiner's use of German it appears that German is treated as the default language for the examination. In Excerpt 2, SE explains the rules for the languages to be used during the examination:

Excerpt 2, Working languages

```
01    SE:   also wir ham grad noch in der studienordnung nachgekuckt,
            well we have just yet  in the program rules     looked up

02          da    steht (.) eh dass dis exam'n hh in:- de::n (0.3)
            there says        that this exam     in    the (pl.)

03          oder (.) der       oder de:n    arbeitsprachen
            or       the(sg.)  or   the(pl.) working languages

04          des    projektes gehalten werden soll,
            of the project   held     be     should

            well we have just looked it up in the program rules
            it says there that the exam should be conducted in the
            working language or languages of the project

05    StM:  hn:.

06    SE:   .hhhh das  heisst wir haben also: e:h man kann ja sagen
                  that means  we  have        one can     say

07          dass engels englisch          auch: 'ne arbeitsprache ist,
            that English (Danish) English also   a  working language is
      GES:  SE GAZE -> ALL STUDENTS, BY END OF HIS TURN  GAZE -> StR

            that means we could say that English is a working
            language too

08    StR:  [h↓m¿]
      GES:  NODS

09    SE:   [·hh]h das heisst /wenn jemand von euch lust hat
                   that is    if   one    of  you  like has
      GES:                    /SE SPREADS HIS ARMS OUT WIDELY

10          englisch zu reden,
            English to speak

            so if one of you wants to speak English

11    StR:  hnnnn.
      GES:  StR POINTS THREE TIMES TO HERSELF
```

```
12    StR:   ·hnhha [hh

13    SE:           [the(hh)ere she wa(hh)s
      GES:   SE POINTS TWICE WITH BOTH HANDS TO StR

14    SE:    [ehh hhe hhe hhe hhe hhe he] xx [=

15    StR:   [ahh hha hha hha hha hha   ]    [I: will:

16    SE:    hhe hhe hhe hhe oka:y
```

SE remarks in lines 1–4 that the program regulations state that the examination should be held in the working language(s) of the project. Without giving any account, he comments that English can be said to be a working language for the project. When in line 9–10 he draws the consequence that any of them would be allowed to speak in English, he looks from one student to the other and by the end of his turn is looking towards StR, who responds nonverbally by pointing to herself three times. SE seems to comment on this—unfortunately, it is unclear what he says in line 13—and mimics StR's gesture by pointing twice towards her. Both participants start laughing before StR ultimately says that she will speak English.

Note that SE gives only a very general explanation of the "working languages" rule. He does not tell StR directly that she is allowed to speak English. However, English is introduced as the second option (*auch: ne Arbeitsprache* [also a working language]) and its legal background for use, its legitimacy or warrant, is deduced from the general program regulations. We note that SE does not design this explanation as especially for StR (although he ends up looking at StR), and his wording does not explicitly refer to StR. The comments are presented instead as applicable generally to all participants. But when StR appoints herself as intending to use English, SE in line 13 and the following laughter shows that StR's response was expected. In his interpretation of the rules, SE defines a kind of ideal linguistic market where speakers are free to choose whatever language best suits them, and SE presents their possible choices as acceptable and workable.

As it turns out, in the way this declaration is received by StR, the parties show their understanding that *she* is the one for whom this rule is activated and that she intends to make use of it through using English. So, it seems that this is actually not a free language market but rather an imbalanced allocation of languages with StR in focus for English. Certainly, SE and the students have discussed the matter of language choice earlier and do it here again for the record—and possibly for the co-examiner. They seem to share a silent expectation created by their paper that German is the language of the examination. In this light, the very first utterances on the recording (Excerpt 1) show the students doing multilinguality while the examiners treat German as the language of the examination. SE's explanation of the program regulations has shifted the focus from an orientation to German as the common language to a possibility of language choice.

It is here that we direct our attention: How do participants actually accomplish language choice to meet the moment-to-moment contingencies of interaction, such as topic management and speaker selection? How do participants orient to the relevance of language choice for participation? When setting out the procedures for the examination, SE explicitly sets a goal, a kind of local interactional "policy" as follows: *h- es geht ja darum dass ihr sagen könnt was ihr sagen wollt* [the idea is that you can say what you want to say].

Such a policy suggests that speakers are free to choose whatever language best suits them, but how can language choices be organized to allow all participants to contribute equally, to ensure that all participants can say what they want? How is the policy interpreted and accomplished in situ? In short, how realistic and achievable in practice is an ideal linguistic democracy that "you can say what you want to say in the language of your choice"? The practical interactional consequences of the policy are unclear. For example, is the policy understood to mean *one speaker—one language*, that is, does a speaker choose a language and then stick with this language? Alternatively, is language choice dependent on topic, that is, that certain topics are handled in one language, others in a different language? Or could it even mean that "anything goes," that is, that any speaker at any point can choose any of the working languages?

In the remainder of this chapter, we examine how the participants themselves manage such matters in the course of interaction to conduct a multilingual examination. This will point us to some organizational challenges which multilinguality seems to create.

Language and participation: Practices

SE explicitly sets out that German and English are both to be considered the "official working languages." This does not say anything about who is to speak which language, to whom, and when, or about what. We are interested in how the participants orient to such matters as an ongoing and relevant task for conducting the examination and, in particular, for organizing participation. During the 75 minutes of the oral examination, all participants but one use both German and English—apart from some minor switches into Danish. The other participant, StR, speaks English. As we discussed in our analysis of Excerpt 2, the issue of free language choice is designed specifically for her, but we will see that it generates particular challenges in the interaction.

Self-initiated language choice

After establishing the procedures for the examination, both SE and CoE hand over the floor to the students.

Excerpt 3, Start with my presentation

```
01   SE:   /.hhh bitte das wort ist hh euer[s:. hh
                 please  the word is       yours
            well the floor is yours
     GES:  / SE SPREADS ARMS WIDELY, GAZE -> STM AND STL

02   CoE:                                  [geh ma' lo:s.
                                            go just ahead
                                            just go ahead

03          (.)
     GES:  STL POINTS TO HER LEFT

04   SE:   .hhhhh ja:.
                  yes

05   StM:  ich denk mal [  wir  ] werd[-
            I   think     we    will
     GES:  SE POINTS AT STM. STL AND STM GAZE -> STR

06   StR:                [I think]    [I'll just start with

07                 [my ] presentation,

08   StM:  [ja.]
            yes

09          (.)

10   StM:  okay.

11   StR:  in English.
```

In lines 1 and 2, the examiners SE and CoE relinquish (very explicitly) the floor to the students who are each expected in turn to deliver a short presentation. The examiners, however, do not direct a request towards a specific student. It seems though that StR is to be the first presenter. StL points to her left (line 3), and as StM verbally accepts the floor on the students' behalf (line 5), both StL and StM turn their heads towards StR, who then starts to talk in overlap with StM, looking briefly to her right towards the other two students. In their bodily behavior, the students display the decision they have made about who of them will deliver the first presentation.

While StM in line 5 responds in German, that is, in the language in which the sequence initiating talk had been produced (by SE and CoE, lines 1–2), StR switches into *English*. According to the earlier stated rules, German and English are both official languages, but it does not seem to be as straightforward as that. We note that StR not only starts speaking English, but mentions the language of her choice, making it a salient matter. We wonder why she would be doing this here. She already has been speaking in English, so mentioning this explicitly seems to indicate that although switching the language in this sequential position may not necessarily need an account, it at least needs to be mentioned. We see StR's behavior as evidence that, for her, German and English are not simply interchangeable, but that German is treated as the default language, and English as the marked one. Using English warrants a mention. But this is not the whole story as we will see in the next excerpt.

Language choice for selection of next speaker

Excerpt 4 occurs at a pivotal moment for the examination. The three students have each given their individual presentations in their language of choice (StR in English, StM and StL in German). Subsequently, SE comments for several minutes, in German, on issues arising from the three presentations and relative also to the students' written project (written in German). In the following segment, we see SE come to the end of this period of comments, as he hands the floor back to the students for their responses, and to initiate further discussion. He concludes by identifying two issues for the students to address, ultimately presenting these as two questions. We pick up SE's talk as he ends his turn:

Excerpt 4, Who would like to volunteer?

```
01   SE:    .hhh also das sind jetzt zwei £fragen=
                    well these are  now  two    questions
             well that's now two questions
        GES: SE BRINGS HANDS TOGETHER AND SPREADS THEM WHILE GAZE ->
             STUDENTS

02   SE:    =ghhe ghhe-hhe .HHHhhh

03          (.)

04   SE:    e::::::h
```

```
05          (.)

06   CoE:  ↓*ja*
           yes
     GES:  CoE POINTS -> STUDENTS

07   SE:   ja.
           yes
     GES:  SE WAVES HANDS, BRINGS HANDS DOWN, STOPS WAVING

08          (0.5)
     GES:  StL LOOKS TO HER LEFT

09   SE:   und (.) es brauchst /du //nicht
           and      it  need    you  not

10         unbe[dingt zu beantwor]ten=
           necessarily to answer
     GES:  SE WAVES HANDS         /POINTS -> StL AND StM
                                  //StM looks down

           and you (sg.) don't necessarily have to answer it

11   CoE:      [x x x auch      ]=
                       too
     GES:  CoE WAVES HAND LEFT TO RIGHT -> STUDENTS

12   SE:   =also
           well

13   CoE:  =[eine frage] (zu sein)
            a question   to be

           xxxx to be a question as well

14   StL:  [  mmh    ]

15   SE:   ja. hhh [hh  ]
     GES:  StM NODS, SE NODS AT StR

16   StL:           [hm m]

17          (1)
     GES:  SE GAZE FROM StL -> StR

18   SE:   wer möchte. /ehh //*he e e or* (.)
           who likes
           who would like to
     GES:              /SE GAZE -> StR
     GES:                    //StL LOOKS BRIEFLY TO HER LEFT
```

```
19   SE:  who would like to volunteer /.hhhh hhhhhh
     GES: SE LOOKS DOWN                /GAZE -> StR.
                                       /StL RAISES HAND

20   StL: °mmf° vielleicht /weil e::hm: der (.) ausgangspunkt
                maybe       because            the point of departure
     GES:                   /StR GAZE -> StL
```

In the talk directly preceding Excerpt 4, SE formulated complex questions but had not yet appointed a specific student to respond. During the whole sequence, the students show no active recipient behavior. They sit frozen in their seats and look at SE. When SE ends his talk at line 1, he waves his hands left to right in front of his body in an apparent inviting gesture and flashes his gaze around the table. At this point, any student could self select to answer, but all three retain their body position without movement. From line 2 onwards, we see SE waiting for a student's response, and he is joined by CoE who also waves his hands invitingly. The students still sit without movement. In lines 6 and 7, CoE and SE quite demonstratively withdraw from speakership (*ja* [yes]), and SE brings his hands down in resting position. The floor is now wide open for any student to respond.

In the following 0.5 second silence (line 8) StL—who had been talking at length before this episode—moves and turns left to look towards StM and StR. This could be taken as indicating for everybody that she is scrutinizing the scene for visible evidence of possible next speakers, possibly seeing if the path is clear to deliver an answer herself. At least SE treats StL's movement as potentially preparatory to her self selecting, and he heads this off by telling her that she need not be the one to answer (lines 9–10). SE accompanies his talk with repeatedly waving his open hands towards all three students, hands flat in front of his body, each moving to and fro from left to right, so embodying through gesture his openness to a different next respondent. Also, CoE moves his right hand from left to right while pointing across from StL to StR (line 11). At this point (line 9), StM bodily withdraws by looking down, leaning back, and bringing his hand up to his mouth. StR still sits without any movement.

The examiners' talk and hand gestures would seem to invite all of the students to self select and come forth with an answer. However SE's gaze seems to end up several times at StR in transition relevant position (lines 15, 17, 18), while StR sits motionless and without any reaction. From lines 11 to 15, the examiners again make efforts to elicit a response, and during the one second pause at line 17, the floor is again wide open for the students to respond.

When no response is forthcoming, after some gestural effort, in line 18 SE verbally asks for one of the students to produce an answer, seeking a "volunteer," but again without appointing a specific student. We note that StL at this point again gazes to her left, which might be an attempt to clarify who is going to deliver the answer, but StR still sits in a frozen position. At the end of line 18, SE switches to English (or) and repeats his invitation in English in line 19. When doing this he lowers his gaze, and just as he ends his turn brings his gaze up first to StR, the student who (in the examination) speaks only in English. At this point StL raises her hand and takes the floor. When StL has said her first word, StR moves and looks right in StL's direction.

How can we understand what is going on? During the interaction in Excerpt 4, the examiners stick to their procedure not to appoint a specific student as a responder. On the contrary, they tell one of the students that she need not be the one to respond, and through expansive inviting gestures make visible that any student is entitled to respond. However, even though the examiners verbally and bodily relinquish the floor, no student self selects as speaker, and StM and StR do not engage in any pre-talk activity such as shifting their body position, moving their gaze, or otherwise clearing with their fellow students who is going to be the responder. Both sit out the challenge, the pursuit of a response which is consecutively sharpened by the examiners (cf. Pomerantz, 1984b).

At the end of the excerpt, when SE switches into English, we see him orienting to the impact and relevance of language choice for possible participation. The choice of English now puts pressure also on StR to respond because English in this examination is *her* language. So SE makes a response from StR maximally relevant and possible, in terms of language choice, and allows its absence to be noticeable and accountable as were the absent responses from her German-using student colleagues to the previous talk in German. StR now has no interactional space to hide. Note that SE is looking down when he speaks English, withdrawing his gaze from possible recipients until the end of his turn. Gazing throughout his turn towards StR could even more strongly appoint her as the next speaker (Lerner, 2003). Note that SE does not redo the substance of his question and commentary in English, only the invitation to respond. That is, SE treats previous talk in German as understandable and recoverable for StR, as sufficient for StR to develop a response. The only matter to be "fixed" is her potential speakership. But as we see, StR successfully resists the examiners' many attempts to draw her into the interaction. It is StL who eventually responds. Evidence that StL understands an emerging pressure for StR to be next speaker is that before talking (line 20) she visibly signals her own readiness to accept speakership, as an alternative to StR, by raising her hand (line 19).

Excerpt 4 is followed by several minutes of a lively discussion between SE, StL, and StM. During this sequence, StR displays bodily recipient behavior (e.g., nodding). When the topic draws to an end—but before there has been any closing—CoE cuts into StM's ongoing talk (lines 5 and 6).

Excerpt 5, I'd like to ask you a question

```
01    SE:    aber aber jedenfalls jedenfalls nicht die mächtige[n
             but  but  in any case in any case not the  powerful
             but not in any case the powerful

02    StM:                                                    [nein
                                                               no

03           nein [das ist nicht (da:s) die /(maleid)losen
             no    it  is  not   (it)    the    (??)

04    StR:   [nein
              no
      GES:                       /CoE RAISES HAND, POINTS -> StR
                                 StR GAZE -> CoE, StM'S GAZE SHIFTS
                                 BETWEEN SE AND CoE

05    StM    und die*:*[eh
             and the

06    CoE:            [eh I'd like to: (.) ask you a question

07           'n English th[en,

08    StR:                [jah(h)

09    CoE: because in your:: presentation you said e::h

10           (0.7)
```

StR's recipient token *nein* [no] in line 4 is actually her first verbal contribution for a very long time. She hasn't said a word since the ongoing topic was started in Excerpt 4. Immediately after, we see CoE's hand coming up and point towards StR. This movement draws the gaze of StR and StM, the current speaker, who abandons his turn and the floor. Then enters CoE with a classical preliminary (pre-pre) construction (Schegloff, 1980) which projects an upcoming question later in the talk and explicates, while speaking English, that this question will be in English.

In Excerpt 5, CoE initiates a very different principle for speaker allocation compared to what we have seen so far. While earlier questions and invitations to the students to talk were directed towards the whole group, and the examiners insisted on allowing self selection of next speaker, here CoE appoints the next speaker by gesture, an address term (*you*; cf. Lerner, 1996), and by choice of language. He also presents the forthcoming question as belonging to StR's epistemic domain, to what she is entitled to know and comment on (Heritage, 2002; Heritage & Raymond, 2005; Raymond & Heritage, 2006), since he says that the question originates in her earlier presentation. While the language switch in Excerpt 4 was one resource in zooming in on a specific student, here language switch is used on top of other resources for speaker selection.

At this point, about one third of the way into the examination, the situation has changed from having two languages as the officially declared working languages for all speakers, to a situation where languages are allocated to specific speakers. English is the language chosen, even explicitly so, to bring StR into the discussion. The shift in contextualization for language choice is quite dramatic, as we can observe in the five excerpts, given below in order of occurrence in the interaction:

> In Excerpt 1, we observe free language choice as CoE starts in German and the students use German, English, and Danish to respond;
>
> In Excerpt 2, English is sequentially tied to StR as a non-default language choice (she self-identifies as the one to use English—*I will*);
>
> In Excerpt 3, StR switches to English while explicitly mentioning the choice of language;
>
> In Excerpt 4, English is chosen as the last resort to bring StR into the talk; and
>
> In Excerpt 5, the switch into English is connected with other ways of appointing StR as the next speaker, and the language choice is again explicitly mentioned.

This new situation has been accomplished by the whole group, but StR has been particularly significant. Excerpt 4 seems especially critical. We have seen StR successfully resist taking speakership in the face of interactional pressure and hereby bringing the examiners into a difficult situation. In an examination, everybody in the whole group has to participate to display competence. It is not acceptable for a group member to hide and so not contribute. In Excerpt 4, when self-selection for a specific person is made more obviously relevant, and the person still resists taking the turn, the examiners are faced with a dilemma. In Excerpt 5, CoE, as the external examiner, solves this dilemma by explicitly appointing StR as the next speaker by targeting his question directly at her.

Having assigned languages to speakers has also, in our view, a potential for exclusion. The discussion has so far been held in German, and StR has not joined the talk. German has emerged as the language of the other four participants, and English as StR's language. In order to bring StR into the discussion as an active speaker at this time, the examiners have to address her specifically in English. The participants seem to have achieved a clear matching of languages and participants: The two examiners speak mainly German but switch into English to appoint StR as the next speaker, while StL and StM speak German. For the students, the practice of *one speaker—one language* seems to have been established.

Language choice for alignment
In Excerpt 5, line 4, we note another interesting detail: StR clearly says *nein* [no]—which is German. If English had been her sole language, she should have

said *no*. But although English had been assigned to her as her language of interaction, she now speaks German. Why is that? We note that StR's utterance is placed inside talk between SE and StM, which is in German. With her *nein* [no], StR aligns with the previous speaker, StM, who has just enthusiastically agreed with SE. In this alignment activity, StR does not change language but retains the language of the previous speaker and so makes salient that it joins the same action.

This observation fits with a closer analysis of Excerpt 1, to which we return here.

Excerpt 1 (repeated), Summer holiday

```
01    CoE:   so heute habt /ihr sommer (.) urlAUb¿
             so today  have you summer        holiday
             so today you're on summer holidays
      GES:                  /StM, StR GAZE -> CoE

02           (0.5)
      GES:   CoE GAZE -> STUDENTS

03    StM:   ja:
             yes

04    StR:   [mm  ]

05    CoE:   [ehh ] hhe hhe.

06    StL:   not /yet, not [↑yet.
      GES:       /GAZE -> CoE

07    CoE:                 [NOT YET.

08    StR:   det ville vær' de:jligt¿
             that would be great
```

CoE inquires in line 1, in German, about the students' summer holiday and StM replies with a *ja:* [yes]. CoE's laughter in line 5 can be heard as a sequence closing which overlaps with StR's *mm* (line 4) that supports StM's reply. Now in line 6 StL produces a disagreement with StM's positive response, which could also fit as a response to CoE's question. The disagreement is in English. StL says something which can be heard as building on and disaligning from StM's previous response, and at the same time as a dispreferred response (Schegloff, Jefferson, & Sacks, 1977; Pomerantz, 1984a) to CoE's question in line 1.

As in the initial observation, we see a practice at work according to which speakers follow previous speakers in their choice of language. Language choice carries a potential for alignment (or disalignment) with the previous speaker.[3]

We will refer to this practice as *language consistency across turns*. This is the practice to which the participants orient in Excerpts 3 and 5 when they not only change language but explicitly mention that they change to English. In Excerpt 6, another instance of this practice comes into focus.

After Excerpt 5, CoE talks for about 2 minutes to explain his question and finishes with an either-or question. Here begins our next excerpt:

Excerpt 6, Auf Deutsch oder auf Englisch [In German or in English]

```
01     CoE:  is it a ga::p¿ or is it a positive conflict¿
02           between the category: and the empirical work,
03           (.)

04     CoE:  °in your (.) report.°
05           (0.7)

06     StR:  em:::::::: (1.6) ·th (0.4) I think that ah:::hH
07           (1.2) ehm::::: (0.8) I think that- (.) that (1)
08           the f- ehm::::h (0.3) tha:- the bo- (.) the
09           postmodern society of the fragmen: .Hhhhhh-tation
10           part and the complexity some is something that ·hhh
11           that the::: °*em*° (0.3) people=w'll (.) definitely
12           l-learn from:h (0.3) in::: in:::: uhm (0.8) ↑in
13           for example the DDR but i:t's it's right↓ hhhhh
14           it's still very::::*::* very::::: (0.4) ehm:::::
15           (0.7) th traditional: and ·hhhh and eh:::: (0.5) ·hhh
16           ehm:::::: (2) ehm::::: (2.3)
17           o' I (can som[( )              [ehh hhe hheh ·hhh]

18     CoE:            [/or you can also [//(          here)
       GES:            /CoE GAZE AND POINTS -> StL
                                        //StL GAZE -> CoE,
                                        //StM GAZE -> StL

19     CoE:  [xx] [ref[lection] [(eh es)] also auf Deutsch
                                          well  in German

20     StL:  [n¿] [u:hn[nn:. ]  [  xx  ]

21     CoE:  oder auf Eng[lisch]
             or in English
             now, in German or in English

22     StL:              [ ja¿ ]
                           yes

23     CoE:  das:::(so[llst du do](hh)ch.) hh[e ·hh
             it        should you
             you should yeah
```

```
24    StL:              [  ja:    ]              [I: just say it
25         now in English¿ hh e-=I think the::::: the dangers
26         with all this possibilitie:s hhhh /tha:t [e]:::h the
      GES:                                /StM NODS
27         danger of postmoderni:sm¿ ·hhhh is: that

28    StR:                                                    [hn]

29    StL: the manager becomes managed himself (.) by all this
30         possibilitie:s
```

In lines 6–16, there are numerous signs that StR is having trouble producing a coherent and substantial response. There are moments of hesitation, instances of cut-off and restarted talk, numerous silences (including long ones [Jefferson, 1989] of 1.6 and 2.3 seconds), and generally her talk ends up going nowhere in particular. Evidence that CoE hears it this way is that he starts up, while StR is still talking, to select another student (StL) to continue and complete the response. In line 17, CoE looks towards StL, points to her, and invites her (line 18) to take over the answer. Here, StR responds by breaking into laughter (line 17).

Our interest here is that when selecting StL as the next speaker, CoE explicitly presents to her the option to speak in German (line 19). That is, CoE gives StL the option to continue in a language other than the one StR had been using (English) to begin the response. Language choice is made explicit for its possibility for change the current language of use.

CoE switches from English to German over the course of his talk to StL, to select her as next speaker. He begins with *or you can also (here) xx reflection (eh es)*, but then continues with *also auf Deutsch oder auf Englisch*. [well, in German or in English]. As he begins in English, CoE aligns with the language of StR (the last speaker) and with the language of the topic, that is, the language in which he himself had formulated the task (his question). However, this orientation to language choice competes with the orientation to *one speaker—one language*, which for StL is German. So, by switching to German as he builds his talk, explicitly to offer to StL the possibility to switch to German, CoE now meets the orientation to *one speaker—one language*. He also allows StL, in *response*, to now meet the orientation to *language consistency across turns*. Switching language over the course of an extended turn at talk now allows StL, as the selected next speaker, to balance the two competing orientations to language choice and speaker designation.

This does not compel StL to switch to German, and indeed she does not, although she does *begin* in German when acknowledging her selection as next speaker, *ja* [yes] (lines 22 and 24).[4] However, while CoE continues in German, StL instead switches to English and explicitly says that she will continue in English. So we see that by beginning in German, StL orients both to *one speaker—one language*, her own examination language being German, and also to *language consistency across turns*, as she responds to talk from CoE which had switched to German (line 19). She then responds to CoE's earlier question, directed to StR, in English. Again, one option is for StL simply to give her response in English, but instead she makes her language choice salient, as something worth remarking upon.

We can consider what StL does in terms of the interactional effect or possibilities of her language choice for English. Recall that StL is being called on now to complete the faltering and ultimately abandoned response begun by her student colleague, StR. Recall also that StR was responding to talk from CoE that was originally targeted specifically at her. So, by choosing to use English, StL can maximize the possibility for her talk now to be heard as connected to, following from, and building upon, StR's previously abandoned talk. StL can present her own and StR's contributions as hearably part of the same response through their consistent choice of a common language, English, when another language was possible and even prompted. In this way, StL can allow StR to retain some possible co-ownership of the response to CoE's question.

In this sense, while StL is not orienting to *one speaker—one language*, because her examination language is German, she might be orienting to *language consistency across turns*, in that the original question from StL, posed to her student colleague StR, was in English, and that the original response, begun by StR, was also in English. So StL has grounds for using the same language as StR, because the two students' contributions can be heard together as constituting one collaboratively built response. In support of this possibility, we note some parallel wording in their responses. StR had struggled to articulate ideas on "postmodernism" and "fragmentation" and "complexity," and then StL begins her contribution along similar lines, with her initial focus on *the dangers with all this possibilitie:s .... the danger of postmoderni:sm¿* (lines 25–27). The direction of StL's talk seems at least sympathetic to the substance of the talk that StR had struggled to produce.[5]

Importantly also, by choosing English, StL makes it at least possible for StR to return to the discussion at some later point, perhaps when she has collected her thoughts, unaccountably without requiring a language switch. StL leaves the interactional door open. That is, had StL used German, as invited to by CoE, and in keeping with the two orientations for language choice, then in order to return to the discussion, StR would need herself to go against the orientation to *language consistency across turns*. StR would have to contribute in English when the talk had switched to German. So StL's choice of English makes it possible for StR to return to the discussion by talking unproblematically in English. StL's choice of English shows an orientation to *maintaining* StR's possibility for participation, where CoE's prompt for German had not done so.

So we can see that language choice has implications for possibilities for participation, and how participation is managed, for just how and when it is that who can speak to whom, and about what. We observe that the participants manage the interaction so that they enable each other to say what they want.

Discussion: Language choice as social practice

In the beginning of this examination, one examiner (SE) states that German and English are the two languages which may be used during the examination (Excerpt 2). However, already in his wording it becomes obvious that German is the unmarked language of use: He says it in German. We followed over several excerpts how this general rule is gradually replaced by a practice in which each of the students is assigned to one language of use. We argued that there is a more general practice at work here as well, according to which the next speaker uses the language of the previous speaker. We suggest that moments where language choice becomes salient reveal how the participants are apparently managing these *two competing practices for language choice*. Choosing to use German or English is not something that can be done simply and easily, once and for all, and subsequently be taken for granted, but rather is oriented to by the participants throughout, and is dependent on the moment-to-moment interactional contingencies for speaker designation and participation.

We consider in more detail the consequences of both practices for language choice which the participants have to negotiate.

One speaker—one language
1. language change at speaker switch is the unmarked case
2. no switch of language at speaker change is accountable

For the students, language choice is manifest in the language used for the presentation. StR presents first and does so in English, and then StM and StL both present in German. Language change at speaker change is the unmarked case because the participant speaks in their chosen language for this examination. So, the two staff speak in German, the two German-English speaking students who presented in German also speak in German, and the English-only speaking student who presented in English speaks in English. In this practice, the marked or accountable case is where there is no switch of language at speaker change so that the participant does not switch to speak in their chosen language. In the examination, this occurs when a "German-using" participant speaks in English. By *marked* or *accountable* we mean that there are some interactional grounds for a participant *not* to use their selected language for this examination, as for example, aligning or disaligning with the previous speaker.

Language consistency across turns
1. no language switch at speaker change is the unmarked case
2. if the speaker uses his/her best language, and it differs from the previous speaker's, it is accountable

In the second practice, the incoming speaker uses *the language of the previous speaker* (Auer, 1984; Gafaranga, 2007). This practice ensures continuity of language across turns such that a response, or next talk, is made in the language of the initiating or preceding talk. Here, no language switch at speaker change is the unmarked and unaccountable case. However, this practice competes with the first practice at moments where *language consistency across turns* would involve a participant using a language other than their own selected language. This is a particular issue for StR, who presented in English and in this examination is only participant speaking in English.

So, when should language be changed or not be changed? A participant might switch language to make a specific participant a potential next speaker. That is, English might be used to select a participant as next speaker who has English as their preferred examination work language, in this case one of the students (StR). Or, German can be used to select a participant as next speaker who has German as their preferred examination work language, as in the case of the two staff members or two of the students (StL, StM). Switching language presents that new language as relevant for next talk, and so for a speaker of that language to be the relevant next speaker, as in Excerpt 6. A participant might switch language to avoid making the previous speaker necessarily the next speaker, that is, language switch can avoid excluding the other possible language and so can open up speakership. For example, where a previous participant had spoken in German, by switching to English the current speaker can present someone other than the previous speaker as a possible next speaker, and the English-only-speaking participant need not be the only candidate. By allowing for selection of other-than-previous speaker it is also possible that one of the German-and-English speaking participants is a relevant next speaker, in English. Finally, a participant might change to the *language of the previous speaker*. That is, here a German-and-English speaking participant might switch to English where they had previously spoken in German, if the last speaker is the English-only participant (StR). This maintains continuity in English and ensures that the English-only participant remains able to contribute as a possible next speaker.

The specific environment in which this talk is placed is an examination. The abstract policy about language choice ("two working languages") must be reconciled with the practice of what we could call *language consistency across turns*. This situation clearly challenges StR. If she followed the practice of choosing the language of the previous speaker, she would need to speak German, in which she apparently has little competence. Switching the language would be easier if she were to disagree with the previous speaker—but since they defend a jointly written text, she might not want to do or indicate this. So she is disadvantaged in taking turns freely and as a consequence is not taking part in the discussion. This again presents the examiners with a challenge, since they do not know if StR's silence is due to a lack of content knowledge or due to the demanding language choice situation. So the examiners need to bring StR into the talk, and as we have seen, they create a new practice according to which languages are assigned to speakers. Now we see the multilingual situation making problematic the purpose of the examination: to assess the students according to their subject competence and project work. Since choice of language apparently has to do with issues of participation, multilingual examinations, as in our data, introduce particular interactional complexities when compared to monolingual examinations. Yet we saw how the participants skillfully managed competing motivations for language consistency and language choice, jointly to accomplish the examination.

Conclusion

We have examined the video recording of a multilingual group examination where German and English work as the official languages. The examination was conducted according to a locally (here-and-now) proclaimed policy allowing participants to choose freely from the available languages to be able always to say what they want to say, and so be unhindered by personal limitations in one or other language. We identified and examined a range of both verbal and embodied resources, over the course of the examination, on which participants drew to manage matters of language choice and participation (speakership and recipiency) while seeking to display and determine students' performance and disciplinary competence.

Conducting the examination in two official languages required participants to realize a division of labor between these languages on a local moment-to-moment basis. Language choice was inevitably tied to participation for establishing who could contribute, on what they could contribute, when and how they could contribute, and how their contributions could be responded to and acted upon. Specifically, we noted the significance of two practices for language choice: *one speaker—one language* and *language consistency across turns*. We saw how participants negotiated their orientation to these two practices and managed moments where the practices were in competition.

We have seen therefore how ideals or policies in institutions are actually accomplished by participants in situ through processes of interaction. A specific institutional ideal to each participant—to speak the language of their choice—required of them to constantly negotiate and bring into play different languages.

To this end, participants drew moment-to-moment on their own L2 competence, and attended to others' L2 competencies, to support and accomplish the activity. In multilingual settings, participants deploy in very flexible ways their linguistic resources. In line with previous research about language learning in interaction (c.f. Eskildsen, this volume; Brouwer & Wagner, 2004; Hellermann, 2008), it is likely that participation in multilingual encounters itself compels complex forms of language use that can enhance the L2 competencies of the participants.

Acknowledgments

We are grateful to our colleagues, Hartmut Haberland, Gabriele Kasper, Janus Mortensen, and Gabriele Pallotti, for suggestions which have improved this text. We thank also the *Research Center for Cultural and Linguistic Practices in the International University (CALPIU)*, at Roskilde University in Denmark, and the Center's Chair Prof. Bent Preisler, for supporting our collaboration for this research. An earlier version of this chapter appeared in Haberland et al. (2008).

Notes

1. Janus Mortensen made the recordings, and we are grateful to him for allowing us to use the data.
2. In our transcriptions, we include a line for gesture and other embodied conduct, which is signaled to the left by "GES:".
3. Also interesting is StR's switch to Danish in her comment to StL. StR is certainly not disaligning with StL and might have used English, which is the language she will later use throughout the examination. But StR might also know that StL does understand Danish, and using Danish can signal the current exchange as informal talk separate from the formal examination environment.
4. As with other instances in our data, as a native English speaker with some German competence, and a native German speaker fluent in English, we hear this unproblematically as German "*ja.*"
5. As an aside, possible further evidence is available from the full transcription and the video data. While StL continues to develop her response as an extended turn, StR makes verbal and visible embodied claims to agreement and co-ownership of the response, for example nodding and saying *mm* and *yes*.

References

Auer, P. (1984). *Bilingual conversation*. Amsterdam: John Benjamins.
Auer, P. (Ed.). (1998). *Code-switching in conversation: Language, interaction and identity*. London: Routledge.
Brouwer, C. E., & Wagner, J. (2004). Developmental issues in second language conversation. *Journal of Applied Linguistics, 1*, 29–47.

Eskildsen, S. W. (this volume) The L2 inventory in action: Conversation analysis and usage-based linguistics in SLA.

Gafaranga, J. (2001). Linguistic identities in talk-in-interaction: Order in bilingual conversation. *Journal of Pragmatics, 33*, 1901–1925.

Gafaranga, J. (2005). Demythologizing language alternation studies: Conversational structure versus social structure in bilingual interaction. *Journal of Pragmatics*, 37, 281–300.

Gafaranga, J. (2007). Code-switching as a conversational strategy. In P. Auer & Li Wei (Eds.), *Handbook of multilingualism and multilingual communication* (pp. 279–313). Berlin: Mouton de Gruyter.

Gumperz, J. (1982). *Discourse strategies*. Cambridge: Cambridge University Press.

Haberland, H., Mortensen, J. Fabricius, A., Preisler, B., Risager, K., & Kjærbeck, S. (Eds.). (2008). *Higher education in the global village: Cultural and linguistic practices in the international university.* Roskilde: Department of Culture and Identity, Roskilde University.

Have, P. ten (2007). *Doing conversation analysis: A practical guide* (2nd ed.). London: Sage.

Hellermann, J. (2008). *Social actions for classroom language learning.* Clevedon: Multilingual Matters.

Heritage, J. (2002). Oh-prefaced responses to assessments: A method of modifying agreement/disagreement. In C. Ford, B. Fox, & S. Thompson (Eds.), *The language of turn and sequence* (pp. 196–224). New York, NY: Oxford University Press.

Heritage, J., & Raymond, G. (2005). The terms of agreement: Indexing epistemic authority and subordination in talk-in-interaction. *Social Psychology Quarterly, 68*, 15–38.

Higgins, C. (2009). "Are you Hindu?" Resisting membership categorization through language alternation. In H. Nguyen & G. Kasper (Eds), *Talk-in-interaction: Multilingual Perspectives* (pp. 111–136). Honolulu, HI: National Foreign Language Resource Center, University of Hawai'i.

Hutchby, I., & Wooffitt, R. (2008). *Conversation analysis* (2nd ed.). London: Polity Press.

Jefferson, G. (1989). Preliminary notes on a possible metric which provides for a "standard maximum" silence of approximately one second in conversation. In D. Roger & P. Bull (Eds.), *Conversation: An interdisciplinary perspective* (pp. 166–196). Clevedon: Multilingual Matters.

Lerner, G. (1996). On the place of linguistic resources in the organization of talk-in-interaction: "Second person" reference in multi-party conversation. *Pragmatics, 6*, 281–294.

Lerner, G. (2003). Selecting next speaker: The context-sensitive operation of a context-free organization. *Language in Society, 32*, 177–201.

Li Wei. (1998). The "why" and "how" question in the analysis of conversational code-switching. In P. Auer (Ed.), *Code-switching in conversation: Language, interaction and identity* (pp. 156–179). London: Routledge.

Li Wei. (2002). "What do you want me to say?" On the conversation analysis approach to bilingual interaction. *Language in Society, 31*, 159–180.

Li Wei. (Ed.). (2005). Conversational code-switching [Special issue]. *Journal of Pragmatics, 37*(3).

Muysken, P. (2000). *Bilingual speech: A typology of code-mixing.* Cambridge: Cambridge University Press.

Myers-Scotton, C. (1993). *Duelling languages: Grammatical structure in codeswitching.* Oxford: Clarendon Press.

Pomerantz, A. (1984a). Agreeing and disagreeing with assessments: Some features of preferred/dispreferred turn shapes. In J. M. Atkinson & J. Heritage (Eds.), *Structures of social action: Studies in conversation analysis* (pp. 57–101). Cambridge: Cambridge University Press.

Pomerantz, A. (1984b). Pursuing a response. In J. M. Atkinson & J. Heritage (Eds.), *Structures of social action: Studies in conversation analysis* (pp. 152–163). Cambridge: Cambridge University Press.

Raymond, G., & Heritage, J. (2006). The epistemics of social relations: Owning grandchildren. *Language in Society, 35*, 677–705.

Schegloff, E. A. (1980). Preliminaries to preliminaries: "Can I ask you a question?". *Sociological Inquiry, 50*, 104–152.

Schegloff, E. A. (2006). Interaction: The infrastructure for social institutions, the natural ecological niche for language, and the arena in which culture is enacted. In N. J. Enfield & S. C. Levinson (Eds.) *Roots of human sociality: Culture, cognition and interaction* (pp. 70–96). Oxford: Berg.

Schegloff, E. A., Jefferson, G., & Sacks, H. (1977). The preference for self-correction in the organization of repair in conversation. *Language, 53*, 361–382.

Sebba, M., & Wootton, A. J. (1998). We, they, and identity. Sequential versus identity related explanation of code-switching. In P. Auer (Ed.), *Code-switching in conversation: Language, interaction and identity* (pp. 262–289). London: Routledge.

10 Employing Multilingualism for Doing Identity Work and Generating Laughter in Business Meetings: A Case Study

Monika Vöge
University of Potsdam, Germany

Introduction

Multilingualism and/or language alternation[1] has been demonstrated to be a conversational resource (Alfonzetti, 1998; Auer, 1984; Li Wei, 2002) and an instance of practical social action (Gafaranga, 1999). Interactants change between languages in order to achieve different interactional goals as, for example, claiming group membership (Gafaranga, 2001), rejecting affiliation with group members (Cashman, 2001), and proposing identity-related accounts for language choice (Sebba & Wootton, 1998). This chapter examines three sequences in multilingual business meetings in which participants employ multilingualism as a resource for membership categorization, and how they, through categories orienting to multilingualism, bring about organizational and epistemic authorities (Raymond & Heritage, 2006) as well as local identities. The chapter further discusses how interactants generate laughter by making multilingualism relevant, and how they use this laughter for affiliation, disaffiliation and issues of group constellation.

Among multilingual speakers, language choice is a social activity and a membership categorization device (Gafaranga, 2001, 2005). The theoretical concept of membership categorization (Sacks, 1974, 1995) views social identities as resources that speakers actively deploy in interaction.

Membership categorization analysis (MCA) shows that identity is not something people are, but "something they do" (Widdicombe, 1998, p. 191). "Identities are negotiated in and through social interaction, are interactionally accomplished objects" (Gafaranga, 2001, p. 1915). Sacks (1995) argues that through the "very central machinery of social organization" (LC1; p. 40) participants construct social identity in interaction. Participants do not carry identity with them as an external inflexible device.

Identity is constructed for the "self" and ascribed to others. Also, a person's multilingualism can be made relevant in interaction as an identity category—or not. Wagner (1998) states,

> since membership is a sociological category, non-nativeness can not be used ... without delivering proof that non-nativeness also is a relevant, sociological category. Seen as mere non-natives, the participants [in a particular second language acquisition study] seem to act in a socially empty room. (p. 108)

It seems evident from experience that in order to achieve intersubjectivity with others, neither unblemished grammatical structures nor standard pronunciation is required. Linguistic identity is part and parcel of social identity; it is the conversational structure that establishes the social structure. To be a "foreign language speaker" is thus not at all times relevant in interaction, but can be made relevant at any time.

The data analyzed in this chapter are taken from a context that is both multilingual and institutional. Institutional frameworks that are particular to specific institutional contexts play a decisive role for the analysis in this chapter. The organizational positions of the participants have influence on their individual rights and obligations. These are realized through interactional activities, activities that shape the local identities of the interactants. Raymond and Heritage (2006) describe the connection between local identities and the design of interactional activities and show how ownership and epistemic responsibilities are realized in interaction:

> By looking at how persons manage the rights and responsibilities of identities—the territories of ownership and accountability that are partly constitutive of how identities are sustained as identities—we are witnessing a set of resources through which identities get made relevant and consequential in particular episodes of interaction. (p. 700)

In the institutional setting of a business meeting, not only epistemic but institutional/organizational and other kind of authorities come into play. This chapter presents examples of how participants locally activate and implement epistemic and organizational authorities through their interactional activities in an institutional multilingual setting. The interrelatedness of multilingualism, local identities and institutional interaction is described by Drew and Heritage (1992):

In each case, considerations of social identity and task reconfigure the interpretative "valence" that may be attached to particular actions in institutional contexts by comparison to how they are normally understood in ordinary conversation. Still more tangled and complex interpretative issues arise in interactions ... where participants to an institutional interaction ... do not share common cultural or linguistic resources. (p. 24ff)

These "tangled and complex issues" are at the core of this chapter, as it provides an analysis of multilingualism in an institutional context (see also Kurhila, 2004; Torras & Gafaranga, 2002) in regard to identity work in an institutional environment.

The chapter puts emphasis on laughter in multilingual talk-in-interaction by examining sequences in which the laughable is connected to multilingualism. Laughter has been shown to constitute a central resource in doing identity work (Glenn, 2003; Jefferson, 1985; Jefferson, Sacks, & Schegloff, 1987). It shapes participation and plays an important role when participants orient to work-relevant identities (Dannerer, 2002; Haakana, 1999; Markaki, Merlino, Mondada, & Oloff, 2010; Vöge, 2010). Since laughter works as an adjacency pair (Jefferson, 1979), it can be managed in a sequence that includes or excludes co-present participants by affiliating or disaffiliating with it (O'Donnell-Trujillo & Adams, 1983). The analyses in this chapter will show that by laughing, participants can activate or challenge identity-building activities and even infringe on social norms (Coser, 1960). "Laughter, then, may not always be a matter of flooding out, to be accounted for as something that happens to a speaker such that he *can't help lau:gh*, but can be managed as an interactional resource, as a systematic activity" (Jefferson, 1985, p. 34).

Focusing on the relevance of the multilingual setting when it comes to generating laughter, the chapter provides evidence for the various interactional consequences laughter has in a multilingual business setting. Three cases of laughter in which the participants display their orientation to multilingualism, generate laughter from this orientation, and then use this as a resource in doing identity work, are investigated. The phenomenon is not frequent in the corpus, which is the main reason why this chapter is designed as a case analysis. Of course, a single case analysis holds the imminent risk of showing just that, a phenomenon occurring in just a few cases. A larger number of data extracts would certainly be beneficial for the findings' validity. However, as many conversation analytic studies have shown, a single case analysis can have "the capacity to explicate single episodes of action in interaction as a basic locus of social order" (Schegloff, 1987, p. 101). Single case analyses occasionally turn out to have some novel or enlightening features. This chapter aspires to widen our knowledge about coherences of multilingualism, identity work, and laughter in interaction.

Ethnographic background

The data for this chapter consists of 15 hours of video recordings, comprising 14 business team meetings within the human resources department of a major international financial service company. The meeting's participants come from Germany, Russia, Argentina, and the United States. The company's official language is English, and all participants have sufficient English language proficiency. Nevertheless, the meeting's language is mostly German, since all team members' first language (L1) is German with the exception of the departmental leader Simon (L1 Hebrew/English), and the intern Tamara (L1 Russian). Simon uses the team meetings as an occasion to improve his German and has asked explicitly that the team members continue speaking German.

In all meetings, members of the team participate and report on current activities. On average, the meetings last about an hour and involve no more than 11 people: the team members (4–8 employees, including the intern), the departmental leader (Simon), his secretary (Laura), and a maximum of two apprentices.

During the data collection period, the team was subjected to a change in leadership and several other major personal changes. The segments analyzed in this chapter stem from a period of approximately eight weeks in which the team lacks a direct, regularly present sub-team leader. In this period, Simon, the departmental leader, attends the team meetings on an irregular basis to perform leadership duties.

Case 1, In German: Making multilingualism relevant for orientation to epistemic and institutional authorities

In the first case, In German, the meeting's participants show orientation to multilingualism through a language switch and a metalinguistic negotiation of language. The epistemic and organizational authorities of the local identities are made relevant through the orientation to multilingualism and a particular recipient design. Together these factors serve as a basis for the collaboratively generated laughable.

Case 1 shows an instance in which one team member (Melanie) presents new ideas for re-structuring the area for which she is responsible. Just before the segment, a language alternation from German to English has occurred. This alternation was initiated by Melanie, who explained a specific topic to Simon due to his lack of understanding. That sequence is now closed and Melanie begins to distribute handouts in English in preparation for her forthcoming report.

Employing Multilingualism for Doing Identity Work and Generating Laughter 241

Figure 1. Case 1 "In German" seating order, meeting 011013. Faces are blurred to protect privacy.

Excerpt 1, Case 1 "In German," 1 LGH 011013, 0:30:36

```
01   Melanie:    it's it's just ehm (.) if you go through
02               its eh the objectives and then its
03               de:tailed into r:e:sources some of them-
04               *Melanie furrows brows
                 *(0.2)
                           *Melanie looks up from papers, first
                            to Simon, then into round
05   Melanie:    in deutsch* oder in englisch
                 in german     or    in english
06               was wol[l(nse)
                 what want youF
                 "in German or in English what do you(F) want"
                                   *Simon nods
07   Simon:             [in deutsch. *abba imma
                         in German of course
08   Melanie:    eh[m
09   (Nora):       [ehehe[hehe
                               *Wilma smiles
10   Anke:                     [haha[ha*haha          ]
11   Tamara:                        [hha[hhahha       ]
12   Laura:                             [hhahha       ]
                                   *Melanie looks down at her papers
13   Melanie:                        [*zuerST die £ZIE(h)LE(h)£
```

```
14                    (.) dann die verschiednen quellen
                          then the different     sources
```

Note: asterisk=onset point, £=smile voice, YouF=second person singular formal ("*Sie*" in German, pronounced here as /se/). Non-vocal activities are described on a separate line placed above speech transcription.

Multilingualism in institutional teams can be made relevant in many ways (Asmuß, 2002; Mondada, 2004). In Case 1, the team openly orients to multilingualism through the metalinguistic topicalization by one of the participants (Melanie, lines 5/6). After three English turns, Melanie asks Simon directly *in Deutsch oder in Englisch, was wolln se* [in German or in English, what do you (F) want]. She carries out a self-repair by interrupting herself (line 3), and then, after a short break of 0.2 seconds, by initiating language alternation from English to German. With this change into German, she orients to Simon's earlier expressed preference.[2]

Case 1 shows how interactants can make use of a multilingual setting as a resource for orientation to local identities through making their respective epistemic and institutional authorities relevant. Melanie and Simon cooperatively orient to Simon's organizational authority as the person highest in hierarchy. In the beginning of her turn in line 5, Melanie looks at Simon; towards the end she turns her gaze towards all participants around the table. Through gaze and body posture it becomes apparent that Melanie's question is directed at Simon, and that she, together with the team, is awaiting Simon's response. Subsequently, Simon takes the turn and makes a decision about language choice. The participants thus co-construct and make evident Simon's local identity as "head of team" or "person highest in hierarchy."

The linguistic material in Melanie's turn makes obvious that her turn is directed at Simon. Melanie chooses a specific form of address in line 6. The address form *Sie* (displayed as "youF" [you formal] in the transcript) is the formal address format in German (in contrast to the informal form *du* [you]). Usually, it is common practice in the team to address colleagues with the informal address form *du*+first name. Only Simon is addressed by all team members with *Sie*+first name. Through her choice of the formal address format, Melanie implies the local identities "boss" and "subordinate" and the relationship between those local identities. Her turn clearly contrasts with other address forms used in the team. This contrast is possible in German, but not in English, where the address form *you* does not allow the difference between formal and informal. By changing into German, Melanie makes this contrast possible.

The implicit formality Melanie has created through the form of address is then breached by Melanie using the colloquial expression *was wolln se* [what do youF want] (the colloquialness being expressed through the "sloppy" production of the address form *Sie* [se]). Through the semantics of the modal verb *want*, she still expresses and reveals that it is in fact Simon who has the final word on all decisions. Being the person highest in the hierarchy, he has the epistemic authority to enforce his preferences.

So far, an analysis of membership categories has shown how a multilingual setting can be a resource for interactants when orienting to epistemic and institutional authorities, thereby bringing about local identities. Focusing on the analysis of laughter, it becomes obvious that Simon's answer in line 6 receives laughter and is thus categorizable as a laughable (Vöge, 2008). Now, to understand how Simon's contribution can become a laughable, it is necessary to have a closer look at how the relevant membership categories in relation to multilingualism and the institution generate a resource for laughter.

Simon answers Melanie in overlap at the first possible point of completion and gives a clear directive to continue in German. Simon is not an advanced speaker of German and all team members know this. Simon's membership in the category "foreign language speaker" is crucial in giving his turn in line 7 the potential for a laughable because he toys with that category. By using colloquial elements (*abba imma* [of course]), produced with a slightly exaggerated open quality of the final vowel and an emphasized nonchalant tone of voice (stressing of *deutsch* [German]), Simon is "doing" being an expert language user and contrasts in that way his local identity as a learner of German. The colloquial expression *abba imma* [of course] in his second pair part to Melanie's question has an implicative sense of 'keep it coming.' Thus Simon makes his categorization as "learner of German" a subject of irony and mocks the fact that he is being categorized as "foreign language speaker": His alleged deficiency in German is contrasted by his capability of producing a turn like a first language user in terms of speed, choice of words, prosody, and timing.

Melanie orients to Simon's epistemic authority as "the boss" by clearly selecting Simon as the recipient of her question. Simon contrasts and simultaneously underscores his identity of being "the boss" through the colloquialness of his answer *abba imma*. Further, he makes a clear decision (or rather, confirms it, since he made this decision prior to the meeting, see endnote 2) in terms of language choice *in deutsch, abba imma* [in German, of course].

The analysis of the membership categories has shown that Simon's turn is laughable through the orientation to, and the toying with, the membership categories "boss" and "foreign language speaker," which both have been made relevant by Melanie in her question.

When looking at group interaction and constellation, it is noteworthy that Nora is the first to laugh after Simon's turn (line 9). Although it was Melanie who stated the question, she does not laugh and tries to continue with her report (line 8). During the whole sequence she stays in a serious mode, almost somewhat "on hold" between lines 5 and 13.[3] In line 13, it becomes observable that Melanie did notice the laughter sequence but does not participate in it. Acknowledging the humorous "in-between" sequence with a few laugh particles within her speech, she takes up her turn from line 1, to then go into a serious mode—literally "back to business". Apart from Nora, the other team members laugh or smile as a reaction to Simon's turn in line 7. They may orient to Simon's local identity as a boss—the team jointly laughs about a joke from the boss—yet they influence the group constellation through their activities: They are affiliating with Simon and at the same time disaffiliating with Melanie by not following her agenda.

In Melanie's activities, an infringement of social rules comes to pass. She puts a local social rule, which has previously been established, up for discussion: the issue of the preferred language choice in the meetings. It is well known to the team that Simon wishes to use the meetings as an opportunity to practice his German. The meeting's participants always communicate in German. Nevertheless, Melanie inquires about language choice and thus breaches a local social rule that the person highest in hierarchy, Simon, had established. The team deals with this breach through laughter—Simon produces a laughable and the other participants (except Melanie) laugh. Thus, in collaboration with the team, Simon has found a safe way for both him and Melanie to deal with the trespass.

Case 2, You will miss us: Using regional and local identities for creating affiliation through laughter

In Case 2, You will miss us, two language alternations occur: one from standard German to a regional dialect (line 6), and one from German to English (line 24). The analysis reveals how interactants orient to the membership categorization "Multilingual Speaker" through repair and employ this orientation for building affiliation. Analyses show how co-participants can utilize this orientation to deconstruct approaches for affiliation by creating a laughable on this very basis. Both language alternations are initiated by the same person (Melanie) and build the basis for the affiliation with the team's head (Simon) on the basis of shared regional foreignness.

In the following extract, the team reacts to Corinna's announcement of leaving the team and the company. In the preceding 12 minutes, Corinna had announced her upcoming change of position. Melanie is commenting on Corinna's career decisions and the consequences that it will have for both her and the team. She then launches into a side sequence with Simon.

Figure 2. Case 2 "You will miss us" seating order, meeting 010928. Faces are blurred to protect privacy.

Excerpt 2, "You will miss us" LGH 010928, 0:12:28

```
01    Melanie:    was   man   gelernt  hat   das  in  praxis
                  what  one   learned  has   that in  practice
                                          *Corinna smilingly nods*
02                umzusetzen=is doch    *fantastisch*
                  put          is indeed fantastic*
                  "putting into practice what one has
                  learned that's really fantastic"
03    Corinna:    ja
                  yes
                  *Simon turns gaze away from Melanie
                  towards Claudia, turns upper body towards her
04    Simon:      *hm?,
05                (1.3)
                       *Ulrike turns gaze towards Melanie
                            **Corinna turns gaze towards Melanie
06    Melanie:    des  *du    **uns vermisst des (0.1) wisse mer=
                  that  youIF   us  miss    that       know  we
                  "we know that you'll miss us"
07    Corinna:    =na    [da-
                  well   there
                        [*Ulrike turns gaze downwards,
                          then lifts head laughing loudly
```

```
08    Ulrike:            [*HAHAha[hahh he [hehe
                              *Madita leans backwards
09    Madita:            [*hahahh
10    Corinna:           [>davon könnt ihr
                            that can   youPL
                              *Ulrike turns gaze
11                              towards Corinna
                         au- <davon könnt *ihr    ausgehen
                         ass- that   can   *youPL assume
                         "you bet"
12                       hhhehe[hehe
13    (Ulrike:)                [hhehhehh
14                       (0.2)
15    Melanie:           ganz    klar    ehehehe[e
                         entirely clear
                         "totally"
                                         [*Corinna turns gaze away
                                             from Melanie
                                             makes a face
                                             lifts shoulders
                                             turns gaze towards Laura
16    Laura:                             [*nein. wir werdn=
                                           no.  we  will
                                    *Simon turns gaze towards Laura
17                       =[se  auch vermissn*
                           her too  miss
                         "no. we'll miss her too"
18    Corinna:           [.HHH[H hhhokhhee
                              "okay"
19    Melanie:                [ja
                               yes
20    Corinna:           °da    ham    wir noch ( [    )°
                          there have   we  still
21    Simon:                                    [so.
                                                 alright
                            *Simon looks at Corinna,
                              Corinna looks at him
22                       (1.*0)
23    Corinna:           [so
                          alright
                            *Corinna turns gaze    ***Ulrike turns gaze
                            towards Melanie          towards Melanie
                                **Simon turns gaze towards Melanie
24    Melanie:           [wa*s it** too much of*** dialect?
25                       (0.2)
                            *Ulrike and Corinna turn
                             gaze towards Simon
```

```
26   Simon:      .dhh* nu:a de:  letzte satz     isch
                       only the  last   sentence I
27               habe nisch verstandn
                 have not   understood
                 *Ulrike and Corinna turn
                  gaze towards Melanie
28   Melanie:    *oh I said that (.) we know that (.)
                             *Ulrike slowly turns gaze away
29               she will miss* us
                                  *Ulrike and Corinna turn
                                   gaze towards Melanie
30   Simon:      a:h ahha and eh >how did you say it<?*
31               (0.8)
                        *Ulrike and Corinna
                         turn gaze towards Madita
                                ** Madita laughingly swings
                                   upper body forwards
32   Madita:     °des *de°-  **hehE[HEHA
                                    that you
                                          *Melanie leans forward
                                           to Madita
33   Melanie:                       [*wa(h)s    was
                                         what       what
34   Madita:                        [HA hahahahahahehehe
                              *Corinna laughingly
                               leans forward
35   Corinna:                       [hehHEHE*HE .th.hhe th
                                         *Ulrike laughingly
                                          turns away upper body
36   Ulrike:                        [HAHAHA*HAHAheheh
37   Simon:      £thehewha(ha)t£
38   Madita:     i(h)ich wo(ho)ltte dic(h)h ko(hh)piern
                 I         wanted      you      copy
39               .HHH (aber mir gelingt   das)
                      (but  me  succeeds  that)
40               [nich so schön  wie dir    HEHEH[ehehe
                 [not  as beautiful as  you
                 "I wanted to copy you but I (can't
                  quite manage it) as well as you do"
41   Ulrike:     [£das geht nich£
                    that goes not
                  "that doesn't work"
42   Simon:                                         [thehehe
43   Madita:     .hhh das original is immer
                       the original is always
                 *Ulrike shifts gaze from
```

```
44                      *besser hmhmhehe .thhh
                         better
                                              *Simon slightly leans
                                               forward in Melanie's
                                               direction
45      Melanie:        I sai- eh ich e hab gesagt* wir wissen
                            I             have said    we know
46                      (.) dass sie uns vermisst
                            that she us   misses
                        "I said we know that she'll miss us"
47      Simon:          a:hhh okay
48      Melanie:        [ja
                         yes
49      Simon:          [aber [sie  hat (0.2) sie  haben das:
                         but   youF has       youF have  that
50      ( ):                  [£ja:h£
                               yeah
51      Simon:          s:e- eh (.) <du:   [habst das> sehr schnell
                        ver-         youIF +have that  very fast
52      Melanie:                          [°(hast)°
                                            (have)
53      Simon:          °gemacht° [eh >gesagt<
                         done          said
                        "but youF +have- eh youF have ver- youIF +have done that
                        said that very fast"
54      Melanie:                  [ja
                                   yes
55      Melanie:        ja=
                        yes
56      (Laura):        =EE:Hhe[eheh
57      Ulrike:                [nhhehhehh[ehhehh
58      Melanie:                          [WE:ll if I say something
59                      really emotio[nal it comes   in my   o]wn
                                     *Simon makes a face,
                                      head back
                                    ** Simon points at himself
                                       shoulders raised
60      Simon:                       [>*jajaja<ja::>°jaja°<**]
                                       yeahyeahyeah
                                     *Simon lets hands
                                      drop on table
61      Melanie:        dialect you know*
62      Simon:          °stimmt.°
                         that's right
63                      (.)
64      Simon:          °okee.°
                         okay
```

Note: +word = a non-existing word-from.

The first language alternation happens in line 6, after Melanie has complimented Corinna on her future position. Melanie announces to Corinna, who has made her leaving known, *dess du uns vermisst des wisse mer* [that you will miss us we know]). This turn is produced in a dialect from the area around Stuttgart. In the team, Melanie is the only one who speaks this dialect. Melanie's turn is contrasted from other turns through this use of dialect and builds a resource for creating an affiliation based on membership categories. As Egbert

(2004) has shown, even minor-seeming regional linguistic differences can serve as a basis for membership categorization. By producing her turn in dialect and marking it as being produced in that way, Melanie makes the membership categories "foreign language speaker" and "regional stranger" relevant for herself. Through that, she seems to strive for affiliation with Simon.

The second language alternation in line 24 takes the form of a repair initiation and marks the change from German into English. Melanie asks a question about whether her earlier turn was comprehensible (in line 6): *was it too much of dialect*? Simon replies in German (line 26), thus resisting Melanie's initiation to alternate languages. This is in line with Auer's (1988) observation about code-switching: "After code-switching, it is the newly introduced language that will be taken up by the co-participant. This is only a conversational preference, not an absolute 'rule' or 'norm'" (p. 203). In reaction to Simon's statement that his only trouble was in understanding the last sentence, Melanie interprets 'last sentence' as referring to her turn in regional dialect (line 6) and translates it into English. By doing this, she designs her utterance to single out Simon as a recipient.[4] This is apparent not only from the language choice but also from her gaze. By alternating to English and asking Simon specifically whether he understood her utterance (line 24), she makes the categories "foreign language speaker" and "regional stranger," which she activated for herself in the first language alternation, also relevant for Simon. Her activities open up a dialogue structure and thus make the affiliation between Melanie and Simon even more feasible.

With regard to membership categorizations displayed by the interactants for themselves and others, it is interesting that Simon, with his resistance towards Melanie's language alternation in line 26, also resists being categorized as an "incapable foreign language speaker" who would need to be spoken to in his L1. He does further work in this direction in lines 49/51/53 where he comments on the way Melanie produced her dialect turn, diagnosing what his trouble was. Simon identifies the speed of her utterance, not the dialect, as the trouble source. These diagnoses of the trouble, or "post mortems" (Egbert, 2004) "occur after trouble resolution and are used by participants to draw a connecting line between the trouble and some other feature involved in the interaction. This is sometimes used for membership categorization" (p. 1475). Simon's German turn in line 49ff does not come without effort as it includes four repairs: three self-initiated, self-completed repairs,[5] and one other-initiated, other-completed repair by Melanie. The latter one occurs in line 52. The trouble source for this repair lies in Simon's incorrect declination of the verb 'have.' This error is not corrected by Simon himself but by Melanie in overlap his ongoing talk. As Kurhila (2001) notes, such repair sequences in native-nonnative speaker interaction are "managed so as to intrude upon the talk in progress as little as possible" (p. 1108). Nevertheless, Melanie carries out a doubly-dispreferred action: Schegloff, Sacks, and Jefferson (1977) describe the preference for self-initiation of repair, and as Melanie other-initiates and other-completes, this repair doubles the dispreference. Although this is mitigated by low volume, Melanie's repair activities assist her in categorizing Simon as a non-native speaker of German.

In lines 45/46, Melanie repeats her turn from line 6 in standard German, after a false start in English. This is a further move towards constructing Simon as an inept speaker of German who needs to be addressed in English or in standard German and who is unable to understand a dialectal variety. However, Simon's request *how did you say it* (line 30) was probably a request to re-hear the turn in the dialect, which is also how one other team member (Madita) interprets it. Simon's request thus sounded like an attempt to be introduced to the community of dialect speakers.

In line 58ff when Melanie gives 'emotions' as the reason for her use of dialect, Simon agrees with Melanie's argument regarding 'emotionality' on the content level, but does so in German and thus defies her on the sequential level again. Repeatedly, he is reluctant to accept Melanie's initiation of language alternation. One could say that Simon declines the categorization as "incapable foreign language speaker," a category that Melanie apparently pursues to make relevant for him. Simon thus disaffiliates, but accepts to share with her the category "capable foreign language speaker," and affiliates with her on that level. Melanie uses her regional dialect as a resource for emotionality, which suggests that she feels "at home" in both languages, her dialect and standard German. In agreeing with her, Simon implies that this is also true for him and his multilingualism. Still, Simon resists the language alternation and keeps using German, even though Melanie had previously given an account for her using dialect in English (line 58ff). He affiliates in regard to content (he states to know the phenomena) but disaffiliates in regard to sequence structure (he declines the language switch; see Auer, 1988). Simon nonvocally balances out the emerging discrepancy between decline and acceptance by expressing total agreement via embodied actions (pointing at himself, raising his shoulders in agreement) and facial expressions (line 60).

When Melanie gives emotionality as the reason for her employing her regional dialect (line 58ff), she speaks English again and thereby chooses Simon as the recipient of her turn. In this way she makes a further attempt to strive for affiliation with the boss, an institutional identity Melanie implicitly confirms through the recipient design of her activities.

Regarding the interactional consequences of laughter that are generated from membership categories orienting to multilingualism and the institutional setting, lines 32–44 show how laughter can assist interactants in this particular environment in attaining disaffiliation and dealing with breaking local social institutional rules. Madita, the student worker, takes over a turn Melanie was asked to produce in line 32. In opening a side sequence, she seems to interfere with Melanie's membership categorizations and her affiliation work with Simon. In line 30, Simon had finally complied with Melanie's language alternation into English. He even inquires further and asks Melanie to linguistically describe her turn from line 6: *and eh >how did you say it<?* Repair operations of this kind, quasi 1:1 repetitions, are difficult for the producer of a trouble source, and Melanie hesitates to satisfy the requirement. A gap of 0.8 seconds occurs (line 31), then Madita self-selects as next speaker although the address form *you* in Simon's turn can only be meant to address Melanie. She starts copying Melanie, then interrupts herself after two short sounds *dess de* [that you], the first two sounds in Melanie's original turn in line 6. She then breaks off laughingly.

In annexing Melanie's turn, Madita damages Melanie's identity work. Putting an end to the gap, she breaks into the dialogue structure that Melanie created for herself and Simon and makes the issue of using dialect and employing a foreign-language-using identity for affiliation laughable by breaking out into explosive laughter. Although Madita affirms Melanie's identity as a "multilingual speaker" by making it relevant, she at the same time devitalizes Melanie's attempts to categorize Simon as an "incapable foreign language speaker" by indicating that even native speakers of German who may be able to reproduce dialect might not do it as well. Through that, she implies that while native speakers may not need a translation, they may also have difficulties understanding dialect.

Melanie's own membership categorization makes her now the target of a laughable instead of delivering the resources for affiliation. All participants, including her boss, jointly laugh about the joke that builds on her use of dialect. Madita succeeds in employing the dialect as a resource for a laughable, preempts the serious explanation that Melanie gives for her using dialect (line 59, emotional) and thus deconstructs Melanie's affiliation work.

Looking more closely at the group constellation and group interaction, it becomes observable that Melanie does not share the laughter at any point during the side sequence (with the exception of an early orientation to laughter in her repair initiation *before* she understands what Madita is doing, line 33), but almost everyone else does. Consequently, it is Melanie who closes the laughter sequence by producing a serious next turn in second position to Madita's account (line 38ff). Melanie seems to ignore both content and tone of Madita's contribution and starts her turn (line 45) in English *I sai-*, then carries out a self-repair and reproduce her turn from line 6 in standard German. This nearly has the effect of interactionally deleting the laughter sequence, as if the immediate previous turn would have been Simon's question in line 30 *and eh > how did you say it<?* Through these activities Melanie distances herself further from the team. By not joining the laughter and almost ignoring the whole sequence, Melanie is positioning herself outside of the group.

Despite Melanie's declination to laugh along, Madita's laughter is joined by Corinna and Ulrike at an early point in overlap. This laughter is on the verge between "laughing with" (Madita) and "laughing at" (Melanie). "Laughing at" has the potential to be a face threatening act and can infringe local social rules (Glenn, 1995). Looking at Madita's next turn after the occurrence of the laughable in line 38 (I wanted to copy you but I can't quite manage it, line 38ff), one can observe that she in fact orients to this potential danger: She attempts to atone for the damage that she might have caused by producing the laughter side sequence. Laughingly she gives an account of her activities and tries to excuse her potentially face threatening action by combining a compliment for Melanie with self-deprecation. This works to buffer the dispreferred activity. Nevertheless, the infringing quality of the laughter remains perceptible.

Case 2 has shown how regional and linguistic identities can be made relevant in order to achieve affiliation. Further, it has shown how laughter generated from linguistic and institutional membership categories can help to disaffiliate a person from a group and how such laughter can assist in breaching social rules, while it at the same can be employed to buffer this very infringement.

Case 3, Private: Being boss and the publication of laughables—dealing with inappropriateness

The analysis of Case 3, Private reveals how the interactants orient to the membership category "multilingual speaker" through repair and employ this orientation for building affiliation. Further, Case 3 shows in what ways multilingualism is used as a resource for orientation to local identities in terms of epistemic authorities (Raymond & Heritage, 2006) and institutional authorities. This is similar to what was observable in Case 1, In German and Case 2, You will miss us. The analysis of laughter shows again how making relevant the membership category "multilingual speaker" for others generates a laughable. The resulting laughter affects the group constellation and makes it possible for the interactants to infringe on local social rules.

At first glance, it may seem as if "inappropriate behavior" is not necessarily a part of business interaction. In Case 3, though, it becomes obvious that participants can orient to each other in an inappropriate way and that such interactional behavior has consequences in regard to membership categories, local identities, and affiliation.

The transcript is displayed in two parts. The data extract is taken from the same meeting as Case 1. Melanie reports about a certain topic that Simon would like to end at this point (closing implicit *so* [Meier, 1997], in line 1). He asks Melanie to present on this at another time in a meeting with a more exclusive group of participants. To convey this, he uses the expression *vielleicht wir können über diese Thema privat sprechen* [maybe we can talk about this in private] (line 1). The German use of *privat* turns out to be tricky in this context: Melanie makes Simon's minimal mistake publicly available through repair and implies an inappropriate innuendo.

Excerpt 3, Case 3 "Private" Part 1, LGH 011013, 0:47:09

```
01   Simon:      so .hh vielleicht wir können  über    diese
                 so     perhaps     we  can    about   this
                          *Simon drops
                           his hand on the table
02                thema (.) [*privat  sp[rechen und dann ein
                  topic      private  talk      and then  a
03   Melanie:               [ja          [ja
                            yes          yes
04   Simon:      [pf (.) (         )
                 "so perhaps we can talk about this
                  issue in private and then a (pf)"
                 [*Melanie furrows     **Simon rests
                  brow                   head on hand
05   Melanie:    [*p:rivat nit.    [**aber
                  private not       but
06   Simon:                        [priva:t,
                                    private
07   Melanie:    £sp[äter(hh)£=
                    later
                 "yes not in private but later"
08   Laura:         [unter    uns
                    between   us
                 "by ourselves"
                                  *Melanie winks
                                   at Simon
09   Melanie:    =hehehehe↑[HE^HE^ [HE^*HA^ [HA^
```

In Case 3, it is not the usage of another language that makes the orientation to multilingualism visible, but an other-initiated, other-completed correction of a single word. The rebuffering of Simon's usage of *privat* in line 1 by Melanie in line 5 (not in private) draws attention to the fact that something is amiss with the word private. Melanie's suggestion for an alternative, *später* [later], which she offers smilingly in line 7, amplifies this notion. Simon's usage of *privat* in German makes possible an innuendo: In German the word carries the semantic meanings[6] *(a) confidential; (b) familiar, domestic, homely; (c) not official, not public.* The semantics allows an innuendo but does not make it inevitable. The occurrence of this other-initiated, other-completed repair is interesting as it does not occur "when mutual understanding [is] jeopardized" (Hosoda, 2006, p. 44). However, through Melanie's interactional activities (repair, smiling, laughter), she points to the trouble source and subtly implies an innuendo. In doing so, she breaches both the institutional setting and the hierarchical structure.

Although it is not necessary for the sake of intersubjectivity to explicitly identify the trouble source in this case (see Jefferson, 2007, on non-correction

gratuity), Melanie decides to make Simon's non-native usage publicly available with an other-initiated, other-completed repair. Her repair is thus potentially problematic in terms of
- The preference for self-correction (Schegloff et al., 1977): An other-initiated, other-completed repair is twice dispreferred;
- The ethnographic and local structure of the team, with Simon being at the top of the hierarchy and Melanie being the newest member of the team in terms of seniority. She declines a directive from her boss (to talk about an issue between the two of them), breaks out of the interactional frame set by Simon, and opens an insertion sequence;
- The possible face threat by referring to Simon's lack of fluency in German and thereby making him a candidate laughable; and
- The hint towards something inappropriate (*privat* as in the context of something ambiguous): Melanie moves on a level which is implicitly inapt.

Although her other-initiated, other-completed repair and the resulting publicizing of the inappropriateness are potentially problematic, Melanie achieves affiliation through her activities nonetheless. While holding the risk of a dispreferred activity and thus the defamation of her boss, Melanie's activities enable her to get closer to Simon—or at least give the impression that they are close. In their paper on laughter in the pursuit of intimacy, Jefferson et al. (1987) describe this phenomenon:

> The introduction of improper talk may have an interactional basis. That is, it is a convention about interaction that frankness, rudeness, crudeness, profanity, obscenity, etc. are indices of relaxed, unguarded, spontaneous; i.e., intimate interaction. That convention may be utilised by participants. That is, the introduction of such talk can be seen as a display that speaker takes it that the current interaction is one in which he may produce such talk; i.e., is informal /intimate. Further, the introduction of such talk may be ... a consequential, programmatic action. (p. 160)

Melanie makes use of this convention: When she offers an alternative for *privat*, she does so smilingly with post-utterance laughter (line 7). As an embodied action, she blinks at Simon while laughing. Thus, she invokes a sense of conspiracy between her and Simon that serves to create a "we"-group. The aspired affiliation is stressed through laughter, embodied actions and looks, and is based on the orientation to multilingualism through the orientation to erroneous foreign language use.

The analysis of the next part of this stretch of talk (displayed in part two of the transcript) gives further insight into how a multilingual setting is a resource for interactants when bringing into existence local identities as well as institutional and epistemic authorities. The focus here is on Simon, Melanie, and Laura (Simon's assistant).

Excerpt 4, Case 3 "Private" Part 2 (simplified)

```
5/7   Melanie:   ja  p:rivat nit. aber £sp[äter(hh)£=
                 yes private not. but      later
                 "yes not in private but later"
08    Laura:                            [unter   uns
                                         between us
                 "by ourselves"
                                      *Melanie winks
                                       at Simon
09    Melanie:   =hehehehe↑[HE^HE^[HE^*HA^[HA^
10    Laura:              [£unter     uns£
                           between us
                 "by ourselves"
11    Simon:                       [UNTer   [uns
                                   [BETWEen [us
                 "by ourselves"
12    Laura:                                [n:hhe[he
13    Simon:                                      [was  is
                                                   what is
14               [privat=
                  private
                 "what does private mean"
15    Nora:      [Eh:hhehh
16    Melanie:   =^hha[:h
                      *Melanie turns gaze
                       smilingly to Laura
17    Laura:     [*privat  is  bei [ihnen z- eh
                  private  is  at  [youF  a- eh
18    Madita:    [(           )    [°ins bett.°=
                                    into bed
19               =>HAha<[ha:hh
20    Laura:           [zu    hau-   ]
                        at    ho
                                       *Anke throws head
                                        back, laughs silently
                                        with open mouth
21    Simon:                      [intimisch?* ]
                                  +intimate
                 "intimate"
22               hehe=
23    Melanie:   =[>hahhahh<  ^HE^HA^HA^
                  *Wilma looks at Simon, smiles
24    Laura:     [*nEIn £zu hau:se zu hau:se£
                   no    at home   at home
                             *Simon lifts one hand
```

```
25    Simon:      ja  sie  können  *zu  hause
                  yes  youF  can      at  home
26                [hehe £bei uns  zu m(h)i(h)r  nach
                        at  us     to me         at
27    Melanie:    [HEHEhehe.hhh
                                  *Simon shifts gaze from
                                  Melanie to papers on table
28    Simon:      hause  k(h)ommen*=
                  home    come
                  "yes you can come home to us home to me"
29    Melanie:    =.HHhehhehh[.HHH
                  *Simon points  **Simon leans
                    at papers        backwards
                  in front of him
30    Simon:      [*wir können  **über  diese  thema
                    we   can        about this  topic
                  *Melanie hugs her arms,
                  slowly stops laughing
31                *sprechen.  aber,
                    talk        but
                  "we can talk about this topic. but"
32                (0.2)
33    Simon:      ja.
                  yes
34                (0.2)
35    Simon:      ein paar änderungen und ich [denke
                  a   few  changes     and  I   think
36    Melanie:                                  [ja
                                                 yes
37    Simon:      sie  können  das  in ressortgespräch=
                  youF  can    that in departmental meeting
38    Melanie:    =okee=
                  okay
39    Simon:      =ehm (.) [präsen[tieren.
                                   present
                  "a few changes and I think you can
                  present that in the department meeting"
40    Melanie:              [hmh?  [okee
                                    okay
```

Note: +word = a non-existing word-from.

Simon's membership categorizations as "foreign language speaker," "man," and "boss" are crucial in making his turn a resource for affiliation. Melanie makes use of and plays with these categories. With her correction of *privat*, Melanie orients to Simon's identity as a foreign language speaker. The implication of the innuendo works here because of the obvious difference in gender and the general assumptions of flirting and/or inappropriate behavior between men and women at work. Simon's organizational authority as "boss" becomes relevant through Simon's own actions: His directive that the topic is better discussed in private (line 1) signals that he is in the position to give directives. His next directive in line 35 shows that it is he who makes decisions about which topics are to be discussed in the department leaders' meeting.

After having reached the climax of the sequence—and interestingly, it is Simon who helps the joke on his behalf to its climax as will become obvious below—Simon elegantly manages to move away from the implicit inappropriateness through self-repair. In this moving out of inappropriateness, Simon's local identity of "boss" shows again. The analysis reveals how swiftly he is able to achieve distance from the inappropriateness and to turn a potential mocking into an affiliative activity: In lines 26/28, he smilingly offers Melanie to come to his home to discuss the matter, on the surface going along with her innuendo, but inviting her *to our place*, thus making the membership category "married person possibly with family" relevant for himself, including his wife/family as hosts and excluding the assumption that his invitation could be in any way romantically inspired. He then smilingly self-repairs the pronoun from *us* to *me*, but he already has achieved the dissipation of the romantic or sexual innuendo. In line 30, Simon manages to completely leave risky waters and bring the interaction "back on track." With no trace of laughter or smile, he connects to his turn from lines 1–4[7] and repeats that he and Melanie can talk about this topic. His body posture is directed at the papers in front of him, thus signaling involvement in the work activity. Towards the end of Simon's turn in line 31, Melanie only hesitantly leaves laughter mode and Simon delays his turn in lines 32 and 34 with pauses of 0.2 seconds each, perhaps to give Melanie time to move out of the laughter sequence with him. In lines 37/39 Simon suggests that Melanie should present the topic in the *Ressortgespräch*, an executives' meeting. He is back in the institutional frame and has taken Melanie with him. In his way of handling the potentially risky situation, Simon displays the institutional authority of a superior. He has competently moved out of a situation that could have been potentially problematic for him.

Having analyzed how Simon makes his hierarchical position a social reality, it becomes obvious that Melanie's teasing also plays on Simon's organizational position. Making publicly available the mistake and thus drawing attention to a potential laughable is both more risky and incisive if the trouble source's producer has such a high position in the team. Melanie acts antipodal to hierarchy. Coser (1960) shows that humor and teasing from bottom to top in an institutional team can be a means to invert hierarchy. Melanie plays with this inversion and uses it as a further means to achieve affiliation.

When looking at Laura's conduct (Simons' secretary), it is worth noting that she also does identity work in order to display institutional and epistemic authority. It is observable in her activities that she realizes her structural role as Simon's assistant and her relative closeness to him interactionally: She is the first one to help him out of a potentially tricky situation. In line 8, she offers in overlap a harmless explanation for *privat*. She smilingly remains involved without joining the laughter. In response to Simon's question *was ist privat* [what does private mean], line 13/14, she is the first to reply. Here, too, she offers an innocent[8] description of *privat* —*zu Hause* [at home]. When the laughter is at its climax in lines 18–23, Laura repulses the sexual innuendo with a loudly produced *nein* [no], line 24. Interactionally she creates distance to the inappropriateness for both herself and Simon and removes him from the line of fire.

Focusing on the laughter occurring in this extract, it is Melanie's repair in lines 5/7 that makes the laughable publicly available. Simon's membership categorizations as "foreign language speaker" and also as "male" and "boss" are not only essential in making his turn a resource for affiliation, but also for making it a potential laughable. The subsequent collaborate activities of the participants draw even more attention to Simon's minor mistake and thus make the resulting sexual innuendo and laughter possible. Hence the participants (with the exception of Laura) make the trouble source accessible as a laughable for all participants. The first step in making the alleged mistake publicly available and thus, as an innuendo, laughable for all is made by Melanie through her other-initiated, other-completed repair in lines 5/7, which she produces with a tongue-in-cheek tone. Madita carries out the second step: Her off-stage-remark that she produces in line 18, silent but clearly audible, makes the inappropriateness of *privat* explicit—to a degree which could not be any more explicit. *Ins Bett* [into bed] as an alternative for *privat* has an unmistakably sexual connotation and makes this accessible for all members. The ambiguity of *privat* is thus extinguished and innuendo is no longer implicit but made explicit for all. This can be seen as an infringement on local social rules. Madita's off-stage commentary serves to accelerate the sequence and to annihilate the ambiguity.

When looking at how the team moves in and out of the laughter sequence, the influence of laughter on the group interaction and constellation becomes palpable. The team members collaboratively make the laughable publicly available through lines 5, 7, and 18 (discussed above), through laughter (line 15, Nora; line 21, Anke), smiles (line 24, Wilma), and smile voice (lines 10, 24, Laura). Then Simon helps the laughter to its climax upgrading the explicitness. He gives an even stronger substitute for *privat*, *intimisch* [intimate] (line 21). Unlike Madita, Simon utters his suggestion loudly and it is clearly audible for all interactants. The adjective *intimate* carries in German an almost clinical connotation and is, especially in contrast to Madita's figurative description, very direct. Although grammatically not fully correct no attempts of repair are made. The word-merge from *intim* (German) and *intimate* (English) with the German/English ending *-isch/–ish* is understood without problems by Simon's co-participants. Subsequent to *intimisch* Simon produces post-utterance laugh particles and thus recognizes the "joke on his behalf" and joins it, turning the "laughter about him" into "laughter with him" by participating in the joke. Melanie's almost ecstatic laughter in line 23 marks the climax of the laughter sequence.

Case 3, Private, has shown how inappropriateness, invoked through categorizing the other as "foreign (faulty) language user," can be a resource for laughter and affiliation. As in all three cases, the realization of institutional membership categories and organizational authorities through the orientation to multilingualism has been revealed.

Concluding remarks

This chapter has shown how the orientation to multilingualism as a members' category can be a resource in doing identity work in terms of institutional authorities and organizational identities. The case analysis has revealed that a bi- or multilingual identity is not necessarily a "transportable identity" (Zimmerman, 1998), but it is occasioned and employed to achieve interactional goals. The orientation to multilingualism has an influence on the local identities in a business team and their relations with each other. "Language itself is a social structure; language preference itself structures society" (Gafaranga, 2005, p. 298). This is true for the particular social setting of a business team. Interlocutors shape the institutional environment they interact in through language preference and the orientation to multilingualism. Drew and Heritage (1992) have a point in saying that social identity work gets "more tangled and complex where participants to an institutional interaction ... do not share common cultural or linguistic resources" (p. 24). It also gets very interesting and resourceful.

Multilingualism as a members' category can be made relevant by participants for self or other in aspiration of affiliation or disaffiliation, and to establish institutional and epistemic authorities, thus bringing about local identities. In all three cases, institutional and epistemic authorities were realized in orientation to multilingualism. In Case 1, In German, this is done through the specifically addressed question about language preference and the subsequent directive by the person highest in the hierarchy. In Case 2, You will miss us, this occurs through a recipient design that selected exclusively the person highest in the hierarchy as the only recipient to a dialectal turn, thus building an attempt to form an affiliation by making relevant the categorization "local/regional foreigners" for self and other. In Case 3, Private, the realization of organizational and epistemic authorities happens through Simon's management of a laughter sequence which is based on an inappropriateness and invoked by his subordinates, and through the subsequent directives Simon gives. All of these analytic results support the claim that multilingualism provides rich resources for bringing into existence local identities with their respective organizational and epistemic authorities in institutional interaction. Through language choices and the orientation to multilingualism, interlocutors are doing "being boss" and "being subordinate," and thus create the social reality of a business meeting.

In every case, the laughter is generated from the orientation to multilingualism as a members' category. In Case 1, the laughable was the second pair part to the inquiry about language preference, an answer that was given in a distinctive "first language user" manner. In Case 2, the laughable turned out to be first a dialectal turn and then the mocking repetition of it. In Case 3, it was a trouble source due to the inappropriate word usage of a foreign language speaker, and the other-initiated, other-completed repair of it. Further, in all three cases laughter has been shown to have vast influence on group interaction and group constellation. In all three cases, the group constellation was affected by who laughs along, who does not laugh along, and who might be "laughed about" (Glenn, 1995). The analyses have thus furnished further results to prove that laughter has both affiliative and disaffiliative qualities, and that these can be employed by the interactants adequately. It has been shown that laughter plays an important role for participants when orienting to work-relevant identities as well as to work-relevant relations and aspired affiliations, like the one between superior and subordinate, and that participants make use of this interactional tool accordingly.

Laughter seems to enable participants to activate but also to challenge membership categorizations that others have brought about for self or other. The analyses have provided evidence that laughter employs interactants with a tool to either breach local social norms or deal with those infringements, while at the same time supplying them with a resource that can achieve affiliation with others, or demolish attempts to build affiliation. In Case 1, it was the previously local social rule of the meeting's language choice that was challenged. Case 2 showed an example of mocking a colleague's dialect and through that breaking into an attempted dialogue structure, and Case 3 revealed the moving in and out of inappropriateness through laughter. The chapter has thus demonstrated how laughter can constitute a somewhat "protected area" in multilingual business meetings for both breaching local social rules and cushioning these infringements.

Acknowledgments

I am indebted to Maria Egbert, Kristian Mortensen, and the editors of this volume for helpful and constructive comments on earlier versions of this chapter.

Notes
1   This chapter does not contribute to the discussion of terminology in regards to the difference between code-switch, language switch/change, and transfer. For this

discussion, see for example Auer (1984, 1988) and Gafaranga (1999). Throughout this chapter I will use the term Gafaranga (2001, 2005) uses as an umbrella term when referring to "any occurrence of two languages in the same conversation" (Torras & Gafaranga, 2002): "language alternation."

2   The transcript below shows how Simon expresses this preference. The instance shows the first time Simon participates in a team meeting (2 weeks prior to the incidence in Case 1). In this meeting, he gives a directive in regard to what language should be used in the team meeting (line 2; there has been information about that before [not on tape]) and reason for his being there (lines 7/8).

Excerpt 5, Business meeting, 010928, 0:00:20

```
1 Simon:    so ich denke mich wir müssn fortfahren in
            alright I think we have to continue
2           deutsch fortfahren aber wenn es zu
            to continue in German but when it gets to
3           kompliziert für mich ich spreche englisch,
            complicated for me I will speak English,
4           aber (.) deshalb isch habe keine große teil
            but (.) that is why I won't contribute
5           zu    £mache[n hehehe
            a £great dea[l
6 Melanie:         [HEhe
7 Simon:    ich bin hier zu lernen und verstehn
            I am here to learn and to understand
8           was ist los in LifeLongLearning,
            what is going on in ((the Triple L Team)),
```

3   This might have to do with the fact that Melanie's question could have been related to the English handout.

4   It is worth noticing that Melanie initiates the translation for Simon with *oh* (line 28), thus implying that this twist in the interaction is somewhat unexpected for her (Heritage, 1984), although it was Melanie herself who launched the repair initiation (line 24). Through Melanie's interactional activities in line 28, it now seems as if the initiative for repair lies with Simon.

5   The three self reapirs are concerning (a) the modal verb *haben* [have]: Simon uses the third person singular form *hat* instead of the second person singular form in formal address terms *haben*; (b) the form of address: instead of using the formal form of address *Sie*, he employs the informal form *du* which is common in the team (the reason for this might be the problematic differentiation between the terms of address for English speakers, and also the difficulty with the ongoing turn, because Simon is usually the only one who addresses everyone in the team with the formal *Sie*); and (c) the participle *gemacht*: Simon corrects the rather unspecific participle *gemacht* [made] into the more specific *gesagt* [said].

6   Source: Duden Fremdwörterbuch (Foreign Word Lexicon, 1990).
7   The same is observable in Case 2, "You will miss us" from line 45 onwards.
8   'At home' as an equivalent to 'private' is especially innocent in comparison to what Madita offers in line 18: 'into bed.'

References

Alfonzetti, G. (1998). The conversational dimensions in code-switching between Italian and dialect in Sicily. In P. Auer (Ed.), *Code-switching in conversation: Language, interaction and identity* (pp. 180–214). New York, NY: Routledge.

Asmuß, B. (2002). Nationale Stereotype in internationalen Verhandlungen [National stereotypes in international business negotiation]. In M. Becker-Mrotzek & R. Fiehler (Eds.), *Unternehmenskommunikation* [Corporate communication] (pp. 59–88). Tübingen: Narr.

Auer, P. (1984). *Bilingual conversation*. Amsterdam: John Benjamins.

Auer, P. (1988). A conversation analytic approach to code-switching and transfer. In M. Heller (Ed.), *Code-switching: Anthropological and sociolinguistic perspectives* (pp. 187–213). Berlin: Mouton de Gruyter.

Cashman, H. R. (2001). Identities at play: Language preference and group membership in bilingual talk in interaction. *Journal of Pragmatics, 37*, 301–315.

Coser, R. L. (1960). Laughter among colleagues. *Psychiatry, 23*, 81–95.

Dannerer, M. (2002). Allen Ernstes scherzen? Formen und Funktionen von Scherzen und Lachen in innerbetrieblichen Besprechungen. [Seriously joking? Forms and functions of jokes and laughter in in-company meetings]. In M. Becker-Mrotzek & R. Fiehler (Eds.), *Unternehmenskommunikation* [Corporate communication] (pp. 89–115). Tübingen: Forum Fachsprachen Forschung.

Drew, P., & Heritage, J. (Eds.). (1992). *Talk at work*. Cambridge: Cambridge University Press.

Duden Fremdwörterbuch [Foreign word lexicon]. (1990). Mannheim: Bibliographisches Institut.

Egbert, M. (2004). Other-initiated repair and membership categorization—Some conversational events that trigger linguistic and regional membership categorization. *Journal of Pragmatics, 36*, 1467–1498.

Gafaranga, J. (1999). Language choice as a significant aspect of talk organisation: The orderliness of language alternation. *Text, 19*, 201–225.

Gafaranga, J. (2001). Linguistic identities in talk-in-interaction: Order in bilingual conversation. *Journal of Pragmatics, 33*, 1901–1925.

Gafaranga, J. (2005). Demythologising language alternation studies: Conversational structure vs. social structure in bilingual interaction. *Journal of Pragmatics, 37*, 281–300.

Glenn, P. J. (1995). Laughing *at* and laughing *with*: Negotiation of participant alignments through conversational laughter. In P. ten Have & G. Psathas (Eds.), *Situated order—Studies in the social organization of talk and embodied activities* (pp. 43–56). Boston, MA: University Press of America.

Glenn, P. J. (2003). *Laughter in interaction*. Cambridge: Cambridge University Press.
Haakana, M. (1999). *Laughing matters. A conversation analytical study of laughter in doctor-patient interaction*. Helsinki: Department of Finnish Language, University of Helsinki.
Heritage, J. (1984). A change-of-state token and aspects of its sequential placement. In J. M. Atkinson & J. Heritage (Eds.), *Structures of social action* (pp. 299–345). Cambridge: Cambridge University Press.
Hosoda, Y. (2006). Repair and relevance of differential language expertise in second language conversations. *Applied Linguistics, 27,* 25–50.
Jefferson, G. (1979). A technique for inviting laughter and its subsequent acceptance declination. In G. Psathas (Ed.), *Everyday language studies in ethnomethodology* (pp. 79–96). New York, NY: Irvington Publishers.
Jefferson, G. (1985). An exercise in the transcription and analysis of laughter. In T. Van Dijk (Ed.), *Handbook of discourse analysis, Vol. 3: Discourse and dialogue* (pp. 25–34). London: Academic Press.
Jefferson, G. (2007). Preliminary notes on abdicated other correction. *Journal of Pragmatics, 39,* 445–461.
Jefferson, G., Sacks, H., & Schegloff, E. (1987). Notes on laughter in the pursuit of intimacy. In G. Button & J. R. E. Lee (Eds.), *Talk and social organisation* (pp. 152–205). Clevedon: Multilingual Matters.
Kurhila, S. (2001). Correction in talk between native and nonnative speaker. *Journal of Pragmatics, 33,* 1083–1110.
Kurhila, S. (2004). Clients or language learners—Being a second language speaker in institutional interaction. In R. Gardner & J. Wagner (Eds.), *Second language conversations* (pp. 58–74). London: Continuum.
Li Wei. (2002). "What do you want me to say?" On the conversation analysis approach to bilingual interaction. *Language in Society, 31,* 159–180.
Markaki, V., Merlino, S., Mondada, L., & Oloff, F. (2010) Laughter in professional meetings: The organization of an emergent ethnic joke. *Journal of Pragmatics, 42,* 1526–1542.
Meier, C. (1997). *Arbeitsbesprechungen: Interaktionsstruktur, Interaktionsdynamik und Konsequenzen einer sozialen Form*. [Workmeetings: Interactional structure, interaction dynamics, and consequences of a social form]. Opladen: Westdeutscher Verlag.
Mondada, L. (2004). Ways of "doing being plurilingual" in international work meetings. R. Gardner & J. Wagner (Eds.), *Second language conversations* (pp. 18–39). London: Continuum.
O'Donnell-Trujillo, N., & Adams, K. (1983). *Hehe* in conversation: Some coordinating accomplishments of laughter. *Western Journal of Speech Communication, 47,* 175–191.
Raymond, G., & Heritage, J. (2006). The epistemics of social relationships: Owning grandchildren. *Language in Society, 35,* 677–705.

Sacks, H. (1974). On the analysability of stories by children. In R. Turner (Ed.), *Ethnomethodology: Selected readings* (pp. 216–232). Harmondsworth: Penguin.

Sacks, H. (1995). *Lectures on conversation (1964–72)* (G. Jefferson, Ed.). Cornwell: T. J. Press Ltd.

Schegloff, E. A. (1987). Analyzing single case episodes of interaction: An exercise in conversation analysis. *Social Psychology Quarterly, 50,* 101–114.

Schegloff, E., Sacks, H., & Jefferson, G. (1977). The preference for self-correction in the organization of repair in conversation. *Language, 53,* 361–382.

Sebba, M., & Wootton, T. (1998). We, they and identity. Sequential versus identity-related explanation in code-switching. In P. Auer (Ed.), *Code-switching in conversation: Language, interaction and identity* (pp. 262–286). New York, NY: Routledge.

Torras, M., & Gafaranga, J. (2002). Social identities and language alternation in non-formal institutional bilingual talk: Trilingual service encounters in Barcelona. *Language in Society, 31,* 527–548.

Vöge, M. (2008). *All you need is laugh—Interactional implications of laughter in business meetings* (Unpublished doctoral dissertation). University of Southern Denmark.

Vöge, M. (2010) Local identity processes in business meetings displayed through laughter in complaint sequences. *Journal of Pragmatics, 42,* 1556–1576.

Wagner, J. (1998). On doing being a guinea pig—A response to Seedhouse. *Journal of Pragmatics, 20,* 103–113.

Widdicombe, S. (1998). Identity as an analysts' and participants' resource. In C. Antaki & S. Widdicombe (Ed.), *Identities in talk* (pp. 191–206). London: Sage Publications.

Zimmerman, D. H. (1998). Identity, context and interaction. In C. Antaki & S. Widdicombe (Ed.), *Identities in talk* (pp. 87–106). London: Sage Publications.

Bridging the

Interactional/Linguistic Divide

11 Italian Learner Varieties and Syntax-in-Interaction

Michela Biazzi
University of Pavia, Italy

This chapter investigates Italian second language talk by speakers of different learner varieties (henceforth LVs) in a specific type of institutional encounter, namely general practice medical consultations. Focus is drawn on their use of syntactic structures in two specific interactional contexts: co-constructions and the opening sequence of the encounter.

The theoretical foundation draws on work about syntactic competence in LVs within second language acquisition (SLA), studies on spontaneous learning[1] in the interlanguage framework (Klein, 1986; Selinker, 1972), and on research at the interface of syntax and interaction in first language conversations (Ford, Fox, & Thompson, 2002; Fox, 2007; Fox, Hayashi, & Jasperson, 1996; Fox & Jasperson, 1995; Hakulinen & Selting, 2005; Hayashi, 1999; Kärkkäinen, Sorjonen, & Helasvuo, 2007; Lerner, 2004; Lerner & Takagi, 1999; Ono & Thompson, 1995; Thompson & Couper-Kuhlen, 2005; Schegloff, 1979; Selting, 2000).

This study explores the possibility of bridging the gap between two different approaches to second language talk: work on the acquisition of a second language from a developmental perspective,[2] where second language speakers (henceforth L2Ss) are mainly assessed according to their morphosyntactic performance in elicited data, either monologic narratives or interviews (Dimroth & Starren, 2003; Doughty, Bymes, Connor-Linton, Spielmann, & Tyler, 1997; Doughty & Long, 2000; Hendriks, 2005; Klein & Perdue, 1992, 1997;

Larsen-Freeman & Long, 1991; Perdue, 1993, 2000); and a conversation analytic and interactional linguistic[3] approach to second language conversations, aiming at investigating interactional competence from an emic perspective in naturally occurring data (*Issues in Applied Linguistics*, 2000; Gajo & Mondada, 2000; Kramsch, 2003; Leather & van Dam, 2003; Mondada & Pekarek Doehler, 2000; Pekarek Doehler, 2000; Wagner & Gardner, 2004; Young, 2008). One of the fundamental principles of the latter approaches is the constitutive role of social interaction in language acquisition and development, which brings along a redefinition of the notion of *language acquisition* itself. Following Pekarek Doehler (2000),

> [language acquisition] is not just learning a linguistic system and its communicative norms; it is more appropriately described in terms of the development of the ability to participate into social practices—and, consequently, it must be studied within specific social practices. (p. 7, my translation)[4]

As a consequence, the role of the researcher is to identify and describe in detail language practices as they are deployed sequentially and to consider them as social practices and instances where learning may take place.

The LV approach and the interactional approach to SLA both treat the learner's deviations from the target language norm in a similar way, that is, as potential indexes of the systematicity of the learner's variety "as opportunities to apply his abilities to collaboratively solve problems, and as potential instances for the elaboration of a linguistic repertoire appropriate to the learner's concrete communicative needs" (Pekarek Doehler, 2000, p. 13, my translation).[5] Such a rejection of the "deficit model" in favour of "the normality of second language conversations" is a founding principle of the CA approach to second language talk in Wagner and Gardner (2004, pp. vii-x, 1–4).

Studies on the morphosyntactic competence of Italian L2Ss have been carried on since the mid-eighties (Bernini & Giacalone Ramat, 1990; Giacalone Ramat, 2003) within the comparative study of SLA set up by the European Science Foundation Project (ESF) on adult language acquisition (Perdue, 1993), essentially based on the LV approach.[6] Following the ESF project, a number of studies have compared learners of different target and source languages performing in monologic narrative tasks based on similar visual inputs (Hendriks, 2005). Many studies on Italian L2 are also based on a corpus of longitudinal interviews with untutored adult learners of Italian, collected from the mid-1980s to the mid-1990s (Andorno, 2000). However, these interviews have been treated most of the time as if they were monologic data since the native interviewers' turns were transcribed but not usually included in the analysis. The overall purpose of these studies has been to set morphosyntactic, lexical, and textual parameters to describe the stages learners of different first languages (L1) go through when learning a second language (L2) and examine which patterns are universal (independent of source and target languages), which ones are language-specific or may correlate with other sociolinguistic variables of the learner, and finally, if different levels of analysis may correlate with one another.

The main research question of this study is whether interactional structures develop across different LVs, as it has been observed for the use of L2 morphosyntactic and lexical features (Klein & Perdue, 1992; Perdue, 1993). Furthermore, the study investigates to which extent the use of different interactional formats may be explained in terms of the speakers' competence in the syntactic structures of the L2 and, on the other hand, which formats cannot be explained in terms of syntactic competence only, suggesting that more than linguistic issues may be at play. The attempt to use different approaches to second language talk and acquisition brings along a number of theoretical and methodological issues, for example, the notions of *learning* and *acquisition*, *competence* and *performance*, *speaker* and *learner* on the one hand, and the different types of data investigated and analytic procedures, on the other.

Data and methodology

The present research draws on a corpus of 19 audio-recorded[7] interactions between general practitioners (henceforth GPs) and migrants seeking general medical services in a health centre for undocumented foreigners.[8] All the GPs are Italian L1 speakers (4 male and 1 female) whereas the patients (henceforth Ps) are all L2Ss of Italian and come from a variety of countries, as shown in Table 1: five Ps are from Ecuador, three Ps each from Albania, Romania, and Moldova, two from Togo, and one each from the Ukraine, Morocco, and Peru.

Table 1. Length of consultations and participant variables

		participants			
	consultation	general practitioner[9]		L2 speaker	
no.[10]	length (minutes)	gender	gender	country of origin	L2 speaker learner variety
3	11:01	AM	F	Moldova	pre-basic
8	11:55	CM	F	Ecuador	pre-basic
1	5:50	AM	F	Moldova	basic
12	6:22	DF	F	Togo	basic
9	2:00	CM	M	Ecuador	basic
14	8:09	DF	F	Ecuador	basic
2	3:70	AM	M	Togo	basic
7	9:53	BM	F	Albania	basic/post-basic
11	8:00	DF	F	Ukraine	basic/post-basic

continued...

Table 1. *(cont.)*

		participants			
		general practitioner[9]	L2 speaker		
consultation no.[10]	length (minutes)	gender	gender	country of origin	L2 speaker learner variety
19	8:00	EM	F	Peru	basic/post-basic
10	11:00	DF	F	Ecuador	basic/post-basic
16	5:30	EM	F	Ecuador	basic/post-basic
6	10:24	BM	F	Romania	post-basic
5	4:90	AM	M	Morocco	post-basic
13	13:38	DF	F	Albania	post-basic
15	4:51	EM	M[11]	Romania	post-basic
17	7:23	EM	F	Moldova	post-basic
20	2:37	EM	M	Romania	post-basic
4	2:37	AM	F	Albania	post-basic

However, the analysis that follows will not consider the different L1s of the Ps nor whether they have learnt Italian in a tutored and/or untutored context. Its main concern is the L2Ss' LV at the time of the consultation (Table 1, right-hand column). This is why the interlocutors will be mainly referred to as L1 and L2 speakers, highlighting only one of their multiple identities and for the purpose of analysis (Linell & Luckmann, 1991). In fact, following Antaki and Widdicombe (1998), identity work is constantly negotiated in interactions since multiple identities and asymmetries may interact and be made relevant by participants throughout the exchange. So, the analysis is limited in that it does not take into account the participants' identity work from their perspective, or other linguistic types of resources. On the other hand, the choice is dictated by the analyst's need to narrow down the scope of the investigation coherently with the research questions.

The first preliminary step of the present work is the assessment of the Ps' LV.[12] A LV of the target language consists of the target language means available to the learner at a given time. The fully-fledged target language may then be considered to be the final LV in which the organizing principles and their interaction have reached their fullest complexity. A LV is characterized by a double *systematicity*, both in its internal organization at a given time and in the transition from one variety to the next over time (Klein, 1986, p. 29).

The notion of *basic variety* was the outcome of a large cross-linguistic field investigation sponsored by the European Science Foundation, the ESF Project (Klein & Perdue, 1992, 1997; Perdue, 1993), whose main finding was that "all our learners, irrespective of source and target language, develop a particular way of structuring their utterances which seems to represent a natural equilibrium between the various phrasal, semantic, and pragmatic constraints" (Klein & Perdue, 1992, p. 311). The following features characterize the basic variety: regular phrasal patterns such as NP-V-(NP), NP-Cop-NP/Adj/PP, V-NP (restricted to presentationals), or NP-NP-V, which may be preceded or followed by adverbials of time and space. Utterances are mainly structured around an infinite verb (the so-called *infinite utterance organization*); they follow the *focus last* pragmatic principle—according to which the *comment* follows the sentence *topic*—and the *controller first* semantic principle, where the controller is the entity which controls the event (usually a human or animate entity, often the agent; Klein & Perdue, 1992, pp. 312–313; Perdue, 1993, pp. 30–32).

Before reaching this level, real beginners studied by the ESF project went through the non-finite utterance organization stage, which characterizes the *pre-basic variety*. At this stage "nominals are put into a relationship with a 'predicative' nominal, adverbial, adjective, or particle; or simply introduced into learner's discourse with optional contextualization thanks to a temporal or locative adverbial" (Klein & Perdue, 1992, p. 313). The use of gestures and references to the situational context are pervasive. The lexicon is essential and includes a limited number of function words (some personal pronouns, conjunctions, and frequent adverbs and some negation and assertion particles).

The step beyond the basic variety is the development of a finite utterance organization, a common feature of *post-basic varieties*, which, unlike pre-basic and basic varieties, are less uniform among learners and more sensitive to the source and target languages involved. Among other things, the ESF project observed a development in the following features common to post-basic learners with respect to the basic variety: referential means (especially in the use of the third person pronoun system), focalization devices, verb morphology, and means for subordination (Klein & Perdue, 1992, pp. 315–323).

In the present study, assessing the L2Ss' LV on the basis of naturally occurring interactions proved to be anything but an easy task. The type of data and their collection methodology represent the main problems in applying the notion of LV to the corpus. The limited amount of talk available for each L2S (one single medical consultation) and its non-elicited nature are the two main limits of the data used for the present research. First, as mentioned in the previous section, the notion of LV originated from work on mainly monologic and elicited data (Klein & Perdue, 1992, 1997; Perdue, 1993), aimed at triggering the use of specific linguistic structures and devices while neutralizing (or at least controlling, as far as possible) other linguistic and non-linguistic variables. This was not the case for the present corpus of institutional encounters, apart from its homogeneity with regard to the institutional context and hidden agenda of the exchanges and the institutional roles of the participants.

Second, the small amount of talk available for each L2S does not allow an accurate and comprehensive profile of the speaker's language competence. As a matter of fact, the single occurrence of a specific grammatical structure does not necessarily imply that it represents a productive means in the speaker's interlanguage, an index of the developmental restructuring of the LV system, nor that the speaker would use it appropriately and productively in other communicative contexts. On the other hand, the fact that some linguistic structures were not produced during the consultation does not necessarily mean that they do not belong to the L2S competence. In other words, in the analysis that follows one should always bear in mind that the assessment of the L2Ss' LV based on one single naturally occurring exchange can provide but a rough picture of the speakers' competence.

In the third column of Table 1, the Ps are arranged along a continuum according to the LV they belong to. In order to place the L2Ss along the interlanguage continuum shown in Table 1, the following criteria were used: *the type of utterance organization* (nominal, non-finite, finite), *the use of function-words, nominal and verbal morphological agreement*, and *the use of dependent clauses*. Nevertheless, sometimes—in 5 cases out of 19 (Table 1, speakers 7, 11, 19, 10, and 16)—it was not possible to place the L2S at one single level because of lack of sufficient data. As a consequence, the intermediate class of *basic/post-basic speaker* was used. This is a less precise assessment but a more cautious and realistic attitude towards the data. Furthermore, this is coherent with the dynamic and non-discreet nature of the notion of LV, which is best represented by a continuum of varieties with faded boundaries from one variety to the next.

Despite the limits in applying the notion of LV to interactional data, this category proved to be useful to the research aims. First, LVs are mainly defined with respect to morphosyntactic parameters, which is coherent with the present study's interest in the use of syntactic structures in interaction. Second, most studies on the acquisition of Italian by adult migrants use the notion of LV as a common reference point (Giacalone Ramat, 2003),[13] which makes it possible to compare the results of the present research with other studies on Italian L2.

Before turning to the analysis of specific interactional contexts, the following paragraphs will briefly hint at some general features of the Ps' interlanguage systems as they are reflected in the medical encounters investigated. Examples 1 to 6 exemplify each of the three LVs.

In Examples 1 and 2, both L2 speakers rely mainly on pragmatic and lexical means, which is typical of the prebasic variety. In fact, their talk does not show any systematic use of the target language morphosyntactic structures.

Example 1, File 3 Pre-b

```
1    PA0:    i::::::::::::::: eh::: bisogne::::   eh eh eh
             *I                eh   *need:F.PL    eh eh eh
2            .hhh doctor       dentiste
                  doctor.M.SG  dentist:*F.PL
             "I::::::::::::::: eh::: need::::  eh eh eh a
             dentist"

3            (0.4)

4    PA0:    i::::  mi        è                  poca
             *I     1SG.DAT   be:IND.PRS.3SG     little:F.SG
5            poca         mtch    a  tossa              eh  [eh
             little:F.SG mtch   *to cough:*F.SG  eh   eh
             "I::::  have  a  little  little  mtch  cough  eh
             eh"

6    DO0:                                              [eh sì
             eh yes
7            (.) TANTE        COSE       (.)    [TANTI
                 many:F.PL   thing:F.PL         many:M.PL
8            PROBLEMI        MAMMA MIA!
             problem:M.PL    EXC
             "[eh yes (.) many things (.) [many problems
             my god"

9    PA0:                                       [oh tanti
                                                oh  many:M.PL
10           cose         tante     (.)  ium=
             thing:F.PL   many:F.PL
             "[oh many things many (.) ium="

11   DO0:    tutti       seri             serissimi!
             all:M.PL    serious:M.PL     very serious:M.PL
             "all serious very serious!"

12   PA0:    .hh

13           (0.4)

14   DO0:    va bene. (.) d'accordo.
             ok           ok
             "that's right. (.) ok."

15   PA0:    a            tosse        bisogna              po
             *to          cough:M.SG   need:IND.PRS.3SG     *of
16           medicinu                mie    (.)    eh
             medicine:*ACC.SG        my:F.PL       eh
```

```
17              come i uze        prindio            come::
                as I *already     *take:IND:PRS.1SG as
18              (mtch) caramelle caramielle uze::
                       candy:F.PL candy:F.PL *already
                "I need a medicine for my cough (.) eh
                since I already take ( ) some candies"

19     DOO:     °°( )°°((to the researcher))

20              (0.6)

21     DOO:     va bene. d'accordo. adesso la
                okay    okay        now     3SG.ACC.CRT
22              visito              un
                examine:IND.PRS.1SG a:M.SG
23              momento     signora. (.) venga
                while:M.SG madam:ADR     come:IMP.3SG
24              sul          lettino    che
                on the:M.SG couch:M.SG that
25              proviamo          la         pressione.
                test:IND.PRS.1PL the:F.SG pressure:F.SG
                "that's right. ok. now I'm going to examine
                you madame. (.) come on the couch for checking
                your blood pressure"

26     PAO:     ai ai e   forse così bisogne    lettina!
                      and maybe so   need:*F.P couch:*F.SG
                "(ai ai) and maybe so you need a couch!"
```

Example 2, File 8 Pre-b

```
1      DOO:     [okè
                 ok
                "[okè"

2      PAO:     [di dove:::::: me[:
                 of where      1SG.DAT
                "where:::::: me[:"

3      DOO:                    [io adesso le
                                I  now    3SG.DAT.CRT
4               faccio              le         quattro
                do:IND.PRS.1SG the:F.PL four
```

```
5              richiestei
               prescription:F.PL
               "[now I'm going to write you the four
               prescriptionsi"

6              (0.5)

7     DOO:     e       lei         va              al
               and     3SG.CRT     go:IND.PRS.3SG  to the:M.SG
8              CUP                 a
               reservation centre  to
9              prenotarle.
               book:INF.CLIT.3PL.ACC.F
               "and you go to the hospital reservation
               centre to book them."

10             (0.3)

11    PAO:     CUP (.)              prenotalei
               reservation centre   *book:INF.CLIT.3PL.ACC.F
               "the hospital reservation centre (.) to
               book themi"
```

In Example 1, the L2S's talk is characterized by a strong L1 interference at the lexical level (e.g., the use of particles such as *po* [for/of] and *uze* [already], lines 15 and 17–18) and in word order (lines 4 and 15). Moreover, the use of the verb *bisogne/bisogna* [need] (lines 1, 15, and 26) is probably merely formulaic. Turning now to Example 2, one notices a pervasive use of nominal (verbless) utterances and a considerable reliance on the juxtaposition of lexical items by the L2S (lines 2 and 11), which provides no evidence of the speaker's knowledge of the target language syntactic categories.

Instead, the utterances by the following two speakers in Examples 3 and 4 are often built around a verbal predicate and its arguments, although verbal and nominal morphology and function-words (e.g., articles and prepositions) are often missing or deviant, with a clear predominance of unmarked morphological forms. Their utterances mainly follow the pragmatic principle *focus first* and the semantic principle *controller first*.

Example 3, File 2 B

```
1     PAO:    °sono                   andato
              be:IND.PRS.1SG.AUX      go:PTCP.PST.M.SG
2             al'                     ospedale° (.) [↓però
              to the:M.SG             hospital:M.SG    but
              "I went to the hospital (.) [↓but"
```

3	DO0:	[mh
4	PA0:	°dopo° la medicina
		after the:F.SG medicine:F.SG
5		fa male ancora.
		do:IND.PST.3SG pain:M.SG still
		"after the medicine it still hurts."
6		(5.0)
7	PA0:	ha (.) questo con
		have:IND.PRS.3SG this:M.SG with
		"it has (.) this one with"
8		(3.5)
9	DO0:	↓mhm↑
10	PA0:	°°questo (qua)°°
		this:M.SG here
		"this one (here)"
11	DO0:	messo questo?
		put:PTCP.PST.M.SG this:M.SG
		"did you put this one?"
12	PA0:	sì:: (.) quattro (.) quattro gior[ni
		yes four four day:M.PL
		"yes (.) four (.) four days"
12	DO0:	[↓mhm↑
13		(0.2)
14	PA0:	così:::
		so
		"like that"
15	DO0:	>(poi)< c'è ancora
		then there be:IND.PRS.3SG still
16		dolore.
		pain:M.SG
		">(then)< it still hurts."

```
17      PA0:    prima    non  è                   così
                before   NEG  be:IND.PRS.3SG      so
                "before it wasn't like that"

18               (0.3)

19      DO0:    [mhm.
```

Example 4, File 16 B/Post-b

```
1       PA0:    anche   l'           altro            dottore::     ce
                also    the:M.SG     other:M.SG       doctor:M.SG   PLE
2               l'             ho                    una         cosa
                CLIT.3SG       have:IND.PRS.1SG      a:F.SG      thing:F.SG
3               qui  (.)  e    io   sempre  me
                here       and  I    always  1SG.DAT
4               schiacciava                  no.
                squeeze:IND.IPFV.3SG         DSP
                "the other doctor:: as well I've got
                something here and I used to squeeze it"

5               (1.5)

6       PA0:    questo       qui¿
                this:M.SG    here
                "this one¿"

7               (0.8)

8       DO0:    eh  adesso  aspetta            un       mo-         ah
                eh  now     wait:IMP.2SG       a:M.SG   *moment     ah
9               sì.  (.)  fa                   vedere.
                Yes        make:IMP.2SG        see:INF.PRS
                "eh now wait a mi- ah yes. (.) let me see"

10      PA0:    mhm::

11               (9.0)

12      PA0:    prima     teneva                  così.  (.)  como
                before    hold:IND.IPFV.3SG       so            *like
13              questi         qui    no.
                this:M.PL      here   DSP
                "before they were like that (.) like these
                ones."
```

```
14    PS0:    (2.0)

15    PA0:    io  sempre  me                     schiaccia:va↑
              I   always  *1SG.DAT.REFL          squeeze:IND.IPFV.3SG
              "I used to squeeze it"
```

For example, in Example 3, temporal meaning is conveyed through a lexical means (*prima* [before], line 17). In Example 4, verbal morphology is limited to the third person singular morpheme (*schiacciava* [squeezed], lines 4 and 15, and *teneva* [held], line 12), lacking appropriate subject-verb agreement. One may thus conclude that these speakers still rely on the pragmatic and lexical mode (which is typical of pre-basic varieties), but, at the same time, are also developing towards the syntactic mode (Givón, 1979), which characterizes post-basic varieties. In fact, this movement between the pragmatic mode and the syntactic mode represents one of the central features of the basic variety (Klein & Perdue, 1997; Perdue, 1993).

Finally, Examples 5 and 6 show Ps whose talk is both morphosyntactically and textually richer and more target-like: Verbal morphology codes a wide range of temporal, aspectual, and modal values, despite the persistence of some morphosyntactic inaccuracies (e.g., wrong auxiliary selection in Example 5a, lines 11–12; articles missing in 5a, lines 10–11; and deviant subject-verb agreement in Example 6, line 1).

Example 5, File 17 Post-b

(a)

```
1    DO0:    cos'      hai?
             what      have:IND.PRS.2SG
             "what's your problem?"

2    PA0:    .hh sono                       andata
                 be:IND.PRS.1SG.AUX         go:PTCP.PST.F.SG
3            al              mare       (.).hh tre       anni
             to the:M.SG     sea:M.SG          three     year:M.PL
4            fa (.)  e    dopo     che     sono
             ago     and  after    that    be:IND.PRS.1SG.AUX
5            arrivata                a     casa       mhm
             arrive:PTCP.PST.F.SG    to    home:F.SG  mhm
6            preso                   un'         abbronzatura
             take:PTCP.PST.M.SG      a:F.SG      tan:F.SG
7            perfetta         ma    .hhh (.)   qua     sulle
             perfect:F.SG     but              here    on the:F.PL
```

```
8              bra-[ccia
               arm:F.PL
               ".hh I went to the seaside (.) .hh three
               years ago (.) and after I came home mhm got
               a perfect tan but .hhh (.) here on my arms"

9      DOO:    [adesso vediamo.
               Now     see:IND.PRS.1PL
               "now we'll have a look"

10             (0.6)

11     PAO:    m'           hanno
               CLIT.1SG.DAT have:IND.PRS.3PL.AUX
12             rimasta                le
               remain:PTCP.PST.F.SG   the:F.PL
               "I still have the"

13             (0.4)

14     PAO:    punti         bianchi↑
               spot:M.PL     white:M.PL
               "white spots"
```

Example 6, File 20 Post-b

```
1    PAO:   ha                       preso
            have:IND.PRS.3SG.AUX take:PTCP.PST
2           questi::   eh dicevano          di fare
            this:M.PL  eh say:IND.IPFV.1PL of do:INF.PRS
3           per forza↓ (.) la(.)     corposcopia      e
            for force      the:F.SG *colposcopy:F.SG and
4           la biopsia.
            the:F.SG biopsy:F.SG
            "he took these:: eh they said I had to
            have(.) a (.) colposcopy and a biopsy"
5           (0.5)
6    PAO:   >e abbiamo              già<
            and have:IND.PRS.1PL.AUX already
7           l'              ho                   già
            CLIT.3SG.ACC have:IND.PRS.1SG.AUX already
8           prenotato              telefonicamente per
            book:PTCP.PST.M.SG     by phone        for
```

| 9 | lunedì.
Monday
">and we've already< I've already booked it by phone for Monday" |

Moreover, unlike the previous patients, these post-basic speakers produce some dependent clauses, as in Examples 5a, 5b, lines 4, and in Example 6, line 2.

From the examples above, it becomes evident that the assessment of the Ps' interlanguage, based exclusively on their naturally occurring talk in one single exchange, cannot be more detailed nor comprehensive.

Bearing in mind the limitations of the preliminary assessment grounded on the notion of LV, the following sections will present the results of the investigation on co-constructions and on the opening sequence of each encounter in the corpus. Due to the above mentioned coarse-grained assessment of the L2Ss' LV, in the following paragraphs the analysis will be mainly based on the comparison of the interactional practices of two broader groups: the less advanced speakers (Group 1), including pre-basic to basic/post-basic speakers (Table 1), and the more advanced speakers (Group 2), with the seven post-basic speakers only (Table 1). Specific observations on the varieties included in Group 1 (e.g., the pre-basic level) will be added whenever appropriate.

Co-constructions

In conversation analysis and interactional linguistics, the notion of co-construction[14] is strictly related to the categories of turn constructional unit (henceforth TCU) and transition relevance place (henceforth TRP).[15] Co-constructions are TCUs which are jointly constructed across turns by more than one speaker (Lerner, 1991; see also Ikeda and Ko, this volume), not to be confused with utterance extensions or *increments*, which are additions to an already complete clause (Couper-Kuhlen & Ono, 2007; Schegloff, 1996). The present study identifies co-constructions as syntactically based. According to Kärkkäinen et al. (2007), co-constructions offer the syntactician "a perspective on syntactic structuring as an interactive and dynamic process" (p. 355). In their comparative study on the role of clauses as "interactionally warranted units" in Japanese and English, Thompson and Couper-Kuhlen (2005) look at co-constructions together with next-turn onsets and turn-unit extensions as contexts showing the speakers' orientation to clausal formats and "their variable grammatical projectability" (p. 497) in the two languages. Following Ono and Thompson (1995), by looking into these formats and their regularities in the allocation of turns, the analysis that follows aims at studying when and how conversationalists jointly orient to syntactic constructs in interaction, and more specifically to abstract *constructional schemas*, such as NP VP NP or NP VP

NP PP when completing another speaker's utterance. Moreover, from an SLA perspective, the syntax of co-constructions could be regarded as a parameter to assess interactional competence in a second language.

Co-constructions are prototypically two-pair part templates, consisting of a preliminary component (Example 7, line 1) and a final component (Example 7, line 3), each one usually delivered by different speakers.[16]

Example 7, File 9 B

```
1    PAO:    non      posso
              NEG      can:IND.PRS.1SG
              "I can't"

2             (0.5)

3    DOO:    respi[rare?
              breathe:INF.PRS
              "brea[the?"
```

The preliminary component typically projects the constituent of the second pair-part and does not usually end up in a transition relevance place, whereas the final component usually does. Projection (Auer, 2005) may act at different levels: syntactically, semantically, lexically, and/or pragmatically. In Example 7, the preliminary component consists of a conjugated modal verb (*posso* [I can]), which in Italian must be followed by an infinitive verb. So, in Example 7, the projection trajectory imposes a restriction in the appropriate choice of the second pair-part at the morphosyntactic level.

Instead, in Example 8, the preliminary component (*dunque tu sei andata qui dal?* [well you went here to the?], lines 1–2) projects both the part of speech to follow (a noun) and, though to a much lesser extent, some of its semantic properties (human and medical specialist).

Example 8, File 15 Post-b

```
1    DOO:    mtks dunque  tu      sei
                   well    you    be:IND.PRS.2SG.AUX
2             andata                qui    dal?
              go:PTCP.PST.F.SG  here from the:M.SG
              "well you went here to the?"
3    PAO:    sono                 andata              a
              be:IND.PRS.1SG.AUX  go:PTCP.PST.F.SG    to
4             un          consultorio            familiare.
              a:M.SG      guidance centre:M.SG   familial:M.SG
              "I went to a family gui[dance centre."
```

Furthermore, following Koshik (2002), such content questions as *dunque tu sei andata qui dal?* [so you went here to the?] may also be regarded as Designedly Incomplete Utterances (henceforth DIU), where the practitioner provides the syntax and the lexicon for the answer. From a syntactic point of view, the doctor's question represents the preliminary component of a TCU completed by the interlocutor. So, such DIU have been included in the counting of co-constructions because these question-and-answer adjacency pairs represent TCUs produced jointly by the participants. The fact that the practitioner may intentionally leave the question incomplete for pedagogical purposes deals with the function of such co-constructions. In other words, in identifying co-constructions as syntactically based, what really matters is not so much the speaker's intentions (for example, the fact that these questions are intentionally left incomplete for pedagogical purposes or for any other reason) but their syntactic format and participant structure.

Co-constructions are common in contexts such as the *if-then* compound, parenthetical inserts, lists, quotations, assisted explaining, and storytelling (Kärkkäinen et al., 2007; Lerner, 1991). In the present data, most co-constructions occur in contexts of assisted explaining, where the P explains the symptoms, problems and needs and the GP either inquires about the P's problem or provides bureaucratic information. Consider, for example, the P's attempt to explain his health problem in Example 7 and the GP's inquiry in Example 8.

In the analysis that follows, it is important to differentiate co-constructions on the basis of the presence or absence of recycled chunks from the preliminary component in the second pair-part. So, completions which add the final component without recycling any constituent from the preliminary component, as in Example 7, line 3, will be called *additive completions*, while completions which recycle part of the preliminary component (the predicate *sono andata* [I went] recycles the predicate *sei andata* [you went] in the previous doctor's turn) and thus anchor the final component to the first pair-part, as in Example 8, line 3, will be called *anchored completions*.

Apart from the syntax of recycling, the collection of co-construction sequences will be analyzed according to the following criteria: *directionality, turn allocation format, syntactic cohesiveness,* and *type of syntactic constructs*. The five criteria have been chosen in order to analyze co-constructions following two main trajectories, namely their interactional and syntactic deployment. On the one hand, *directionality* and *turn allocation format* focus on the distribution of participants and turns in co-constructions; on the other hand, the last three criteria are concerned with their syntactic format and are coherent with the syntactically-based notion of co-constructions adopted in the present research. In fact, following studies on the syntax of recycling in repairing (Fox et al., 1996; Fox & Jasperson, 1995; Hayashi, 2003; Uhmann, 2001), the analysis turns to the syntax of repairing in co-constructions and, more specifically, deals with syntactic regularities in the above mentioned "anchored completions," where part of the previous turn is recycled. This is probably the aspect of co-constructions (among the ones considered in this chapter) that best suits the research aim to work at the syntactic and interactional interface. Recycling is then seen as an interactional linguistic device available to the speakers in order to jointly obtain syntactically bound co-constructions.

Before proceeding with the analysis of co-constructions, a further methodological clarification is to be made. Since this chapter aims at finding out whether (and, if so, to what extent) co-constructions correlate with the speakers' LV, the investigation that follows will focus on the L2S's contribution to co-constructions. Nevertheless, one cannot do without including in the analysis the GP's contributions to co-constructing, whether they are preliminary, final or non-final components, in order to examine how the native participant's contribution is either projected or completed by the L2 interlocutor.

Directionality
Directionality refers to whether it is the L1 or L2 speaker who provides the final component. In Example 7, it is the native speaker who completes the previous turn, while in Example 8, it is the nonnative participant who delivers the final component. In some cases (4 in the corpus), an insertion sequence may occur between the preliminary component and the final one. It usually consists of one or more attempts (or completion units[17]) by both speakers to deliver the final component. For instance, in Example 9 (line 11), the GP completes the P's TCU (lines 1–3) after three attempts by the P (lines 5, 8, and 10) and one by the GP himself (line 7).[18]

Example 9, File 8 Pre-b

```
1     PAO:    [anche anche a q-  a         qui:::
              also   also   at   at        here
2                     ((touching her breast)) questo
                                              this:PRO.M.SG
3                     tengo              un::
                      hold:IND.PRS.1SG   a:M.SG
                      "also also at h- at here:::
                      ((touching her breast))this I have a::"

4     PSO:    (0.5)

5     PAO:    como   un                 tumore        nel
              *like  a:M.SG             tumor:M.SG    in the:M.SG
                     ((rubbing her belly))
                     "like a tumor in the ((rubbing her belly"
```

```
6    PS0:    (1.4)

7    DO0:    TIENE              [un?
             hold:IND.PRS.3SG   a:M.SG
             "you have a?"

8    PA0:                                [(seno)
                                         breast:M.SG
             "(breast)"

9    PS0:    (0.3)

10   PA0:    como   una       u[na
             *like  a:F.SG    a:F.SG
             "like a a"

11   DO0:                     [un       nodulo?=
                              a:F.SG    lump.M.Sg
             "a lump?"

12   PA0:    =sì sì (.)
             "yes yes"
```

Table 2 shows the number of completion units produced in co-constructions by each speaker in each consultation.

Table 2. Completion units in co-constructions

L2 speaker	learner variety	completion units by L1Ss	completion units by L2Ss
3	pre-basic		
8	pre-basic	3	2
1	basic	1	1
12	basic	1	1
9	basic	1	
14	basic	3	
2	basic	1	
7	basic/post-basic		2
11	basic/post-basic	1	
19	basic/post-basic	2	6
10	basic/post-basic	3	
16	basic/post-basic		
6	post-basic	1	
5	post-basic		2
13	post-basic	1	3

15	post-basic	1	1
17	post-basic		2
20	post-basic		
4	post-basic	2	2
total		21	22

On the whole, there are 43 co-constructions, 21 completed by the GPs and 22 by the Ps. The majority of co-constructions in the consultations with pre-basic and basic speakers are completed by the L1 speaker (10/14). By contrast, the number of co-constructions completed by the P increases and slightly outnumbers the GP's completions in exchanges which involve more advanced speakers (basic/post-basic and post-basic speakers; 18/29). This suggests a tendential relationship between morphosyntactic development and the ability to take a more active interactional role in the encounter, which is displayed in the ability to semantically and syntactically complete the interlocutor's turn.

Turn allocation format

In CA, the turn-allocation component deals with the distribution of turns among the participants in a given activity (Sacks, Schegloff, & Jefferson, 1974, pp. 702–703). In the present work, two features of the turn allocation component in co-constructions are taken into account: turn allocation cues at the end of the preliminary component, that is, signals indicating a trouble source and eliciting the interlocutor's completion, and overlapping at the onset of the completion unit.

Among the signals triggering turn continuation and selecting next speaker, there are pauses (Example 10), hesitations <eh> (Example 11), weakly rising intonation <¿> (Example 12), shift to high pitch <↑> (Example 13), rising intonation <?> (Example 14), and elongated ending <:> (Example 15). In some cases, as in Examples 12, 14, and 15, more than one elicitation cue may occur in sequence.

Example 10, File 9 B

```
1    PA0:   non      posso
            NEG      can:IND.PRS.1SG
            "I can't"

2             (0.5)

3    DO0:   respi[rare?
            breathe:INF.PRS
            "brea[the?"
```

Example 11, File 4 Post-b

```
1    PA0:  ho                      fatto
           have:IND.PRS.1SG.AUX    do:PTCP.PST.M.SG
2          l-     eh:::
           *the eh
           "I had t- eh:::"

3    DO0:  la          visita      per la
           the:F.SG    exam:F.SG   for the:F.SG
4          gravidanza?
           pregnancy:F.SG
           "the pregnancy consultation?"
```

Example 12, File 13 Post-b

```
1    PA0:  devo                  far
           must:IND.PRS.1SG      do:INF.PRS
2          l'          ecografia↑
           the:F.SG    ultrasound:F.SG
           "I must have an ultrasound↑"

3    PS0:  (2.5)

4    PA0:  per     me.
           for     1SG.OBL
           "for me"

5    DO0:  per te↑
           for 2SG.OBL
           "for you↑"

6          (1.0)

7    DO0:  mhm. che          sei::::::::¿
                that:REL     be:IND.PRS.1SG
           "mhm. you are::::::::¿"

8          (1.5)

9    PA0:  adesso sono              sedici   settimane.
           now    be:IND.PRS.3PL    sixteen  weeks
           "now I'm in week sixteen."
```

Example 13, File 15 Post-b

```
1    DO0:   mhm. perché    questa        cosa           di
             mhm  because   this:F.SG     thing:F.SG     of
2            andare     in caritas              non mi
             go:INF.PRS in charity centre       NEG 1SG.DAT
3            sembra-                  tu  dov'  è
             seem:IND.PRS.3SG         you where be:IND.PRS.3SG
4            che        sei
             that:COMP  be:IND.PRS.2SG.AUX
5            seguita¿                 al↑
             treat:PTCP.PST.F.SG      to the:M.SG
             "mhm. because this idea of going to the
             charity centre I don't think- you where are
             you treated¿ at the↑"

6    PA0:   in:::::  eh consultarorio
             in       eh *guidance centre:M.SG
             "in::::: eh family guidance centre"
```

Example 14, File 8 Pre-b

```
1    PA0:   [anche anche a q-  a         qui:::
              also  also  at   at        here
2            ((touching her breast))  questo
                                      this:PRO.M.SG
3            tengo                    un::
             hold:IND.PRS.1SG         a:M.SG
             "also also at h- at here:::
             ((touching her breast))this I have a::"

4    PS0:   (0.5)

5    PA0:   como un              tumore        nel
             *like a:M.SG        tumor:M.SG    in the:M.SG
             ((rubbing her belly))
             "like a tumor in the ((rubbing her belly))"

6    PS0:   (1.4)

7    DO0:   TIENE              [un?
             hold:IND.PRS.3SG   a:M.SG
             "you have a?"

8    PA0:                          [(seno)
                                    breast:M.SG
             "(breast)"
```

```
9       PS0:    (0.3)

10      PA0:    como     una       u[na
                *like   a:F.SG    a:F.SG
                "like a a"

11      DO0:                        [un        nodulo?=
                                    a:F.SG    lump.M.Sg
                "a lump?"

12      PA0:    =sì sì (.)
                "yes yes"
```

Example 15, File 14 B

```
1       DO0:    mi           dica!
                1SG.DAT     tell:CONJ.PRS.3SG
                "how can I help you"

2       PA0:    io lei        me          aveva
                I  3SG.CRT   1SG.DAT    have:AUX.IND.IPFV.3SG
3               fatto::
                do:PTCP.PST
                "I you had me do"

4       PS0:    (0.2)

5       PA0:    [°°(me           ha
                   *1SG.DAT    have:AUX.IND.PRS.3SG
6               detto           che
                tell:PTCP.PST  that:COMP
7               faciamo)°°
                do:IND.PRS.1PL
                "you told me that we do"

8       DO0:    [gli        esami=
                the:M.PL   exam:M.PL
                "the exams"

9       PA0:    =sì ha                          fato
                yes have:AUX.IND.PRS.3SG    *do:PTCP.PST

10              esami.
                exam:M.PL
                "yes I had the exams"
```

In the data, hesitations and long word endings at the end of the first part of a co-construction are used by both L1 and L2 speakers, while rising intonations and pauses are employed respectively by L1Ss and L2Ss only. The fact that the L1S elicits the interlocutor's completion in the form of a question, besides being a feature common to native-nonnative discourse, may also be regarded as indexing the GP's interactional dominance in this type of institutional encounter, which gives him or her the interactional right to ask content questions in order to deliver the diagnosis and make prescriptions. Such content questions as *che sei::::::::¿* [that you are¿] in Example 12, line 7, and *TIENE un?* [you HAVE a?] in Example 14, line 7, are also instances of DIUs (Koshik, 2002), often found in pedagogical discourse, where the more expert speaker lays a scaffold by providing the syntax and the lexicon for the answer.

Rising intonations and pauses may also be triggered by different trouble sources: on the one hand, the GP's need to get the missing information; on the other hand, the P's need for the interlocutor's help in order to overcome linguistic trouble. In other words, the rising intonation by the L1 speaker tends to occur in case of content gaps, while the L2S's pauses, hesitations, and long word endings are more likely to indicate lexical gaps.

Table 3 displays the number of turn allocation cues and overlaps.

Table 3. Frequencies of turn allocation cues and overlaps

	cue −		cue +		overlap −		overlap +		total	
	no. of occurrences	%	no. of occurrences	%	no. of occurrences	%	no. of occurrences	%	no. of occurrences	%
L1	8	38	13	62	10	48	11	52	21	100
L2Ss Group 1	8	67	4	33	5	42	7	58	12	100
L2Ss Group 2	3	30	7	70	4	40	6	60	10	100
total	19	44	24	56	19	44	24	56	43	100

In the entire corpus, more than half of the completion units (56%) are triggered by trouble cues at the end of the preliminary TCU component, which may be regarded as an index of the collaborative nature of most completions in the data. This means that the interlocutor tends to deliver the solicited completions, namely he or she tends to take the turn in response to a turn allocation cue triggering the completion unit. However, the less advanced speakers (Group 1) frequently take the turn and deliver the completion component in absence of any turn allocation cue (unsolicited completions; 67%), while this happens to a lesser degree in Group 2 (30%) and in in the case of the L1 speakers (38%). The more advanced speakers are similar to the L1Ss in their tendency to deliver completion units following a trouble cue at the end of the interlocutor's turn. This suggests that appropriately eliciting the interlocutor's completion and appropriately decoding turn allocation cues may be regarded as potential indicators of different degrees of interactional competence.

As shown in Table 3, 56% of the completion units are delivered in overlap, with little variation across groups. A combination of the two parameters (turn allocation cues and overlapping) is summarized in Table 4.

Table 4. Turn allocation cues and overlaps combined[19]

	Type 1 C− O−	%	Type 2 C− O+	%	Type 3 C+ O+	%	Type 4 C+ O−	%	total	%
L1Ss	2	10	6	29	5	24	8	38	21	100
L2Ss Group 1	3	25	5	42	2	17	2	17	12	100
L2Ss Group 2			3	30	3	30	4	40	10	100
total	5	12	14	33	10	23	14	33	43	100

One third of the overall completions follow the decoding of a cue triggering the participant's final component in no overlap (33%, Table 6, Type 4); in another third, the onset of the completion is delivered in overlap and is not preceded by any trouble cue (Table 4, Type 2). In 23% of all completion units, cues and overlapping co-occur, for example when, after a hesitation or a pause, both speakers start speaking at the same time. In 12% of them, there are neither cues nor overlapping. Table 4 also shows that the L1Ss and more advanced L2Ss share a similar proportion of completion units delivered in no overlap after a trouble cue (38% and 40% of type 4), while in the less advanced group, the proportion of completion units in overlap without trouble cue is higher (42% of type 2 against 17% of type 4).

Example 16 exemplifies three of the four types of the above mentioned allocation modes: In line 6, the latching with neither turn allocation cue nor overlapping falls within type 1; in line 8, the onset of the completion in overlap, not preceded by any turn allocation cue, fits type 2, while type 3 (the co-occurrence of turn allocation cue and overlapping) is shown in line 11.

Example 16, File 19 B/Post-b

```
1     DOO:   poi      c'        è
             then     there be:AUX.IND.PRS.3SG
2            stato                  un        momento
             stay:PTCT.PST.M.SG     a:M.SG    moment:M.SG
```

```
3              che         tu   facevi (.)           eh
               that:COMP   you  do:IND.IPFV.2SG
4              l'       X  o    il Y ((names of drugs))
               the:M.SG    or   the:M.SG
5              e   in più    ti             davano
               and moreover  2SG.DAT.CLIT   give:IND.IPFV.1PL
6              anche=
               also
               "then in the past when you were taking (.)
               eh X or Y and in addition they also gave you"

7    PA0:      =l'      A (name of drug)[i::
               the:M.SG
               "A (name of drug)"

8    DO0:                                   [il
                                             the:M.SG
9              V (name of drug)e    la::
                               and  the:F.SG
10             [la::
               the:F.SG
               "V a::nd a::nd"

11   PA0:      [i V- eh V (.)      tutti     e     due.
               the:M.PL            all:M.PL  and   two
               "V- eh V (.) both of them."
```

Syntactic cohesiveness

The parameter of *syntactic cohesiveness* looks at whether the syntactic constituents and phrases of the completion unit respect the grammatical constraints projected by the preliminary component. The literature on grammatical patterns found in co-constructions is quite limited and is mainly based on English (Szczepek, 2000a, 2000b), Japanese (Hayashi, 2003) and Finnish (Helasvuo, 2004). In their comparative study of grammatical constraints in co-constructions in English, Japanese, and Finnish, Kärkkäinen et al. (2007, pp. 364–370) observed the following:

> The grammatical characteristics of the language under study set certain constraints on the kinds of co-constructions that can exist in that language. With regard to co-constructions, constraints on linear organization (especially word order) are of course particularly relevant. Also relevant are the grammatical means by which co-participants are able to project the future trajectory of the turn. (p. 364)

Thompson and Couper-Kuhlen (2005) argued that English is an *early projection* language where "speaker transitions in joint turn construction are, as a rule, seamless" whereas Japanese is a *delayed (or late) projection* language in that "a Japanese co-participant may supply the secondary component, but typically only following a noticeable pause and often accompanied by an acknowledgment token" (pp. 493–494). As for Italian, there is no systematic account of grammatical projectability. One of the few studies on co-constructions in Italian L1 from a grammar-in-interaction perspective is Orletti (2007), based on TV talk/reality shows and conversations between adults and language-impaired children in speech therapy sessions. In addition to clause-size patterns, the researcher found occurrences of co-constructions at word level, suggesting that the notion of projectability can be to the morphological level. The author also demonstrated how solicited and unsolicited co-constructions are templates accomplishing different social actions.

In order to clarify the concept of syntactic cohesiveness as it is used in this chapter, consider Examples 17 and 18. They both represent deviant cases in the corpus, in the sense that they are semantically coherent but syntactically non-cohesive continuations of the first speaker's TCU.

Example 17, File 1 B

```
1    DO0:   [eh? (.) CON   QUESTE       CARTE          QUA (.)
             eh        with this:F.PL paper:F.PL    here
2                   va                  [dentro
             go:IND.PRS.3SG.CRT     inside
             "eh? (.) with these papers here (.) you get
             into"

3    PA0:                           [oculista
                                    eye-specialist:M.SG
             "[eye-specialist"

4    DO0:   e    le              dan                per
             and  3SG.DAT.CRT    give:IND.PRS.3PL   for
5           l'            oculista              e     per
             the:M.SG    eye-specialist:M.SG    and   for
6           il            dentista         le
             the:M.SG    dentist:M.SG     3SG.DAT.CRT
7           danno                   l'          appuntamento
             give:IND.PRS.3PL      the:M.SG    appointment:M.SG
8           e    le              dicono             dove
             and  3SG.DAT.CRT    tell:IND.PRS.3PL   where
```

```
9                   andare. (.) VA BENE?
                    go:INF.PRS   ok
                    "and they give you the appointment for the
                    eye-specialist and for the dentist and they
                    tell you where to go. (.) ok?"

10      PA0:        °°ho
                    have:IND.PRS.1SG.AUX
11                  capito                       (tutto)°°
                    understand:PTCT.PST.M.SG everything
                    "°°I understood (everything)°°"
```

In Example 17, the L2 speaker's completion unit consists of the bare noun *oculista* [eye-specialist] instead of the target-like PP *dall'oculista* [to the eye-specialist]. The lexical item in isolation does not make explicit the syntactic link between the two components of the co-construction, while the full PP would index not only awareness of the argument structure of the verb *andare* [go] but also knowledge of the verb dependency rules. The GP's self-completion in the following turn with the recycling of the bare noun within its PP (*e le dan per l'oculista e per il dentista le danno l'appuntamento* [and they give you for the eye-specialist and for the dentist the appointment], lines 4–6) adjusts the interlocutor's candidate completion (*oculista* [eye-specialist]) both syntactically and pragmatically: Not only is the P's continuation syntactically inappropriate, but the GP's formal and content repair in lines 4–9 shows that it is also pragmatically inadequate.[20]

Example 18, File 19 B/Post-b

```
1       DO0:    .hhh ADESSO tu      vuoi↑               cioè
                     now    you     want:IND.PRS.2SG    well
2               ti            ha[n
                CLIT.2SG.DA   have:IND.PRS.3PL
                "hhh NOW you want↑ well they have"

3       PA0:                    [sto               prendie↑ndo:::
                                 stay:IND.PRS.1SG  take:GER.PRS
4               il [X
                the:M.PL
                "I'm ta↑king X"
```

In Example 18, the L2 speaker, despite orienting to the semantic content of the GP's TCU (the drugs he was prescribed), completely restructures the clause projected by the interlocutor and changes the perspective on the projected scene. This results in a borderline case of co-construction, where the P's syntagmatically non-cohesive completion (lines 3–4) may also be considered as a rephrasing belonging to a new TCU and not simply as a completion of the previous one.

Table 5 shows that all L1Ss' completion units and 90% of those by L2Ss are syntactically cohesive with respect to the preliminary component of the co-construction sequence. Non-cohesive units are to be found almost exclusively in the less advanced varieties (42%).

Table 5. Completion units with and without syntactic cohesion

	syntactic cohesion	%	no syntactic cohesion	%	total
L1Ss	21	100			21
L2Ss Group 1	7	58	5	42	12
L2Ss Group 2	9	90	1	10	10
total	37	86	6	14	43

So, in the data investigated, non-cohesive co-constructions represent deviations from the general tendency to orient to the syntactic cohesiveness of completions. The first type of deviations, exemplified in Example 17, where one constituent (the article or the preposition) is missing or is nontarget-like, clearly correlates with a nonnative syntactic competence. On the other hand, deviations consisting of clausal restructuring, as in Example 18, do not necessarily mean poor syntactic competence in the target language. On the contrary, they may reveal a higher degree of textual competence in the L2 speaker's ability to change perspective.

A look at the constituent types of the completion units (Table 6) indicates that they mainly consist of single phrases.

Table 6. Constituent types of completion units

	L1Ss no. of occurrences	%	L2Ss Group 1 no. of occurrences	%	L2Ss Group 2 no. of occurrences	%	total
NP	8	38	7	58	3	30	18
PP	3	14	1	8	5	50	9
VP (bare)			1	8	1	10	2
ADJP	2	10					2
VP+NP(PP)	5	24					5
clause	3	14	3	25	1	10	7
total	21	100	12	100	10	100	43

This overall tendency is more evident in the completions of the L2 speakers (75% in Group 1 and 90% in Group 2) than in those of the L1 speakers (62%), who, in five cases (24%), recycle a complex VP and in three instances (14%) an entire clause (see also Table 7 below). Whether it is the single post-verbal constituent to be added or the VP to be recycled as well, both completion templates highlight the interactional relevance of the verb argument structure in projecting the semantic and syntactic format of the TCU completion.[21] This finding also reveals the speakers' orientation to the previously mentioned clausal constructional schema, NP VP NP (PP), typical of Italian unmarked word order, SVO.

Now consider how the two Ps co-construct their request in the following example:

Example 19, File 15 Post-b

```
1      PA0:   sono              io (.) eh    io
              be:IND.PRS.1SG    I            I
2             ho                fatto
              have:AUX.IND.PRS.1S  do:PTCT.PST
3             eh:: gli esami        per   sei    mesi (.)
              the:M.PL exam:M.PL    for   six    month:M.PL
4             adesso dovrei                 andare
              now    must:COND.PRS.1SG  go:INF.PRS
5             dal              mhm dal
              to the:M.SG          to the:M.SG
              "it's me (.) eh I had eh:: the tests six
              months ago (.) now I should go to the mhm
              to the"

6             (0.7)

7      PA1:   °°dall'          epatologo°°
              to the:M.SG  pathologist:M.SG
              "to the pathologist"

8      PA0:   dall'         epatologo (.)        e
              to the:M.SG  pathologist:M.SG    and
9             mi              mi              serve
              1SG.Dat.CLIT  1SG.Dat.CLIT   need:IND.PRS.SG
10            una       carta         che:::
              a:F.SG    paper:F.SG    that
              "to the pathologist (.) and I need a
              prescription that"

11     D00:   ((quietly reads the results))
12            hai              fatto
              have:AUX.IND.PRS.2SG  do:PTCP.PST
```

In Example 19, line 7, one of the Ps recycles the preposition (*dal* [to the], line 5) from the previous turn before delivering the missing lexical item (*epatologo* [pathologist]). The candidate completion is ratified by the interlocutor, who repeats the PP before introducing another TCU (lines 8 to 10). The completion component in line 7 constructs a syntactically cohesive unit in that the recycling of the phrasal head (the preposition) anchors the completion to the TCU in progress.

A consideration of the three examples that follow shows how the more advanced speakers' contributions to co-constructions may take the form of complex syntactic constructs. In Example 20, the L1 speaker's additive completion in line 4 (the first component of the co-construction chain) is ratified in the next turn (lines 6–8) by the recycling of the negation (*non* [not]) followed by a brand new declarative clause (*non è potuto andare* [I couldn't go]), which in its turn introduces a causative clause (*perché stava male* [because I was sick]).

Example 20, File 19 B/Post-b

```
1    PA0:   devo                  deve-
            must:IND.PRS.1SG      must:IND.PRS.3SG
2           deveva                fare          la
            *must:IND.IPFV.3SG    do:INF.PRS    the:F.SG
3           gastroscopia↑      °de       controllo°
            gastroscopy:F.SG   *of       check:M.SG
            "I have to has- had to have a gastroscopy↑"

4    DO0:   però non l'                   hai::¿
            but  NEG 3SG.ACC.CLIT         have:IND.PRS.2SG.AUX
5           non¿=
            NEG
            "but you didn't:::¿ didn't¿="

6    PA0:   =non è                       potuto
             NEG be:IND.PRS.3SG.AUX      can:PTCP.PST.M.SG
7           andare     perché  stava              male::
            go:INF.PRS because stay:IND.IPFV.1SG  bad
8           adesso io senza    lavoro¿
            now    I  without  job:M.SG
            "I couldn't go because I was sick:: now I'm
            unemployed¿"

9           (0.8)
```

In Example 21, the L2S shows his interactional competence in actively participating in the co-construction in two ways. First, the lexical recycling of the VP (*ho bisogno* [I need]) in the first completion component (line 5) is preceded by a brand new declarative sentence (*non me l'hanno timbrato* [they didn't receipt it], lines 2–4), which embeds the recycled chunk in a causal dependent clause. Furthermore, in lines 8–9, he adjusts the GP's candidate completion (*l'appuntamento* [the appointment]) and delivers the appropriate completion (*la lettera* [the letter]) while rephrasing the point he made in the previous turn (*non me l'hanno timbrato* [they didn't receipt it] in lines 2–4 becomes *per timbrarlo* [to receipt it] in lines 9–10).

Example 21, File 4 Post-b

```
1      DOO:    ha                       [bisogno
                have:IND.PRS.3SG         need:M.SG
                "you need"
2      PAO:                             [non      me
                                         NEG      1SG.DAT.CLIT
3              l'               hanno
                3SG.ACC.CLIT     have:IND.PRS.3PL
4              timbrato              perchè:::
                stamp:PTCP:PST        because
5              ho                       bisogno   di
                have:IND.PRS.1SG         need:M.SG of
6              prendere         prima:::
                take:INF.PRS     before
                "they didn't sign it because
                I need to take first"

7      DOO:    °l'         ap[puntamento°
                the:M.SG    appointment:M.SG
                "an appointment"

8      PAO:                [la        le-         sì   la
                            the:F.SG  the:F.PL    yes  the:F.SG
9              lettera       qui    per
                letter:F.SG   here   for
10             timbrarlo                     così    anche
                stamp:INF.PRS.CLIT.3SG.ACC    so      also
11             mercoledì d- devo
                Wednesday    must:IND.PRS.1SG
12             fare         l'         ecografia            così   per
                do:INF.PRS   the:F.SG   ultrasound:F.SG      so     for
13             non venire              ancora=
                NEG come:INF.PRS        again
                "the the yes the letter I came here to get it
                signed also on Wednesday I'll have an ultrasound
                so in order not to have to come again"

14     DOO:    =ho                  capito.
                have:IND.PRS.1SG     understand:PTCP.PST
                "I see."
```

In Example 22, the P's post-basic syntactic competence in Italian is displayed in more than one way. Not only does the speaker recycle the definite article before delivering the missing argument of the previous turn (*il docciaschiuma* [the shower foam], line 2)[22] with the appropriate article-noun morphological agreement, but she also topicalizes it by placing the object at the beginning of the sentence (*il docciaschiuma ho preso* [the shower foam I took], lines 2–3), which is quite unusual in Italian learner data. So, the L2S overcomes the pervasive *controller first* and *focus last* principles of basic varieties.

Example 22, File 17 Post-b

```
1    DOO:   e   utilizzi:::      il           eh::↓
            And use:IND.PRS.2SG  the:M.SG eh
            "and you u:::se the eh::↓"

2    PAO:   il         docciaschiuma ( )
            the:M.SG   shower foam:M.SG
3           ho                       preso
            have:IND.PRS.1SG.AUX  take:PTCP.PRS.M.SG
4           [perché
             because
            "I bought the shower foam [because"

5    DOO:   [eh sì beh  ma  tanto non serve
             eh yes well but anyway NEG need:IND.PRS.3SG
6           a   niente [( )  .hhh no↑ dovresti
            to nothing               NEG must:COND.PRS.2SG
            "[eh yes well but anyway it's useless [( )
            .hhh you shouldn't"

7    PAO:              [non so
                        NEG know:IND.PRS.1SG
8           >ho                     preso<
            have:IND.PRS.1SG.AUX take:PTCP.PST.M.SG
9           perché↑ SONO            andata
            because be:IND.PRS.1SG go:PTCP.PST.F.SG
10          al        dottore   io a casa      no¿
            to the:M.SG doctor:M.SG I at home:F.SG NEG
11          m'        hanno
            1SG.DAT.CLIT have:IND.PRS.3PL.AUX
12          dato                    le        pastiglie
            give:PTCP.PRS.M.SG the:F.PL pill:F.PL
```

```
13          m'              hanno
            1SG.DAT.CLIT    have:AUX.IND.PRS.3PL
14          detto               che         l'
            tell:PTCP.PRS.M.SG  that:COMP   the:M.SG
15          anno        prossimo        (ia)    quando
            year:M.SG   following:M.SG          when
16          prendo              l'          abbronzatura
            take:IND.PRS.1SG    the:F.SG    tan:F.SG
17          si      copre                   e
            REFL    cover:IND.PRS.3SG       and
18          sparisce.
            disappear: IND.PRS.3SG
            "I don't know >I bought< because↑ I went
            to the doctor at home ok¿ they gave me pills
            they told me that next year when I get a tan
            it'll cover up and disappear."
```

After highlighting some syntactic regularities in co-constructions, the analysis will now look closely at one interactional feature of co-constructions, namely the syntax of recycled chunks in *anchored completions*.

Syntax of recycling

This section considers whether the speaker who provides the completion repeats part of the previous turn before completing it. Work on L1 conversations in German, English, Japanese, and Finnish (Fox et al., 1996; Fox & Jasperson, 1995; Hayashi, 2003; Uhmann, 2001) singled out recurrent recycling patterns in repairing. For example, Uhmann (pp. 388, 396) identified two principles of recycling in same-sentence self-repair in German conversations: the *functional head rule* and the *no gap rule*. According to the former, "self-repairs are preferred if the accomplishment of repair starts with the repetition of the functional head which immediately c-commands the repairable" (p. 388). According to the latter, "to avoid discontinuous structures, all constituents following the repairable up to the initiation of self-repair have to be repeated in the syntactic loop" (p. 396). Generally speaking, the existence of regular templates in repairing demonstrates, first, the conversationalists' preference for syntactically cohesive constructs and, second, an overall orientation to the syntactic structure of TCUs, in terms of constituent and clause boundaries.[23]

Nevertheless, the universal value of such principles of recycling are challenged in a cross-linguistic perspective. In fact, a first comparative study of self-repair in English, German, Japanese, and Finnish by Kärkkäinen et al. (2007) suggested that "ways of initiating and doing self-repair in a given language seem to be deeply interwined with the kind of morphosyntactic practices the language users have available" (p. 355). For example, morphological repair was found in Japanese and Finnish, but not in English. Moreover, the scope of backing up in the utterance may vary from one language to the other. For example, English allows clausal recycling, while Japanese seems to allow the backing up of internal constituents only (pp. 346, 352).

This section will look closely at the phenomenon of other-recycling (that is recycling of the previous speaker's turn) first in co-constructions and later, more in general, throughout some of the consultations. It will focus on the syntactic format of the recycled items and check whether L2 speakers perform differently according to their LV.

In the present collection of co-constructions, recycling occurs in about half of the completion units investigated, equally distributed among L1 (11/21) and L2 speakers (10/22). The counting of recycling occurrences includes instances of both functional and lexical recycling. As a consequence, there are cases where the L2 speaker recycles the part of speech (e.g., the preposition) but not its lexicalization, as in Example 23 (*in* instead of *al*, line 6).

Example 23, File 13 Post-b

```
1    DO0:   mhm. perché    questa      cosa        di
            mhm  because   this:F.SG   thing:F.SG  of
2           andare         in caritas              non
            go:INF.PRS     in charity centre       NEG
3           mi             sembra-         tu    dov'
            1SG.DAT.CLIT   seem:IND.PRS.3SG you   where
4           è              che             sei
            be:IND.PRS.3SG that:COMP       be:IND.PRS.2SG.AUX
5           seguita¿                       al↑
            treat:PTCP.PST.F.SG            to the:M.SG
            "mhm. because this idea of going to the
            charity centre I don't think- you where are
            you treated¿ at the↑"

6    PA0:   in::::: eh consultatorio
            in      eh *guidance centre:M.SG
            "in::::: eh family guidance centre"
```

Table 7 shows the types of recycled chunks from the interlocutor's previous preliminary component. Minimal recycling chunks consist of single constituents or phrases whereas multi-chunk recycling includes the recycling of a string of at least one phrase followed by a full phrase or a constituent (article or preposition) of another phrase. As shown in Table 7, all the units recycled by the less advanced speakers (Group 1) are minimal chunks, either single constituents (such as negation particles or articles) or single phrases (such as NPs).

Table 7. Types of recyclings in completion units

recycling in completion units		L1Ss	%	L2Ss Group 1	%	L2Ss Group 2	%
minimal recycling	single constituent (Art[24]/P/N/Neg)	5	45	3	75	2	33
	single phrase (NP/PP)	1	10	1	25	2	33
multi-chunk recycling	governing functional head (VP+ Art/P or NP+P)	5	45			2	33
	no. of recycling/ no. of completion units	11/21 (52%)	100	4/12 (33%)	100	6/10 (60%)	100

As an example, consider lines 5 and 10 in Example 24 (repeated below from the previous section), where the P recycles the indefinite article (*como un/una* [like a/a]) only.

Example 24, File 8 Pre-b

```
1    PA0:   [anche anche a q-  a        qui:::
             also   also  at      at   here
2                  ((touching her breast)) questo
                                          this:PRO.M.SG
3           tengo                  un::
            hold:IND.PRS.1SG       a:M.SG
            "also also at h- at here:::
            ((touching her breast))this I have a::"

4    PS0:   (0.5)

5    PA0:   como   un              tumore        nel
            *like  a:M.SG          tumor:M.SG    in the:M.SG
            ((rubbing her belly))
            "like a tumor in the ((rubbing her belly"

6    PS0:   (1.4)

7    DO0:   TIENE                   [un?
            hold:IND.PRS.3SG        a:M.SG
            "you have a?"
```

```
8    PAO:                            [(seno)
                                      breast:M.SG
              "(breast)"

9    PSO:    (0.3)

10   PAO:    como    una      u[na
             *like   a:F.SG   a:F.SG
             "like a a"

11   DOO:                            [un       nodulo?=
                                      a:F.SG   lump.M.Sg
             "a lump?"

12   PAO:    =sì sì (.)
             "yes yes"
```

In contrast, more advanced speakers (Group 2) recycle a wider range of syntactic constructs, including multi-chunk formats (such as VP+preposition), as in Example 25.

Example 25, File 4 Post-b

```
1    DOO:    ha                [bisogno
             have:IND.PRS.3SG   need:M.SG
             "you need"
2    PAO:                            [non    me
                                      NEG    1SG.DAT.CLIT
3            l'              hanno
             3SG.ACC.CLIT    have:IND.PRS.3PL
4            timbrato           perchè:::
             stamp:PTCP:PST     because
5            ho                 bisogno   di
             have:IND.PRS.1SG   need:M.SG of
6            prendere        prima:::
             take:INF.PRS    before
             "they didn't sign it because
             I need to take first"

7    DOO:    °l'          ap[puntamento°
             the:M.SG     appointment:M.SG
             "an appointment"

8    PAO:                  [la       le-         sì la
                            the:F.SG the:F.PL   yes the:F.SG
```

```
9             lettera     qui     per
              letter:F.SG here    for
10            timbrarlo                       così    anche
              stamp:INF.PRS.CLIT.3SG.ACC so   also
11            mercoledì d- devo
              Wednesday must:IND.PRS.1SG
12            fare        l'         ecografia          così per
              do:INF.PRS  the:F.SG   ultrasound:F.SG so    for
13            non venire             ancora=
              NEG come:INF.PRS       again
              "the the yes the letter I came here to get it
              signed also on Wednesday I'll have an ultrasound
              so in order not to have to come again"

14   DOO:    =ho                    capito.
              have:IND.PRS.1SG      understand:PTCP.PST
              "I see."
```

The higher syntactic complexity of recycling constructs by the latter group is closer to the L1Ss' recycling formats, which often include the recycling of the VP together with the dependent NP or PP, exemplified in Example 24 (line 7). The recycling of the functional head governing the completion unit may represent an index of the learners' syntactic competence in terms of orientation to the dependency and verb/noun argument structure in formatting the completion unit.[25]

In order to look deeper into the relationship between the syntactic format of the recycled constituents and the Ps' LV, next turn other-speaker recycling formats outside of co-constructions will be analyzed in four consultations from the corpus (Table 8).[26] Simple numerical differences among groups should not be taken as a valid indicator since the size of the three corpora is not balanced. What is more significant are functional and formal differences.

Table 8. Recycled constituents in speaker groups

	L1S	%	Group 1	%	Group 2	%
N	5	26	7[27]	35	1	8
ADJ			1	5		
ADV	1	5				
NP	2	11	6	30	2	15
PP	3	16	6	30	2	15
DEMP	2	11			2	15
VP	3	16				
NP+PP					1	8
VP+NP/PP	2	11			5	38
clause	1	5				
no. of other-recycling	19	100	20	100	13	100

The two groups differ with respect to recycling in more than one way. A first look at formal differences (Table 8) indicates that the two groups differ with respect to the syntactic format of recycled chunks. 60% of the pre-basic speakers' recyclings consist of single phrases (NP or PP), and 40% are represented by single constituents, either bare nouns (35%, equal to 7 occurrences) or adjectives (1 occurrence). This indicates their weak orientation to phrase boundaries together with the inclination to orient mainly to the lexical content of the TCU and not so much to its syntactic format. It also demonstrates a lower orientation to the syntactic cohesion of their talk with the previous turn, which is especially true for PP, where half of the prepositions are missing,[28] as in 26d. On the other hand, more advanced speakers use a wider range of formats, where the recycling may also involve the functional head of the NP or PP (the VP in 38% of the recycled chunks) as in 27c. Their orientation to the syntactic context of the recycled chunks results in a more cohesive sequence.

Example 26

(a) File 3 Pre-b

```
1    DO:    venga              sul              lettino
            come:IMP.3SG   on the:M.SG   couch:M.SG
2           signora
            madam:ADR
            "come on the couch madam"

3    PA:    lettina
            couch:*F.SG
            "couch"
```

(b) File 3 Pre-b

```
1    DO:    è                      ancora un       po' alta
            be:IND.PRS.2SG   still   a:M.SG   bit high:F.SG
2           signora
            madam:ADR
            "it's still a bit high madam"

3    PA:    ancora un po' alta
            still  a:M.SG bit high:F.SG
            "still a bit high"
```

(c) File 3 Pre-b

```
1    DO:  come vede                         sono
as        see:IND.PRS.3SG.CRT  be:IND.PRS.3PL
     quattro esami
     four    exam:M.PL
          "as you can see there are four exams"

2    PA:  quattro esami
          four    exam:M.PL
          "four exams"
```

(d) File 8 Pre-b

```
1    DO:  e    questa       va
          and  this:F.SG    go:IND.PRS.3SG.CRT
2         al p- el     primo       piano
          to the:M.SG  first:M.SG  floor:M.SG
     "and with this one you go to the f- to the first floor


3    PA:  pri[mo p
          first:M.SG
          "fir[st f"

4    DO:  [in ospedale
          in hospital:M.SG
          "to the hospital"

5    PA:  in ospedale           devo
          in hospital:M.SG  must:IND.PRS.2SG
6         andare
          go:INF.PRS
          "to the hospital I have to go"
```

(e) File 8 Pre-b

```
1    DO0: e    lei       va                  al
          and  3SG.CRT   go:IND.PRS.3SG  to the:M.SG
2         C                    a
     reservation centre to
3         prenotarle.
          book:INF.CLIT.3PL.ACC.F
     "and you go to the hospital reservation
          centre to book them."
```

```
4              (0.3)

5      PAO:   C (.)                    prenotale¿
              reservation centre *book:INF.CLIT.3PL.ACC.F
              "the hospital reservation centre (.) to
              book them¿"
```

Example 27, File 17 Post-b

(a)

```
1      DOO:   e °°allora non [ti°°
              and so       NEG   2SG.DAT.CLIT
              "and °°so you [don't°°"

2      PAO:              [e   allora=
                          and so
                          "[and so"

3      DOO:   =NON  DEVI         più   fare        la
              NEG   must:IMP.2SG more  do:INF.PRS  the:F.SG
4             la          l'         abbronzatura.
              the:F.SG    the:F.SG   suntan:F.SG
              "you MUSTN't get a tan anymore"
```

(b)

```
1      DOO:   e    lei          invece?
              and  3SG.ACC      instead
              "and what about her?"

2      PAO:   lei          invece     ogni  tanto       accusa
              3SG.ACC      instead    every much:M.SG   feel:IND.PRS.3SG
3             dei     dolori     in    parte       bassa
              some    pain:M.PL  in    part:F.SG   below:F.SG
              "now and then she feels some pain in her lower belly"
```

(c)

```
1      DOO:   (mtks)  dunque  tu    sei
                      well    you   be:AUX.IND.PRS.2SG
2             andata              qui     dal?
              go:PTCP.PST.F.SG    here    from the:M.SG
              "well you went here to the?"

3      PAO:   sono                     andata↑              a
              be:AUX.IND.PRS.1SG       go:PTCP.PST.F.SG     to
              un       consultorio                familiare.
              a:M.SG   counseling centre:M.SG     family:ADJ.M.SG
              "I went to the family counseling centre "
```

The two groups also differ in the functions of their recycling. The less advanced speakers recycle part of the previous speaker's turn as a resource either to show their understanding, as in 26a to 26d, or ask for clarification (26e), whereas a wider range of interactional functions, including taking the floor (27a) and anchoring their turn to previous talk (27b and 27c), are to be found in Group 2 only.

To sum up, a first investigation of formal and functional tendencies in L1S-L2S co-constructing and recycling suggests that the syntactic format of recycling both in co-constructions and outside of them may be relevant in the study of how L2 speakers activate their syntactic competence when they use the L2 in authentic interactional contexts, in order to achieve a number of interactional and textual goals, such as turn-taking, co-constructing, anchoring and delivering cohesive talk. Further analysis is needed to investigate target-like and nontarget-like recycling in and outside of co-constructions on by the L2Ss, and recasts and error correction (or avoidance of them) by L1Ss.

Opening sequence

As a further test of the initial hypothesis about possible correlations between morphosyntactic competence and performance in interactional exchanges by L2Ss, the following section will look at another type of sequence, namely the opening sequence of the encounter and more precisely the sequence where the P explains the reason for coming to the medical consultation. It is usually preceded by the GP's elicitation, which may either immediately follow a salutation turnor be delivered within the same turn, as in Example 28.

Example 28, Salutation + elicitation particle

(a) File 2 B

```
        °°ciao°°  ALLORA  ( )
        "°°hi°°   so  ( )"
```

(b) File 4 Post-b

```
        <buon>giorno (.) sì ( )
        "<good>morning (.) yes ( )"
```

Core and optional elements may be identified in the GP's first elicitation turn:

[salutation] + [address term] + **elicitation particles and/or request** + [address term]

The optional components are salutations (29b and 29c) and address terms (which may either precede or follow the explicit request, 29g and 29f), whereas the core elements are elicitation particles and requests (29a), which may co-occur (29g). The GP elicits the P's problem presentation through a series of more or less explicit means ranging from *allora/sì* [so/yes] (29a, 29b, and 29c) to *mi dica* [tell me] (29e, 29f, and 29g) and *tu per che cosa sei qui adesso?/quale è il motivo della sua visita?* [why are you here now?/which is the reason for this consultation?] (29d and 29g).

Example 29

(a) File 3 Pre-b

>   ALLORA!
>   "So"

(b) File 2 B

>   °° ciao°° **ALLORA**
>   "°° hi°° so"

(c) File 4 Post-b

>   <buon>giorno (.) sì
>   "<good>morning (.) yes"

(d) File 16 B/Post-b

>   allora. (.) **tu per che cosa sei**
>   so   you for what   be:IND.PRS.2SG
>   **qui adesso?**
>   here now
>   "So. (.) What brings you in today?"

(e) File 14 B

>   **mi   dica!**
>   1SG.DAT.CLIT tell:IMP.3SG.CRT
>   "how can I help you"

(f) File 6 Post-b

>   mi   dica   signora.
>   1SG.DAT.CLIT   tell:IMP.2SG   madam:ADR
>   "how can I help you madam"

(g) File 9 B

>   signor Osvaldo   mi   dica
>   mister:ADR Osvaldo   1SG.DAT.CLIT   tell:IMP.3SG.CRT
>   un   po' (.) qual è   il
>   a:M.SG   bit   which be:IND.PRS.3SG the:M.SG
>   motivo   di questa   visita?
>   reason:M.SG of this:F.SG consultation:F.SG
>   "Mr Osvaldo (.) what is the reason for your visit today"

There usually follows the P's response, which, in some cases, may be delayed by a pause (0.6 to 4.0 seconds) followed by a further request by the GP, as in Example 30, lines 4–5.

Example 30, File 2 B

```
1     DOO:    °°ciao°°  ALLORA
              "°°hi°°   so"

2             (4.0)

3     PAO:    (    )=

4     DOO:    eh. (.) qual è              il
                      what be:IND.PRS.3SG the:M.SG
              "       what's the problem?"
5             problema?
              problem:M.SG

6             (0.4)

7     PAO:    ( ) qua::  eh::  non  lo
                  here   eh    NEG  3SG.ACC.CLIT
8             so?              così
              know:IND.PRS.1SG so
              "( ) here:: eh:: I don't know? like that"
```

In the P's response to the GP's request, the four different sequential constructs in which the P explains the reason why he or she needs a medical consultation are exemplified in Table 9:

Type 1: the P completely relies on the GP's assistance (Example 30)
Type 2: the P partially relies on the GP's help (Example 31)
Type 3: the P autonomously explains his or her need in more than one turn (Example 32)
Type 4: the P autonomously explains his or her need in one single turn (Example 33)

Table 9. Problem elicitation sequences

	sequences
Type 1	GP's elicitation (pause) (P's attempt to answer) (pause) (GP's elicitation) (pause) P's answer (pause) GP's acknowledgment token/diagnostic question
Type 2	GP's elicitation (pause) (GP's elicitation) P's initiation (pause) GP's completion (pause) P's ratification (GP's ratification)
Type 3	GP's elicitation (pause) P's answer (pause) (GP's elicitation) (pause) P's answer (pause) P's answer (GP's continuer) (pause) P's answer (pause) P's answer (GP's continuer) (pause)

Type 3 *(cont.)*	P's answer (pause) P's answer (pause) P's answer (pause) P's answer GP's ratification
Type 4	GP's elicitation (pause) P's answer (pause) GP's acknowledgment token

Example 31, File 4 Post-b

```
1     DOO:   <buon>giorno (.) ↑sì
             "<good>morning (.) ↑yes"

2            (2.6)

3     PAO:   ho              fatto              l-    eh:::
             have:IND.PRS.1SG do:PTCP.PST.M.SG *the eh
             "I had th- eh:::"

4     DOO:   la         visita              per
             the:F.SG   consultation:F.SG   for
5            la         gravidanza?
             the:F.SG   pregnancy:F.SG
             "the pregnancy consultation?"

6            (0.4)

7     PAO:   eh:: sì.
             "eh:: yes."
```

Example 32, File 12 B

```
1     DOO:   mi         dica
             1SG.DAT    tell:IMP.3SG.CRT
             "what can I do for you"

2            (0.6)
```

```
3      PAO:  °°sì¿°°
             "°°yes¿°° "

4      DOO:  qual è              il         problema?
             what be:IND.PRS.3SG the:M.SG problem:M.SG
             "what's wrong with you?"

5            (0.8)

6      PAO:  i:: il         problema     è
                the:M.SG problem:M.SG be:IND.PRS.3SG
7            che:
             that:COMP
             "the problem is that"

8            (0.5)

9      PAO:  io:: ho::                  problemi    di
             I    have:IND.PRS.1SG problem:M.S of
10           mestrua(liazioni)
             *menstruation:F.PL
             "I have menstrual problems"

11     DOO:  mhm¿
             "mhm¿"

12           (1.5)

13     PAO:  >solo che<       sono                  io
             only that:COMP be:IND.PRS.1SG.AUX I
14           andata:::
             go:PTCP.PST.F.SG
             ">the only thing is that< I went:::"
```

Example 33, File 3 Pre-b

```
1      DOO:  ALLORA
             so

2            (4.0)

3      PAO:  allora mi            bisogni
             well   1SG.DAT.CLIT *need:IND.PRS
```

```
4              medicino        con    [le           pressione
               *medicine:M.SG with   the:F.PL      pressure:F.SG
               "well I need some medication for high
               blood pressure"

5    DOO:                             [eh!
```

Since it was not possible to find any clear correlation between the type of GP's elicitation and the degree of autonomy of the P's response, one may hypothesize that the latter may depend on a number of other linguistic and non-linguistic factors. Table 10 matches the above mentioned four response types with the LV of the P who produced them in order to test its relevance for the P's degree of autonomy in delivering his request. In the fourth column, the type of P's response is simplified into the binary parameter of autonomy, types 1 and 2 being <−autonomous> and types 3 and 4 being <+autonomous>.

Table 10. Patient response Type and autonomy in different learner varieties

L2 speaker	learner variety	response type	autonomy
3	pre-basic	4	+
8	pre-basic	4	+
1	basic	4	+
12	basic	3	+
9	basic	2	−
14	basic	2	−
2	basic	1	−
7	basic/post-basic	1	−
11	basic/post-basic	1	−
19	basic/post-basic	1	−
10	basic/post-basic	4	+
16	basic/post-basic	4	+
6	post-basic	4	+
5	post-basic	3	+
13	post-basic	3	+
15	post-basic	3	+
17	post-basic	3	+
20	post-basic	3	+
4	post-basic	2	−

Leaving aside collaborative answers jointly produced in co-construction formats (type 2), where the GP's idiosyncratic tendency to intervene may play a significant role, the present analysis will now compare the Ps who completely failed to provide an answer to the GP's request (type 1) and those who succeeded in doing so (types 3 and 4). A first glance at Table 10 shows that there is no clear correlation between the response type and the LV and, more precisely, between the autonomy of the response and the speaker's morphosyntactic competence. All post-basic speakers explain autonomously in one (type 4) or more than one turn (type 3) the reason for being there, but this is also true for the two pre-basic speakers and four (out of 10) basic speakers. This shows that less advanced speakers too can autonomouly explain the reason why they need a medical consultation. As a consequence, a low morphosyntactic competence may not necessarily imply the inability to achieve one's interactional goal, such as explaining one's need in institutional encounters. L2Ss may use other resources compensating for their limited morphosyntactic means.

A careful look at the two pre-basic speakers' responses in Example 34 shows that both speakers succeed in delivering their responses mainly thanks to their lexical means. In 34a, the P manages to explain her need in one single turn despite the fact that the syntactic format may reveal a poor mastery of the target language morphosyntax[29] and/or a possible interference from the L1. The wrong coding of the semantic roles of the verb *avere bisogno di* [need], where the experiencer is coded in the indirect object clitic pronoun (*mi* [me]) instead of the subject pronoun (*io* [I]), is probably modeled on the speaker's L1.[30] In 34b, the other pre-basic speaker's response consists of a single bare noun (*gastrite* [gastritis], line 5), which explains the pathology and enables the GP to narrow down the subsequent diagnostic questions.

Example 34

(a) File 3 Pre-b

```
1      DOO:    ALLORA!
               "So"

2              (4.0)

3      DOO:    qual'  è                     il            motivo
               which  be:IND.PRS.3SG        the:M.SG      reason:M.SG
4              [della           visi]ta¿
               of the:F.SG     consultation:F.SG
               "what brings you here today"

5      PAO:    [(°°ehm°° )]      gast°i-° gastriti
                                                    gastritis:*PL
               "ehm     gast°i-° gastritis"

6              (0.7)
```

7	DO0:	gastriti
		gastritis:*PL
		"gastritis"

Instead, failure to respond to the GP's request is primarily due to lexical gaps. In Example 35 a to d, the P (a basic/post-basic speaker) leaves the sentence incomplete and signals the beginning of a word search through a long word ending, a pause or a hesitation marker (*sì ha fatto e::: boh* [yes has done eh:: I don't know]; *io fatto: (0.8) andata a fare::* [I did: (0.8) gone to do::]; *ho fatto l- eh:::* [I did t- eh]; *io lei me aveva fatto::* [I you had done me]; *me ha detto che faciamo::* [you told me we do::]). Interestingly, all speakers use the generic verb *fare* [do] independently of the GP's elicitation format. Furthermore, in 35e, the P introduces the symptoms by means of a deictic pronoun (*qua* [here]) and then admits he cannot be more detailed in lexicalizing his health problem (*non lo so? così* [I don't know? like that]).

Example 35

(a) File 7 B/Post-b

1	PA0:	guarda io c' ho
		look:IMP.2SG I PLE have:IND.PRS.1SG
2		tanti problemi dottore.
		many problem:M.PL doctor:ADR
		"well I've got many problems doctor"
3	DO0:	((laughs)) [allora ((reads quietly))
		okay
4	PA0:	[( )
5	DO0:	( ) ha fatto?
		have:IND.PRS.3SG.CRT do:PTCP.PST
6	PA0:	sì ha fatto e:::
		yes have:IND.PRS.3SG do:PTCP.PST and
7		boh.
		Well
		"yes I had and::: don't know"
8	DO0:	allora (.) vediamo un po'.
		okay see:IMP.1PL a:M.SG bit
		"okay let's take a look"

(b) File 11 B/Post-b

```
1    DOO:   allora
             "well"

2           (1.0)

3    PAO:   io fatto:
            I  do:PTCP.PST.M.SG
            "I had"

4           (0.8)
```

Thus, what really endangers communication in these specific interactional contexts is not so much a low morphosyntactic competence in the L2 but specific lexical gaps. This hypothesis is corroborated by the fact that two Ps who fail to explain their need in the opening sequence (files 7 and 11) succeed in delivering two further requests (a heart test and a pressure test) later on in the exchange since they know how to lexicalize them, as shown in Example 36.

Example 36

(a) File 7 B/Post-b

```
1    DOO:   allora
             "well"

2           (4.0)

3    PAO:   ma   le            ho
            but  3SG.CRT       have:IND.PRS.1SG.AUX
4           detto              dottore        scusa
            tell:PST.PTCT.M.SG doctor:ADR     sorry
5           per fare           anche un       controllo
            for do:INF.PRS     also  a:M.SG   check:M.SG
6           eh de li           cuore          perché sempre io
            eh of *the:PL      heart:M.SG     because always I
7           vado               del            medico
            go:IND.PRS.1SG     of the:M.SG    doctor:M.SG
8           [così a  S.C.      .hhhhhh
             well in S.C.
            "but I also asked you doctor sorry **to have
            a heart test** because I always go to the
            doctor [well in S.C.(nearby town).hhhhh"
```

9   DO0:   [mhm
              "[mhm"

(b) File 11 B/Post-b

1   DO0:   le   chiedo   la
              3Sg.DAT.CRT ask:IND.PRS.1SG   the:F.SG
2   visita   ginecolo[gica↑
              consultation:F.SG gynecological:F.SG
              "I'll give you a prescription for a gynecologist"

3   PA0:   [eh sì anche io voglio
                                         yes also I want:IND.PRS.1SG
4   mhm voglio   misurare
                   want:IND.PRS.1SG   measure:INF.PRS
5   pressione↑
               pressure:F.SG
               "eh yes I want mhm want to measure my blood pressure too"

6   DO0:   sì sì sì.   la
              yes yes yes 3SG.F.ACC.CLIT
7   misuriamo.
               measure:IND.PRS.1PL
               "yeah yeah yeah we'll measure it."

To sum up, the analysis suggests that the accomplishment of certain interactional tasks such as explaining one's needs in an institutional encounter (e.g., one's health problem or symptoms in a medical consultation) is more strictly dependent on the speaker's lexical competence in the L2 rather than on the morphosyntactic competence.[31] This tentative conclusion triggers the need for a deeper investigation both of L1 and L2 lexical competence at the lexical and interactional interface (Hakulinen & Selting, 2005).

Concluding remarks

This chapter has explored whether interactional sequences, such as co-constructions and the opening of a GP medical consultation, may correlate with the L2Ss' LV.

The study has singled out interactional and syntactic regularities in clear cases of syntactically bound co-constructions by speakers of different Italian LVs. By focusing on the syntax of recycled chunks in *anchored completions*, the analysis has shown that the syntax of recycling in co-constructions tends to correlate with the speaker's morphosyntactic proficiency in the L2. More generally, the syntax of co-constructing (with or without recycling) may be regarded as a potential cue to investigate the interactional proficiency of L2Ss, namely how syntactic competence in the L2 differently shapes the online development of interactional sequences. Further work is needed to determine to which extent L2Ss' co-construction (and recycling) templates follow a developmental path and to what degree the grammatical projectability of L1 and L2 affects the acquisition of co-constructing (and recycling) in a second language.[32]

At the same time, the study has not found any strong correlation between the sequential format of the opening sequence and the speaker's morphosyntactic competence. In fact, pre-basic speakers, too, can autonomously state their need provided they know how to lexicalize it. This finding suggests that L2Ss can handle the task or goal of some particular activity by simply appealing to their lexical resources. The proposal here is preliminary and merely suggestive, but the evidence indicates that in the interactional contexts investigated, lexical proficiency seems to be more interactionally relevant than syntactic competence. In other words, inadequate lexical competence (e.g., of a specialized lexicon) may seriously endanger the achievement of one's interactional goals, which is not necessarily the case for low morphosyntactic competence in the L2. Conversely, high morphosyntactic competence is not necessarily a predictor of a successful interactional performance.

These tentative research findings raise more general theoretical questions about the nature of interactional competence, about how universal versus language-specific co-constructing and recycling practices in L1 and L2 affect second language talk, and about what L2Ss need to learn in order to become competent in diverse interactional contexts. The nature and the amount of data so far investigated are not enough to tackle these issues, which go beyond the scope of this chapter. Cross-linguistic work is needed to provide sound hypotheses as to the universal vs. language-specific nature of interactional practices and their role in the acquisition of a second language.

Notes

1   "The term *spontaneous learning* is used to denote the acquisition of a second language in everyday communication, in a natural fashion, free from systematic guidance. A prototypical case is that of a Turkish worker who settles in a West European country not knowing a single word of the local language and who manages to acquire—through his sporadic and unsystematic social intercourse with the broader society—some knowledge of the language" (Klein, 1986, p. 16). Sometimes *spontaneous* learning is referred to as *untutored* learning (vs. *tutored* or *guided* learning).

2   One of the most influential studies, which prompted methodological reorientations in SLA research, is the ZISA (Zweisprachenwerb italienischer und spanischer

Arbeiter) project, conducted at the University of Hamburg in the late 1970s (Meisel, Clahsen, & Pienemann, 1981). One major finding of the research was the developmental sequence of the acquisition of word order rules in German L2. More generally, it was found that, although ILs are highly variable, acquisition orders and developmental sequences show a high degree of uniformity (Larsen-Freeman & Long, 1991, p. 270).

3   Briefly, the three founding principles of interactional linguistics are that "grammar organizes social interaction," "social interaction organizes grammar," and "grammar is a mode of social interaction" (Ochs, Schegloff, & Thompson, 1996, pp. 33–41). In this perspective, not only does grammar represent a central resource for doing social interaction, but it constitutes types of activities in itself.

4   "[L'acquisition d'une langue] ne peut être réduite à l'apprentissage ni d'un système ni de règles communicatives, mais apparaît comme le développement de la capacité même de participer à une pratique sociale—et doit par conséquent être étudiée à l'intérieur de cette pratique" (Pekarek Doehler, 2000, p. 7).

5   "comme occasions de mise en œuvre pratique des capacities de résolution collaborative des problèmes, et comme lieux potentials de l'élaboration d'un repertoire variable et adapté aux besoins communicatives pratiques" (Pekarek Doehler, 2000, p. 13).

6   For a detailed account of its aims, methodology, and results see Perdue (1993), volumes I and II.

7   They have been transcribed in CLAN (MacWhinney, 1994) using the Jeffersonian CA conventions.

8   The data were audio-recorded by the author in the course of participant observation in 2003 for her dissertation research on Italian native-nonnative discourse. The consultations were collected in Lombardy (Northern Italy) with the full informed consent of the participants.

9   Each general practitioner is identified by a code (A, B, C, D, E) and gender (M, F). So, for example, AM stands for doctor A, who is a male. Doctors A and D are in their late thirties, B and E are in their late fifties, and C is in his sixties.

10 The L2 speakers are numbered after the file of the consultation. So, for instance, speaker 3 is the patient in file 3, which is the third consultation in chronological order.

11 This consultation is attended by two patients (a couple), one of whom (the female, PA1) rarely speaks. The coding refers to the male, who takes a more active role.

12 One of the first empirical studies based on the concept of LV is the Heidelberg Research Project for Pidgin German (Klein & Dittmar, 1979).

13 The *Common European Framework of Reference for Languages* (Council of Europe, 2001) could represent an alternative model with its six-level functional-pragmatic scale, defined in terms of what the speakers can do in an L2. However, the grammatically-based LV model is more coherent and has a better fit with the research aims, which are primarily concerned with the use of specific syntactic structures in interaction.

14 Co-constructions have been studied from a variety of perspectives, mostly based on English, Japanese, and Finnish data. Sacks (1992) refers to them as *collaborative built sentences*; Lerner (1991) names them *sentences-in-progress*; Ono and Thompson (1996) use the term *co-construction*; Thompson and Couper-Kuhlen (2005) talk about *joint utterance constructions*; Szczepek (2000a, 2000b) calls them *collaborative productions*.
15 For a discussion of the notions of TRP and TCU see Selting (2000).
16 Between the two prototypical (minimal) components there may occur other non-final completion units (see Example 9 and endnote 15).
17 In this chapter, *completion unit* will be used as a hyperonym of *final component*. A completion unit may be either final (if it ends up in a transition relevance place, as in Example 9, line 11) or non-final (if it requires further completions, as in the same fragment, lines 5, 6, 8 and 10).
18 In the counting of completion units, each speaker's completion attempt counts as a single occurrence. So Example 10 includes 3 completion units by the L2 speaker and 2 by the L1 speaker.
19 C=cue; O=overlap
20 Before going to the eye specialist, the P is supposed to fix an appointment at the hospital reception desk.
21 Cordin and Lo Duca's (2003, pp. 67–120) comparison of the acquisition of verb argument structure by first and second language speakers of Italian has shown, among other things, a common tendency to "argument reduction," that is to leave verb arguments unexpressed where they are pragmatically inferable, whereas first and second language learners may differ in the choice of the preposition to express the argument, which is more frequently accurate (that is, target-like) in L1 learner varieties (Cordin & Lo Duca, 2003, pp. 81–94). For a crosslinguistic approach to the L1 acquisition of verb argument structure in other languages see also Bowerman and Brown (2008) and Gagarina and Gülzow (2008).
22 It also represents an instance of *terminal item completion* (Hayashi, 1999), which differs from the final component in that the former delivers the final constituent only (e.g., the noun) of a phrase (e.g., NP) whose first constituent (e.g., the article) has already been delivered by the first speaker.
23 Similar tendencies were found in a wider corpus of Italian native-nonnative naturally occurring interactions, which includes other types of institutional encounters and ordinary conversations as well (Biazzi, 2008).
24 Indefinite and definite articles.
25 This tendency is coherent with the *functional head principle* discovered for German L1 by Uhmann (2001, p. 388).
26 Group 1 refers to the two pre-basic speakers (files 3 and 8, Table 1) and Group 2 applies to files 5 and 17 (Table 1), which involve two post-basic speakers.
27 One from an NP and six from a PP in the previous turn.

28 Except for "*in*+N", where the preposition *in* is usually recycled. On the other hand, the PP may be understood as a single lexical item, a result of speech segmentation problems. For a detailed account of the acquisition of prepositions in Italian as L2 see Bagna (2004).
29 Wrong gender morpheme of the word *medicino* [medicine] (masculine) instead of the feminine *medicina*; wrong determiner-noun agreement *le pressione* [the pressure] (plural-singular), where the article is in the plural and the noun in the singular; use of wrong preposition *con* [with] instead of *per* [for].
30 The Russian construct *mnje nuščna* [I need]. On the other hand, it could represent a marked construction, possibly overlapping with the Italian *mi serve* [I need.]
31 This is not to say that the degree of autonomy in the P's response depends exclusively on the L2S's linguistic competence. It may also rest on a number of other non-linguistic factors, such as familiarity with the interlocutor, the institutional context and/or with a specific speech event, or reluctancy due to the type of health problem.
32 Although it is premature to establish whether Italian is an early or late projection language or whether it belongs to yet a third type, a first insight into the data so far investigated shows that most of the completion units by both first and second language speakers are postverbal constituents, which shows the centrality of the predicate in turn projection. Moreover, completion units often come after a cue (e.g., hesitations, pauses, rising intonations), which would place Italian closer to a late projection language. On the other hand, in the data unsolicited co-constructions are not so rare, which may suggest that the turn allocation format in co-constructions may be "early" or "late" according to the different social action they perform.

References

Andorno, C. (Ed.). (2000). *Banca dati di italiano L2* [Databank of L2 Italian]. Pavia: Università di Pavia.
Antaki, C., & Widdicombe, S. (1998). *Identities in talk*. London: Sage.
Auer, P. (2005). Projection in interaction and projection in grammar. *Text, 25*(1), 7–36.
Bagna, C. (2004). *La competenza quasi-bilingue/quasi-nativa. Le preposizioni in Italiano L2* [Near-bilingual/near-native competence. Prepositions in L2 Italian]. Milano: FrancoAngeli.
Bernini, G., & Giacalone Ramat, A. (Eds.). (1990). *La temporalità nell'acquisizione di lingue seconde* [Temporality in second language acquisition] Milano: FrancoAngeli.
Biazzi, M. (2008). Riformulazioni tra parlanti L1–L2 di italiano: tra grammatica e interazione [Reformulations among L1-L2 Italian speakers: Between grammar and interaction]. In G. Bernini, L. Spreafico, & A. Valentini (Eds.), *Competenze lessicali e discorsive nell'acquisizione di lingue seconde* [Lexical and discourse competence in second language acquisition] (pp. 511–540). Perugia: Guerra.

Bowerman, M., & Brown, P. (Eds.). (2008). *Crosslinguistic perspectives on argument structure. Implications for learnability.* Hillsdale, NJ: Erlbaum.

Cordin, P., & Lo Duca, M. G. (2003). *Classi di verbi, valenze e dizionari. Esplorazioni e proposte* [Verb classes, valencies and dictionaries. Explorations and proposals]. Padova: Unipress.

Council of Europe. (2001). *Common European framework of reference for languages.* Cambridge: Cambridge University Press.

Couper-Kuhlen, E., & Ono, T. (2007). Incrementing in conversation. A comparison of practices in English, German and Japanese. In E. Couper-Kuhlen & T. Ono (Eds.), Turn continuation in cross linguistic perspective [Special issue]. *Pragmatics, 17*(4), 513–552.

Dimroth, C., & Starren M. (2003). *Information structure and the dynamics of language acquisition.* Amsterdam: John Benjamins.

Doughty, C. J., Byrnes, H., Connor-Linton, J., Spielmann, G., & Tyler, A. (1997). *Profiling the Georgetown University advanced foreign language learner.* Washington, DC: Georgetown University.

Doughty, C. J., & Long, M. H. (2000). Eliciting second language speech data. In L. Menn & N. Bernstein Ratner (Eds.), *Methods for studying language production* (pp. 149–177). Mahwah, NJ: Lawrence Erlbaum.

Ford, C., Fox, B., & Thompson, S. (2002). *The language of turn and sequence.* Oxford: Oxford University Press.

Fox, B. (2007). Principles shaping grammatical practices: An exploration. *Discourse Studies, 9*(3), 299–318.

Fox, B., Hayashi, M., & Jasperson, R. (1996). Resources and repair: A cross-linguistic study of syntax and repair. In E. Ochs, E. Schegloff, & S. Thompson (Eds.), *Interaction and grammar* (pp. 185–237). Cambridge: Cambridge University Press.

Fox, B., & Jasperson, R. (1995). A syntactic exploration of repair in English conversation. In P. W. Davis (Ed.), *Alternative linguistics. Descriptive and theoretical modes* (pp. 77–133). Amsterdam: John Benjamins.

Gagarina, N., & Gülzow, I. (Eds.). (2008). *The acquisition of verbs and their grammar. The effect of particular languages.* Dordrecht: Springer.

Gajo, L., & Mondada, L. (2000). *Interactions et acquisitions en contexte* [Interaction and acquisition in context]. Fribourg, Switzerland: EUFS.

Giacalone Ramat, A. (Ed.). (2003). *Verso l'italiano. Percorsi e strategie di acquisizione* [Towards Italian. Acquisition paths and strategies]. Rome: Carocci.

Givón, T. (1979). *On understanding grammar.* New York, NY: Academic Press.

Hakulinen, A., & Selting, M. (Eds.). (2005). *Syntax and lexis in conversation: Studies on the use of linguistic resources in conversation.* Amsterdam: John Benjamins.

Hayashi, M. (1999). Where grammar and interaction meet: A study of co-participant completion in Japanese conversation. *Human Studies, 22,* 475–499.

Hayashi, M. (2003). *Joint utterance construction in Japanese conversation.* Amsterdam: John Benjamins.

Helasvuo, M. (2004). Shared syntax: The grammar of co-construction. *Journal of Pragmatics, 36*(8), 1315–1336.
Hendriks, H. (2005). *The structure of learner varieties.* Berlin: Mouton de Gruyter.
Ikeda, K., & Ko, S. (this volume). Choral practice patterns in the language classroom.
Kärkkäinen, E., Sorjonen, M., & Helasvuo, M. (2007). Discourse structure. In T. Shopen (Ed.), *Language typology and syntactic description. Volume II: Complex constructions* (pp. 301–371). Cambridge: Cambridge University Press.
Klein, W. (1986). *Second language acquisition.* Cambridge: Cambridge University Press.
Klein, W., & Ditttmar, N. (1979). *Developing grammars.* Berlin: Springer.
Klein, W., & Perdue, C. (1992). *Utterance structure. Developing grammars again.* Amsterdam: John Benjamins.
Klein, W., & Perdue, C. (1997). The basic variety. *Second Language Research, 13*(4), 301–347.
Koshik, I. (2002). Designedly incomplete utterances: A pedagogical practice for eliciting knowledge displays in error correction sequences. *Research on Language and Social Interaction, 35*(3), 277–309.
Kramsch, C. J. (2003). *Language acquisition and language socialization: Ecological perspectives.* London: Continuum.
Larsen-Freeman, D., & Long, M. (1991). *An introduction to second language acquisition research.* London: Longman.
Leather, J., & van Dam, J. (2003). *Ecology of language acquisition.* Dordrecht: Kluwer Academic Publishers.
Lerner, G. (1991). On the syntax of sentences-in-progress. *Language in Society, 20,* 441–458.
Lerner, G. (2004). On the place of linguistic resources in the organization of talk-in-interaction: Grammar as action in prompting a speaker to elaborate. *Research on Language and Social Interaction, 37*(2), 151–184.
Lerner, G., & Takagi, T. (1999). On the place of linguistic resources in the organization of talk-in-interaction: A co-investigation of English and Japanese grammatical practices. *Research on Language and Social Interaction, 37*(2), 151–184.
Linell, P., & Luckmann, T. (1991). Asymmetries in dialogue. Some conceptual preliminaries. In I. Markova & K. Foppa (Eds.), *Asymmetries in dialogue* (pp. 1–20). Hemel Hemstead: Harvester Wheatsheaf.
MacWhinney, B. (1994). *The CHILDES project: Tools for analyzing talk. Volume I.* Pittsburg, PA: Carnegie Mellon University. Retrieved September 2010, from www.childes.psy.cnu.edu/
Meisel, J., Clahsen, H., & Pienemann, M. (1981). On determining developmental stages in natural second language acquisition. *Studies in Second Language Acquisition, 3*(1), 109–135.
Mondada, L., & Pekarek Doehler, S. (2000). Interaction sociale et cognition située: quels modèles pour la recherche sur l'acquisition des langues? [Social interaction and situated cognition: Which models for language acquisition research?]. *Acquisition et Interaction en Langue Etrangère, 12,* 147–174.

Nonnative discourse. (2000). [Special issue]. *Issues in Applied Linguistics, 11*(1).
Ochs, E., Schegloff, E., & Thompson, S. (Eds.). (1996). *Interaction and grammar.* Cambridge: Cambridge University Press.
Ono, T., & Thompson, S. (1995). What can conversation tell us about syntax? In P. W. Davis (Ed.), *Alternative linguistics. Descriptive and theoretical modes* (pp. 213–271). Amsterdam: John Benjamins.
Ono, T., & Thompson, S. (1996). Interaction and syntax in the structure of conversational discourse: Collaboration, overlap, and syntactic dissociation. In E. H. Hovy & D. R. Scott (Eds.), *Computational and conversational discourse: Burning issues—An interdisciplinary account* (pp. 67–96). Berlin: Springer.
Orletti, F. (2007). Enunciati a più voci: La conversazione fra grammatica ed interazione [Utterances with multiple voices: Conversation between grammar and interaction]. In M. Pettorino, A. Giannini, M. Vallone, & R. Savy (Eds.), *La comunicazione parlata. Atti del congresso* [Spoken communication. Proceedings of the conference] (pp. 1221–1235). Napoli: Liguori.
Pekarek Doehler, S. (2000). Approches interactionnistes de l'acquisition des langues étrangères: Concepts, recherches, perspectives [Interactionist approaches to foreign language acquisition: Concepts, research, perspectives]. *Acquisition et Interaction en Langue Etrangère, 12,* 3–26.
Perdue, C. (Ed.). (1993). *Adult language acquisition: Cross-linguistic perspectives.* Cambridge: Cambridge University Press.
Perdue, C. (Ed.). (2000). The structure of learner varieties [Special issue]. *Studies in Second Language Acquisition, 22*(3).
Sacks, H. (1992). *Lectures on conversations.* Oxford: Blackwell.
Sacks, H., Schegloff, E. A., & Jefferson, G. (1974). A simplest systematics for the organization of turn-taking for conversation. *Language, 50*(4), 696–735.
Schegloff, E. (1979). The relevance of repair to syntax-for-conversation. In T. Givón (Ed.), *Syntax and semantics, vol. 12: Discourse and syntax* (pp. 261–285). New York, NY: Academic Press.
Schegloff, E. (1996). Issues of relevance for discourse analysis: Contingency in action, interaction, and co-participation context. In E. H. Hovy & D. R. Scott (Eds.). *Discourse processing: An interdisciplinary perspective* (pp. 3–35). Heidelberg: Springer.
Selinker, L. (1972). Interlanguage. *International Review of Applied Linguistics, 10*(3), 201–231.
Selting, M. (2000). The constructing of units in conversational talk. *Language in Society, 29,* 477–517.
Szczepek, B. (2000a). Formal aspects of collaborative productions in English conversation. *Inlist, 17.* Retrieved May 2010 from http://inlist.uni-konstanz.de.
Szczepek, B. (2000b). Functional aspects of collaborative productions in English conversation. *Inlist, 21.* Retrieved May 2010 from http://inlist.uni-konstanz.de.
Thompson, S., & Couper-Kuhlen, E. (2005). The clause as a locus of grammar and interaction. *Discourse Studies, 7*(4–5), 481–505.

Uhmann, S. (2001). Some arguments for the relevance of syntax to same-sentence self-repair in everyday German conversation. In M. Selting & E. Couper-Kuhlen (Eds.), *Studies in interactional linguistics* (pp. 373–404). Amsterdam: John Benjamins.
Wagner, J., & Gardner, R. (Eds.). (2004). *Second language conversations.* London: Continuum.
Young, R. F. (2008). *Language and interaction.* New York, NY: Routledge.

Appendix: Glossing abbreviations

*	nontarget form
1	first person
2	second person
3	third person
ACC	accusative
ADR	address term
AUX	auxiliary
CLIT	clitic pronoun
COMP	complementizer
COND	conditional
CRT	courtesy form
DAT	dative
DSP	discourse particle
EXC	exclamation
F	feminine
GEN	genitive
GER	gerund
IND	indicative
INF	infinitive
IPFV	imperfective
M	masculine
NEG	negation
OBL	oblique
PL	plural
PLE	pleonastic
PRS	present
PST	past
PTCP	participle
REFL	reflexive
REL	relative
SG	singular

12 The L2 Inventory in Action: Conversation Analysis and Usage-Based Linguistics in SLA[1]

Søren Wind Eskildsen
University of Southern Denmark

Introduction

This chapter finds itself at a junction in Second Language Acquisition (SLA) research. As an attempt at analyzing and describing the interplay between contextual factors (i.e., "the social language learner") and individual psycholinguistic factors (i.e., "the cognitive language learner"), it follows, in some respects, an increasing tendency to view second language (L2) learning as both a social and a cognitive achievement (e.g., Atkinson, 2002; Block, 2003; de Bot, Lowie, & Verspoor, 2007; N. Ellis & Larsen-Freeman, 2006; Firth & Wagner, 1997; Kramsch, 2002; Lantolf, 2000; Lantolf & Thorne, 2006; Larsen-Freeman, 2007; Larsen-Freeman & Cameron, 2008; Watson-Gegeo, 2004; Zuengler & Miller, 2006). In other respects it has fewer parallels. As a longitudinal case study of a Mexican-Spanish speaking classroom learner of English, it tracks *both* linguistic and interactional development over a period of almost two years. As such, it finds its closest equivalents in similar longitudinal case studies of interactional competence development (e.g., Hellermann, 2007; Hellermann & Cole, 2009). However, it also breaks a new path as it attempts to combine analytical tools from conversation analysis (CA) with usage-based linguistics (UBL), a framework for investigating linguistic development in language learning (for L1, see e.g., Dabrowska & Lieven, 2005; Goldberg,

2006; Lieven, 2009; Lieven & Tomasello, 2008; MacWhinney, 2004; Tomasello, 2000, 2003; for L2, see e.g., Bybee, 2008; N. Ellis, 2002; N. Ellis & Cadierno, 2009; Eskildsen, 2009; Eskildsen & Cadierno, 2007; Goldberg & Casenhiser, 2008). In so doing, it tries to capture the relationship between interactional environments and action sequences on the one hand, and the individual accumulation of linguistic resources in L2 learning on the other.

In order to investigate over time this emergent inventory of L2 resources as it is put to use, a performance-based model of language knowledge is needed as a frame of reference. Useful for capturing the fluidity of linguistic patterns as they emerge ontogenetically, the method and theory of the UBL tradition cover a number of functional-cognitive linguistic theories united in the rejection of certain dualisms in (applied) linguistics, among these the syntax-lexis distinction and the competence-performance distinction. UBL also assumes that language structure emerges from usage events, and that language learning is a bottom-up, usage-driven, and experiential process (e.g., N. Ellis, 2002; Langacker, 2000; Tomasello, 2000; Tummers, Heylen, & Geeraerts, 2005). This means that there is an important coupling between what language learners encounter in real life interactions and what they learn. The assumption that language knowledge and language use, interaction and cognition, and individuality and sociality are mutually constitutive makes UBL especially fruitful for the present endeavor in two ways: (a) it allows for a simultaneous focus on social aspects of use and individual aspects of cognition, and (b) it opens up towards a complementary methodological and theoretical relationship with CA.

In concrete linguistic terms, according to Tummers et al. (2005), UBL subscribes to a "maximalistic language model in which abstract grammatical patterns and the lexical instantiations of those patterns are jointly included, and which may consist of many different levels of schematic abstraction" (p. 228–229). Language knowledge is seen as a structured inventory of symbolic units, that is, form-meaning patterns (Langacker, 1987) of varying complexity stored on multiple levels of abstractness, ranging from fixed multi-word expressions (MWEs; e.g., *I dunno*) to partially schematized patterns or "utterance schemas" (Tomasello, 2000; e.g., *I don't Verb*) to fully abstract language knowledge (e.g., *NP AUX NEG VERB*; N. Ellis, 2002; Tomasello, 2003). Learning a language, then, is an item-based process (MacWhinney, 1975; Tomasello, 2000) of extracting regularities among linguistic patterns in a slow and piecemeal fashion along a trajectory of increasing schematicity of language knowledge from formulas via partially abstract patterns to fully abstract constructions.

In UBL, it is generally assumed that a profitable and empirically justifiable approach to language learning research, be it L1 or L2, should start from observing specific linguistic facts in action, primarily concrete MWEs and partially concrete utterance schemas. This methodology implies for L2 learning research that no reference should be made to an abstract level of language knowledge unless it can be empirically substantiated to exist for the linguistic patterns and L2 users under investigation (Eskildsen, 2009; Eskildsen & Cadierno, 2007). This point of departure is reflected in the insight that linguistic knowledge is emergent in nature, constantly under construction, and in flux as usage environments change (e.g., Bates & MacWhinney, 1988; Hopper, 1998). In these changing environments, type and token frequencies are thought to determine matters of psycholinguistic entrenchment and schematicity of recurring expressions and constructions. In Tomasello's (2003) words, token frequency is frequency of a concrete expression which "in the language learner's experience tends to entrench that expression in terms of the concrete words and morphemes involved," whereas type frequency "of a class of expressions determines the abstractness or schematicity of the resulting construction" (p. 107). The maximalistic nature of the linguistic inventory, however, guarantees that what is learned as specific is not necessarily replaced over time by the more abstract constructional knowledge acquired; rather, abstract patterns and their specific instantiations may cohabitate in the grammar, which implies that specific linguistic patterns co-exist psycholinguistically alongside more abstract schematizations of the same patterns (e.g., Achard, 2007; Langacker, 2000).

Usage-Based Linguistics in SLA

UBL constitutes an important contribution to SLA because its holistic views on individuality and sociality are compatible with a view of language learning that potentially encompasses both social and cognitive perspectives on learning, an aspect that is becoming increasingly important within the SLA field (e.g., Larsen-Freeman, 2007). So far, however, the UBL trajectory of learning, from formulas towards increasing schematicity, suggested by N. Ellis (2002) as a default guide to investigating L2 development, has only been applied to SLA in few longitudinal studies. Bardovi-Harlig (2002), in a response to N. Ellis, examined future expression by 16 learners of English and found two phenomena indicating that the path is only partially valid for SLA: (a) the role of formulas in initial development was found to be limited; and (b) the use of formulas was found not to diminish ontogenetically. The first phenomenon, Bardovi-Harlig concedes, may be due to the fact that initial formulaic use is too brief to be detected in her corpus. In terms of the second finding, Bardovi-Harlig does not acknowledge that the existence of the formulas in advanced stages of learning in fact supports the validity of the suggested path of acquisition insofar as it is connected with the cohabitation in the grammar hypothesis. Bardovi-Harlig does conclude, however, that N. Ellis' proposed path of acquisition presents a richer view of SLA development than a starting point that excludes formulas.

Studying the development of *do-negation* by a Mexican-Spanish speaking learner of English, Eskildsen and Cadierno (2007) found positive evidence for the UBL path of acquisition, with the system emerging in acquisition characterized as the gradual abstraction of regularities that link expressions as constructions. *Do-negation* learning was found to be initially heavily reliant on one specific instantiation of the pattern, *I don't know*, with productivity gradually increasing as the underlying knowledge seemed to become increasingly abstract, as reflected in type and token frequencies. *I don't know* was also found to be stable throughout development suggesting its entrenchment as a MWE. These findings thus suggest that L2 learning is indeed item-based, that expression entrenchment is dependent on token frequency (as in the case of *I don't know*) and that more abstract pattern and construction learning is dependent on type frequency, as expected.

In a recent longitudinal study on the same student, this time focusing on *can*-patterns, Eskildsen (2009) found no conclusive evidence that L2 development implies reaching a level of fully schematic linguistic knowledge. The observed linguistic patterns were found to be interrelated in terms of partially concrete utterance schemas but could not be shown to be linked as fully abstract constructions in ontogenesis. Linguistic productivity, the study suggested, seems to be guaranteed by a rich inventory of linked utterance schemas rather than the learning of increasingly complex combinatorial rules or increasingly schematized linguistic knowledge. In other words, it might not be the case for all kinds of linguistic patterns that their learning is a matter of endlessly abstracting regularities. Initially in development, the focal student's *can*-utterances were found to be dominated by a few concrete interrelated patterns, MWEs such as *I can write* and *can you write*, rendering language learning item-based in accordance with UBL. Furthermore, the data revealed that these MWEs were inextricably linked with certain interactional contexts, suggesting a locally contextualized view of L2 learning, and showing interaction to be a constant source of cognitive reinforcement (i.e., entrenchment) and renewal for the MWEs and utterance schemas in the individual linguistic repertoire. In other words, the study, proposing an emergentist outlook on development, suggested that language learning is a process indistinguishable from language use.

Outline of the chapter

Further exploring matters pertaining to the intersection of use and learning, this chapter will undertake a dual analysis of L2 interaction as it attempts to trace linguistic and interactional development in a Mexican L2 learner of English. First, I introduce the data and the linguistic inventory of the focal student, including the

MWE under investigation. The following two sections are then concerned with the interactional analysis in which I go through a set of extracts covering a time-span of approximately one year. After a discussion of the main findings, I move on to analyze the linguistic developmental issues in my focal student, using the UBL framework, before presenting my conclusions in the final section.

Present study

Data

The data source for the study is the Multimedia Adult English Learner Corpus (MAELC),[2] which consists of audio-visual recordings of classroom interaction in an English as a Second Language (ESL) context. The classrooms in which the recordings were made were equipped with video cameras, and students were given wireless microphones on a rotational basis; the teacher also wore a microphone (Reder, 2005; Reder, Harris, & Setzler, 2003). Consisting of recordings from July 2003 through July 2005, this is a longitudinal case study of Valerio,[3] an adult Mexican male learner of English whose L1 is Spanish. The final database of the inquiry consists of transcripts from approximately 30 sessions (each consisting of three hours of recordings, not all of which has been transcribed) in which Valerio is either wearing a microphone or sitting next to someone wearing a microphone. This transcribed database has not been coded for linguistic category information, which means that only searches based on exact and concrete sequences of either letters or words are possible. The uses reported on in this chapter do not include uses that are being specifically practiced in grammar tasks in the classroom at the time of recording.

Taking cognitive portability of concrete linguistic patterns as its starting point, the present study investigates the interplay between interactional circumstances and L2 development by focusing on a recurrent linguistic pattern and its interactional deployment over time. The pattern under investigation is the *auxiliary do*-pattern, not including the *do-neg* pattern. An overview of Valerio's linguistic inventory, insofar far as *aux-do* is concerned, is presented in the appendix. The data displayed in the appendix are described and discussed further below; the important thing to note at this stage is the primary empirical observation that there seems to be an initially recurring formula, *what do you say*—a fixed multi word expression (MWE), here operationalized as *a recurring string of words used for a relatively coherent and constant communicative purpose* (Eskildsen, 2009; Eskildsen & Cadierno, 2007). The use of this MWE over time, and the notion that it may constitute the developmental seed of a more generic *aux-do* pattern, are investigated in turn in the following, starting from the point of tracing the MWE in action to show the co-emergence of interactional contingencies and specific features in the linguistic inventory of my focal student.

Zooming in on the inventory in use

One way to get at these interactional contingencies is to put the data under the scrutiny of a conversation analysis (CA) inspired analysis to investigate issues pertaining to sequential placement. In the interest of clarity, it should be stressed that this investigation is not strictly CA; rather, some concepts often used in micro-analysis have been borrowed for the present purposes. The epistemological common-ground shared by the present research and proponents of micro-analysis for L2 studies (e.g., Firth & Wagner, 2007) is the conceptualization of language learning as emergent, constant, and never-ending. This shared epistemology between the present approach and a CA-inspired approach to L2 studies has informed the following investigation of whether "a micro-analysis of second language conversations can enhance our understanding of what it means to talk in another language, by broadening the focus beyond the sounds, structures and meanings of language to encompass action sequences, timing and interactivity" (Wagner & Gardner, 2004, p. 14). In other words, Schegloff and Sacks' (1973) insight that conversation is organized in action sequences, and the ensuing discovery that what people accomplish through language depends on the sequential positioning of linguistic items, is what makes micro-analysis relevant for the study of L2 interactional data.

So, in the analyses which follow, the target utterance is the MWE *what do you say*, the focus being on what it does and where it does it in terms of its sequential position and the orientations of the participants. An initial overview of the data reveals that the MWE, when viewed over time, is used to perform four different functions. In the order they appear chronologically in the data they are (a) *invitation for help*; (b) *display of doing thinking*; (c) *reference to a past interactional event*; and (d) *elicitation of opinion*. Table 1 presents an overview and reference point for the various MWE instantiations under investigation and extracts analyzed in the following. As Table 1 displays, the extracts are presented in an order which reflects both chronology and pragmatic function of the MWE.

Table 1. MWEs by function, chronology, and extract representation

MWE function	data appearance	extract representation
invitation for help	July–August 2003	1, 2, 4
display of doing thinking	July 2003–March 2004	2, 3, 5
reference to past action	August 2003–June 2005	6, 7, 8
elicitation of opinion	March–July 2004	9, 10, 11

The interest, then, lies in the interplay among the MWE, sequential organization, and social activity. On a more epistemological note, the current interest is also in the interplay between the social nature of the classroom interactions and the nature of the contributions of the individual participants in interaction, the underlying assumption being that these co-develop in an equal partnership, as it were, in which none is given prominence over the other.

The MWE as invitation for help or display of doing thinking?

Extract 1 below is from Valerio's very first day in ESL class. In the preceding discourse, a task in which participants talk about favorite holidays / days of the year, Valerio (Va) has been "interviewing" Angelica (An), who does not immediately begin to interview him back. Instead, Valerio now self-selects as the next speaker (line 1) to tell Angelica about his favorite day of the year, which turns out to be his wedding anniversary. Please note that intra-turn pauses marked in the transcripts are action-filled (e.g., the students are writing) unless otherwise noted in the analyses. In the transcripts, words between slashes are to be read phonetically, following IPA conventions.[4]

Extract 1, July 01, 2003

```
01     Va:    ((writes)) xxx aih ((slaps himself on
02            mouth)) uh .hh for me: December (1) eight
03     An:    ((writes)) December ((writes)) December?
04     Va:    eight (3) because (1) is (1) anniversary?
05     An:    ((writes)) uhuh ((looks up at Valerio))
06            (2)
07     Va:    for the /mæriɪd/?
08            (2)
09     An:    anniversary
10     Va:    for the /mæriɪd/?
11     An:    for is para ((waving hand))
12     Va:    for ((frowns)) (2) um:
13            (5)
14     An:    xxx ((turns to her own desk, writes))
15     Va:    agh: ((leans over to see what An writes))
16 ->         (4) teacher what do you say for
17            (2)
18     An:    anniversary[: and marry ((pointing at=
19     Va:               [for anniversary /mæriɪd/?
20     An:    =Valerio))
21     Te:    it's it's anniversary.
22     Va:    anni[versary?
23     Te:        [wedding anniversary
24     An:    wedding? ((picks up paper))
25     Va:    wed[ding?
26     Te:       [wedding (+) so let [me write it down=
27     Va:                           [wedding (1) ah=
28     Te:    =for you  ]
29     Va:    =yeah yeah]
```

```
30      Te:     wedding [anniversary
31      Va:             [wedding is here ((shuffles paper,
32              writes)) no (2) uhuh ((points to board,
33              looks at An)) wedding anniversary (1) is
34              wedding anniversary
35      An:     ((writes))
```

In line 4, Valerio uses the term *anniversary* which, after a 3 second pause in which Angelica writes down Valerio's answer, is acknowledged by Angelica (line 5). Then there is a pause, indicating trouble (line 6), before Valerio goes on to add *for the /mærɪɪd/?*. The rising intonation in this turn may suggest a certain tentativeness on Valerio's part as to how to express the term "wedding anniversary." Following another pause, Angelica repeats *anniversary* in line 9, which Valerio seems to treat as a repair initiation as he offers a repetition of *for the /mærɪɪd/?* (line 10) as solution candidate. The immediate focus of Angelica's repair, however, seems to be Valerio's use of *for*, and she gives him the Spanish equivalent *para* in line 11. Valerio frowns, repeating *for* (line 12), and Angelica turns around to her own desk, seemingly leaving the problem unsolved (line 14).

Valerio then leans forward to see what Angelica is writing and summons the teacher, who is already approaching the pair (lines 15–16). Using the MWE *what do you say (for)*, Valerio explicitly invites the teacher to help solve the word search (Brouwer, 2003). The two students go on to co-construct the word search, indexing it as a joint problem (lines 18–20), and the teacher gives the target phrase, wedding anniversary (lines 21–28). The sequence is eventually closed down successfully as the students treat the teacher's repair as the item they were looking for (lines 27–35).

Below, in Extract 2, an interaction occurring 17 days later, Valerio uses the MWE twice for a related purpose, first with his partner in the task, next with another classmate in a brief side sequence requiring a summons (as was the case in the previous interaction in which Valerio summoned the teacher). In the task the students are instructed to talk about what they did the day before. Prior to the extract, Valerio has told Angelica that he went to the dentist. We enter the interaction as this sequence is closed by Valerio in line 1, as he, partly in Spanish, concludes that they are done talking about "yesterday," which he sums up in the utterance *he visit dents*. The third person usage, it should be noted, is task-specific; the students are supposed to collect information from each other so the third person probably comes from Angelica's writing.

Extract 2, July 18, 2003

```
01      Va:     bueno yesterday ya. yes. he visit dents.
02              (2) for evening?
03              (1)
```

```
04      An:     (muchas) cosas hicistes? ("(many things)
05              you have done?")
06      Va:     mhm estuve en la casa de xxx ("I was at
07              xxx's house")
08      An:     xxx
09      Va:     ah entonces es (("then it's")) I have (1) I
10 ->           am ho:: (2) I hoh what do you say. ((looks
11              away)) ha:ve I'meh I brdrdrdr (1) in my
12              home (3) ((looks back)) the morning in my
13              home and visit dents ((points to An's
14              paper))
15      An:     no es [next
16      Va:           [visit dents
17      An:     next del dentista
18      Va:     no next fue visitar al dentista ("I
19              visited the dentist")
20      An:     y luego ("and then")
21      Va:     I visit ((writes))
22      An:     ((writes)) and (2) in the morning (3) es
23              que xxx visit c: correcto? ("is visit
24              correct?")
25      Va:     ((looks in electronic dictionary)) to be?
26              (1) qué es el verbo to be? ("what is the
27              verb 'to be'?") Estar?
28      An:     uh:h
29              ((both look in electronic dictionary))
30      Va:     estábamos no da ("'we were' doesn't work")
31              hmhm (17) ((looks in ED)) Lore ((makes eye
32              contact with Lorenza who sits across the
33 ->           room)) what do you say estuvo
34      Lo:     estuvo? (1) I went?
35      Va:     I went?
36      Lo:     uhuh
37      Va:     alright thank you (1) ya más fácil ("very
38              easy")
39      Lo:     si si sabe cómo se escribe? ("yes yes do
40              you know how to write it?")
41      Va:     I went ((nods, looking at Lore))
```

Valerio then goes on to introduce the next topic, namely what he did in the evening (line 2). This Angelica responds to by further inquiring about Valerio's activities (lines 4–5). In the following turn, Valerio says in Spanish that he was at somebody's house (inaudible name), which Angelica responds to in another inaudible turn (lines 6–8). This is followed by Valerio refocusing on the task, also partly in Spanish, *entonces es I have* (line 9). The next part of the turn is marked by speech perturbations such as pauses and a stretched vowel sound in *I am ho:*, indicating trouble and initiation of self-repair (Schegloff, Jefferson, & Sacks,

1977). Valerio then uses the target expression *what do you say* pronounced with slightly falling intonation (line 10). As opposed to the previous interaction, however, this time the MWE is not used as an invitation for help, and it is not oriented to as such by the co-participant. Instead, Valerio here makes it public that he is "doing thinking," as Houtkoop-Stenstra (1994) called it (quoted in Brouwer, 2003, p. 538), while keeping the floor. This is achieved by means of the vowel stretching, a common pre-indicator of a word search (Schegloff, 1979), and by using the MWE, but also by means of other modalities, such as falling intonation and, especially, by avoiding eye contact (see also Mori & Hasegawa, 2009). In the previous turn exchange in Spanish, there was eye contact between the participants; however, as Valerio starts searching for the word, his gaze wanders off (line 10). Accordingly, Angelica does not intervene in Valerio's word search, and it seems he does not expect her to. The eye contact is re-established later in Valerio's turn, during the 3 seconds pause in line 12, at which stage the focus is no longer on the word search but back on the task itself. They then seem to be summarizing what information Angelica has retrieved from Valerio (lines 12–21), and then Angelica, lines 22–23, initiates a new search for a lexical item as she seems to express doubts that *visit* is the right verb; this turn, unfortunately, is partially inaudible. In lines 23–31, the students seem to be cooperating to find the right verb, but their lack of success in this eventually results in Valerio employing the MWE in a manner similar to Extract 1 above where he first summons the intended recipient, Lorenza, before asking for the specific lexical item (lines 31–33). The summons, which receives a non-verbal answer in that mutual gaze is established, and the MWE *What do you say* (line 33) open the side sequence in which Lorenza and Valerio agree on a solution to the lexical problem (lines 33–38). While the term given by Lorenza is not the English equivalent to *estuvo*—"he was" would be the most fitting term here—the function of the MWE is very clear to her. The sequence is eventually closed by Valerio appreciating Lorenza's help (line 37) and Valerio's nodding (line 41) in response to Lore's question in Spanish *sabe cómo se escribe?* [do you know how to write it?] in line 39.

At this stage, then, we have three instances of the MWE, two of which recur in comparable sequences where Valerio explicitly invites a co-participant to help carry out a lexical inquiry. The third instance also takes place in a lexical search environment, but it is carried out in a manner which is not invitational as Valerio uses it to display that he is "doing thinking."

In the next extract, recorded 1 month and 12 days after Extract 1, the MWE is used with *how* rather than *what*, which makes for a more native-like pattern. However, as this *how do you verb*-pattern is not found again in Valerio's data, it cannot be said to substitute the existing pattern, nor can I argue empirically that this interaction constitutes a first step towards a new emergent pattern in Valerio's inventory. Therefore, I do not, for the present purposes, distinguish between the two.

Extract 3, August 12, 2003

```
1    Te:   here is bread
2    Va:   hm
3    Te:   here is some bread ((showing them book))
4          (1)
5    Va:   for
6    Ol:   xxx ((looks in teacher's book, nods))
7    Te:   mhm
8    Va:   teacher
9    Ol:   ((looks up from teacher's book))
10   Te:   mhm
11   Va:   here is bread (.) all debr all de:hm
12   Ol:   ((looks down))
13   Va:   .hhh in Mexico [is different names in:=
14   Ol:                  [((looks toward Valerio))
15   Va:   =((points to teacher's book)) the brea:d or
16         for the: ((looks in Ol's direction)) nhah
17 ->      ((slight laughter)) how do you say .hhh
18 ->      ((looks down)) how do you say *panadería*
19         ((looks up)) (2) for the make (1) bread?
20   Te:   mhm a bakery
```

Leading up to this extract, the teacher has been assisting Valerio's partner Olivia (Ol) with a troubling word, *bread*. This item, part of a sentence which the students are asked to complete in the task, did not seem to present any problems to Valerio. As Olivia acknowledges the teacher's help (line 6), Valerio summons the teacher (line 8), gets a verbal response (line 10), and, perhaps recycling the teacher's turn in line 1, starts talking about different breads (line 11). At this stage, Olivia has reoriented as she shifted her gaze from the teacher's book towards Valerio (line 9), and an interactional space has been established in which the two students and the teacher co-participate. Olivia and the teacher are both potential recipients of Valerio's turn, Olivia as implied by her gaze, and the teacher as implied by her recipiency token in line 10. Valerio's turn in line 11 contains the first trouble indicator as marked by a stretched vowel in *all de:hm*, at which point Olivia leaves the established interactional space, turning her gaze downwards. Valerio then restarts his turn *.hhh in Mexico is...,* line 13, following which Olivia realigns with Valerio as she turns her gaze towards him, seemingly moving from the status of non-addressee to that of potential addressee (line 14).

Following the next trouble indicator, the stretched vowel in *the:* (line 16), the MWE, used twice, sits mid-turn as a display of doing thinking (lines 17–18). It is difficult to tell if Valerio's head-turning towards Olivia (line 16) constitutes a search for support because it follows the trouble indicator but precedes the trouble, and because Valerio previously summoned the teacher (line 8) for a reason which is yet to be revealed. Following the "slight laughter" (lines 16–

17), the two consecutive MWEs are employed in a manner so as to suggest that, more than anything, Valerio is gradually withdrawing from the interactional space which he has shared with the teacher since the summons-and-answer pair in lines 8–10. The first MWE, in line 17, is uttered with a fast transition via in-breath and a shifting eye gaze away from the co-participants into the second instantiation of the MWE, suggesting that he is here signaling "more to come" (Schegloff, 1996). In that sense, given the lack of reaction from Olivia and the fast transition into the second instantiation of the MWE, the shifting gaze suggests that he is momentarily excluding primarily the teacher, but probably also Olivia, from recipiency. Both are re-established as potential recipients as Valerio looks up immediately following the second MWE and co-occurring with the Spanish *panadería* (line 18). The teacher then gives her solution candidate (line 20) after Valerio has elaborated on what he is after (lines 18–19).

Extract 4, below, was recorded on the same day as Extract 3. It gives another example of the MWE as used as an invitation for help. The students are doing a task in which they have been instructed to add logical *but*-clauses to main clauses written on hand-outs. Previously in the interaction there has been some task-solving and a pause, following which Valerio now opens a new sequence as he begins to read from the task sheet.

Extract 4, August 12, 2003

```
01      Va:     in this country ((reading in a whisper,
02              leaned back))
03      Ol:     ((writes))
04  ->  Va:     I no under[stand. .hhh what do you say.=
05      Ol:              [((increasingly orienting to=
06      Va:     =((sits up))]
07      Ol:     =Valerio))  ]
08              ((mutual eye contact))
09      Va:     in this country ((looks down at paper,
10              starts reading aloud))
11      Ol:     ((looks down at paper))
12      Va:     you can orden some (1) /ki:nds/?
13      Ol:     /ki:nds/
14      Va:     of food (1) by telephone /bu:t/ but
15      Ol:     ((reading)) but it's better cook in your
16              house  (1) es mejor cocinar en tu casa?
17              humhumhum ((laughter))
18      Va:     ((moves shoulders up and down)) hmhm
19              [((nods, taps paper with pen))]
20      Ol:     [order some xxx                ]
21      Va:     .hhh order [some kind order]
```

```
22   Ol:                    [xxx                    ]
23   Va:    order [some /ki:nds/                    ]
24   Ol:          [((leans towards Valerio))] yes?
25   Va:    order some /ki:nds/ what do you. order
26          some /ki:nds/
27   Ol:    order [some
28   Va:          [bueno order. yes. some [/ki:nds/]
29   Ol:                                  [some    ]
30          some /ki:nds/ ((opens electronic dictionary))
31          no atrapé xxx (("didn't catch xxx")) (1)
32          [some /ki:nds/. /ki:nds/? some /ki:nds/ xxx
33   Va:    [looks in electronic dictionary
34          ((whispers))
35   Ol:    ((looking at Valerio)) xxx (2) ((looks
36          down))
37   Va:    ((shows Olivia electronic dictionary))
38   Ol:    xxx
39   Va:    a:::::::::hh (1) bu:[::::
40   Ol:                        [xxx ((writes, looks
41          at Valerio's paper, puts down pencil))
42   Va:    bu:: alright ((erases, hits table with
43          side of hand 4 times, writes I don't like
44          because it has different taste))
```

At first, leaning back, Valerio reads in a whisper (lines 1–2; *in this country*) while Olivia is busy writing (line 3). Then Valerio gradually changes posture as he starts to sit up straight while simultaneously saying *I no understand. .hhh what do you say* (line 4). Olivia reacts to *I no understand* and Valerio's changing posture by increasingly, and in overlap with Valerio's body movements, orienting to him (line 5). The two students' changing postures eventually result in physical alignment, and a mutual interactional space has been established, as displayed by the mutual eye contact (line 8). Valerio then begins to read aloud from what appears to be the troubling sentence on the task sheet (line 9). As Valerio thus reorients towards the written sheet, Olivia follows suit and orients to *her* task sheet (line 11). The actual reading starts in line 12, the task sentence being "(in this country) you can order some kinds of food by telephone, but...". Valerio mispronounces both "order" (*orden*) and "kinds" (/ki:nds/) but, perhaps reacting to the 1-second pause and Valerio's rising intonation on /ki:nds/, Olivia seemingly ignores *orden* and repeats /ki:nds/, perhaps indexing it here as a potential trouble source (line 13). At this point in the interaction, however, the students do not orient further to this item. Instead, when Valerio has finished reading the sentence aloud (line 14), Olivia offers her solution to the task (lines 15–17) by proposing a way to complete the 'but'-clause. After 3 seconds of pondering over Olivia's solution (marked by the shoulder movements), Valerio accepts it (acknowledgment token *hmhm* and *nodding* in line 18).

Having thus produced a solution to the task, the students reorient to the task wording, *order some kind* (lines 20–23). Even though in line 21, Valerio pronounces *kind* correctly, it would seem that /kiːnds/ is being established as a troubling item as both Valerio and Olivia increasingly orient to this specific item, with Valerio reading from the text and Olivia eventually leaning into his physical space (lines 23–26). In line 25, Valerio seems to almost employ the MWE as he utters *what do you.* in-between repetitions of the task text, *order some* /kiːnds/. Olivia then repeats *order some* (line 27), which Valerio, in line 28, overlaps with *bueno order. yes.* followed by another mispronunciation of 'kinds' in *some* /kiːnds/. This turn seems to act as a specification that *order* is not the problem while bringing *some* /kiːnds/ further into focus by way of Valerio's repeating it from his previous turn. In the following turn, Olivia repeats *some* /kiːnds/, following which she looks in her electronic dictionary and expresses, in Spanish, "not having caught" something (line 31; partially inaudible). This "something" would seem to be /kiːnds/ as Olivia is very focused on this item in line 32. The students have thus collaboratively 'unframed' /kiːnds/ from its original context in the task sentence, as they have brought it into focus (Brouwer, 2004).

In lines 33–37, the students are concerned with dictionary use followed by Valerio's emphatic change of state token (*aːːːːːːːh*, line 39; Heritage, 1984) and his writing his task-solution, started by *buːː* (line 39; Valerio's default way of pronouncing 'but' is /buːt/, as also seen in line 14), and continued by a repetition of *buːː* in line 42. Finally, Valerio completes the sentence, writing *but I don't like because it has different taste*. Even though the original lexical problem is not evidently solved, which Goodwin and Goodwin (1986) found to be an acceptable outcome of word searches, the increasingly co-constructed focus on /kiːnds/ throughout the interaction followed by Valerio's change-of-state and production of a task-solution suggest that they achieve a form of agreement on the trouble-item. The students, then, after having agreed on Olivia's task-solution and co-identified /kiːnds/ as the trouble-source initially causing Valerio to invite Olivia to help him, end up with individual solution candidates. At this stage, the students do not share their sentences with the teacher, so an assessment remains elusive. The students themselves do not orient any further to this task.

The next extract, recorded 8 months and 9 days after Extract 1, shows that the MWE as a tool to perform a private word search is retained over time. The students are involved in a task intended to elicit the short answer forms "yes I do" and "no I don't" as yielded by questions about likes and dislikes. We enter the interaction as Valerio asks his fellow classmate Danny, who is from China, about Mexican food (line 1).

Extract 5, March 09, 2004

```
01      Va:    d'you like m: eh food Mexican?
02             (2)
03      Da:    maybe but I didn't uh ((starts making a
04             waving gesture with right hand)) but I do
05             not taste
06      Va:    ((nods))
07      Da:    maybe
08  ->  Va:    you ((nods briefly)) you::: ts (1) what do
09             you say. ((looks down)) (1) you eating mex
10             you eating food Mexican?
11      Da:    no ((shakes head)) never
```

In lines 3–5, Danny offers a diplomatic *maybe but I do not taste* to Valerio's question. Valerio nods in acceptance (line 6), and Danny repeats the *maybe* (line 7). Then Valerio, after giving a brief nod in response to Danny's second *maybe*, embarks on what turns out to be an elaborative question containing our target expression (lines 8–10). In this extract, the MWE is yet again used by Valerio to display that he is doing thinking. The MWE again follows speech perturbations, it is uttered with falling intonation, and it is followed or accompanied by some kind of inward physical presence (he looks down). The co-participant does not interrupt; the MWE used as a display of doing thinking seems to waiver a transition relevant place.

So far, we have seen that the MWE is linked to certain sequential environments in which it performs certain activities and from which it derives its functions—these things hang together and they are what the participants primarily seem to be orienting to. The data have shown that the MWE may be used to ask for help (teacher/peer) or as a display of doing thinking, a public display of accountable behavior to inform co-participants that no help is explicitly requested. The explicit invitation for help is always pre-indexed by some kind of interactional work, either a summons, a gesture, or a gaze or any of these in combination. Keeping in mind the interactional preference for self-repair (Schegloff, Jefferson, & Sacks, 1977), the findings therefore tie in well with the co-participants not getting involved unless specifically summoned. It was found that if Valerio is physically disengaged from the current activity, either looking down/away or in other ways physically out of alignment with the task, there is a tendency that the MWE is self-oriented, but still displaying accountable behavior. This is sometimes, though not consistently, also reflected in falling intonation. It seems that the co-participants are more concentrated on bodily posture and aspects of eye gazing when dealing with Valerio's orientation in his lexical problem-solving activities. When it is other-oriented, the problem-solving initiated by the MWE may not always be straightforward, but the problem-solving activity it instigates is fairly quickly agreed on collaboratively in all cases. What ties all usages of the target MWE together is that it works as a self-initiated repair in lexical inquiry situations—the solution may come out as an other-repair but only if specific interactional work has been carried out to accomplish this.

The MWE as reference to past action

In the following extract analyses, we shall see that the MWE increasingly performs other functions, although they still retain traces of previous usage. Extracts 1–4 above documented that Valerio used the MWE in word search environments from the first day in class. Approximately seven weeks into Valerio's career as a language learner in this classroom, he starts using the phrase in a new environment where he uses the MWE to make a reference to an interactional contribution previously made by a co-participant.

Extract 6 below shows the first example of this usage in the data. Recorded in August 2003, it falls approximately seven weeks before Extract 5 above, so chronologically there is overlap between Valerio's different uses of the MWE. This is an important empirical observation. It suggests that the various instantiations of the MWE emerge from the same source, psycholinguistically, and hence it suggests that all the instantiations are one linguistic item that is carried across interactional barriers, rather than a series of unrelated, instantaneous interactional phenomena. I will return to this issue in the discussion below.

On the day of the recording of the interaction in Extract 6, one of the students brought her young daughter to the class. Prior to the extract, the students in the interaction—Olivia (Ol), José (Jo), and Valerio (Va)—have been doing some group work, and the teacher has come to their table to evaluate their work. During this evaluation, the teacher comments that the little girl is cute, which spawns questions about the word "cute" and what adjective to use about boys instead of girls. The teacher then explains that you can use the same word when talking about boys, but when the boys get older it may be more appropriate to use "handsome." This is line 1 in the extract.

Extract 6, August 15, 2003

```
01      Te:     pretty for a girl [and handsome for a boy
02      Va:                       [pretty. ((nodding))
03      Te:     ((leaves to write on board))
04      Jo:     xxx
05      Te:     [bupbupbupbupbup ((to child in class))
06      Jo:     [xxx
07              (1)
08   -> Va:     what do you say for bo boy
09              (1)
```

```
10    Ol:    [for boy?
11    Te:    [handsome
12    Va:    handsome?
13    Te:    handsome mhm
```

In overlap with the teacher, Valerio attends to the word *pretty* by repeating it and nodding (line 2). The teacher leaves the students' table to go and write the new words on the board, and on her way she makes some babbling sounds to the child (line 5). In overlap with these two actions, José makes two unintelligible comments (lines 4 and 6). Following a pause, Valerio then deploys the MWE, in line 8, to display an orientation to what the teacher had said a few turns earlier. Another pause ensues, following which Olivia repeats the final part of Valerio's turn, *for boy*, with rising intonation, thus aligning with Valerio's orientation and indexing his inquiry as a joint problem (lines 9–10). In overlap with Olivia's turn, the teacher offers *handsome* as an appropriate answer to their inquiry (line 11). Valerio repeats the word with "try-marking" intonation (Sacks & Schegloff, 1979), and the teacher confirms by repeating *handsome*, followed by an acknowledgment token, in response (lines 12–13). Following the interaction, there is further work on the item *handsome*, but for the present purpose it suffices to note that Valerio successfully deploys the MWE in a new environment; he uses it to refer to an action carried out by a co-participant a few turns earlier in the interaction and his co-participants orient to his action as such.

While this use resembles an other-initiated repair inasmuch as it contributes to a problem-solving activity, the problem it solves is not a matter of failed mutual understanding or lacking intersubjectivity. The co-participants have already achieved mutual understanding—they all "know" that they are talking about adjectives that express 'cuteness' in relation to boys and girls—so this use of the MWE, rather than initiating an other-repair, primarily achieves the function of referring to a past event, in this case to a specific lexical item used in a prior turn. In this respect, resembling an explicit word search marker (Brouwer, 2003), this new use of the MWE also carries traces of the lexical search environments discussed in the previous section.

In the interaction in Extract 7 below, Valerio uses the MWE to orient to something which Iago, a class mate and task partner here, did earlier in the interaction. The students are solving a task concerned with the difference between *lend* and *borrow*. In the course material, the students are introduced to a range of different nouns which they are supposed to use as they practice lending/borrowing requests. Earlier in the interaction, the object of the borrowing/lending request had been "eggs." Iago seemed to find this amusing, and instead of practicing the request, Iago, laughing, asked if Valerio *had* eggs. Valerio's answer was *sure*, but instead of making requests about borrowing or lending the eggs, they moved on to the next noun in the course material. Now, Valerio seems to be referring to this past interactional event concerning the eggs. One of the resources used to achieve this is the MWE (line 4).

Extract 7, November 04, 2003

```
01     Va:    ah do you ask question for the eggs
02            ((points to book)) more (1) time
03     Ia:    ((giggles))
04  -> Va:    what do you say? ((points at Ian
05            throughout this turn and Ian's next turn))
06     Ia:    okay uh u:h (1) can you lend me the: [heh]
07     Va:                                         [no ]
08            is can you lend (1) is ((looks in book))
09     Ia:    yeah
10     Va:    can I borrow ((pointing at Ian))
```

In the first two lines in the extract, Valerio asks Iago to make the borrow/lend request with eggs as the object. Iago giggles (line 3) perhaps recalling the past event, which he seemed to find amusing, but he does not respond to Valerio's question. Then, in line 4, Valerio reformulates, using our focal expression accompanied by a finger-pointing gesture which suggests that not only is Valerio referring to a past event in the interaction; he seems to be holding Iago accountable for some previous action. As mentioned, when their interaction had first revolved around eggs, Iago did not make the actual request in accordance with the task activity. In this extract, Iago's response (line 6) is characterized by speech perturbations and pauses, suggesting trouble in delivering a relevant next action. Valerio keeps his finger pointed at Iago throughout Iago's turn, and does not terminate this gesture until he takes the floor again verbally as he, in lines 7–8, begins other-repairing Iago's *can you lend me the:*. In other words, Valerio deploys the MWE not only to orient to a previous utterance made by Iago, he seems to challenge (Koshik, 2003) the correctness or relevance of that previous utterance. This is displayed in the pointing gesture but also in expression of disagreement in the following turn (lines 7–8), in which he argues in favor of using *borrow* rather than *lend*. Following the extract, the interaction then seems to become a more principled discussion of the difference between *lend* and *borrow*, which is finally closed as Valerio acknowledges that Iago is right after all, apologizes, and thanks him for his help.

Recorded more than one year and a half later, Extract 8 below displays the long-term use of the MWE as a means to refer to a previous action by a co-participant. Valerio and his partner, Mary, are talking about things that have changed in their lives since moving to Portland. Mary has been telling Valerio about her different jobs, both in a tea shop in Portland and in different contexts in her home country. Line 1 in the extract is the end of the turn in which she says that back home she worked in different places, but in Portland she has only worked in a tea shop.

Extract 8, June 30, 2005

```
01      Ma:     I only work at this tea shop
02      Va:     tea shop.
03      Ma:     yeah
04      Va:     tea shop i:s is eh (2) is the ehm (1) is eh
05  ->          the what do you say before?
06              (1)
07      Ma:     tseh it's like a: coffee shop?
08      Va:     it's is a restaurant?
09      Ma:     ((nods)) [yeah.
10      Va:              [coffee shop?
11      Ma:     yeah yeah yeah. it's kind of coffee shop.
12              you make drink? [((gestures pouring)) xxx
13      Va:                     [((nods)) the same the
14              same for the starbucks and [you can:=
15      Ma:                                [((points at
16              Va)) yeah like that
```

Valerio then repeats *tea shop* (line 2), which receives an acknowledgment token from Mary (line 3). Valerio's turn in lines 4–5, however, suggests that his previous turn might have been a first attempt at "unframing" the item to make it a matter of focus (Brouwer, 2004). The beginning of this turn is characterized by non-lexical speech perturbations and pauses. Simplified, Valerio makes three attempts to express something about the tea shop: *tea shop is () is the () is the* before using the MWE to ask for help by referring to an utterance previously made by Mary. This time Valerio adds *before*, making it very explicit that he is referring to a past event. After a 1.0 second pause, Mary explains that it is like a coffee shop, an utterance which aligns with Valerio's focus on the concept of 'tea shop' by way of proposing an explanation of the term, but at the same time the try-marking intonation suggests that she is not entirely sure what previous event Valerio is aiming at. Mary's turn is thus reminiscent of what Kurhila (2006, p. 155) calls a "candidate understanding" of a previous turn, "used to check the level of shared knowledge between the participants." As such, it constitutes the first pair part of an adjacency pair, requiring confirmation or rejection. Valerio's next turn, however, does not seem to provide this. Instead, he proposes another explanation of the concept of "tea shop," suggesting that it is a restaurant (line 8). Mary nods and says *yeah* in agreement (line 9), in overlap with which Valerio repeats *coffee shop* with rising intonation (line 10), seemingly in response to Mary's turn in line 7. This response, however, neither confirms nor rejects Mary's candidate understanding, but is treated as a complex question functioning as both a comprehension check which Mary confirms (*yeah yeah yeah*) and an inquiry about the nature of a 'coffee shop' / 'tea shop' which Mary orients to by explaining, verbally and in terms of gesturing, to Valerio that it is a place where you can get something to drink (lines 10–12). Valerio then nods in acceptance, thereby confirming Mary's previous candidate understanding and thus providing the second pair part that has been pending since line 7, as he compares 'coffee shop' to a chain of coffee shops, which Mary also agrees with (lines 13–16). We thus see two adjacency pairs within the base adjacency pair whose first pair part is in line 7 and whose second pair part is in line 13. The first adjacency pair, in lines 8–9, is a question-answer sequence relating to the topic of the overall interaction; it is thus not a traditional insertion sequence which serves to equip the speaker of the projected second pair part with new information needed to respond to the first pair part of the base adjacency pair (Hutchby & Wooffitt, 2008; Schegloff, 2007). The second adjacency pair is an insertion sequence in the form of a candidate understanding (line 10) and a confirmation (lines 11–12). Schematically, the sequential progression looks like this (from line 7):

line 7	Ma:	FPP 1	
line 8	Va:	FPP 2	
line 9	Ma:	SPP 2	
line 10	Va:		FPP3
lines 11–12	Ma:		SPP3
line 13	Va:	SPP1	

While the *before*, which Valerio adds to the *what do you say* in line 5, firmly situates the reference of the utterance within this interaction, and Mary's response to it also stays within the topical confines of their interaction so far (although it does not point back to any specific previous utterance she has made), the function of the MWE here highlights the interrelatedness of the functions of the MWE as 'asking for help' to solve a lexical problem and "referring to past interactional event." In this interaction, the MWE seems to perform both functions successfully.

The MWE used to elicit an opinion
The first instance of Valerio using the MWE as a means to elicit a co-participant's, as captured on tape, took place in the following interaction. In this interaction, Valerio is summoned by the teacher to have a little talk on how things are going in class and which level he should most profitably attend next semester. In this ESL class, students attend levels A-D, A being beginning and

D being intermediate (there are no advanced levels; see Brillanceau, 2005; Reder, 2005). Sometimes students repeat the same level before advancing (hence the teacher's question in line 5 concerning *how many times* Valerio has been in level C). At this stage the relevant discussion for our focal student is whether to advance from C to D.

Extract 9, March 09, 2004

```
01      Te:     okay (1) would you like to stay in level
02              cee or try level dee
03      Va:     ehm (2) I like level dee but I don't know
04 ->           (1) what do you say (1)((gesturing)) [mmm
05      Te:                                          [how
06              many times have you been in level cee
07      Va:     two
08      Te:     just two times (1) three times is okay
09      Va:     ((nods))
```

The teacher starts out by asking Valerio what level he wants to attend (lines 1–2). Following an *ehm*, he gives a possible answer, after which he deploys the MWE (line 4) to elicit the teacher's opinion on the matter. The teacher, initiating an insertion sequence to obtain further information before responding to Valerio's question, asks him how many times he has done level C (lines 5–6). Valerio tells her twice (line 7) which she deems as insufficient for him; he is better off spending another term in level C (line 8). The MWE thus worked as a successful way of eliciting a co-participant's opinion and Valerio nods in agreement (line 9). Following the interaction, Valerio makes a further inquiry about the class, but the agreement is not changed.

Approximately two months later, the following interaction takes place, in which the MWE is employed four times. The students have been instructed to correct four sentences which the teacher has retrieved from classroom writing samples. Prior to our point of entry into the interaction, the students have all individually written down the exemplar sentences. The teacher has encouraged the students to correct the sentences in pairs, and Sal and Valerio have just begun to go over the first example. In line 1, Sal opens with a turn-initial *okay,* indexing the beginning of a new sequence (Kasper, 2004), and reads the first sentence out loud:

Extract 10, May 14, 2004

```
01      Sa:     ((orienting to paper)) okay you should
02              listeni:ng to old generation
03      Sa:     ((looks at Valerio))
04 ->   Va:     what do you say
```

```
05                  (1)
06      Sa:         you know it has- it- these are these are
07                  le learning mistakes. these are not right
08                  ((pointing to paper))
09                  (1)
10      Va:         this is no right?
11      Sa:         no at's right.
12  ->  Va:         and? (.) what do you say
13      Sa:         what?
14                  (1)
15  ->  Va:         what [do you say]
16      Sa:              [I I just I] I ju- I just read these
17                  sentence ((pointing to Va's paper))
18  ->  Va:         and what do you say
19      Sa:         .hh I s I I think this would be listen (1)
20                  you should listen to old genera[tion
21      Va:                                       [yeah (1)
22                  you should listen old generation or to old
23                  generation
```

After reading the sentence, Sal looks up at Valerio (line 3), perhaps trying to elicit his thoughts on the sentence. Valerio, on the other hand, employs the MWE, perhaps trying to elicit Sal's opinion about the sentence. After a pause, indicating trouble, Sal embarks on an explanation concerning the sentences on their sheet and the task at hand (lines 6–8). It would seem that from Sal's perspective, intersubjectivity, that is, mutual understanding of the task at hand, is yet to be established. Another pause ensues, following which Valerio recycles parts of Sal's previous turn, *no(t) right*, to perform what Sal hears as a comprehension check, and Sal confirms his understanding (lines 9–11). In Sal's turn in line 11, it should be noted, the pronoun sounds like a "that" without the word-initial consonant (hence the transcription of the utterance as *at's right*). Valerio, in line 12, then repeats the MWE following a turn-initial *and* with rising intonation, suggesting that Valerio does know what the task is about and that he is trying to elicit Sal's opinion on the target sentence. Sal, however, initiates self-repair (line 13) and Valerio repeats the MWE as a candidate solution (line 15). Then, in lines 16–17, partially in overlap with Valerio's candidate solution, Sal again orients to the situation as a repair activity, as he seems to offer another explanation of the task and how to go about solving it as a candidate solution. In line 18, Valerio once more uses the MWE following a turn-initial *and*, and, displaying that intersubjectivity has been established, Sal gives his opinion on the grammaticality of the sentence, and Valerio agrees (lines 19–23).

In the extract below, the MWE is used for the same purpose. The students are discussing by how many individuals the world's elderly population is increasing on a monthly basis. This extract starts in the middle of a long interaction in which Iago has shown his reluctance to answer the question, saying to both the teacher and Valerio that he does not know and that he is incapable of giving a sensible estimate. We enter the interaction at a point where Valerio proposes *maybe* as a means to initiate giving an estimate; at least that is how the co-participants respond to Valerio's *maybe* in line 1.

Extract 11, May 14, 2004

```
01     Va:    maybe ((pointing to paper))
02     Te:    maybe okay that's a ge- that's a good
03            thank you[u
04     Ia:             [oh maybe. [okay.
05     Te:                        [maybe: b[y:
06     Ia:                                 [okay in my
07            opinion
08     Te:    in my op yes:((reaches towards Ian))
09     Va:    [yeah
10     Ia:    [yes
11     Te:    yes [xxx
12     Ia:        [yeah in my opinion. [that
13     Va:                             [good! ((pointing
14            at Ian))
15     Ia:    that's bee ((pointing to Valerio's paper))
16     Va:    what is your opinion?
17     Ia:    heh in my opihinion ((laughing voice))
18     Va:    °what is your opinion°. three hundred
19            thou:sand?
20     Ia:    it's u:h (.) the elderly population is
21            increasing b[y:
22     Va:                [a month
23     Ia:    by
24     Va:    a month?
25     Ia:    three [hundred
26     Va:          [maybe three hundred
27     Ia:          [thousand
28 ->  Va:          [what do you say? (1) three hundred
29            thousand?
30     Ia:    I guess
31     Va:    okay
```

The teacher supports Valerio (line 2) and Iago, in turn, changes his orientation to the task at hand in line 4, *oh maybe okay,* perhaps as a result of Valerio offering *maybe* as a way to initiate an expression containing an estimate or to express uncertainty; the change is evidenced by the *oh* token (Heritage, 1984). Iago then complies by offering *in my opinion* (lines 6–7) as a possible means to express his estimate, which receives positive assessments from both the teacher and Valerio (lines 8–14). In line 15, Iago actually gives his opinion on the matter, namely that 'answer B' in the task is the most appropriate one. For some reason, Valerio does not orient to this and goes on to specifically ask for Iago's opinion (line 16, line 18) and later, using the MWE (line 28), repeats the request for Iago's opinion on the matter. Interestingly, Valerio performs the first request for Iago's opinion in line 16 by using the phrase *what is your opinion?*, which has been afforded by the interaction. He repeats the phrase in line 18 in a more quiet voice and with slightly falling intonation, implying that it might be private speech (Lantolf & Thorne, 2006). They eventually end up agreeing (lines 16–31) on the number 300,000 (which is one of three options given in the task). In line 28, Valerio again asks for Iago's opinion, this time using the MWE; the use of the MWE even here, in an interaction which previously afforded the useful native-like phrase *what is your opinion,* suggests its entrenchment as a means to ask a for a co-participant's opinion.[5]

Discussion

Summing up, the MWE was initially used in lexical enquiry sequences. The orientation to the MWE in these cases by the co-participant was found to be dependent on whether or not it was accompanied by a summons or an active physical presence, primarily via eye gaze. If not, it was treated as a display of "doing thinking." These uses could be found in the data from July 03 through March 04 (Extracts 1–5). Seven weeks after the first use of the MWE as an invitation to help Valerio solve a lexical problem, a new use of the MWE emerges as Valerio starts using it to ask for, or even challenge (cf. Extract 7), something previously done or uttered by the co-participant. This form of usage is found in the data from August 2003 through July 2005 (Extracts 6, 7, and 8). Spring 2004 marks the emergence of the other form of other-oriented usage for which the MWE is used, as Valerio starts using it to ask for other people's thoughts or opinions on whatever task is at hand. This usage is found in the data from March through July 2004 (Extracts 9–11).

In accordance with the core assumption in UBL and emergentism that linguistic patterns are always traceable to previous usage, the different MWE uses overlap chronologically, just as they overlap in terms of their respective pragmatic functions, with later uses carrying residues of previous usage. The initial repeated use of the MWE in activities of asking for help was demonstrated in Extracts 1, 2, and 4. The second environment is similar to the initial one in so far as it carries traces of doing a lexical enquiry; however, the interactional load it carries changes substantially as Valerio uses it to display that he is doing thinking, performing a private word search. This usage was demonstrated in Extracts 2, 3, and 5. The third environment still carries traces of the lexical enquiry dimension, but instead of solving Valerio's production problems, this usage primarily displays a focus on something previously uttered by a co-participant. This use was demonstrated in Extracts 6, 7, and 8. The example in Extract 8, however, showed that the function of *referring to a past action* might also work to solve a lexical problem, thus sharing some features with the function of *asking for help*. Likewise, the final use of the MWE, which was described as *elicitation of thoughts or opinion*, carries traces of the invitation for help to the extent that both uses work to elicit another person's cognition. This use was displayed in Extracts 9–11.

Each of these different contexts, then, has been shown to call upon the use of the "what do you say"-MWE. The recurrent activity of asking for help has been argued to play an important role in terms of initial routinization of the MWE. As such, the data have shown the need for a theory of L2 learning which embraces both social and cognitive processes. The social processes are seen in terms of the changing interactional environments as well as in the importance of how Valerio's co-participants orient to his different MWE usages. These social processes seem to be important for the initial entrenchment of the MWE. The use of the expression in new environments, on the other hand, is dependent on different processes, cognitive in nature, which allow interactional abilities to become individually portable, implying that some aspects of linguistic behavior are retained by the individual and carried across contextual barriers in acquisition (Larsen-Freeman, 2004). I argue that the psycholinguistic unitary status of the expression, and thus the likelihood of its being portable, is supported by the fact that there is chronological overlap among the various environments in which it is used. The expression's unitary status is further supported by the syntactic variety in two usages, not included in the transcribed extracts (cf. endnote 6), "I understand what do you say" and "I don't understand what do you say." This unitary status might be one of the reasons why Valerio uses it often and is capable of transporting it into new interactional environments. However, instances like *how do you say* and *what did you say* also show an incipient process of diversification, possibly leading to further generalization of the *aux-V* structure. In other words, although it can be hard to tell precisely when or where, as it is a gradual shift, the MWE, at some point, becomes more generally deployable, as the linguistic inventory of the focal student changes along with the changing nature of the locally occurring social interactions in the classroom.

These findings also resonate with some of the implications in Hellermann (2007), in which a classroom learner of L2 English was found to pick up from a peer and recycle the specific utterance *I talk to you* in identical sequence positioning in subsequent interaction. Hellermann's study constitutes a window onto the dual routinization of social activity and linguistic utterance (Kanagy, 1999), supporting a view of learning as situated in participation. In Hellermann's study *I talk to you* recurred in task openings, an activity inherent to the language classroom as a community of practice. The MWE investigated here could also be seen as initiating an activity of the language classroom as community of practice, namely an invitation for help in a lexical search. In Valerio's case it would seem, then, that the initial entrenchment of the MWE was dependent on successful participation in a certain activity in the community of practice of the language classroom.

The parallels between Hellermann's results and those of the present study do not end here, however. Hellermann (2007) goes on to speculate that "strategies used and learned in one situation may be applicable to other situations" (p. 92), and this is precisely what the extracts presented here have shown. For the MWE *what do you say*, then, it seems that what was at one point routinized in one sequential environment of asking for help, a practice in the language classroom, later came to be employed in quite different situations—but situations carrying traces of previous usage. In the two initially occurring environments, it was used as a self-initiated repair that could potentially come out as an other-repair if additional interactional, multi-modal work had been carried out, but in later environments it was used first as a reference to a past action carried out by a co-participant and then as a means of eliciting a co-participant's opinion.

The data, then, show that the MWE in time becomes available to Valerio in more than one practice, ultimately pointing to the need for a chronological distinction between situated performance and generic linguistic productivity. The former is local and social; the latter need not be. Therefore, the performance-competence distinction might be viewed in terms of a time-scale where *performance* is always and everywhere situated in the here-and-now world of the speakers, and *competence* is emergent as ever-changing ontogenetic sediments of linguistic experience. In this context, the stuff of learning is thought to be that which is recycled over time and/or carried across contextual boundaries (Eskildsen, 2009; Larsen-Freeman, 2004, 2006). This allows for an investigative framework for L2 learning which acknowledges both social, co-constructed and individual experience to investigate how "grammar and social interaction organize one another" (Schegloff, Ochs, & Thompson, 1996, p. 33), and is in alignment with a view of language learning as centrally a matter of *interactional competence*, that is, L2 users'/learners' ability to employ (co-constructed) abilities (e.g., linguistic expressions and sequential routines) in interactional practices (see Hellermann, 2007, and references cited there). Language learning as interactional competence development can be conceived as doing things in a real world, using language in action, while gaining a more evolved inventory of resources which transcend the moment. This latter concept seems to be in agreement with Lantolf and Thorne (2006) who propose that "learning an additional language is about enhancing one's repertoire of fragments and patterns that enables participation in a wider array of communicative activities" (p. 17).

In the case of the present data, all uses of the MWE are instances of the linguistic inventory in action; however, as the initial use of the MWE is gradually expanded, spilling over into other communicative activities, the pattern can no longer be said to be exclusively linked to a specific environment. It becomes deployable in a number of related environments instead. This calls for an elaboration of Larsen-Freeman's (2004) conceptualization of learning as that which is carried across contextual boundaries. *What do you say* is carried across contextual boundaries, time-wise, but only so to a certain extent content-wise; the usage of the MWE still seems to be restricted to the kinds of environment discussed here. However, the utterance schema that emerges from the MWE, namely the more general *do-schema*, while a sediment of those interactional contingencies, is much more generally applicable and not, in terms of use, dependent on a narrowly defined conversational setting. In other words, there seems to be a continuum of usability, from the very fixed one-to-one correlation between environment and expression (as displayed by the initial use of the MWE investigated here), via the usability of a MWE in related environments (as shown in the development of the MWE investigated here), to a more general applicability of more general utterance schemas (Eskildsen, 2009) which may be carried across both content-defined and time-defined contextual boundaries.

Development in terms of increased productivity as briefly outlined may be displayed in a more quantitative manner. Recalling the UBL methodology of type and token frequencies, Table 2 below presents an overview of type-token ratio development for the *aux do*-pattern under investigation here and, on the right hand side, a representation of the weight of the MWE *what do you say* in relation to the total number of tokens. Tokens are the total number of *aux-do* instantiations whatever the constituents. Types denote the different kinds of instantiations; in this table they are distinguished according to both pattern type, main verb, and tense. This means that *do you like* and *what do you like* are distinguished, as are *do you like* and *do you say*, and *do you say* and *did you say*. A high type-token ratio therefore represents a high degree of productivity across patterns.

Table 2. Overview of aux do-usage

period of recording	tokens	types	t/t ratio	number of instantiations of the MWE 'what do you say'
Summer 2003	17	7	0.41	8 (ratio: 0.47)
Autumn 2003	13	7	0.54	3 (ratio: 0.23)
Winter 2003–04	9	6	0.67	3 (ratio: 0.33)
Spring 2004	36	13	0.36	10 (ratio: 0.28)
Summer 2004	22	12	0.55	2 (ratio: 0.09)
Summer 2005	24	18	0.75	1 (ratio: 0.04)

The presence of the MWE is striking, representing the first three uses of the *aux do* pattern and 47% of all *aux do* usages in the first period of recording, the Summer of 2003. In that sense, it is reasonable to suggest that this is the pattern that sparks off the use/acquisition of more varied and productive *do*-patterns. It constitutes the seed of an emergent pattern. The role of the MWE in relation to the emergent pattern is depicted numerically in the column on the right.[6] The MWE displays a descending tendency of occurrence in the data from 47% of all *do* usage initially, via a fairly stable presence at around 25–30% during the next three recording periods, to a quite abrupt plunge to the brink of disappearance towards the end of the data collection period. Linguistic patterns go in and out of experience; an idea which is at the core of the emergentist assumption that interaction is a constant source of renewal for the individual linguistic inventory, this goes well with a locally contextualized notion of language knowledge in which linguistic expressions are seen as fundamentally tied to specific situations (i.e., interactionally contingent).

Two parallel developmental tendencies are evident, then: increasing type-token ratio suggesting increased productivity and, reflexive of this, relative decreasing MWE usage. These tendencies, however, are non-linear; fluctuation is the norm as the data confirm the waxing and waning of linguistic patterns as demanded by changing environments (e.g., Eskildsen, 2009; Hopper, 1988; Larsen-Freeman, 2006; Thelen & Bates, 2003). This is especially evident in the type-token ratios which suggest a lower degree of schematicity in Spring and Summer 2004 than in Winter 2003/2004. This unpredictability of linguistic behavior and development concurs with empirical findings and theoretical discussions in the SLA literature dating back to the late 1970s (e.g., Cancino, Rosansky, & Schumann, 1978; R. Ellis, 1990, 1994; Huebner, 1985; Meisel, Clahsen, & Pienemann, 1981; Tarone, 1983, 1990; Young, 1988). Thus supporting variability and non-linearity as empirical phenomena in L2 development, the present study argues that in terms of frames of reference it is fruitful to adopt an approach viewing such phenomena as core principles, namely UBL and emergentism (e.g., N. Ellis, 2007; Hopper, 1998; MacWhinney, 2006; Tomasello 2003). In so doing, the present research finds kinship in recent SLA research inspired by cognitive linguistics (N. Ellis & Cadierno, 2009; Robinson & Ellis, 2008), chaos/complexity theory (Larsen-Freeman, 1997; Larsen-Freeman & Cameron, 2008), and dynamic systems theory (De Bot, Lowie, & Verspoor, 2007; Larsen-Freeman, 2006; Thelen & Bates, 2003; Verspoor, Lowie, & van Dijk, 2008; see also N. Ellis & Larsen-Freeman, 2006; and MacWhinney, 1998 on the relationship between these frameworks).

Table 3 (Appendix) shows in more detail the emergent nature of *aux do*-pattern development. From Table 3, it is evident that the most advanced uses are traceable to previous experience; the linguistic inventory is constructed in this stepping-stone fashion as the emergent individual grammar is called upon in a variety of usage events (Eskildsen, 2009; Langacker, 2000). Table 3 also displays the item-based nature of the learning trajectory from the MWE toward a richer inventory of interrelated linguistic expressions and patterns, perhaps increasingly schematic structures. It is beyond the scope of the present chapter to go into a detailed discussion concerning the degree of schematicity of the underlying language knowledge in the inventory, which is a vexing issue (Eskildsen, 2009; Lieven, Behrens, Speares, & Tomasello, 2003). For this particular pattern it seems that *do you Verb* is the kernel, an utterance schema, *do you* seemingly a totally fixed part for some time until the emergence of the past tense form and the expansion of the pattern in terms of the use of personal pronouns. This initial pattern development is seen in the first three recording periods, with past tense usage found in the data for the first time in Autumn 2003, and the personal pronoun expansion recorded for the first time with the use of *he* in Winter 2004. At the same time, the pattern is also used with an increasingly diversified inventory of *wh*-question markers and, in 2005, in a new syntactic variety, *what x do you like?*.

In 2005, there are also two instantiations of a present tense third person usage of the auxiliary verb. However, this presents an uncertain issue insofar as these are the only recorded instances of this use, and Valerio does not conjugate the auxiliary verb. Interestingly, but outside the scope of this chapter, *(it) doesn't matter* also seems to be an entrenched, frequently employed MWE in Valerio's inventory, emerging in May 2004, but there does not seem to be any obvious link between the negated use of the third person form *does* and Valerio's potential for employing the same form, *does*, in non-negated contexts. This issue aside, the data have shown that for Valerio the utterance schema *do you verb* seems to emerge from the MWE *what do you say* and expand towards an increasingly schematized and diversified inventory of language knowledge, as new closely related patterns emerge. It may also be noted that the initially occurring patterns (e.g., *what do you say* and *do you like*) are retained and put to use on and off throughout development, alongside the use of the more differentiated structures, supporting the previously mentioned cohabitation in the grammar hypothesis.

Aux-do development, then, item-based in nature, seems to hinge on an initially highly recurring MWE.[7] Table 3 reveals the further existence of other potential MWE candidates, namely *what do you write, do you like, do you have*, which are temporally unstable; *what do you write, what/when do you use* recurred in Spring 2004; and *do you have* is the recurring expression making for the high number of tokens in Summer 2004 (cf. Table 2). This instability, or fluctuating nature of the MWEs, was also an issue in Eskildsen (2009), where it was found that Carlos's (another classroom student) *can*-pattern emergence was traceable to a few initially recurring MWEs—all of which eventually disappeared from the data. The explanation for this fluctuation was found in the recurrent classroom activities in which the MWEs were deployed. When such activities were not on the agenda, the MWEs were seemingly discharged.

Conclusions and perspectives

Recent CA-oriented classroom research has argued that recurring social actions serve as sites for the development of language for social practices (Hellermann & Cole, 2009). What we see here corroborates with and expands on that insight. We have an action sequence in which some social action is carried out (e.g., doing a lexical inquiry), coupled with a fixed expression. Over time, this fixed expression is extended to be used in other contexts, as the focal student, Valerio, improved his productivity based on activities in the social world of the classroom practices. The analysis has demonstrated how L2 learning research can benefit from a holistic view of L2 development which does not principally separate learning and use, taking into consideration participation in social interaction as well as psycholinguistic notions of cognitive portability of linguistic resources in terms of acquisition. On a speculative note one might pose the question if early learning is more characterized by a correlation between socio-interactional environments and linguistic expressions than advanced learning, but that is a point for future research. In fact, it will be necessary to undertake a closer scrutiny of the nature of the changing environments in which people expand on their linguistic resources and develop their linguistic inventories (Firth & Wagner, 2007).

Linguistic behavior may be social in nature, but sociality should not necessarily be given prominence over individuality. Rather, the two should be seen as mutually constitutive. These data do not support the idea that individual linguistic development is driven solely by social actions which afford new utterances and constructions, but show that (a) certain expressions at certain points in time sit in certain environments, with sociality and interactional requirements informing the nature of the language used, and that (b) reused linguistic material (recurrent MWEs) may act as guides in introducing the participant to new social actions. The microanalytic tools inspired by CA are immensely useful for teasing out situated interactional phenomena, but seem inadequate in terms of handling the usage-based emergence of schematically sanctioned linguistic productivity of the kind investigated here (but see, e.g., Forrester, 2008; Markee 2008; Wootton, 2006, for approaches to developmental CA studies). In order to investigate the portable nature of linguistic items, these being primarily MWEs and utterance schemas, other analytical methodologies and frameworks are necessary. I have proposed UBL as one such framework to complement the interactional research methodology, resulting in a promising way to investigate the emergent linguistic inventory in action.

Notes

1. The research reported on here forms part of ongoing longitudinal investigations into the usage-based nature of learning English as a second language and is partially funded by a grant from the VELUX Fonden Foundation. I thank Gabriele Pallotti, Johannes Wagner, Gabriele Kasper, and an anonymous reviewer for insightful comments. Needless to say, any remaining flaws are my responsibility.
2. MAELC was compiled and is maintained at The National Labsite for Adult ESOL (known locally as the Lab School). The Lab School was supported, in part, by grant R309B6002 from the Institute for Education Science, U.S. Dept. of Education, to the National Center for the Study of Adult Learning and Literacy (NCSALL) and was a partnership between Portland State University and Portland Community College. I thank Steve Reder and all the staff at the Lab School for granting me access to the data and helping me logistically. This research would not have been possible without their hospitality and assistance.
3. Valerio is a pseudonym.
4. I would like to thank Sylvie Cifuentes for assisting me with the Spanish translations. A few notes on the transcripts: Pauses are measured in full seconds only, because my access to the data does not allow for more precise timing. Methodologically, I am aware that from a CA perspective this seems to represent a serious flaw in the data, but for the analyses carried out in this chapter, increased precision of pause timing is not required. Spoken Spanish is written in *italics*, translations given in citation marked parentheses. All names are pseudonyms.
5. Another interesting observation in relation to Valerio's *what do you say* is that Ian actually, a few turns later, repeats it to ask for Valerio's opinion.
6. The number of MWE instantiations exceeds the number of MWEs analyzed in the previous section. The extracts investigated here are representative of all intelligible interactional uses of the MWE in the data, but in the interest of saving space the data have not been exhaustively extracted and analyzed here.
7. In fact, there might be one more MWE, namely *do you like np/V/ø*; so there may be two items from which the emergence of the pattern originates. The initial existence of two exemplar patterns does not change the view of development as item-based, however.

References

Achard, M. (2007). Usage-based semantics: Meaning and distribution of three French "breaking" verbs. In M. Nenonen & S. Niemi (Eds.), *Collocations and idioms 1: Papers from the First Nordic Conference on Syntactic Freezes, Joensuu, May 19–20. Studies in Languages, 41* (pp. 86–99). Joensuu: Joensuu University Press.

Atkinson, D. (2002). Toward a sociocognitive approach to second language acquisition. *The Modern Language Journal, 86*, 525–545.

Bardovi-Harlig, K. (2002). A new starting point? Investigating formulaic use and input in future expression. *Studies in Second Language Acquisition 24*(2), 189–198.

Bates, E., & MacWhinney, B. (1988). What is functionalism? *Papers and Reports on Child Language Development, 27,* 137–152.

Block, D. (2003). *The social turn in second language acquisition.* Edinburgh: Edinburgh University Press.

Brillanceau, D. (2005). Spontaneous conversation. A window into language learners' autonomy. *Focus on Basics, 8a,* 22–25.

Brouwer, C. E. (2003). Word searches in NNS-NS interaction: Opportunities for language learning? *The Modern Language Journal, 87,* 534–545.

Brouwer, C. E. (2004). Doing pronunciation: A specific type of repair sequence. In R. Gardner & J. Wagner (Ed.), *Second language conversations* (pp. 93–113). London: Continuum.

Bybee, J. (2008). Usage-based grammar and second language acquisition. In P. Robinson & N. C. Ellis (Eds.), *Handbook of cognitive linguistics and second language acquisition* (pp. 216–236). New York, NY: Routledge.

Cancino, H., Rosansky, E., & Schumann, J. (1978). The acquisition of English negatives and interrogatives by native Spanish speakers. In E. Hatch (Ed.), *Second language acquisition* (pp. 207–230). Rowley, MA: Newbury House.

Dabrowska, E., & Lieven, E. (2005). Towards a lexically specific grammar of children's question constructions. *Cognitive Linguistics, 16,* 437–474.

de Bot, K., Lowie, W., & Verspoor, M. (2007). A dynamic systems theory approach to second language acquisition. *Bilingualism: Language and Cognition, 10,* 7–21.

Ellis, N. C. (2002). Frequency effects in language processing—A review with implications for theories of implicit and explicit language acquisition. *Studies in Second Language Acquisition 2(2),* 143–188.

Ellis, N. C. (2007). Dynamic systems and SLA: The wood and the trees. *Bilingualism: Language and Cognition, 10(1),* 23–25.

Ellis, N. C., & Larsen-Freeman, D. (2006). Language emergence: Implications for applied linguistics—Introduction to the special issue. *Applied Linguistics, 27,* 558–589.

Ellis, N. C., & Cadierno, T. (2009). Constructing a second language: Introduction to the special section. *Annual Review of Cognitive Linguistics, 7,* 111–139.

Ellis, R. (1990). A response to Gregg. *Applied Linguistics, 11(4),* 384–391.

Ellis, R. (1994). *The study of second language acquisition.* Oxford: Oxford University Press.

Eskildsen, S. W. (2009). Constructing another language—Usage-based linguistics in second language acquisition. *Applied Linguistics, 30(3),* 335–357.

Eskildsen, S. W., & Cadierno, T. (2007). Are recurring multi-word expressions really syntactic freezes? Second language acquisition from the perspective of usage-based linguistics. In M. Nenonen & S. Niemi (Eds.), *Collocations and idioms 1: Papers from the First Nordic Conference on Syntactic Freezes, Joensuu, May 19–20. Studies in Languages, 41* (pp. 86–99). Joensuu: Joensuu University Press.

Firth, A., & Wagner, J. (1997). On discourse, communication, and (some) fundamental concepts in SLA research. *The Modern Language Journal, 81,* 285–300.

Firth, A., & Wagner, J. (2007). S/FL learning as a social accomplishment: Elaborations on a "reconceptualized" SLA. *The Modern Language Journal, 91,* 800–819.

Forrester, M. A. (2008). The emergence of self-repair: A case study of one child during the early preschool years. *Research on Language & Social Interaction, 41*, 99–128.

Goldberg, A. (2006). *Constructions at work. The nature of generalization in language.* Oxford: Oxford University Press.

Goldberg, A., & Casenhiser, D. (2008). Construction learning and Second Language Acquisition. In P. Robinson & N. C. Ellis (Eds.), *Handbook of cognitive linguistics and second language acquisition* (pp. 197–215). New York, NY: Routledge.

Goodwin, M. H., & Goodwin, C. (1986). Gesture and co-participation in the activity of searching for a word. *Semiotica, 62*, 51–75.

Hellermann, J. (2007). The development of practices for action in classroom dyadic interaction: Focus on task openings. *The Modern Language Journal, 91*, 83–96.

Hellermann, J., & Cole, E. (2009). Practices for social interaction in the language learning classroom: Disengagements from dyadic task interaction. *Applied Linguistics, 30*(2), 186–215.

Heritage, J. (1984). A change-of-state token and aspects of its sequential placement. In J. Atkinson & J. Heritage (Eds.), *Structures of social action: Studies in conversation analysis* (pp. 299–345). Cambridge: Cambridge University Press.

Hopper, P. J. (1988). Emergent grammar and the a priori grammar postulate. In D. Tannen (Ed.), *Linguistics in context* (pp. 117–134). Norwood, NJ: Ablex.

Hopper, P. J. (1998). Emergent grammar. In M. Tomasello (Ed.), *The new psychology of language, Volume 1* (pp. 155–175). Mahwah, NJ: Lawrence Erlbaum.

Houtkoop-Stenstra, H. (1994). De interactionele functie van zacht spreken in interviews [The interactional function of low volume in interviews]. *Gramma/TTT, 3*, 183–202.

Huebner, T. (1985). System and variability in interlanguage syntax. *Language Learning, 35*, 141–163.

Hutchby, I., & Wooffitt, R. (2008). *Conversation analysis. Principles, practices and applications* (2nd ed.). Cambridge: Polity Press.

Kanagy, R. (1999). Interactional routines as a mechanism for L2 acquisition and socialization in an immersion context. *Journal of Pragmatics, 31*, 1467–1492.

Kasper, G. (2004). Speech acts in (inter)action: Repeated questions. *Intercultural Pragmatics, 1*(1), 125–133.

Koshik, I. (2003). Wh-questions used as challenges. *Discourse Studies, 5*, 51–77.

Kramsch, C. (Ed.). (2002). *Language acquisition and language socialization: Ecological perspectives.* London: Continuum.

Kurhila, S. (2006). *Second language interaction.* Amsterdam: John Benjamins.

Langacker, R. W. (1987). *Foundations of cognitive grammar (Volume 1). Theoretical prerequisites.* Stanford, CA: Stanford University Press.

Langacker, R. W. (2000). A dynamic usage-based model. In M. Barlow & S. Kemmer (Eds.), *Usage-based models of language* (pp. 1–63). Stanford, CA: Center for the Study of Language and Information.

Lantolf, J. P. (2000). Introducing sociocultural theory. In J. P. Lantolf (Ed.), *Sociocultural theory and second language learning* (pp. 1–26). Oxford: Oxford University Press.

Lantolf, J. P., & Thorne, S. L. (2006). *Sociocultural theory and the genesis of second language development.* Oxford: Oxford University Press.

Larsen-Freeman, D. (1997). Chaos/complexity science and second language acquisition. *Applied Linguistics, 18,* 141–165.

Larsen-Freeman, D. (2004). CA for SLA? It all depends... *The Modern Language Journal, 88*(4), 603–607.

Larsen-Freeman, D. (2006). The emergence of complexity, fluency, and accuracy in the oral and written production of five Chinese learners of English. *Applied Linguistics, 27,* 590–619.

Larsen-Freeman, D. (2007). Reflecting on the cognitive–social debate in second language acquisition. *The Modern Language Journal, 91,* 773–787.

Larsen-Freeman, D., & Cameron, L. (2008). *Complex systems and applied linguistics.* Oxford: Oxford University Press.

Lieven, E. (2009). Developing constructions. *Cognitive Linguistics, 20*(1), 191–199.

Lieven, E., Behrens, H., Speares, J., & Tomasello, M. (2003). Early syntactic creativity: A usage-based approach. *Journal of Child Language, 30,* 333–370.

Lieven, E., & Tomasello, M. (2008). Children's first language acquisition from a usage-based perspective. In P. Robinson & N. C. Ellis (Eds.), *Handbook of cognitive linguistics and second language acquisition* (pp. 168–196). New York, NY: Routledge.

MacWhinney, B. (1975). Pragmatic patterns in child syntax. *Papers and Reports on Child Language Development, 10,* 153–165.

MacWhinney, B. (1998). Models of the emergence of language. *Annual Review of Psychology, 49,* 199–227.

MacWhinney, B. (2004). A multiple process solution to the logical problem of language acquisition. *Journal of Child Language, 31,* 883–914.

MacWhinney, B. (2006). Emergentism—use often and with care. *Applied Linguistics, 27,* 729–740.

Markee, N. (2008). Toward a learning behaviour tracking methodology for CA-for-SLA. *Applied Linguistics, 29,* 404–442.

Meisel, J., Clahsen, H., & Pienemann, M. (1981). On determining developmental stages in natural second language acquisition. *Studies in Second Language Acquisition, 3*(2), 109–135.

Mori, J., & Hasegawa, A. (2009). Doing being a foreign language learner in a classroom: Embodiment of cognitive states as social events. *International Review of Applied Linguistics in Language Teaching, 47*(1), 65–94.

Reder, S. (2005). The "Lab School." *Focus on Basics, 8*(a), 1–6.

Reder, S., Harris, K. A., & Setzler, K. (2003). A multimedia adult learner corpus. *TESOL Quarterly, 37,* 546–557.

Robinson, P., & Ellis, N. C. (Eds.). (2008). *Handbook of cognitive linguistics and second language acquisition.* New York, NY: Routledge.

Sacks, H., & Schegloff, E. A. (1979). Two preferences in the organization of reference to persons in conversation and their interaction. In G. Psathas (Ed.), *Everyday language: Studies in ethnomethodology* (pp. 15–21). New York, NY: Irvington.

Schegloff, E. A. (1979). The relevance of repair to syntax-for-conversation. In T. Givón (Ed.), *Syntax and semantics: Discourse and syntax, vol. 12* (pp. 261–299). New York, NY: Academic Press.

Schegloff, E. A. (1996). Turn organization: One intersection of grammar and interaction. In E. Ochs, E. A. Schegloff, & S. A. Thompson (Eds.), *Interaction and grammar* (pp. 52–133). Cambridge: Cambridge University Press.

Schegloff, E. A. (2007). *Sequence organization in interaction. A primer in conversation analysis. Volume 1*. Cambridge: Cambridge University Press.

Schegloff, E. A., Jefferson, G., & Sacks, H. (1977). The preference for self-correction in the organization of repair in conversation. *Language, 53*, 361–382.

Schegloff, E. A., Ochs, E., & Thompson, S. A. (1996). Introduction. In E. Ochs, E. A. Schegloff, & S. A. Thompson (Eds.), *Interaction and grammar* (pp. 1–51). Cambridge: Cambridge University Press.

Schegloff, E. A., & Sacks, H. (1973). Opening up closings. *Semiotica, 7*, 289–327.

Tarone, E. (1983). On the variability of interlanguage systems. *Applied Linguistics, 4/2*, 142–164.

Tarone, E. (1990). On variation in interlanguage: A response to Gregg. *Applied Linguistics, 11*(4), 392–400.

Thelen, E., & Bates, E. (2003). Connectionism and dynamic systems: Are they really different? *Developmental Science, 6*, 378–391.

Tomasello, M. (2000). First steps toward a usage-based theory of language acquisition. *Cognitive Linguistics, 11*(1–2), 61–82.

Tomasello, M. (2003). *Constructing a language*. Cambridge: Cambridge University Press.

Tummers, J., Heylen, K., & Geeraerts, D. (2005). Usage-based approaches in cognitive linguistics: A technical state of the art. *Corpus Linguistics and Linguistic Theory, 1–2*, 225–261.

Verspoor, M., Lowie, W., & van Dijk, M. (2008). Variability in second language development from a dynamic systems perspective. *The Modern Language Journal, 92*, 214–231.

Wagner, J., & Gardner, R. (2004). Introduction. In R. Gardner & J. Wagner (Eds.), *Second language conversations* (pp. 1–17). London: Continuum

Watson-Gegeo, K. (2004). Mind, language, and epistemology: Toward a language socialization paradigm for SLA. *The Modern Language Journal, 88*, 331–350.

Wootton, A. J. (2006). Children's practices and their connections with "mind." *Discourse Studies, 8*, 191–198.

Young, R. (1988). Variation and the interlanguage hypothesis. *Studies in Second Language Acquisition, 10*, 281–302

Zuengler, J., & Miller, E. R. (2006). Cognitive and sociocultural perspectives: Two parallel SLA worlds? *TESOL Quarterly, 40*, 35–58.

Appendix: Table 3

L2 inventory in action [following two pages]
Emergence of *aux-do* patterns. In brackets tokens of the form *did*. All main verbs are used in the correct form, except *dance* and *read*, for which Valerio, on these occasions, uses the present participle (*dancing* and *reading*, respectively). In the case of *pay*, used with third person singular in 2005, Valerio says, "What do tax pay for?".

	Summer 2003			Autumn 2003		Winter 2003-2004				Spring 2004	
	What / how do you V	Do you V	Why do you V	Do you Verb	What do/did you V	Do you V	What do you V	Why do you V	What did he V	what do / did you V	Do you V
live											
think											
pay											
know											
drink											
own											
remember											
take											
read											
do											
buy											
shop											
go											
speak										1	1
work										1	
make						1					
write					1 (did)					8 (1 did)	
ask				1		1					
use			1							3	
dance		1									
like		2	3	4	1	2					1
have		1		1							2
repeat		1									
say	8			2	3	3		1	1	10 (1 did)	

Verb	When do you V	Where do you V	Summer 2004	What do / did you	Do you V	Do they verb	Subj do verb	Why did you V	Summer 2005	Do you V	What do / did you V	What do / did 3rd pers sg	Where do you V	What x do you V
live													3	
think											2			
pay												2		
know										1				
drink										1				
own						1								
remember							1							
take					1									
read					1									
do										1				
buy		2												
shop		4												
go		1						1						
speak				3 (did)										
work										1			1	
make														
write														
ask														
use	3										1			
dance														
like				1 (did)	2					1	2			1
have					7	1	1			1	3 (1 did)			
repeat														
say				2						1	1	1 (did)		

Index

A

accountability 238 *See also* accountable
accountable 4, 223, 230, 231, 341, 344 *See also* accountability
acknowledgment 63, 71, 77, 78
  token 55, 340, 343, 345
acquisition order 318
affiliation 8, 75, 237, 244, 249, 260
affordance 38
agreement 54, 55, 56, 58, 59, 62, 71, 75, 76, 77, 78, 97, 127, 178, 234, 250, 278, 340, 345, 347
alignment 5, 8, 20, 62, 66–67, 71, 75, 76–77, 94, 101, 111, 225–226, 339, 341
assessment 31, 34, 46, 48, 54, 55, 56, 58–59, 62, 66, 71, 75, 76, 78, 79, 80, 155, 172, 174, 178, 211, 340

B

business interaction 195, 252

C

categories 237, 243, 249, 251, 252, 256, 259, 275 *See also* categorization
categorization 23, 40, 237, 238, 244, 250, 252, 259 *See also* categories
classroom interaction 111, 135, 136, 139, 157, 163, 206, 331
co-construction 21, 25, 282, 289, 293, 294, 296, 313, 317, 319

code-switching *See* language alternation
competence
  interactional 4, 5, 9, 10, 18, 21, 38, 39, 45, 46, 48, 49, 75, 76, 78, 79, 88, 110, 129, 268, 281, 296, 318, 327, 352
  linguistic 122, 129, 321
completion 180
  candidate 202, 203, 293
  collaborative 202
contiguity 148
correction 113, 170, 186, 196, 203, 253, 254, 256, 307

D

Danish language 136, 212, 215, 219, 225, 233
development 17, 21, 47–48, 49, 75–79, 317, 327, 329, 330, 331, 352–356
disaffiliation 8, 237, 251, 259
disagreement 59, 62, 75, 226, 344
dispreferred 27, 35, 40, 226, 250, 252, 254

E

echoing 6, 165, 175, 181
education 2, 92, 93
English language 20, 49, 89, 113–114, 154, 165, 178–180, 190–193, 197–198,

200, 214, 215–220, 223–233, 240–242, 249–251, 291–292, 330, 331, 352–356
ethnomethodological   3, 4, 10

G

German language   212, 214, 215–232, 242–244, 249–254, 299
gesture   6, 107, 108, 110, 111, 116, 117, 120, 124, 125, 129, 137, 144, 147, 151, 181, 217, 222, 224, 233, 341, 344
grammatical resources   5, 88, 93–94, 97, 99, 100
group   7, 8, 47, 48, 77, 90, 110, 111, 137, 143, 147, 148, 156, 212, 216, 224, 225, 232, 237, 243, 244, 251, 252, 254, 258, 260, 303, 306, 342

H

heritage speakers   5, 87–106
hesitation   24, 27, 28, 40, 41, 127, 154, 184, 188–190, 193, 194, 201, 202, 206, 228, 290, 315
hierarchy   242–244, 254, 257, 259
horizontal comparison   39

I

Icelandic language   186, 189–193, 197, 200, 205
identity   8, 126, 189, 192, 237–266, 270
intersubjectivity   3, 6, 7, 56, 154, 189, 190, 199, 203, 238, 254, 343, 348
Italian language   269–270, 292, 295, 298

J

Japanese language   47, 49–75, 110, 111, 163, 165, 175, 178, 179, 181, 280, 291, 292, 299, 300, 319

K

Korean language   88–89, 90–99, 113, 120

L

language alternation   178–180, 214, 219–220, 223–225, 229–230, 237, 240, 242, 244, 249–251
language expert   195, 200, 206
language learner   8, 38, 192, 195, 200, 204, 206, 327, 329, 342
language learning activity   198
language-oriented activities   204–205
language socialization   18, 38, 45, 48, 75, 77, 79
language switching   See language alternation
laughter   8, 116, 122, 217, 226, 228, 237, 239, 243, 244, 251, 252, 254, 255, 257–260
learning   1–4, 17–18, 77, 109, 117, 122, 128–130, 164, 185, 267–269, 327–330, 332, 351–352
legitimate peripheral participation   48
longitudinal   4, 10, 18, 21, 39, 45, 48, 268, 327, 329, 330, 331, 357

M

material objects   3, 6, 107, 108, 117, 120, 121, 122, 125, 127, 129
membership categorization   237, 244, 249, 251–252, 252
morphosyntax   9, 267–269, 272, 278, 281, 285, 299, 307, 313, 316, 317, 318
multilingual   2, 7, 8, 10, 211, 212, 218, 232, 233, 237–266
multimodal   6, 108, 122, 128, 129
multi-word expression (MWE)   328, 327–364

N

nonverbal behaviors   109–111, 114, 117, 125, 127–130

O

opening sequence   267, 280, 307, 317
ordinary conversation   113–114, 239, 320
orientation to language   204, 229, 230

P

participation 4, 5, 7, 17–44, 94, 147, 157, 164, 185, 195, 205, 211, 212, 214, 218, 223, 230, 232–233, 239
policy 212, 214, 218, 232
proficiency interviews 5, 17, 87–106, 267, 268
progressivity 145, 186, 203, 204
projection 25, 26, 30, 144, 281, 292, 321
prosody 80, 202, 243

R

recipient
  recipient actions 50, 59, 63, 71, 76, 77
  story recipient 45, 62, 76
recycling 282, 293, 296, 299, 300–307, 317, 318, 337
repair 6, 7, 21, 58, 107 134, 152, 154, 157, 171, 188, 200, 202, 244, 249–251, 252–254, 258, 299, 334
  other-initiated 112, 136, 192, 249–250, 253, 254, 258, 260, 343
  self-repair 120, 136, 143, 144, 148, 154, 200, 242, 251, 257, 299, 335, 341, 348
    other-initiated 193
    self-initiated 144, 342
repetition
  echoing *See* echoing
  recycling *See* recycling
response
  delayed 5, 22, 38, 121
  expanded 5, 22, 27, 28, 30, 34, 36, 37, 38, 40, 88, 89, 90–94, 99, 100, 101
  minimal 5, 22, 24, 28, 30, 31, 36, 37, 38, 40, 46, 47, 50, 53, 59, 62, 71, 76, 195

S

scaffolding 3, 77, 78, 79
second language acquisition (SLA) 3, 8, 17, 19, 38, 39, 48, 79, 107, 108, 109, 110, 128, 129, 136, 238, 267, 268, 281, 318, 327, 329, 354
second story 5, 66–67, 71, 75, 76, 77

sequence
  insertion 283, 346, 347
  organization 148
  side 155, 156, 199, 244, 334, 336
SLA *See* second language acquisition (SLA)
sociocultural theory 49
sociolinguistics 2
Spanish language 212, 331, 334–340
storytelling 46, 47, 62, 156, 282
study abroad 5, 45–86
syntax-in-interaction 267–326

T

task 9, 19, 34, 46, 102, 111, 137, 143, 154, 156, 170, 174, 181, 200, 218, 229, 239, 271, 318, 333, 334, 335, 336, 337, 338, 339, 340, 341, 343, 344, 348, 349, 350, 351
TCU *See* turn-construction unit (TCU)
telling 5, 23, 34, 45–86
topic
  initiation 19, 34
  proffer 4, 19, 20, 22–24, 27, 28, 30, 31, 36, 37, 38, 40
transition relevance place (TRP) 188, 201, 280, 281, 320
troubles-talk 25
TRP *See* transition relevance place (TRP)
try-marking 206, 343, 345
turn-construction unit (TCU) 6, 7, 20, 22–24, 27, 31, 34, 37–38, 58, 138, 144–145, 148, 165, 186, 187–190, 195–196, 199–200, 201–202, 203, 204, 280, 282, 293, 295, 299
turn design 175, 181

U

Usage-Based Linguistics (UBL) 327–364

V

vertical comparison 21, 39, 49
video recording 49, 113, 136, 165, 214, 232, 240

Vietnamese language 20
vocabulary
    learning 128, 136, 156
    teaching 135, 136, 143, 156

W

word explanation 6, 136–139, 148, 155, 156, 157

word search 120, 145, 188, 315, 334, 336, 340, 342, 343, 350

writing 18, 20, 40, 147–148, 153, 334, 339, 340, 347

NATIONAL FOREIGN LANGUAGE RESOURCE CENTER
University of Hawai'i at Mānoa

ordering information at nflrc.hawaii.edu

Pragmatics & Interaction
Gabriele Kasper, series editor

Pragmatics & Interaction ("P&I"), a refereed series sponsored by the University of Hawai'i National Foreign Language Resource Center, publishes research on topics in pragmatics and discourse as social interaction from a wide variety of theoretical and methodological perspectives. P&I welcomes particularly studies on languages spoken in the Asian-Pacific region.

TALK-IN-INTERACTION: MULTILINGUAL PERSPECTIVES
HANH THI NGUYEN & GABRIELE KASPER (EDITORS), 2009

This volume offers original studies of interaction in a range of languages and language varieties, including Chinese, English, Japanese, Korean, Spanish, Swahili, Thai, and Vietnamese; monolingual and bilingual interactions; and activities designed for second or foreign language learning. Conducted from the perspectives of conversation analysis and membership categorization analysis, the chapters examine ordinary conversation and institutional activities in face-to-face, telephone, and computer-mediated environments.

430pp., ISBN 978-0-8248-3137-0 $30.

Pragmatics & Language Learning
Gabriele Kasper, series editor

Pragmatics & Language Learning ("PLL"), a refereed series sponsored by the National Foreign Language Resource Center, publishes selected papers from the biannual International Pragmatics & Language Learning conference under the editorship of the conference hosts and the series editor. Check the NFLRC website for upcoming PLL conferences and PLL volumes.

PRAGMATICS AND LANGUAGE LEARNING VOLUME 11
KATHLEEN BARDOVI-HARLIG, CÉSAR FÉLIX-BRASDEFER, & ALWIYA S. OMAR (EDITORS), 2006

This volume features cutting-edge theoretical and empirical research on pragmatics and language learning among a wide-variety of learners in diverse learning contexts from a variety of language backgrounds and target languages (English, German, Japanese, Kiswahili, Persian, and Spanish). This collection of papers from researchers around the world includes critical appraisals on the role of formulas in interlanguage pragmatics and speech-act research from a conversation analytic perspective. Empirical studies examine learner data using innovative methods of analysis and investigate issues in pragmatic development and the instruction of pragmatics.

430pp., ISBN 978-0-8248-3137-0 $30.

PRAGMATICS AND LANGUAGE LEARNING VOLUME 12
GABRIELE KASPER, HANH THI NGUYEN, DINA R. YOSHIMI, & JIM K. YOSHIOKA (EDITORS), 2010

This volume examines the organization of second language and multilingual speakers' talk and pragmatic knowledge across a range of naturalistic and experimental activities. Based on data collected on Danish, English, Hawai'i Creole, Indonesian, and Japanese as target languages, the contributions explore the nexus of pragmatic knowledge, interaction, and L2 learning outside and inside of educational settings.

364pp., ISBN 978-09800459-6-3 $30.

NFLRC Monographs
Richard Schmidt, series editor

Monographs of the National Foreign Language Resource Center present the findings of recent work in applied linguistics that is of relevance to language teaching and learning (with a focus on the less commonly taught languages of Asia and the Pacific) and are of particular interest to foreign language educators, applied linguists, and researchers. Prior to 2006, these monographs were published as "SLTCC Technical Reports."

RESEARCH AMONG LEARNERS OF CHINESE AS A FOREIGN LANGUAGE
MICHAEL E. EVERSON & HELEN H. SHEN (EDITORS), 2010

Cutting-edge in its approach and international in its authorship, this fourth monograph in a series sponsored by the Chinese Language Teachers Association features eight research studies that explore a variety of themes, topics, and perspectives important to a variety of stakeholders in the Chinese language learning community. Employing a wide range of research methodologies, the volume provides data from actual Chinese language learners and will be of value to both theoreticians and practitioners alike. *[in English & Chinese]*

180pp.; 978-0-9800459-4-9 $20.

MANCHU: A TEXTBOOK FOR READING DOCUMENTS (SECOND EDITION)
GERTRAUDE ROTH LI, 2010

This book offers students a tool to gain a basic grounding in the Manchu language. The reading selections provided in this volume represent various types of documents, ranging from examples of the very earliest Manchu writing (17th century) to samples of contemporary Sibe (Xibo), a language that maybe considered a modern version of Manchu. Since Manchu courses are only rarely taught at universities anywhere, this second edition includes audio recordings to assist students with the pronunciation of the texts.

418pp.; ISBN 978-0-9800459-5-6 $36.

TOWARD USEFUL PROGRAM EVALUATION IN COLLEGE FOREIGN LANGUAGE EDUCATION
JOHN M. NORRIS, JOHN McE. DAVIS, CASTLE SINICROPE, & YUKIKO WATANABE (EDITORS), 2009

This volume reports on innovative, useful evaluation work conducted within U.S. college foreign language programs. An introductory chapter scopes out the territory, reporting key findings from research into the concerns, impetuses, and uses for evaluation that FL educators identify. Seven chapters then highlight examples of evaluations conducted in diverse language programs and institutional contexts. Each case is reported by program-internal educators, who walk readers through critical steps, from identifying evaluation uses, users, and questions, to designing methods, interpreting findings, and taking actions. A concluding chapter reflects on the emerging roles for FL program evaluation and articulates an agenda for integrating evaluation into language education practice.

240pp., ISBN 978-0-9800459-3-2 $30.

SECOND LANGUAGE TEACHING AND LEARNING IN THE NET GENERATION
RAQUEL OXFORD & JEFFREY OXFORD (EDITORS), 2009

Today's young people—the Net Generation—have grown up with technology all around them. However, teachers cannot assume that students' familiarity with technology in general transfers successfully to pedagogical settings. This volume examines various technologies and offers concrete advice on how each can be successfully implemented in the second language curriculum.

240pp., ISBN 978-0-9800459-2-5 $30.

CASE STUDIES IN FOREIGN LANGUAGE PLACEMENT: PRACTICES AND POSSIBILITIES
Thom Hudson & Martyn Clark (Editors), 2008

Although most language programs make placement decisions on the basis of placement tests, there is surprisingly little published about different contexts and systems of placement testing. The present volume contains case studies of placement programs in foreign language programs at the tertiary level across the United States. The different programs span the spectrum from large programs servicing hundreds of students annually to small language programs with very few students. The contributions to this volume address such issues as how the size of the program, presence or absence of heritage learners, and population changes affect language placement decisions.

201pp., ISBN 0–9800459–0–8 $20.

CHINESE AS A HERITAGE LANGUAGE: FOSTERING ROOTED WORLD CITIZENRY
Agnes Weiyun He & Yun Xiao (Editors), 2008

Thirty-two scholars examine the socio-cultural, cognitive-linguistic, and educational-institutional trajectories along which Chinese as a Heritage Language may be acquired, maintained and developed. They draw upon developmental psychology, functional linguistics, linguistic and cultural anthropology, discourse analysis, orthography analysis, reading research, second language acquisition, and bilingualism. This volume aims to lay a foundation for theories, models, and master scripts to be discussed, debated, and developed, and to stimulate research and enhance teaching both within and beyond Chinese language education.

280pp., ISBN 978–0–8248–3286–5 $20.

PERSPECTIVES ON TEACHING CONNECTED SPEECH TO SECOND LANGUAGE SPEAKERS
James Dean Brown & Kimi Kondo-Brown (Editors), 2006

This book is a collection of fourteen articles on connected speech of interest to teachers, researchers, and materials developers in both ESL/EFL (ten chapters focus on connected speech in English) and Japanese (four chapters focus on Japanese connected speech). The fourteen chapters are divided up into five sections:

- What do we know so far about teaching connected speech?
- Does connected speech instruction work?
- How should connected speech be taught in English?
- How should connected speech be taught in Japanese?
- How should connected speech be tested?

290pp., ISBN 978–0–8248–3136–3 $20.

CORPUS LINGUISTICS FOR KOREAN LANGUAGE LEARNING AND TEACHING
Robert Bley-Vroman & Hyunsook Ko (Editors), 2006

Dramatic advances in personal-computer technology have given language teachers access to vast quantities of machine-readable text, which can be analyzed with a view toward improving the basis of language instruction. Corpus linguistics provides analytic techniques and practical tools for studying language in use. This volume provides both an introductory framework for the use of corpus linguistics for language teaching and examples of its application for Korean teaching and learning. The collected papers cover topics in Korean syntax, lexicon, and discourse, and second language acquisition research, always with a focus on application in the classroom. An overview of Korean corpus linguistics tools and available Korean corpora are also included.

265pp., ISBN 0-8248-3062-8 $25.

NEW TECHNOLOGIES AND LANGUAGE LEARNING: CASES IN THE LESS COMMONLY TAUGHT LANGUAGES
Carol Anne Spreen (Editor), 2002

In recent years, the National Security Education Program (NSEP) has supported an increasing number of programs for teaching languages using different technological media. This compilation of case study initiatives funded through the NSEP Institutional Grants Program presents a range of technology-based options for language programming that will help universities make more informed decisions about teaching less commonly taught languages. The eight chapters describe how different types of technologies are used to support language programs (i.e., Web, ITV, and audio- or video-based materials), discuss identifiable trends in elanguage learning, and explore how technology addresses issues of equity, diversity, and opportunity. This book offers many lessons learned and decisions made as technology changes and learning needs become more complex.

188pp., ISBN 0-8248-2634-5 $25.

AN INVESTIGATION OF SECOND LANGUAGE TASK-BASED PERFORMANCE ASSESSMENTS
James Dean Brown, Thom Hudson, John M. Norris, & William Bonk, 2002

This volume describes the creation of performance assessment instruments and their validation (based on work started in a previous monograph). It begins by explaining the test and rating scale development processes and the administration of the resulting three seven-task tests to 90 university level EFL and ESL students. The results are examined in terms of (a) the effects of test revision; (b) comparisons among the task-dependent, task-independent, and self-rating scales; and (c) reliability and validity issues.

240pp., ISBN 0-8248-2633-7 $25.

MOTIVATION AND SECOND LANGUAGE ACQUISITION
ZOLTÁN DÖRNYEI & RICHARD SCHMIDT (EDITORS), 2001

This volume—the second in this series concerned with motivation and foreign language learning—includes papers presented in a state-of-the-art colloquium on L2 motivation at the American Association for Applied Linguistics (Vancouver, 2000) and a number of specially commissioned studies. The 20 chapters, written by some of the best known researchers in the field, cover a wide range of theoretical and research methodological issues, and also offer empirical results (both qualitative and quantitative) concerning the learning of many different languages (Arabic, Chinese, English, Filipino, French, German, Hindi, Italian, Japanese, Russian, and Spanish) in a broad range of learning contexts (Bahrain, Brazil, Canada, Egypt, Finland, Hungary, Ireland, Israel, Japan, Spain, and the US).

520pp., ISBN 0–8248–2458–X $30.

A FOCUS ON LANGUAGE TEST DEVELOPMENT: EXPANDING THE LANGUAGE PROFICIENCY CONSTRUCT ACROSS A VARIETY OF TESTS
THOM HUDSON & JAMES DEAN BROWN (EDITORS), 2001

This volume presents eight research studies that introduce a variety of novel, non-traditional forms of second and foreign language assessment. To the extent possible, the studies also show the entire test development process, warts and all. These language testing projects not only demonstrate many of the types of problems that test developers run into in the real world but also afford the reader unique insights into the language test development process.

230pp., ISBN 0–8248–2351–6 $20.

STUDIES ON KOREAN IN COMMUNITY SCHOOLS
DONG-JAE LEE, SOOKEUN CHO, MISEON LEE, MINSUN SONG, & WILLIAM O'GRADY (EDITORS), 2000

The papers in this volume focus on language teaching and learning in Korean community schools. Drawing on innovative experimental work and research in linguistics, education, and psychology, the contributors address issues of importance to teachers, administrators, and parents. Topics covered include childhood bilingualism, Korean grammar, language acquisition, children's literature, and language teaching methodology. [in Korean]

256pp., ISBN 0–8248–2352–4 $20.

A COMMUNICATIVE FRAMEWORK FOR INTRODUCTORY JAPANESE LANGUAGE CURRICULA
WASHINGTON STATE JAPANESE LANGUAGE CURRICULUM GUIDELINES COMMITTEE, 2000

In recent years, the number of schools offering Japanese nationwide has increased dramatically. Because of the tremendous popularity of the Japanese language and the shortage of teachers, quite a few untrained, non-native and native teachers are in the classrooms and are expected to teach several levels of Japanese. These guidelines are intended to assist individual teachers and professional associations throughout the United States in designing Japanese language curricula. They are meant to serve as a framework from which language teaching can be expanded and are intended to allow teachers to enhance and strengthen the quality of Japanese language instruction.

168pp., ISBN 0–8248–2350–8 $20.

FOREIGN LANGUAGE TEACHING AND MINORITY LANGUAGE EDUCATION
KATHRYN A. DAVIS (EDITOR), 1999

This volume seeks to examine the potential for building relationships among foreign language, bilingual, and ESL programs towards fostering bilingualism. Part I of the volume examines the sociopolitical contexts for language partnerships, including:

- obstacles to developing bilingualism
- implications of acculturation, identity, and language issues for linguistic minorities.
- the potential for developing partnerships across primary, secondary, and tertiary institutions

Part II of the volume provides research findings on the Foreign language partnership project designed to capitalize on the resources of immigrant students to enhance foreign language learning.

152pp., ISBN 0–8248–2067–3 $20.

DESIGNING SECOND LANGUAGE PERFORMANCE ASSESSMENTS
JOHN M. NORRIS, JAMES DEAN BROWN, THOM HUDSON, & JIM YOSHIOKA, 1998, 2000

This technical report focuses on the decision-making potential provided by second language performance assessments. The authors first situate performance assessment within a broader discussion of alternatives in language assessment and in educational assessment in general. They then discuss issues in performance assessment design, implementation, reliability, and validity. Finally, they present a prototype framework for second language performance assessment based on the integration of theoretical underpinnings and research findings from the task-based language teaching literature, the language testing literature, and the educational measurement literature. The authors outline test and item specifications, and they present numerous examples of prototypical language tasks. They also propose a research agenda focusing on the operationalization of second language performance assessments.

248pp., ISBN 0–8248–2109–2 $20.

SECOND LANGUAGE DEVELOPMENT IN WRITING: MEASURES OF FLUENCY, ACCURACY, AND COMPLEXITY
KATE WOLFE-QUINTERO, SHUNJI INAGAKI, & HAE-YOUNG KIM, 1998, 2002

In this book, the authors analyze and compare the ways that fluency, accuracy, grammatical complexity, and lexical complexity have been measured in studies of language development in second language writing. More than 100 developmental measures are examined, with detailed comparisons of the results across the studies that have used each measure. The authors discuss the theoretical foundations for each type of developmental measure, and they consider the relationship between developmental measures and various types of proficiency measures. They also examine criteria for determining which developmental measures are the most successful and suggest which measures are the most promising for continuing work on language development.

208pp., ISBN 0–8248–2069–X $20.

THE DEVELOPMENT OF A LEXICAL TONE PHONOLOGY IN AMERICAN ADULT LEARNERS OF STANDARD MANDARIN CHINESE
Sylvia Henel Sun, 1998

The study reported is based on an assessment of three decades of research on the SLA of Mandarin tone. It investigates whether differences in learners' tone perception and production are related to differences in the effects of certain linguistic, task, and learner factors. The learners of focus are American students of Mandarin in Beijing, China. Their performances on two perception and three production tasks are analyzed through a host of variables and methods of quantification.

328pp., ISBN 0–8248–2068–1 $20.

NEW TRENDS AND ISSUES IN TEACHING JAPANESE LANGUAGE AND CULTURE
Haruko M. Cook, Kyoko Hijirida, & Mildred Tahara (Editors), 1997

In recent years, Japanese has become the fourth most commonly taught foreign language at the college level in the United States. As the number of students who study Japanese has increased, the teaching of Japanese as a foreign language has been established as an important academic field of study. This technical report includes nine contributions to the advancement of this field, encompassing the following five important issues:

- Literature and literature teaching
- Technology in the language classroom
- Orthography
- Testing
- Grammatical versus pragmatic approaches to language teaching

164pp., ISBN 0–8248–2067–3 $20.

SIX MEASURES OF JSL PRAGMATICS
Sayoko Okada Yamashita, 1996

This book investigates differences among tests that can be used to measure the cross-cultural pragmatic ability of English-speaking learners of Japanese. Building on the work of Hudson, Detmer, and Brown (Technical Reports #2 and #7 in this series), the author modified six test types that she used to gather data from North American learners of Japanese. She found numerous problems with the multiple-choice discourse completion test but reported that the other five tests all proved highly reliable and reasonably valid. Practical issues involved in creating and using such language tests are discussed from a variety of perspectives.

213pp., ISBN 0–8248–1914–4 $15.

LANGUAGE LEARNING STRATEGIES AROUND THE WORLD: CROSS-CULTURAL PERSPECTIVES
REBECCA L. OXFORD (EDITOR), 1996, 1997, 2002

Language learning strategies are the specific steps students take to improve their progress in learning a second or foreign language. Optimizing learning strategies improves language performance. This groundbreaking book presents new information about cultural influences on the use of language learning strategies. It also shows innovative ways to assess students' strategy use and remarkable techniques for helping students improve their choice of strategies, with the goal of peak language learning.

166pp., ISBN 0–8248–1910–1 $20.

TELECOLLABORATION IN FOREIGN LANGUAGE LEARNING: PROCEEDINGS OF THE HAWAI'I SYMPOSIUM
MARK WARSCHAUER (EDITOR), 1996

The Symposium on Local & Global Electronic Networking in Foreign Language Learning & Research, part of the National Foreign Language Resource Center's 1995 Summer Institute on Technology & the Human Factor in Foreign Language Education, included presentations of papers and hands-on workshops conducted by Symposium participants to facilitate the sharing of resources, ideas, and information about all aspects of electronic networking for foreign language teaching and research, including electronic discussion and conferencing, international cultural exchanges, real-time communication and simulations, research and resource retrieval via the Internet, and research using networks. This collection presents a sampling of those presentations.

252pp., ISBN 0–8248–1867–9 $20.

LANGUAGE LEARNING MOTIVATION: PATHWAYS TO THE NEW CENTURY
REBECCA L. OXFORD (EDITOR), 1996

This volume chronicles a revolution in our thinking about what makes students want to learn languages and what causes them to persist in that difficult and rewarding adventure. Topics in this book include the internal structures of and external connections with foreign language motivation; exploring adult language learning motivation, self-efficacy, and anxiety; comparing the motivations and learning strategies of students of Japanese and Spanish; and enhancing the theory of language learning motivation from many psychological and social perspectives.

218pp., ISBN 0–8248–1849–0 $20.

LINGUISTICS & LANGUAGE TEACHING: PROCEEDINGS OF THE SIXTH JOINT LSH-HATESL CONFERENCE
CYNTHIA REVES, CAROLINE STEELE, & CATHY S. P. WONG (EDITORS), 1996

Technical Report #10 contains 18 articles revolving around the following three topics:

- Linguistic issues—These six papers discuss various linguistic issues: ideophones, syllabic nasals, linguistic areas, computation, tonal melody classification, and wh-words.
- Sociolinguistics—Sociolinguistic phenomena in Swahili, signing, Hawaiian, and Japanese are discussed in four of the papers.
- Language teaching and learning—These eight papers cover prosodic modification, note taking, planning in oral production, oral testing, language policy, L2 essay organization, access to dative alternation rules, and child noun phrase structure development.

364pp., ISBN 0–8248–1851–2 $20.

ATTENTION & AWARENESS IN FOREIGN LANGUAGE LEARNING
RICHARD SCHMIDT (EDITOR), 1996

Issues related to the role of attention and awareness in learning lie at the heart of many theoretical and practical controversies in the foreign language field. This collection of papers presents research into the learning of Spanish, Japanese, Finnish, Hawaiian, and English as a second language (with additional comments and examples from French, German, and miniature artificial languages) that bear on these crucial questions for foreign language pedagogy.

394pp., ISBN 0–8248–1794–X $20.

VIRTUAL CONNECTIONS: ONLINE ACTIVITIES AND PROJECTS FOR NETWORKING LANGUAGE LEARNERS
MARK WARSCHAUER (EDITOR), 1995, 1996

Computer networking has created dramatic new possibilities for connecting language learners in a single classroom or across the globe. This collection of activities and projects makes use of email, the internet, computer conferencing, and other forms of computer-mediated communication for the foreign and second language classroom at any level of instruction. Teachers from around the world submitted the activities compiled in this volume—activities that they have used successfully in their own classrooms.

417pp., ISBN 0–8248–1793–1 $30.

DEVELOPING PROTOTYPIC MEASURES OF CROSS-CULTURAL PRAGMATICS
THOM HUDSON, EMILY DETMER, & J. D. BROWN, 1995

Although the study of cross-cultural pragmatics has gained importance in applied linguistics, there are no standard forms of assessment that might make research comparable across studies and languages. The present volume describes the process through which six forms of cross-cultural assessment were developed for second language learners of English. The models may be used for second language learners of other languages. The six forms of assessment involve two forms each of indirect discourse completion tests, oral language production, and self-assessment. The procedures involve the assessment of requests, apologies, and refusals.

198pp., ISBN 0–8248–1763–X $15.

THE ROLE OF PHONOLOGICAL CODING IN READING KANJI
SACHIKO MATSUNAGA, 1995

In this technical report, the author reports the results of a study that she conducted on phonological coding in reading kanji using an eye-movement monitor and draws some pedagogical implications. In addition, she reviews current literature on the different schools of thought regarding instruction in reading kanji and its role in the teaching of non-alphabetic written languages like Japanese.

64pp., ISBN 0–8248–1734–6 $10.

PRAGMATICS OF CHINESE AS NATIVE AND TARGET LANGUAGE
GABRIELE KASPER (EDITOR), 1995

This technical report includes six contributions to the study of the pragmatics of Mandarin Chinese:

- A report of an interview study conducted with nonnative speakers of Chinese; and
- Five data-based studies on the performance of different speech acts by native speakers of Mandarin—requesting, refusing, complaining, giving bad news, disagreeing, and complimenting.

312pp., ISBN 0–8248–1733–8 $20.

A BIBLIOGRAPHY OF PEDAGOGY AND RESEARCH IN INTERPRETATION AND TRANSLATION
ETILVIA ARJONA, 1993

This technical report includes four types of bibliographic information on translation and interpretation studies:

- Research efforts across disciplinary boundaries—cognitive psychology, neurolinguistics, psycholinguistics, sociolinguistics, computational linguistics, measurement, aptitude testing, language policy, decision-making, theses, dissertations;
- Training information covering program design, curriculum studies, instruction, school administration;
- Instruction information detailing course syllabi, methodology, models, available textbooks; and
- Testing information about aptitude, selection, diagnostic tests.

115pp., ISBN 0–8248–1572–6 $10.

PRAGMATICS OF JAPANESE AS NATIVE AND TARGET LANGUAGE
Gabriele Kasper (Editor), 1992, 1996

This technical report includes three contributions to the study of the pragmatics of Japanese:
- A bibliography on speech act performance, discourse management, and other pragmatic and sociolinguistic features of Japanese;
- A study on introspective methods in examining Japanese learners' performance of refusals; and
- A longitudinal investigation of the acquisition of the particle ne by nonnative speakers of Japanese.

125pp., ISBN 0-8248-1462-2 $10.

A FRAMEWORK FOR TESTING CROSS-CULTURAL PRAGMATICS
Thom Hudson, Emily Detmer, & J. D. Brown, 1992

This technical report presents a framework for developing methods that assess cross-cultural pragmatic ability. Although the framework has been designed for Japanese and American cross-cultural contrasts, it can serve as a generic approach that can be applied to other language contrasts. The focus is on the variables of social distance, relative power, and the degree of imposition within the speech acts of requests, refusals, and apologies. Evaluation of performance is based on recognition of the speech act, amount of speech, forms or formulæ used, directness, formality, and politeness.

51pp., ISBN 0-8248-1463-0 $10.

RESEARCH METHODS IN INTERLANGUAGE PRAGMATICS
Gabriele Kasper & Merete Dahl, 1991

This technical report reviews the methods of data collection employed in 39 studies of interlanguage pragmatics, defined narrowly as the investigation of nonnative speakers' comprehension and production of speech acts, and the acquisition of L2-related speech act knowledge. Data collection instruments are distinguished according to the degree to which they constrain informants' responses, and whether they tap speech act perception/comprehension or production. A main focus of discussion is the validity of different types of data, in particular their adequacy to approximate authentic performance of linguistic action.

51pp., ISBN 0-8248-1419-3 $10.

www.ingramcontent.com/pod-product-compliance
Lightning Source LLC
Chambersburg PA
CBHW052042220426
43663CB00012B/2416